D1603984

Organists

and

Organ Playing

in

Nineteenth-Century
France *and* Belgium

Organists

and

Organ Playing

in

Nineteenth-Century France *and* Belgium

ORPHA OCHSE

INDIANA UNIVERSITY PRESS
Bloomington & Indianapolis

Frontispiece:
Organists at work (clockwise from top): Charles-Marie Widor, Eugène Gigout (Bibliothèque Nationale, Paris), Gabriel Fauré, Camille Saint-Saëns (New York Public Library, Lincoln Center).

The paper used in this publication meets the minimum requirements of American National Standard for Information Sciences—Permanence of Paper for Printed Library Materials, ANSI Z39.48-1984

∞™

Manufactured in the United States of America

Library of Congress Cataloging-in-Publication Data

Ochse, Orpha Caroline, date.
Organists and organ playing in nineteenth-century France and Belgium / by Orpha Ochse
p.   cm.
Includes bibliographical references (p.   ) and index
ISBN 0-253-34161-2
1. Organists—France. 2. Organists—Belgium. 3. Organ—France—Performance—History—19th century. 4. Organ—Belgium—Performance—History—19th century.
ML624.O25   1994
786.5'0944'09034—dc20   94-2589
1 2 3 4 5 00 99 98 97 96 95 94   MN

L'orgue, le seul concert, le seul gémissement
    Qui mêle aux cieux la terre!
La seule voix qui puisse, avec le flot dormant
    Et les forêts bénies,
Murmurer ici-bas quelque commencement
    Des choses infinies!

                      —Victor Hugo

The organ, the only harmony, the only lament that mingles earth with the heavens! The only voice that, with sleeping flood and hallowed forests, could murmur here below some beginning of infinite things!
(*Les Chants du crépuscule: "Dans l'église de * * *"*)

CONTENTS

ILLUSTRATIONS

PREFACE

AFTER decades of neglect, organ music of the nineteenth century is again attracting the interest of performers, scholars, and teachers. While audiences never ceased to appreciate the nineteenth-century works that retained a place in the repertoire, the selection they heard was usually confined to a few of the best-known pieces. Now one begins to encounter a broader cross section of organ music from the forgotten century on recordings and programs.

The recent appearance of new editions and studies has helped stimulate this trend. Most, however, are focused on one composer or a specific aspect of organ music or performance. Like the repertoire, much of the history of nineteenth-century organ music has lingered on the library shelves, gathering dust for half a century or more. For most professional musicians as well as amateurs, information about the nineteenth-century French-Belgian organ school has been limited to the second half of the century. Who or what preceded César Franck has seemed hazy at best, and the over-all pattern of development during the century has usually been lost in a jumble of disconnected details.

The major objective of this study is the presentation of a comprehensive view of the organist's world in nineteenth-century France and Belgium: the situations in which organists studied, lived, and worked; influential organists and their accomplishments, ideas, and attitudes. A few remote paths as well as main highways are explored: glimpses of day-to-day concerns as well as historic events, and disappointments as well as triumphs. In general, the writer has been guided by the question: What was it like to be an organist at that time, in that place?

Lists of compositions and analytical comments about them have been included only incidentally, in relationship to other objectives. Perhaps, however, the description of the setting in which the works were composed will lead to a greater interest in, and appreciation for French-Belgian organ music of the nineteenth century, as well as for the performers of that time.

Our objective is approached along three avenues. The first is devoted to performers, their secular programs, and the developments that led to the modern organ recital. The second avenue describes the organists as church musicians, and the relationship of organ playing to an evolving liturgical environment. The third major concern is the education of the organist, the pedagogical viewpoints of prominent teachers, and the position of organ instruction in the curriculums of leading music schools.

The bibliography includes sources cited and selected additional sources that were particularly useful in the preparation of this study. Books, dissertations, and articles are identified by numbers in square brackets that refer to entries listed in the bibliography. For example, [1, p.5] refers to page 5 of *Souvenirs d'un musicien* by Adolphe Adam.

Musical periodicals were a major source of information, and feature articles of particular interest are listed in the bibliography.

Some official titles of important music schools changed several times during the nineteenth century. These changes have been noted in the history of each school, but in order to avoid unnecessary confusion, familiar English-language titles have been selected to designate the more prominent schools throughout the century: the Paris Conservatory, the Brussels Conservatory, and the Niedermeyer School.

ACKNOWLEDGMENTS

MANY friends and colleagues contributed advice, support, and information during the years this manuscript was in preparation. I should like to thank in particular Agnes Armstrong, Lois Battersby, Robert Capen, Robert Clark, Christine Dispas, James Duncan, Brigitte François-Sappey, Stanley Gauger, Magdalen Gonzalez, Jean and Stephen Gothold, Evelyn Hubacker, Nancy and Albert Jenkins, Wayne Leupold, Jim Lewis, William Little, Kurt Lueders, David McVey, John Near, Frances Nobert, Shirley and Bruce Odou, William Peterson, and Jeanette Wong.

Robert Glasgow deserves a special word of thanks. He was the first to read successive versions of the manuscript, and his insightful comments helped guide its evolution.

A major portion of the material for this book was drawn from the collections of the Organ Historical Society Archive, the Sibley Library of the Eastman School of Music, the Whittier College Library, and the music divisions of the Library of Congress, the Bibliothèque Nationale, and the British Library. I appreciate greatly the generous assistance of the librarians in locating material, and I am particularly indebted to Louise Goldberg (Sibley Library), Philip O'Brien (Whittier College Library), William Parsons (Music Division, Library of Congress), and Stephen Pinel (Organ Historical Society Archive).

Support for an important phase of the research was provided by a grant from the San Francisco Chapter, American Guild of Organists.

Organists
and
Organ Playing
in
Nineteenth-Century
France *and* Belgium

I.
Prelude
Music for a Revolution

FROM the time of the Revolution the political scene in France resembled a roller-coaster. Musicians worked through, around, above, and in spite of the comings and goings of armies, empires, and kings. Yet these happenings affected the lives and careers of musicians in very telling ways, and they also influenced the direction of church music and music education. In a little over a century the following major political changes took place:

1792–95 The National Convention
Abolition of the monarchy; France declared a republic (September 21, 1792). Execution of Louis XVI (January 21, 1793). Reign of Terror (1793–94).

1795–99 The Directory
Republican form of government, overthrown by Bonaparte's coup d'état (November 9, 1799).

1799–1804 The Consulate
Nominally republican, but really a dictatorship under Napoléon.

1804–1814 The First Empire
Napoléon I, Emperor of the French.

1814–48 The Restoration of the Monarchy
Louis XVIII (1814–24). Reign interrupted by Napoléon's return and brief rule (the "Hundred Days," March 20–June 29, 1815). Charles X (1824–30). Louis-Philippe (1830–48).

1848–52 The Second Republic
Prince Louis Napoléon, nephew of Napoléon I, elected president, but gradually assumed the powers of a dictator.

1852–70 The Second Empire
Louis Napoléon became Emperor Napoléon III.

1870–1914 The Third Republic
Napoléon's defeat in the Franco-Prussian War ended his Empire. The Third Republic was formed while German armies marched toward Paris.

Changes in government were rarely accomplished amicably. It was a coup d'état that placed Napoléon I in power in 1799, and another one that crowned Napoléon III emperor in 1852. Revolutions ousted Charles X in 1830 and Louis-Philippe in 1848. Defeat of the French armies in wars with their neighbors toppled Napoléon I in 1814 and Napoléon III in 1870.

Brief but bloody civil wars in the streets of Paris accompanied the revolutions of 1830 and 1848, and dissolved the radical Paris Commune in 1871. Victorious foreign troops marched into the city on March 31, 1814 and July 7, 1815. From September 19, 1870 until January 28, 1871, another generation of foreign troops held the city in siege.

The cost to France of all these conflicts cannot be estimated. Traveling there in 1814, the Englishman John Chetwode Eustace remarked on the number of beggars and the miserable poverty he encountered. He also noted the depopulation and the ruinous state of towns and countryside. He said that most large houses, as well as abbeys and monasteries, seemed abandoned and in a state of dilapidation. A whole generation of young men had been drafted into the army, and by the time Napoléon's adventures came to an end, only old men, women, and children could be seen working the fields. At that time there were reported to be "twelve women to one effective man" [102, pp.6–10].

From 1801 until 1905 the Catholic church in France was state supported and state controlled.[1] Every crunch of the national budget could be cause for anxiety among church musicians, whose livelihood depended on the prosperity of the state. More than once during the nineteenth century church musicians had to retrench, with payrolls cut, music budgets slashed, and positions eliminated. To add to their problems, periodic outbursts of violence in the streets posed serious physical threats to church buildings and organs, to say nothing of life and limb.

The situation in Belgium in the early decades of the nineteenth century was almost as chaotic as it was in France. In 1794 the decisive battle of Fleurus placed Belgium firmly in French hands, and there it remained for a little more than twenty years.

In 1815, the battle of Waterloo took place just south of Brussels, ending Napoléon's power and raising the question of what should become of Belgium. At the Congress of Vienna, Britain and the major European powers decided on the establishment of the Kingdom of the United Netherlands, combining the former Republic of Holland and Belgium under the Dutch king.

Within Belgium, growing discontent with this arrangement led to a revolt in 1830, and to the establishment of an independent Belgium with a constitutional hereditary monarchy. Prince Leopold of Saxe-Coburg was elected king, and was crowned on July 21, 1831. During his reign (1831–65) and that of his son, Leopold II (1865–1909), Belgium enjoyed a period of relative stability.

Somehow, through all the political and military maneuvers, the accompanying social changes and whims of the economy, organists in

France and Belgium managed to push, shove, coax, and coerce their profession from near-annihilation in the period of the Revolution to a renaissance in full bloom by the end of the century.

The French Revolution was like a great tidal wave that permeated every aspect of daily life. When the nineteenth century opened the initial shock was over, but the force of the tidal wave was still very clearly a current event. For organists, there was no "business as usual"; everything had changed.

The power of music as a propaganda tool was not lost on the leaders of the French revolt. "During the violent phases of the Revolution," wrote Donakowski, "musicians enjoyed relative peace if they seemed willing to use their talent to promote the doctrines of the new covenant" [72, p.48]. Many were willing. As a result, countless songs and instrumental pieces were written to commemorate specific battles and heroes, to carry the message of the Revolution to every member of a largely illiterate populace, and generally to keep the flame of enthusiasm burning high.

Jean-François Le Sueur (1760–1837), later the teacher of Hector Berlioz (1803–69), was one of the well-known composers who leaped to the call with hymns and other music for the great revolutionary festivals. Others were Gossec (1734–1829), Catel (1773–1830), Méhul (1763–1817), and Cherubini (1760–1842). These men included leading composers of France's favorite musical genre: opera.[2] Here, too, they proved to be men of the hour, reflecting the spirit of the times with spectacles on patriotic themes.

Meanwhile the church was in a deplorable state. In 1789 the Constituent Assembly had abolished the privileges of the clergy and seized ecclesiastical property. The next year bishops, pastors, and priests were required to take an oath of allegiance to the Civil Constitution. Many fled the country as Christianity became a persecuted religion. The Catholic church was superseded by a succession of government-authorized cults: first the Cult of Reason, replaced in 1794 by the Cult of the Supreme Being (under Robespierre), and then in 1796 by Theophilanthropy (an invention of La Révellière Lépeaux).[3]

Sabatier estimated that there were around two thousand organs in France in 1789. After ecclesiastical estates were taken over by the government, the possessions of monastic establishments were sold. Five hundred twenty-two organs were put on the auction block; 418 of them perished, including the largest organ in France: the 63-stop organ of the abbey of Saint-Martin, Tours. The other 104 survived because they were repurchased by parishes at bargain prices [278, pp.77–78].

In 1795 the National Convention decreed that the sale of organs belonging to the Republic would continue. Since those from the monasteries were already gone, the order referred to parish churches and cathedrals. This was going too far. Some organs were saved because the organists played music for the festivals held every ten days. Attention was also directed to an earlier plan formulated by a *Commission temporaire des arts,* proposing that only small, inferior organs be sold. But it may simply have been the pressure of popular opinion that persuaded the Convention to suspend the order for a while. Some months later a more moderate law provided for the sale of organs which lacked sufficient artistic merit.

The organs spared were often the victims of other problems: lack of maintenance; lack of protection from the elements in buildings that had been damaged; and vandalism. Some organs had been moved from place to place for use in civic ceremonies. The organ builder Somer[4] was in charge of organs for these occasions. Sabatier relates that Somer provided five organs for an outdoor presentation on the Champs de Mars on August 10, 1790 [278, p.79]. Bouvet notes a similar occasion in 1793 for which Somer transported four organs to the site of a festival, and afterward dismantled them and returned them to their original locations [36, pp.138–39, n.1].

Belgian churches and monasteries were subject to the same regulations found in France. Félix estimates that in Brussels alone, fifteen organs belonging to religious orders were lost, probably sold for the price of the materials. The picture was better for parish churches, as repurchase enabled most of them to keep their organs. The churchwardens often bought the church furnishings in their own names in order to save them for a better day, when they could again be used in church [112, p.99].

What kind of music was appropriate for a revolution? The festivals for which Le Sueur and his contemporaries wrote music replaced the celebrations of the church. Often the same music could be used. The Easter hymn O Filii et Filiae, for example, became "Hymn in Honor of the Resurrection of the Estates General." Only a few words had to be changed in the verses, and everyone could join in on the "Alleluias" [72, p.38].

Since the objectives of the festivals were political rather than artistic, music which lent itself to active participation by large crowds was especially useful. Simple melodies with texts set syllabically and consonant accompaniments were ideal. If the tunes were already familiar, so much the better. Ornamentation and contrapuntal complications were out of the question, partly because they were more difficult to perform, and partly because they were associated with music of the aristocracy. The primary concerns were the transmission of the message of the text and its impact on the crowd, both as a verbal communication and as an emotional experience. With an audience of thousands gathered outdoors or in a large church, spoken discourse was of little use in an age before electronic amplification. Music was thus an essential political tool. Processions, costumes, and pageantry also contributed to the dramatic effect of the festivals.

Among the most unusual works of this time were those by Méhul and Le Sueur composed for multiple choirs and orchestras, and performed in the church of the Invalides. Le Sueur's Chant du Ier Vendémiaire an IX (performed on September 23, 1800) used four choirs, each with its own orchestra. One pair was placed in the organ gallery, one in the choir, and one in each side gallery. The space within the church and the stereophonic effects were important elements in the composition, which was an extended patriotic work [225, pp.45–46].

The best-known and most popular musical products of the Revolution, however, were not the elaborate works of famous composers. The song *La Carmagnole* was probably originally a popular air; the tune of *Ça ira* was a contradanse; *Hymne des Marseillais (La Marseillaise)* was composed by a young army officer, Rouget de Lisle (1760–1836).

When the ceremonies and festivals organized by the government were held in churches, the organist was usually expected to play. The famous abbey church of Saint-Denis was reduced to the status of parish church in 1792, and then it became a Temple of Reason. In November 1793 the organist, Ferdinand-Albert Gautier (1748–1825), played for the inauguration of the *Décadis* (ceremonies held every tenth day).[5] His account is recorded by Raugel:

> At the séances décadaires, they assembled in the quire of the Temple of Reason, and there they sang lively songs, clad in diaphanous draperies,—a scene of riot. The tune of *Cadet Roussel* was one of those which I was compelled to accompany as a chorus, as well as several others of the same kind. The *Marseillaise* was not forgotten and was enthusiastically called for, the *Carmagnole* and *Ça ira* formed part of the service. The most remarkable thing about it all was that the maire, a former priest, was in the pulpit singing the verses which the others repeated in chorus. I am not saying this on the report of others: I saw it with my own eyes and heard it with my ears. [Cited in 263, p.43.]

Not all organists were as disturbed as Gautier by their duties during the revolutionary period. Charles Broche (1752–1803), organist of the cathedral at Rouen, seems to have adapted well to the changes. Broche was known as an outstanding performer on both organ and piano. He had studied organ with Desmasures, his predecessor at the cathedral, and then had spent several years in Bologna, Italy, studying counterpoint and fugue with the celebrated Padre Martini. He had been organist at the cathedral of Rouen since 1777, and he also held positions at several other churches. When the Rouen cathedral became a Temple of Reason, Broche remained at his post as organist, and was highly praised by the municipal authorities for his contributions to the civic ceremonies held there. The titles of his compositions for those occasions suggest their character: *Bataille à grands choeurs* with an *Invocation à la Liberté, Hymne à l'Egalité, Hymne aux braves défenseurs de la Patrie,* and some *Couplets patriotiques* [110, p.89].

One of Broche's improvisations was a descriptive piece on the battle of Jemappes, including "the noise of the military instruments, the terrible display of the combat, the clash of the troops, the din of the artillery, the moans of the wounded, of the dying, and the triumphant songs of the victors" [le bruit des instruments militaires, l'appareil terrible du combat, le choc des bataillons, le fracas de l'artillerie, les gémissements des blessés, des mourants et les chants de triomphe des vainqueurs; 110, p.89]. The verve and patriotic fire of his performance thrilled the enthusiastic audience.

In 1793 Nicolas Séjan (1745–1819) and Gervais-François Couperin (1759–1826) made an attempt to establish organ playing as a part of the musical fare of opera-goers. If they had succeeded, it might have created some interesting new professional possibilities for organists in the area of secular music.

When the Opéra moved to the Théâtre de la République et des Arts, two small organs were placed on opposite sides of the hall. They were to be used to play variations on patriotic airs, marches, and accompaniments. For four months Séjan and Couperin played these two organs for all the performances. The small instruments proved inadequate, so Séjan made arrangements for two other instruments to be acquired for the theater. Before they could be moved, the administration of the Opéra took steps to discontinue the use of any organs, using the space instead for loges. Séjan complained to the Committee for Public Instruction that the Opéra administration had even refused to pay him, Couperin, the organ builder (Somer), and the pumpers for their services during the four months. It was his view that the whole problem stemmed from jealousy over the success the organ music had had with the audiences. The salaries were finally paid, but by the Committee for Public Instruction not by the Opéra administration [36, pp.137–46].

Couperin's most famous secular performance occurred at the close of the eighteenth century, at a banquet celebrating Napoléon's campaign in Egypt. Fuller tells us that "in November, 1799, Gervais-François Couperin found himself playing dinner music on the greatest organ in Paris at Saint-Sulpice, while Napoléon and a nervous Directory, which was to be overthrown three days later by its guest of honor, consumed an immense banquet in the nave below" [126, p.141]. The church, transformed into a *Temple de la Victoire*, was profusely decorated with magnificent tapestries, flags, and a superb statue of Victory [34, p.174].

There has been much head shaking over the low level to which organ music was brought during the revolutionary period. Yet to a considerable extent organists were adapting methods, techniques, and music they already knew to the current situation. They already knew how to play programmatic improvisations. A favorite subject was the "Last Judgment" (based on a verse of the Te Deum, *Judex crederis*). One could hear such a piece improvised before the Revolution by Louis-Claude Daquin (1694–1772) [87, pp.120–21]. It was a small step from the portrayal of the end of the world to a description of the latest battle. Such performances were not considered outrageous. Organ music was still in step with the times, and it reflected and responded to popular taste and interests.

France provided inspiration for other musicians, too. The famous Bohemian pianist, Jan Ladislav Dussek (1760–1812), commemorated the end of an era with his salon piece *La Mort de Marie Antoinette*, "complete with a descending glissando to depict the falling of the blade of the guillotine" [257, p.93]. Before long Beethoven could celebrate the defeat of Napoléon's army in 1813 with *Wellington's Victory*, composed in collaboration with Johann Nepomuk Mälzel (1772–1838). Featuring battle music and patriotic songs, its first performance was a smashing success. "From the point of view of the Viennese public . . . the *Battle Symphony* was the composer's finest triumph" [257, pp.53–54].

PART ONE

Performers and Programs

IN THE course of the nineteenth century, interest in secular organ programs grew from modest beginnings to almost unbelievable levels. Although the organ had been used previously in secular performances (e.g., the *Concert spirituel,* and the patriotic festivals organized by the government after the Revolution), it was only rarely heard outside of church services in the early part of the nineteenth century. The organist's special showcase events, Te Deum performances and Noël Masses, were still within a liturgical structure.

By the end of the century Parisians could attend organ recitals in several concert halls, and there were more opportunities for the organist to perform with orchestra than there are today. French virtuosos were touring throughout the Western world, and the vanguard of countless American church music tour groups was experiencing first-hand the wonders of French organ building.

Although the focus in this section is primarily on secular performances and the organists who gave them, one must admit that church-goers heard the same performers and often the same repertoire at Mass on Sunday mornings. Boundaries between sacred and secular were never rigid, and even the most pristine taste permitted a rather generous common ground.

The emergence of secular organ programs was closely linked to the organ-building industry. Organists performed for the public when a new or rebuilt organ was inaugurated in a church and when organs were shown in industrial exhibitions. The demonstration of a new organ in the builder's shop offered another opportunity for a secular performance. When a builder completed an organ that would be sent to another location, he frequently arranged for it to be played several times for invited audiences before it was delivered.

In addition, one occasionally reads of programs given by visiting organists for select audiences, or given by local organists for important visitors. These programs were often more or less impromptu gatherings around the organ bench. The public organ recital for its own sake remained virtually unknown until the last quarter of the century. This secular event had to await the installation of organs in secular locations before it could become an important part of the general musical scene.

Although there were a few exceptions and some borderline cases, public musical programs unrelated to services, festivals, or other celebrations of the church, or to inaugurations of organs, were not generally given in French churches in the nineteenth century. Reviews of organ performances found in nineteenth-century French periodicals sometimes give the modern reader a deceptive impression about the nature of the event. For example, when Jacques Lemmens (1823–81), a Belgian organist, performed in 1852 on the recently installed organ at Saint-Vincent-de-Paul, Paris, his several appearances were given for invited groups of musicians; they were not public recitals. The builder of the organ, Aristide Cavaillé-Coll (1811–99), sent invitations to forty-four musicians to hear Lemmens on February 25, 1852 [73, p.829]. D'Ortigue estimated that some twenty-five to thirty people (including Alkan, Boëly, Franck, and Gounod) actually heard Lemmens at Saint-Vincent-de-Paul. They were not seated in the nave, as a present-day audience might be, but were "as enchained around M. Lemmens, eager to see him handle the colossal instrument" [comme enchaînés autour de M. Lemmens, avides de le voir manier le colossal instrument; 243, pp.181, 185].

A few years later, when one of Lemmens's students, Alphonse Mailly (1833–1918), arrived in Paris, Cavaillé-Coll arranged for several musicians to hear him at Saint-Vincent-de-Paul, but he wrote Lemmens about the difficulties of trying to arrange for a performance in a church. The organ builder regretted that he did not then have a playable organ in his shop on which Mailly could perform [79, no.55, p.42].

The situation had not changed greatly by the final decade of the century. In 1896 Eugène Lacroix (1858–1950) gave a program at Saint-Merry, soon after he assumed the position of organist at that church. A reviewer for *La Tribune de Saint-Gervais* complimented the parish priest for having authorized Lacroix to give the program. He thought it was an excellent example, and regretted that organists were not usually allowed to play recitals in church. In fact, he even suggested that such a program might be given without being followed by an office or a *salut:*[1] for example, after vespers on a Sunday [TSG 2, pp.173–74]. Lacroix's program was terminated by a salut, and could thus be interpreted as an extended prelude to a church ceremony.

The salut was apparently flexible enough to embrace some performances that seem suspiciously close to recitals. For example, *Le Ménestrel* announced that students of the Niedermeyer School would play a fugue by Niedermeyer, a prelude and a sonata by Mendelssohn, and two preludes and a sonata by Bach during a salut solennel at Saint-Louis-d'Antin on March 7, 1875 at 3:45 P.M. [ME 41, p.112].

The term *recital* was not used in France until late in the century. Solo
or small ensemble performances were often called *matinées musicales,* or
soirées musicales, depending on the time of day. These terms might be
used for a program in a private home, a public event in a recital or concert hall, or a program in an organ builder's hall. An organ performance
in a church was usually called an *audition* or a *séance. Audition* (i.e., a
hearing) was a term frequently used for any kind of musical event; *séance*
(session, or meeting), an even broader term, was also in general use for
programs of various kinds. The term *concert* was used much as it is today.
Usually it denoted a program involving ensembles. Toward the end of the
century important organ programs including works with instrumental ensembles were often listed under "Concerts" in the musical press.

The incumbent organist of the church was called the *organiste titulaire*
(or simply *titulaire*). He had charge of the principal organ, or *grand orgue,*
normally located in a *tribune,* or organ gallery over the west door of the
church. He or his deputy played the organ solo music: versets to alternate
with the choir, and more extended pieces at designated places in the
liturgy. The *maître de chapelle*[2] (choir master) was the administrator and
conductor of the choir. After about 1829 many churches installed an
organ or a harmonium in the choir area. It was called the *orgue de choeur*
and was played by the *organiste accompagnateur* (the choir accompanist).
There were variations to this general pattern, influenced by such con-
siderations as the size of the church, whether a choir organ was available,
local custom, and the music budget.

II.
In the Wake of the Storm
1800–1809

CHURCHES were still in the hands of the government when the nineteenth century opened. Some had been closed for more than a decade; others had been used (and often misused) for secular purposes. Some organs had been put in storage; some remained in place but were not playable; others had been destroyed or vandalized beyond repair. In 1801 Napoléon and Pope Pius VII signed the Concordat of 1801, an agreement which restored the legal status of the Catholic church in France. Only then could the slow process of reconstruction begin.

Through it all, a few organists who had begun their careers before the Revolution survived to begin salvaging their profession. Among the more prominent were Antoine Desprez [Després] (c. 1725–1806); Guillaume Lasceux (1740–1831); Nicolas Séjan (1745–1819); Eloi-Nicolas-Marie Miroir (1746–1815); Ferdinand-Albert Gautier (1748–1825); Isaac-François-Antoine Lefébure-Wély [Lefèbre] (1756–1831); François Lacodre, dit Blin (1757–1834); Jean-Baptiste-Nicolas Marrigues (1757–1834); Gervais-François Couperin (1759–1826); and Jacques-Marie Beauvarlet-Charpentier (1766–1834).

Some old traditions of the organ profession filtered down into the early nineteenth century. Leading organists often held several positions simultaneously. Other members of the family and students did much of the actual playing, and the organist was in the position of an administrator, overseeing the organ music in a group of churches.

Most organ positions were held for life, and some were passed down from one generation to the next as an inheritance. The most famous example is the 173-year reign of the Couperin family at the organ of Saint-Gervais, Paris. A young organist might receive an appointment as *survivancier;* that is, he had the right to succeed the incumbent organist (the *organiste titulaire*) when the position became vacant. This practice assured the church of a degree of continuity when an aging organist was no longer able to play. If a position became vacant and the succession was not already determined, the new organist was often chosen by means of a competition.

The idea that an organist had a tenured position was strong enough that some organists were able to reclaim their former positions after churches were reopened for Christian worship in the early years of the century. Thus Lasceux remained at Saint-Etienne-du-Mont, Séjan at Saint-Sulpice, and Couperin at

Saint-Gervais. But in some cases the church no longer had an organ, or an organ no longer had a building. It was years before some damaged buildings were returned to useful condition and supplied with playable organs. Even the better organists had to scramble for enough positions to provide a living.[1]

Whenever a builder completed a major restoration or a new organ, it was customary for a committee to inspect the builder's work. As a part of the examination and approval, or *vérification et réception,* as it was called, one or more organists would play, testing and demonstrating the organ's resources. These events were not really recitals, but often they were open to the public, thus providing the organist with an opportunity to perform outside the structure of a liturgical service. The music was improvised, as was most music played for services.

The nature of the organ inauguration changed greatly during the century, and it eventually included one or two formal recitals as well as the technical examination and reception of the builder's work. But even in the early years, an organ opening could attract an audience, curious to hear the organists as well as the organ.

The first nineteenth-century organ reception in Paris took place in 1800 at the church of Saint-Merry. Extensive repairs had been made to the organ, and the work was examined and approved by five organists: Séjan, Miroir, G.-F. Couperin, Desprez, and Lacodre-Blin [267 p.231].

On January 21, 1802, one could hear the same five organists on the Saint-Eustache organ, installed by Pierre-François Dallery (1764–1833). This organ had formerly been in Saint-Germain-des-Prés, where the organist was Eloi-Nicolas Miroir. The organist followed his instrument to its new location and was then *titulaire* at Saint-Eustache from 1802 until 1812 (without, however, giving up his position at Saint-Germain-des-Prés) [264, pp.45, 195].

On June 19, 1802, the repaired and re-installed organ at Saint-Thomas-d'Aquin was inaugurated by Lacodre-Blin, Desprez, Desquinmare, and Miroir, "to the reiterated applause of the public." This organ had been taken down and "left to decay" in a corner of the Panthéon during the Revolution [264, pp.135–36]. In October 1802 Marrigues was named organist, and he retained that position until his death in 1834. Other openings of rebuilt organs followed at Saint-Roch (1805), Saint-Paul–Saint-Louis (1805), and Saint-Louis-des-Invalides (1807) [264, pp.59, 110, 216].

The confusion created by the Revolution is well illustrated in the history of Saint-Germain-des-Prés. Originally an abbey, it was closed when monastery and convent property was confiscated. Its organ remained intact, although the church building was used as a refinery for saltpeter and gun powder. Thus the organ was available for transfer to Saint-Eustache (see above). No sooner had the instrument been installed in its new home than Saint-Germain-des-Prés was reinstituted as a parish church. The Saint-Eustache clergy had no intention of giving back the organ, so Saint-Germain had to look elsewhere for a suitable instrument. One was obtained from another abbey church, Saint-Victor, and was installed by Jean Somer. This organ had a history going back to the sixteenth century, but it had been transformed in subsequent rebuildings. Somer's restoration began in 1805 and was not completed until 1810. Raugel tells us that by then the four-manual organ of some fifty stops could be considered one of the best in Paris [264, pp.47–48]. Miroir was then the organist.

While all the moving around of organists and organs from one church to another may today seem like a game of musical chairs, the early years of the nineteenth century were anything but entertaining for the French organist who experienced them. A glimpse at the career of Nicolas Séjan illustrates the problems faced by an organist at the top of the profession. No organist of his generation was more frequently singled out for praise by his contemporaries. Alexandre-Etienne Choron (1771–1834), deploring in 1810 the decadence into which the organ had fallen, could still name Séjan as one who followed in the footsteps of the great organists of the past: Couperin, Marchand, Calvière, Daquin [55, vol.1, p.lxxxix].

Guillaume Lasceux's *Nouvelle Suite de pièces d'orgue* (c. 1810) is dedicated to Séjan, with an extravagant tribute, referring to him as "the Haydn of the organ." Lasceux's "Essai théorique" (1809), with verbal text by Traversier, refers to "the matchless Séjan, one of the most fertile improvisers to grace the organ and piano in this century." At Saint-Sulpice, the writer asserts, true connoisseurs and sensitive amateurs could hear the grand genre of organ playing, uniting skill and grace [191, p.37].

Séjan had had a brilliant career before the Revolution. Even the critical

Nicolas Séjan (The British Library, London).

François-Joseph Fétis (1784–1871) could affirm that Séjan had been "the only organist of talent" in Paris in the second half of the eighteenth century[2] [114, vol.8, p.10]. He had studied organ with his uncle Nicolas-Gilles Forqueray (1703–61) and composition with Bordier.[3] In 1760, when he was fifteen, Séjan became organist at Saint-André-des-Arts. At age nineteen he made his debut at the Concert spirituel, and was frequently heard in that series as performer or composer.

In 1772 Séjan was named organist of Notre-Dame, sharing the position with Claude-Etienne Luce, Armand-Louis Couperin, and Claude Balbastre [149, p.52]. He later accumulated additional organ positions, including those at Saint-Séverin (from 1782) and Saint-Sulpice (from 1783). In 1789 or 1790[4] he became organist at the Royal Chapel [114, vol.8, pp.9–10; 109, p.71].

Séjan was appointed professor of organ at the *Ecole royale de chant* in 1789. Fétis tells us that an organ was not acquired because of problems related to the Revolution, so Séjan taught only solfège there [114, vol.8, p.10]. When the Paris Conservatory was founded in 1795, it was again Séjan who was named professor of organ. Whether there was an organ at that institution in those early years remains questionable [84].

Unfortunately, by 1802 the 57-year-old artist had seen his sources of income eroding until there was almost nothing left. In a letter to Fourcroy, Conseiller d'Etat in charge of public instruction, Séjan explained that before the Revolution he had had an income of 3,600 francs from his church positions. All that remained was 450 francs from Saint-Sulpice (where the salary had formerly been 1,200 francs). He had taught in the most illustrious families of France; now that situation was entirely different, and it would be necessary to build a new reputation, an undertaking that would not be possible at his age. His position as organist to the king was swept away in the Revolution, and he had recently been dismissed from the Conservatory, where his salary had been 2,500 francs. In normal times, he could have expected to hold these latter two positions for life and to have been eligible for pensions from them. Having seven children to provide for, Séjan found himself in such unhappy circumstances that he asked if he might be granted a pension like those the government had allotted to some of his colleagues, in recognition of their celebrity and their seniority as artists [cited in 132].

Choron observed that Séjan's position at the Conservatory was cancelled "in disastrous times when there was no longer any hope that the art of the organ could be useful" [dans les tems désastreux où l'on n'espérait plus que l'art de l'orgue pût-être utile]. He noted that Séjan later became organist of Saint-Louis-des-Invalides (in 1806) [55, vol.2, p.310]. None of Séjan's organ music was published during his life. A collection of six of his pieces—three fugues and three noëls with variations—was published between 1819 and 1833.

Séjan's most famous colleague, Gervais-François Couperin, inherited professional positions and renown along with the family name. The mixed reviews of his playing suggest that he catered more to popular taste than to that of connoisseurs. After hearing Couperin play a Mass in honor of Sainte-Cécile at

Saint-Gervais in 1802, J. F. Reichardt fumed: "the instrument is as miserable as the performer! An organist of that type ought not bear the name *Couperin*" [l'instrument est aussi misérable que l'exécutant! Un organiste de cet acabit ne devrait pas s'appeler *Couperin;* cited in 36, p.134]. Fétis said Couperin "was just a mediocre organist and a composer without merit" [ne fut qu'un organiste médiocre et un compositeur sans mérite; 114, vol.2, p.377].

The general public took a different view. People flocked to Saint-Gervais to hear the famous Couperin. A Te Deum he performed in 1810 produced such convincing illusions that everyone applauded, in spite of the sanctity of the place. His playing was colorful, exploiting all the resources of the organ, from imitations of the human voice to thunder effects [34, p.176].

But fame and popularity were not sufficient to enable Couperin to accumulate an estate that would sustain his widow and daughter in later years. Thérèse-Célestine Couperin (1793–1860), the last of the Couperin line, filled the organ position left by her father at Saint-Gervais for a few months in 1826, and she was organist at Saint-François for nearly four years (April 1826 until the beginning of 1830). From then on she gave piano and voice lessons to support herself and her mother. Shortly after the revolution of 1848, Madame Couperin (1775–1862) could describe their situation as "completely ruined," as she negotiated to sell two of the Couperin family portraits for a disappointing 500 francs [36, pp.156–64, 170–71].

The name Beauvarlet-Charpentier perhaps could not compare with Couperin, but it was nevertheless one to command respect in the musical circles of Paris. Jean-Jacques Beauvarlet-Charpentier (1734–94) had been among the best known of the late-eighteenth-century French organists. His son Jacques-Marie was one of the more enterprising organists of the post-Revolution years. At a time when very little organ music was published, seven collections by Jacques-Marie Beauvarlet-Charpentier appeared between the turn of the century and 1822. The five that have been available for study originally carried the designation "Chez l'Auteur"; in other words, he published and distributed them himself. These publications inform us that he was a music and instrument dealer. In addition, the *Journal* (1822) invited inquiries regarding organ cases. Consultation services were also offered for those interested in making additions or repairs to organs, or who wanted to choose a piano.

In the titles of his works published during the Empire, Beauvarlet-Charpentier identified himself as organist of Saint-Paul–Saint-Louis, and of the Missions-Etrangères. In later publications he listed church positions at Saint-Paul–Saint-Louis and Saint-Germain-des-Prés. He remained at Saint-Paul–Saint-Louis until 1831. Subsequently (1831–34) he was at Saint-Eustache.

More definitive testimony is lacking, but the positions Beauvarlet-Charpentier held indicate he was at least an adequate performer. His compositions, meanwhile, suggest that he favored the lighter side of current taste. In addition to organ music, one notes his popular songs (romances), and his descriptive pieces celebrating military victories: some written for piano, or piano and violin, but at least one for piano or organ, *Victoire de l'Armée d'Italie, ou bataille de Montenotte* (1796) [137, vol.40, no.1, pp.3–5].

The *Victoire* . . . , a fourteen-page piece dedicated to Napoléon, is a blow-by-blow portrayal of a battle. There are the usual trumpet calls, marches, patriotic airs, and imitations of battle sounds. A particularly dramatic section, marked *pianissimo,* represents the silent march of 15,000 enemy soldiers on their way to surprise the garrison of 1,500 French. The fortifications are attacked, but reinforcements arrive to save the day. After the battle there are songs of victory, more fanfares, and the French army prepares to march on to other conquests, having won the admiration of the local citizens.

The extant works of Guillaume Lasceux differ from those of Beauvarlet-Charpentier. They bear evidence of a systematic craftsman, approaching the subject of organ playing from a somewhat more professional standpoint. His tributes to Séjan may reflect a shared viewpoint about standards in organ performance.

Lasceux's unpublished "Essai théorique . . ." (1809) and "Annuaire . . ." (1819) are invaluable sources of information about early-nineteenth-century forms, styles, and performance practice. In addition, Lasceux has left us published collections of organ music from both before and after the Revolution, and a manuscript collection of fugues dated 1820.

Important aspects of Marrigues's playing were mentioned in the necrology published shortly after his death (1834) in the *Revue musicale:* "M. Marrigues joined quite remarkable verve and imagination to a brilliant execution on his instrument; his improvisations bore the imprint of originality and genius; his *Te Deum* attracted a great gathering of music lovers and distinguished artists; he possessed to the highest degree the old traditions of the organ, which he observed scrupulously." [M. Marrigues joignait, à une exécution brillante sur son instrument, une verve et une imagination très remarquables; ses improvisations étaient marquées au coin de l'originalité et du génie; ses *Te Deum* attiraient un grand concours d'amateurs et d'artistes distingués; il possédait au suprême degré les antiques traditions de l'orgue dont il était le scrupuleux observateur; RM 14, p.158.]

Marrigues was named *titulaire* of Saint-Thomas-d'Aquin in 1802, subsequently accumulating additional positions at Saint-Nicolas-des-Champs (from 1808) and Saint-Gervais (from 1826) [264, pp.41, 125, 136].

An exact contemporary of Marrigues, François Lacodre-Blin shared his reputation as an outstanding improviser and a defender of the old traditions of organ playing. In his position as organist of Notre-Dame (1806–34) Lacodre-Blin participated in countless ceremonies marking important national events. There were Te Deum performances celebrating Napoléon's victories and later the restoration of the monarchy; there were ceremonies for births, birthdays, weddings, and funerals of famous people; there were the church festivals marked by particularly elaborate services at Notre-Dame. From his tribune

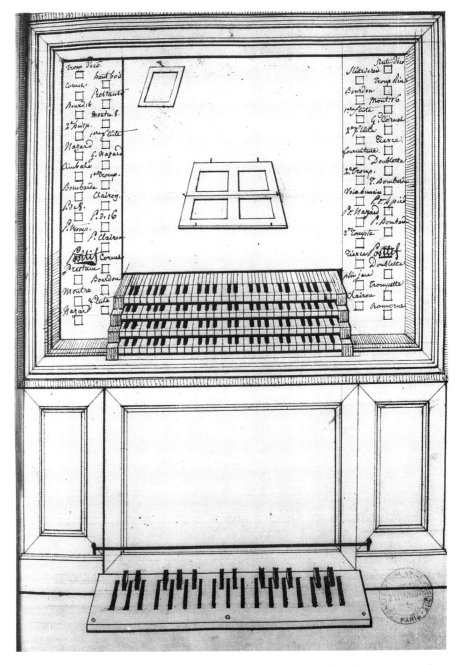

An illustration from Lasceux's "Essai théorique," 1809 (Bibliothèque Nationale, Paris).

high above the west door, Lacodre-Blin saw a turbulent quarter of a century of French history dramatized in the ceremonies for which he played.

Lacodre-Blin was also organist at Saint-Germain-l'Auxerrois from 1791, a position with more problems than pleasures. The revolutionary period had left the organ in deplorable condition, and it was not repaired until 1813 [32, p.87]. Then in 1831 the church was so severely damaged in a riot that it was closed. The 74-year-old organist did not live to see it reopened in 1837, and Saint-Germain-l'Auxerrois did not have another *titulaire* until Alexandre Boë-ly (1785–1858) was named to that position in 1840.

III.
Years of Rebuilding
1810–29

IN 1809 Lasceux's "Essai théorique" warned that the art of organ playing was disappearing from France. There was little incentive for anyone to enter the career of organist, with its uncertain future, low salaries, and scarcity of pupils. Thus the great art of organ playing of the seventeenth and eighteenth centuries was in danger of being entirely forgotten [191, p.7].

The same concerns had prompted the organists of twelve parishes in Paris to write an undated letter to the Minister of Churches. After advising that official of the precarious state of the art of organ playing in France, they proposed a plan. First, the government should raise the salaries of organists to 1,200 francs. Having a reasonable salary, each organist could then be required to select a student from the choir children of the parish and train him in organ playing free of charge. The letter was signed by Couperin, Marrigues, Oudin, Séjan, Lefébure-Wély, Pouteau, Thomelin, Lacodre-Blin, Boulogne and Miroir.[1] Although the total cost to the government would have been modest, the plan was not implemented.

Through much of the second decade of the century fulfillment of the grim predictions seemed all too possible. Preoccupied with the collapse of Napoléon's empire and the restoration of the monarchy (1814–15), the French paid little attention to an endangered art form. Nevertheless, a few events of interest to the organist emerge from the early years of the decade.

On August 27, 1812, Lasceux and Gervais-François Couperin inspected and demonstrated the repairs and additions recently made to the Saint-Gervais organ by Pierre-François Dallery [264, p.122]. By that time an over-confident Napoléon was marching through Russia, and on September 14 he would occupy the Kremlin. He was back in Paris on December 18, his army in shambles and the days of the Empire already numbered.

Paris was invaded by the allied army of France's enemies in March 1814, and it was invaded by Napoléon in his brief bid to regain power the following March. Between invasions, Dallery had completed repairs to the organ at Saint-Germain-l'Auxerrois, and Séjan, Lefébure, and Marrigues were there for the reception of the work on August 8, 1814 [122, p.384]. In spite of such efforts to maintain business as usual, not until after the Battle of Waterloo (June 18, 1815) and Napoléon's subsequent confinement on the island of St.

Helena could France settle down to a period of relative calm under Louis XVIII (until 1824) and Charles X (from 1824 to 1830).

During the confused and troubled years of 1811 to 1815, young François Benoist (1794–1878) had been a student at the Paris Conservatory. He received first prizes in harmony (1811), piano (1814), and composition (1815)— the *Prix de Rome* [249, p.696]. Returning to Paris early in 1819 after three years in Italy, Benoist faced a brighter future than he might have expected. While he had been away, a few encouraging signs related to organ playing had appeared. For example, Dallery had completed some work on the organ at Notre-Dame, which was examined by Marrigues and Lasceux on November 27, 1817 [137, vol.42, no.1, p.19]; and in 1818 there were organ receptions at Saint-Merry and Saint-Jean–Saint-François [264, pp.33, 179].

More important for Benoist were the new organ by Dallery for the Royal Chapel of the Tuileries and the recently completed Grenié organ for the Conservatory (reorganized in 1816 as the *Ecole royale de musique et de déclamation*). On March 31, 1819 there was a competition for the post of organist at the Royal Chapel. The candidates were Caussé, Beauvarlet-Charpentier, Fétis, Louis Séjan (Nicolas Séjan's son), Bergamini, Benoist, Seneitroeffer, and Couperin [82, no.62, p.14]. Benoist and Louis Séjan (1786–1849) were both awarded positions as organists. One can only imagine the disappointment of such veteran performers with notable organ-playing pedigrees as Beauvarlet-Charpentier and Couperin when they learned they were crowded out by the 25-year-old Benoist. To make matters more embarrassing, Benoist was appointed professor of organ at the *Ecole royale de musique* (the Conservatory) the following day.

Whether Benoist really deserved two such distinguished positions remains debatable, but it is clear that he filled both with dignity and tenacity. They gave the organ profession a measure of recognition it badly needed. The position at the Conservatory was especially important, not only in the educational opportunities it opened for young organists but also because it placed the organ in a common environment with other branches of professional music: an important change for an instrument too frequently isolated from mainstream musical developments, at least in the eyes of the general public and the press.

Among the losses to the organ profession in this decade were the death of Eloi-Nicolas Miroir in 1815, the retirement of Lasceux in 1819, and the death of Nicolas Séjan the same year. Louis Séjan succeeded his father as organist at Saint-Sulpice and at Saint-Louis-des-Invalides.

This decade witnessed an important development in organ construction. The new interest in free reeds was symptomatic of the stylistic changes organ composition and performance (as well as organ building) were already experiencing. Traditional organ reeds change pitch if there is a change in wind pressure. Free reeds, on the other hand, speak softer or louder with decreased or increased wind pressure, but they maintain the same pitch. Given a means to control the wind pressure, the performer can vary the loudness of a free-reed stop through a considerable dynamic range. This prospect was very interesting to organists, who were eager to apply to organ performance the subtle shadings and dramatic accents that the piano offered. Some experimental instruments using free reeds had already appeared in other countries, and both Gabriel-Joseph Grenié (1756–1837) and Sébastien Erard (1752–1831) had been working with the idea in France, even before the close of the eighteenth century.

On February 27, 1812, Grenié's new *orgue expressif* was used to accompany the singers in a performance of Zingarelli's *Stabat* at the Tuileries chapel [47, pp.207–208]. A few months later Grenié submitted a proposal for an *orgue expressif* to the administration of the Conservatory [82, nos.58–59, pp.56–57]. The instrument was completed about six years later and was to serve the organ students from Benoist's first class meeting in 1819 until 1871. It had two manuals, with traditional organ flue pipes on one and five sets of free reeds on the other. The twenty-note pedal had two stops: Bourdon (16') and a Flûte (8') [82, no.60, p.73].

The term *orgue expressif* initially referred to an organ that afforded some means of making a *crescendo* and a *decrescendo* without changing registration or manuals. Only later did it denote specifically an instrument using free reeds exclusively, i.e., an instrument of the type generally referred to today as the harmonium.

After the burst of activity in 1819, the organ world seemed to coast along for a few years. In the mid-1820s there was a new flurry of developments, and some new names began to attract attention. Prosper-Charles Simon (1788–1866), a native of Bordeaux, arrived in Paris in 1825. Almost immediately he won recognition for his performance of a Te Deum, including a particularly colorful and dramatic *Judex Crederis,* which took place at Notre-Dame-des-Victoires. The next year Simon was named organist of that church (a post he retained for the rest of his life). In 1827 he became professor of harmony and organ at the Maison Impériale. Later, Simon became organist at Saint-Denis (in 1840) and was employed by the government as an inspector of cathedral and parish organs. An 1855 description of Simon's playing by Georges Schmitt noted particularly his use of unusual registrations and effects, his skill in exploiting the organ's colors, and his facility using the composition pedals [289, pp.86–87].

Benoist's new organ class at the Conservatory had had no instant winners, but finally in 1826 a first prize was awarded to Alexandre-Charles Fessy (1804–56). He had entered the Conservatory in 1813, at age nine, and had first studied piano and harmony, progressing later to the organ class. Fessy was to become one of the better-known Parisian organ performers. He held organ positions at l'Assomption, La Madeleine, and finally (1847–56) at Saint-Roch. He also appeared from time to time in the late 1830s and 1840s as a conductor at the Concerts Valentino, the Concerts Viviennes, and some other concert series of that time. His name was usually associated with programs of a light, popular type [59, pp.68, 92, 234, 254].

In the same year that Fessy received first prize, Louis-James-Alfred Lefébure-Wély (1817–69) played the organ for Mass at Saint-Roch. His father, organist at Saint-Roch, had written the organ music for that occasion, and on the manuscript he noted with pride the accomplishment of his young son:

> This Mass was performed the Tuesday of Easter 1826 by my little son Alfrède, age eight years and four months, on the organ at Saint-Roch, to the satisfaction of those who were present. . . . During the entire Mass he maintained an extraordinary presence of mind that surprised those who were near him at the organ.[2]

> Cette Messe a été Exécutée le mardi de Paques 1826, par mon petit garçon Alfrède, agé de huit ans et quatre mois, sur l'orgue de St. Roch, à la satisfaction des personnes qui étaient présentes. . . . il à [*sic*] conservé pendant toute La Messe, une présence d'esprit extraordinaire qui à surpris les personnes qui étaient près de lui dans l'orgue. [BN MS 14756, p.13.]

One can follow the young organist's progress in the manuscripts of service music by Isaac-François-Antoine Lefébure-Wély. The father documented his son's performances of various manuscripts between 1826 and 1831, noting the date and the boy's age. His careful tutoring was a matter of exceptional concern, as Antoine Lefébure-Wély was struck by paralysis in his left side and was no longer able to perform. His son was his only substitute in the years before his death; in 1831 fourteen-year-old Alfred became *titulaire* at Saint-Roch.[3]

The music Antoine Lefébure-Wély wrote for his son to play is not without interest. Generally in a classic style, it contains a variety of rhythmic figures, independent voice leading, and manual changes that would be difficult for a beginner. One also finds interesting and colorful registrations.

By Easter 1828 young Alfred could play a Magnificat with special "thunder" effects to illustrate the text beginning "Deposuit" ("He has put down the mighty from their thrones"). In the excerpt below (BN MS 13766, p.61), one can see the indications for thunder, a circle cut by a diagonal line, and also the level of difficulty young Lefébure-Wély could manage between ages ten and eleven.

In a manuscript dated January 22, 1829 [BN MS 13356(5)], the organ is used to create a doleful atmosphere for a Requiem Mass. Among the techniques for special effects illustrated or described are clusters of keys in the low register of the pedal; both arms on the manual keys, moving them to produce an undulating sound; sudden outbursts; dramatic silences; and plaintive phrases on the voix humaine alone. Alfred Lefébure-Wély learned his lessons well. In a few years he would be the best-known, most-popular organist of his time.

Another new name on the Paris organ scene was John Abbey (1785–1859). He arrived from England in 1826 to work with Sébastien Erard on an organ to be exhibited the next year at the Exposition de l'Industrie. Abbey stayed on in France, collaborating with Erard for a time, and then working independently. Abbey introduced his French colleagues to various English organ-building techniques and inventions. The swell enclosure, popular in England for over a century, had not previously been used in Paris. Pedal controls for changing stops and an improved winding system also crossed the channel with Abbey.

In describing the Erard-Abbey organ for the 1827 Exposition, Joseph Guédon said it had

a *récit* made expressive by means of venetian-blind slats. The rest of the instrument differed from the old ones only by the arrangement of the mechanism and the power of the sounds. The stops could enter and leave by means of pedals, without one having to interrupt himself to pull or push them.

un *récit* rendu expressif au moyen de lames de jalousie. Le reste de l'instrument ne différait des anciens que par la disposition du mécanisme et la puissance des

Three portraits of
Louis-James-Alfred Lefébure-
Wély (Bibliothèque Nationale,
Paris).

sons. Les registres pouvaient entrer et sortir au moyen de pédales, sans qu'on fût obligé de s'interrompre pour les tirer ou les repousser. [141, p.439.]

The Abbey-Erard organ was described by Fétis as a *grand orgue expressif*, admired by all the connoisseurs. It was such a fine instrument that there was some thought of placing it in the Royal Chapel. However, as it was too large for the space available, Erard set about planning a new organ for that location [RM 6, pp.108–109].

The description by Fétis of the exposition organ is not very clear. He said that the upper manual was the expressive one, which could suggest that it used free reeds. However, he also mentioned the expression pedal, confirming Guédon's description of the *récit* as an enclosed division. Erard's system for controlling the dynamics of free reeds depended on finger pressure rather than a swell pedal. Fétis's use of the term *orgue expressif* is again a general one, in this case referring to an organ with an enclosed division.

This description was part of an introduction to a more extended review of the new Abbey-Erard organ for the Royal Chapel [RM 6, pp.104–10, 129–39]. For the latter instrument Abbey and Erard were joined by Pierre-Joseph Cosyn, who had been Grenié's principal craftsman [82, no.62, p.15]. The organ combined all the latest developments. The first two manuals were enclosed, and dynamic changes were controlled by a swell pedal. The top manual was a division of free reeds, and dynamic changes were effected by finger pressure. There were pedals for coupling divisions and for drawing and retiring stops. Although it had only twelve registers, the effect was said to be that of a much larger instrument.

Fétis mentioned that both Simon and Fessy had played the new organ with fine results, effectively answering criticisms that so many pedal controls might prove an obstacle to improvisation, distracting the organist's attention from his primary objective. Fétis himself was more than enthusiastic: "Either I am very mistaken, or the moment of a revolution in organ music has arrived, a revolution of which the discovery of the *orgue expressif* is the signal." [Ou je me trompe fort, ou le moment est venu d'une révolution dans la musique d'orgue, révolution dont la découverte de l'orgue expressif est le signal; RM 6, p.131.]

François-Joseph Fétis would soon see a revolution, but it wasn't the one he had in mind. Meanwhile, he was making an important contribution of another type to the organ profession. He had founded the *Revue musicale* in 1827, and at that time it was the only Paris journal devoted exclusively to music. In the early years the *Revue* was written almost entirely by Fétis, and it reflected his strong opinions as well as his remarkable store of knowledge. Fortunately, his lifelong interest in the organ prompted him to comment frequently on various aspects of the organ profession. He complained about the Parisian style of plainchant accompaniment (vol.2, p.21), complimented Benoist on the Conservatory organ class (vol.2, pp.68–69), reviewed publications related to the organ (vol.4, p.305), and campaigned for the "true style" of organ playing (vol.4, p.306). One cannot doubt that the musical public gained a new awareness of the organ profession in the pages of the *Revue musicale* and of its successor (to which Fétis also frequently contributed), *Revue et Gazette musicale.*

By the end of the decade it was clear that organ building was moving along at an encouraging pace. Not only were technical and stylistic changes attracting attention, but new organs were appearing more frequently and were serving more diverse interests. In addition to those already mentioned, one can cite the new (1825) 22-stop organ by Louis-Paul Dallery (1797–1870) in the church of the Sorbonne. There it was used in the performances given each Sunday by Choron and his students of the *Institution royale de musique religieuse* [264, p.156]. By 1828 the Protestants of Paris, worshipping in the Oratoire, could sing to the accompaniment of a new organ built by Louis Callinet and Jean Somer, and approved on May 17, 1828 by Beauvarlet-Charpentier and Louis Séjan. The *titulaire* was then Jean-Nicolas Lefroid de Méreaux (1767–1838) [264, pp.157–59].

Meanwhile, what was happening to the performer? This chapter opened with an 1809 lament that there was little incentive for anyone to become an organist. It closes with an 1826 reiteration of the same refrain. Varcollier noted that the organist had to have technical command of the instrument, skill in harmony and composition, and the ability to improvise all that he played: "Well! What does one offer to the ambition of a man who has consumed ten years of his life in such difficult and laborious studies? A salary of 1,000 francs in the principal church of the realm, and of six to seven hundred in the others." [Eh bien! qu'offre-t-on à l'ambition d'un homme qui a consumé dix années de sa vie dans de si fortes et si pénibles études? Un traitement de mille francs dans la première église du royaume, de six à sept cents dans les autres; cited in 133, p.120.]

IV.
The Romantic Dawn
The 1830s

PARIS became a battlefield for a brief time in the summer of 1830. There were 4,054 barricades in the streets, and the fighting left 2,212 dead and 5,451 wounded [14, pp.4–5]. Increasingly repressive measures by Charles X had sparked the short but bloody revolution. In an effort to preserve the constitutional monarchy, liberal members of the chamber of deputies proclaimed Louis-Philippe, duke of Orléans, "King of the French." His reign, known as the July Monarchy, lasted from 1830 to 1848.

The chapel of the Tuileries was destroyed in the July revolution, and the new organ Fétis admired the year before was broken in pieces.[1] Further disturbances on February 13, 1831 resulted in damage to the organ of Saint-Germain l'Auxerrois and the closing of the church for six years [122, p.384]. When Notre-Dame was sacked by rioters in 1830 and 1831, the organ barely escaped destruction [33, p.54].

King Louis-Philippe was anything but helpful to church musicians. He closed the jewel in the crown of French church music, the Royal Chapel, and dismissed its staff of musicians with reduced pensions. He cut almost in half the funds available for salaries of musicians at Notre-Dame, and the position *maître de chapelle* was abolished [33, p.54]. The school of music founded by Choron was another victim of the royal economy measures. In 1825 it had become the *Institution royale de musique religieuse,* and by 1830 it had an enrollment of 150 students [225, p.28]. The new regime so limited its funding that the school could no longer function effectively.

Writing in 1832, Castil-Blaze mourned the loss of Royal Chapel music, in particular, and support for music in general. Artists were starving, he said, and music of quality would disappear from France [47, pp.256–59]. In spite of this gloomy outlook, the July Monarchy did not destroy French music. Enrollment in the Paris Conservatory increased from 289 in 1830–31 to 580 in 1847–48 [249, p.873], and the Conservatory concerts under Habeneck were introducing audiences to the Beethoven symphonies. Paris, with a population of 786,000, was attracting a growing list of virtuoso performers, and its opera was flourishing.

Something new was in the air. The Industrial Revolution was taking hold in France. New inventions and products were making daily living more convenient, and public transportation systems were beginning to offer easier modes of travel. Social issues were bubbling to the surface, and a variety of solutions for society's problems were proposed by the Saint-Simonians and other visionary groups. Even ideas about musical instrument making were changing.

The year 1830 is sometimes cited by historians as a starting point for the Romantic period in French music, with the première of Berlioz's *Symphonie fantastique* (December 5, 1830) as the signal of the new era. Of course, the Romantic period had been in preparation for years. For example, one sees the trend toward bigger, louder sounds with greater emphasis on lower pitches in the orchestra, in organ design, and in organ registration in the second half of the eighteenth century.[2] New voices in the organ and the orchestra contributed to this trend, and also enriched the palette of colors available to composers and performers.

The easy victory of the piano over the harpsichord had been decided before the turn of the century. Performers were delighted with the range of expression it offered, from subtle nuances to grandiose dramatic effects. When organ builders searched for ways to give the organ similar expressive possibilities, theirs was not an isolated interest but a response to contemporary taste. It was a race to see who could best combine the piano's control of dynamics with the organ's sustained tone.

The expanded orchestra and the new and redesigned instruments did not define romanticism, but they were essential tools for the Romantic performer and composer. Even though those tools continued to change, by 1830 the modern musician was ready to use them to communicate with listeners in a more personal way, chipping away at the restraints of traditional forms, textures, and harmonic language, and exploring new ways of combining the musical materials.

Fétis was, after all, on the right track in 1829, when he predicted a revolution in organ music with the "expressive organ" as the sign of change. By 1830 Erard, Grenié, and Abbey had demonstrated that organists could indeed change dynamics and tone color without ever taking their hands off the keys. If the pipe organ with one or more enclosed divisions and the free-reed organ soon went separate ways in matters of structure, they remained siblings as far as practical use was concerned. Throughout the rest of the nineteenth century French organists freely transferred much of their repertoires from one instrument to the other. The designation "for organ or harmonium" on published music was not necessarily a publisher's way of attracting more customers: it was often a perfectly valid statement of an accepted performance practice.

Aristide Cavaillé-Coll's arrival in Paris in 1833 could scarcely have been more timely. The chronological period of his work, as well as his artistic objectives, meshed extremely well with mainstream Romantic developments, and his craftsmanship ensured the high quality of his instruments. In addition, he went to extraordinary lengths to see that his organs were played by artists of his choice, and that organists he considered deserving had opportunities to play his instruments, sometimes for select audiences of musicians, sometimes for the general public. He took great interest in talented young organists and would often arrange for them to be heard on one of his instruments. Cavaillé-Coll probably exerted more influence on the organ profession of his time than any other organ builder before or since.

In 1833 it came as a surprise to almost everyone that this young, unknown provincial builder could snare the contract for a new organ in Saint-Denis. The *Revue musicale* grumbled that there were plenty of good builders whose work was well known [RM 13, pp.369–70]. Cavaillé-Coll was only 22 that year, but many of the people who would participate with him in shaping a new life for the organ in France were also young. Louis-James-Alfred Lefébure-Wély was sixteen; Félix Danjou (1812–66) was 21; Joseph Pollet (1806–83) was 27; Alexandre-Charles Fessy was 29; François Benoist was 39; Prosper-Charles Simon, Louis-Nicolas Séjan, and Alexandre Boëly were all in their forties.

The generation of organists whose careers had spanned the Revolution had almost disappeared. Guillaume Lasceux and Antoine Lefébure-Wély died in 1831, followed in 1834 by François Lacodre-Blin, Jean-Nicolas Marrigues, and Jacques-Marie Beauvarlet-Charpentier. Their careers had encompassed the Consulate, the First Empire, the reigns of Louis XVIII and Charles X, and the beginnings of the July Monarchy. One can but marvel at their tenacity and endurance during a period that offered so little encouragement to the church musician. With them a chapter in the history of French organists had come to a close.

We have already met Benoist, Fessy, and Simon. Let us then turn briefly to the careers of some of the other organists active in Paris during the reign of Louis-Philippe. The youngest member of the new wave of organists, Louis-James-Alfred Lefébure-Wély, was already *titulaire* at Saint-Roch when Cavaillé-Coll arrived in Paris. He had succeeded his father in 1831, even though he was then only fourteen years old. This was the precocious lad who had played for Mass when he was little more than eight; organ playing was his mother tongue.

Alfred entered the Conservatory in 1832. He was awarded second prizes in piano and organ in 1834, and first prizes in both instruments the next year [188, col.11–13]. His association with Cavaillé-Coll began even before the builder had completed his first organ in Paris (1838). In 1836 Lefébure-Wély was heard in a program on Cavaillé-Coll's version of the free-reed instrument, the *poïkilorgue*. In 1839 he demonstrated that instrument two hours a day, four days a week, for the Exposition of Industry [73, p.71].

The careers of Lefébure-Wély and Cavaillé-Coll continued to intertwine for many years. Lefébure-Wély was a colorful, imaginative performer who knew how to show off a new organ to its best advantage. For at least two decades he was Cavaillé-Coll's first choice as recitalist for the inauguration of new organs. In exchange, Cavaillé-Coll was instrumental in forwarding Lefébure-Wély's career, frequently persuading churches to engage him as recitalist, and supporting (or perhaps initiating) his successive appointments as organist at La Madeleine (1847) and Saint-Sulpice (1863).

Joseph Pollet was named *organiste titulaire* of Notre-Dame cathedral in 1834, succeeding Lacodre-Blin. Pollet had had a long association with the music of the cathedral, dating from his entrance in the Notre-Dame *maîtrise* (the choir school) as a choir boy in 1814. He remained a student there until 1824, completing his education at the Paris Conservatory (at that time called the *Ecole royale de musique et de déclamation*) between 1824 and 1832. Meanwhile, he had begun teaching at the Notre-Dame *maîtrise* in 1826. In 1830 he became *maître de chapelle,* and he fulfilled his various responsibilities so well that his appointment as organist was unanimous. Pollet retained the position of organist only until 1841. Then he continued to serve as *maître de chapelle* until his retirement in 1873 [33, pp.70–74].

Jean-Louis-Félix Danjou was organist at the church of Notre-Dame-des-Blancs-Manteaux (1831–34), at Saint-Eustache (1834–44), and at Notre-Dame cathedral (1841–47). At the cathedral he served also as organ professor of the *maîtrise.* Endowed with exceptional intelligence, insight, energy, and dedication, Danjou became one of the most ambitious campaigners of his time for the improvement of church music.

From the time Danjou became organist at Saint-Eustache, his activities and aspirations touched every aspect of church music. As Fenner Douglass summarized them:

> Inspired by a receptive clergy and the group of zealots that quickly formed about him, Danjou soon found himself the leader of a movement for reform, the purposes of which were to restore sacred chant to its ancient dignity, to act against prevailing bad taste and secularization in church music, to organize societies in the provinces to promote those aims, to publish articles and unknown musical masterpieces from the Renaissance and Baroque eras, to raise the standards of organ building and organ repair, and to train a new school of organists who would be capable of reviving the great traditions of the past. [73, p.34.]

Danjou was no mere theorist. He plunged into organ building, and from 1838 or 1839 was artistic director of the Daublaine-Callinet firm (Cavaillé-Coll's most serious competition[3]); he published a periodical from 1845 to 1848, with a final issue in 1854 (*Revue de la musique religieuse, populaire et classique*[4]); he published church music; he engaged in research; and he was the discoverer of the *Montpellier Graduale:* the "Rosetta Stone of medieval neumatic notation" [72, p.356, n.72].

In his periodical Danjou sounded very much like twentieth-century American reformers when he criticized Cavaillé-Coll for trying to imitate orchestral instruments, increase the organ's power, and improve its mechanism at the expense of the historic style of the organ. This style, he pointed out, predated the orchestra and had its own development independent of the orchestra. He believed that the new trend was a violation of the organ's integrity, that it would destroy the organ's essential character, and that it would result in an instrument with a secular orientation inappropriate for the church.

Cavaillé-Coll, sounding very much like the twentieth century's E. M. Skinner, replied that Danjou had summarized his objectives perfectly. He did indeed strive to increase the organ's power, perfect its mechanism, and produce organ stops that would imitate as closely as possible the timbre and character of corresponding orchestral instruments. He felt that he was doing music a favor by replacing "those forests of *nazard, quarte, tierce,* and *cornet* stops that infested the old organs" with his new harmonic stops[5] [ces forêts de jeux de *nazard,* de *quarte,* de *tierce* et de *cornet* dont les anciennes orgues étaient infectées; RMR 3, p.37].

Danjou confronted the organists of Paris as boldly as he had Cavaillé-Coll by bringing Adolf Hesse (1808–63) there to play Bach. Like it or not, French organists could never again isolate themselves from the shadow of German organ music and organ playing that lurked just across the border. For decades after, French organists would be on the defensive about pedal playing, counterpoint, and composed organ music.

One organist in Paris found nothing to fear in the German school: Danjou's friend, Alexandre-Pierre-François Boëly. Like Danjou, Boëly was a scholar as

Jean-Nicolas Marrigues and Alexandre P. F. Boëly at the Saint-Gervais organ. From *L'Echo Musical,* 1919 (Bibliothèque Nationale, Paris).

well as a musician, and he was occupied with his own studies of early music. He was reputed to be the only French organist of his time who had developed a pedal technique adequate for playing the music of Bach.[6] Boëly, too, had other interests, but unlike Danjou's, they did not revolve primarily around church music. He was a pianist, a chamber musician (playing viola), and, above all, a composer.

It is not known just when Boëly became interested in the organ or how he learned to play. He knew Marrigues, the organist of Saint-Gervais, and sometimes substituted for him and (after the death of Marrigues in 1834) for his successor. However, Boëly was never officially on the music staff of Saint-Gervais [122, pp.136–37].

In 1838 Danjou and Boëly were engaged to oversee the restoration by Louis-Paul Dallery of the organ for Saint-Germain-l'Auxerrois. When the work was completed, in August 1840, Boëly was named *titulaire;* this was his only professional position as organist. From 1845 until about 1850 he was also professor of piano at the Notre-Dame *maîtrise.*

Most of his contemporaries would have been amazed to learn that Boëly was the greatest organ composer France had thus far produced in the nineteenth century. Some of his organ music was published in the 1840s, but, as we have noted, most French organists had little or no interest in composed music. Boëly, on the other hand, programmed works of Bach, Couperin, Handel, and Albrechtsberger in organ demonstrations and inaugurations. In bringing the music of great composers of the past to the attention of the public, he was contributing to his own obscurity. Boëly could have used his relatively few performance opportunities to promote his own compositions.[7]

Perhaps the least colorful of the prominent organists of the time was Louis-Nicolas Séjan, the son of Nicolas Séjan. He never attained the stature his father had enjoyed in the organ profession. The necrology written by Maurice Bourges in 1849 rated Louis-Nicolas among the best of second-rank organists in the historic gallery of French organists. New trends in the 1830s and '40s passed him by, and he lacked the imagination or skill to exploit the colorful effects available on the new organs. Nevertheless, he remained the conscientious and respected conservator of an older style. Bourges characterized Louis Séjan's improvisations as clear, orderly, and in a moderate style. If they lacked originality, they never exhibited incoherence or poor taste [RGM 16, p.118].

Louis Séjan's most valuable legacy to the organ profession was the publication of his father's organ pieces. This small collection, containing our only examples of Nicolas Séjan's organ music, was edited by Louis between 1819 and 1833.[8]

The name of Jacques-Claude-Adolphe Miné (1796–1854) is sometimes linked with that of Fessy. In the mid–1830s these two organists collaborated in writing collections of music for church services. They were published periodically in twelve volumes, with the title *Le Guide de l'organiste* (Paris: Troupenas, c. 1835).

Miné entered the Paris Conservatory in 1811 (before Benoist's organ class was initiated) and studied cello and harmony [114, vol.6, p.148]. He was organist-accompanist first at Saint-Etienne-du-Mont (from about 1830), and then at Saint-Roch (1833–43). From 1844 to 1854 he was organist at the cathedral of Chartres[9] [ME 21, no.51, p.4].

Fessy and Miné each published organ methods and additional collections of service music. In those years, when very little music was available for the organist with limited preparation, these publications found a ready welcome. Miné composed or compiled about fifteen collections of organ music, dating from around 1827 to 1854. He also wrote three method books, one of which (*Manuel simplifié de l'organiste . . .*) uses a system of tablature notation that enables a beginning organist to accompany plainchant without knowing how to read normal notation. One organ method and about seven collections of music by Fessy were published (two of the collections posthumously).

Within these publications the struggling organist could find just about anything he needed to know to manipulate the instrument and follow the liturgy, and they contained an abundant supply of easy music for all the situations he might expect to encounter. The quality of the music is quite ordinary (Fessy's music is more interesting than Miné's), but the utilitarian objectives are well satisfied. In 1846 J.-B. Laurens wrote that when someone with no previous musical training wanted to learn to play the organ, his advice was "take Miné." There one would find many easy, agreeable pieces, including some that were "very distinguished and perfectly suitable for church services" [très distinguées et parfaitement convenables au service divin; 193, p.438].

In contrast to the new ideas and new possibilities that sprouted in other areas of music in the 1830s, it was a relatively arid period for organ performance. Only in the last years of the decade did some events of general interest again bring the art of the organ performer to the attention of the public. In May 1838, when Dallery completed repairs and changes in the organ of Notre-Dame cathedral, *Le Ménestrel* reported that principal organists had been invited to try the instrument and judge the organ builder's work.

> Misters Séjan, Boilly [Boëly], Danjou and Gilbert successively took charge of the magnificent instrument, and each performed some fugues, marches, symphonic excerpts, and improvisations that produced a profound impression on the listeners. In all, the testing of the organ was very satisfactory, and Mr. Dallery received abundant praise for the noble perseverance with which he has accomplished this fine work.

> MM. Séjan, Boilly, Danjou et Gilbert se sont successivement emparés du magnifique instrument, et chacun d'eux a fait entendre des fugues, des marches, des fragmens [sic] de symphonies, des improvisations qui ont produit une profonde impression sur l'auditoire. En somme, l'essai de l'orgue a été très satisfaisant, et M. Dallery a recueilli d'amples éloges pour la noble persévérance avec laquelle il a accompli ce beau travail. [ME 5, no.24, p.4.]

Only a few months later, in October, Cavaillé-Coll's first organ in Paris (at Notre-Dame-de-Lorette) was given its *réception*. This was no ordinary event.

An astonished reviewer for *La France musicale* found it hard to believe that such a large audience of music lovers and artists had gathered together out of interest in hearing the organ. The occasion recalled the good old days, when Daquin, Rameau, and Couperin, and, later, Miroir, Nicolas Séjan, and Balbastre used to attract crowds to hear their improvisations [FM 1, no.44, pp.4–5].

Organists for this event were Alphonse Gilbert (1805–70), *titulaire* at Notre-Dame-de-Lorette, Louis-Nicolas Séjan of Saint-Sulpice, Fessy of l'Assomption, and Lefébure-Wély of Saint-Roch. Lefébure-Wély was the star performer. While the reviewer recognized the latter's talent, he advised Lefébure-Wély to give up the light style he had adopted and mend his ways by studying the works of great composers, especially Bach and Handel. But the 21-year-old Lefébure-Wély already knew what *his* public wanted to hear and how to satisfy the popular taste in organ music more effectively than any other performer of his time. He was no more ready to listen to conservative advice than was his twentieth-century counterpart, Virgil Fox.

Reports in *La Revue et Gazette musicale* reveal the differences between the two events. The Notre-Dame reception was a proper affair: the organ was found to be entirely satisfactory, and the artists performed "some pieces of extraordinary merit played in a superior manner" [des morceaux d'un rare mérite supérieurement exécutés; RGM 5, p.203]. In contrast, the situation at Notre-Dame-de-Lorette reminded the reporter of a secular concert, from the large, fashionable crowd to the waltzes and tunes played by "the *pianists*" who tried the new organ. "It is a sad truth, but one must say it: the art of organ playing has fallen into total decadence today." [C'est une triste vérité, mais il faut la dire: l'art de toucher de l'orgue, est en pleine décadence aujourd'hui; RGM 5, p.430.]

The division into two camps—the popular, light, entertaining, and primarily homophonic on one side, and the serious, dignified, and primarily contrapuntal on the other—is well defined in reviews of organ performances. Some organists (Boëly, Danjou, Benoist) were stereotyped as performers of the serious or severe type, and others (Lefébure-Wély, Fessy, Simon) as players of the popular or light type. Writers for the musical press often aligned themselves with one camp or the other, and their slanted reviews need to be interpreted accordingly.

In 1839 several organ builders exhibited their instruments at the Exposition des Produits de l'Industrie: Cavaillé-Coll, John Abbey, and Daublaine et Callinet. They were played during the exposition by various organists, but Lefébure-Wély was selected to play all of them for the jury, a service he also performed at expositions in 1844 and 1849. Cavaillé-Coll and Abbey were awarded bronze medals. After the exposition the Cavaillé-Coll organ was temporarily located in Saint-Roch, where Lefébure-Wély was organist. Prospective buyers (and others) could hear him play it there on Tuesday and Sunday evenings [FM 2, pp.451, 603]. The 31-stop organ by Daublaine et Callinet, constructed under the direction of Félix Danjou, was installed in

Saint-Denis-du-Saint-Sacrement. Marius Gueit (1808–62), a former student of
Lasceux and Marrigues, became the first *titulaire* of this organ [264, pp.175–
76].

While organists and organ builders in Paris were occupied with preparations
for the exhibition in the spring of 1839, one of the more interesting organ
performances took place in the church of Notre-Dame-du-Mont, Marseille.
The organist was Fryderyk Chopin (1810–49), and the occasion was a funeral
service for the celebrated French tenor Adolphe Nourrit (1802–39). Chopin
played "one of those improvisations of which the sad and melancholy character awakened in the soul quite grievous memories" [une de ces improvisations dont le charactère triste et mélancolique réveillait dans l'âme de
bien douloureux souvenirs]. The reviewer implied that the organ left something to be desired and that the artist "by necessity had to limit himself to
throwing a modest flower, but full of fragrance, on that tomb" [a dû
nécessairement se borner à jeter une fleur modeste, mais pleine de parfum, sur
cette tombe]. He observed that George Sand was also in the organ loft [FM 2,
pp.282–83].

V.
Contrasts, Conflicts, and Conquests
The 1840s

IN THE summer of 1841 the first press notice of César Franck (1822-90) as an organist appeared in the *Revue et Gazette musicale* [RGM 8, p.353]. His name was already familiar to readers of the *Revue,* as he had been thrust into public view by an overly ambitious father ever since his Paris debut as a pianist in 1835 [RM 15, p.376]. Even severe critics had acknowledged that young César Franck was a talented pianist and composer, however handicapped by his father's antics to gain attention. But the news that the nineteen-year-old Franck had won second prize as an organ student in Benoist's class would not have attracted more than passing interest, even among organists. Franck's early career as organist was anything but spectacular. It was not until 1845 that he held a professional position, and then it was as organist-accompanist at Notre-Dame-de-Lorette, where Alphonse Gilbert was *titulaire.* He remained in that position until 1853 [276, p.15].

Meanwhile, the spotlight of the organ world was trained not on the Conservatory competition but on an important new organ built by Cavaillé-Coll. In September 1841 the *Revue et Gazette musicale* announced that the *réception solennelle* of the organ for the royal church of Saint-Denis would take place on the 21st at 2 P.M., in the presence of a commission of members of the Institute, charged by the minister of public works to report to him on the merit of this important work. The organ, the "largest and most complete" in France, would be tried in turn by the most able organists [RGM 8, p.415].

The Saint-Denis organ was innovative in many respects, but its most important new feature was the use of Barker machines: pneumatic levers applied to the key action of the *grand orgue* manual. This invention, developed by an Englishman, Charles Spackman Barker (1806–79), made it possible for the organist to couple manuals together without increasing the resistance of the keys. Thus, the organist could use the combined manuals of even a large organ without having to cope with heavy key action. This invention held obvious implications not only for the potential size of organs but also for new directions in organ registration. By an amazing coincidence, Charles Barker arrived in France just in time for his invention to be used by Cavaillé-Coll at Saint-Denis.

The Cavaillé-Coll organ in the cathedral basilica of Saint-Denis (Jim Lewis).

The long-awaited organ reception turned out to be a fiasco. Almost every-thing went wrong. From the report in *La France musicale* we learn that people began to fill the church long before the appointed hour. The commission first inspected the interior of the organ. Then, just when everyone thought the organ would be played, the Canons filed into the choir and began intoning "interminable vespers." Organ versets, which might have added some interest to the service, only increased the boredom and impatience of the public; it seems that the popular Simon, newly appointed organist of Saint-Denis, had been called out of town and had left in his place an organist "of the tenth rank."

Finally the vespers were over. Then, instead of giving the people a chance to hear the organ, the commission asked Lefébure-Wély to play each stop separately. Having stood for more than three hours, the crowd was at the limit of its patience, and the softest stops were accompanied by the noise of "six thousand people" milling around. Ultimately the organist played a *grand choeur,* and everyone left, greatly disappointed with the whole affair. The reviewer suggested that it would have been better to have a private inspection of the organ by the commission followed by a separate public event with performances by leading artists [FM 4, pp.330-31].

This plan, indeed, was widely adopted later. The official utilitarian inspection and testing of the organ gradually faded into the background, and public attention became focused on the inaugural program in which the display of the organ's resources was the primary objective. The secular character of this event might be slightly diluted by a preliminary consecration ceremony, or by attaching it to one of the church's regular services.

No such disturbances as those at Saint-Denis accompanied the 1842 reception of the organ at Saint-Roch, rebuilt by Cavaillé-Coll. Instead, the organist, Lefébure-Wély, managed to scandalize the reviewer of the *Revue et Gazette musicale* by playing a fantasy on themes from Meyerbeer's opera *Robert-le-diable* [RGM 9, p.296].

In the same year, the Cavaillé-Coll organ from the 1839 exposition found a permanent home in a Lutheran church, Les Billettes (located on rue des Archives, formerly named rue des Billettes). The opening program is interesting because its format was typical of many that followed. The organist for this occasion, Sigismund Neukomm (1778–1858), played four improvisations of different types, and a choir sang between each improvisation [FM 5, p.178]. The idea of alternating organ pieces with some other media became a basic principle in the arrangement of organ programs. Vocal solos or choirs often filled the spaces between organ pieces, but instrumental solos might also be heard. Throughout the nineteenth century most organ programs relied on at least one other medium to provide variety. It is clear that the general public was not interested in hearing organ music exclusively, one piece after another. More often than not further variety would be added to the program by including performances by more than one organist.

Neukomm had already played the Cavaillé-Coll organ of the Lutheran church in 1839, while it was at the exposition, and he would be heard from time to time on other Cavaillé-Coll organs during the 1840s. He was well known in Parisian musical circles, and was typically referred to as "the celebrated organist" in press notices of his organ performances.

Sigismund (or Sigismond) Neukomm was born in Salzburg, Austria. He had his first organ lessons there with Weissaner, and he studied composition with Michael Haydn. In 1798 he went to Vienna, where Joseph Haydn became his teacher, mentor, and close friend. His first trip to Paris, in 1809, was brief; but

Neukomm returned the next year and entered the service of Talleyrand, remaining in Paris for four years. From that time his autobiography reads like a whirlwind itinerary. He seemed intent on covering as many miles as possible and writing as much music as possible. At his death, his catalogue of works listed more than two thousand numbers, including some fifty organ pieces.[1]

During the 1840s builders exploited with increasing frequency their opportunities to hold private hearings of new organs in the large rooms, or halls, of their manufactories. In terms of public relations and publicity, these events were beneficial for builders and performers alike. In the spring of 1843 the Daublaine-Callinet firm invited an audience of artists and music lovers to see and hear an organ soon to be installed in the church of Saint-Serge, Angers. Fessy and Séjan demonstrated the features of the organ as well as their own talents [RGM 10, p.143].

Not to be outdone, Cavaillé-Coll then held several hearings of his organ destined for Saint-Jerôme, Toulouse. The performers were Lefébure-Wély and Piétro (or Peter) Cavallo (b. 1819), an organist from Munich who had moved to Paris in 1842. The final program was graced by the presence of Gioacchino Rossini (1792–1868). The popularity of this famous composer in Paris could hardly be overestimated. His presence added luster to any event, and the press was sure to record his reactions. Rossini had been instrumental in Cavaillé-Coll's initial decision to move to Paris, and he retained an interest in the young builder's progress, appearing from time to time at auditions of new organs. On this particular occasion the two organists, one after the other, "charmed and astonished" the audience. Cavallo demonstrated both his contrapuntal skill and his professional acumen when he asked Rossini for a theme on which to improvise a fugue [RGM 10, pp.245, 252–53].

The year 1844 was an eventful one for the organ. At the industrial exposition held in Paris, the two largest French organ companies, Cavaillé-Coll and Daublaine-Callinet, were the only ones exhibiting organs, but each had completed an instrument of particular importance. Cavaillé-Coll entered his recent organ at Saint-Denis. Simon, *titulaire* there, played it on Wednesday and Sunday afternoons from 3 to 4 P.M. during the exposition [FM 7, p.167]. A smaller (eighteen-stop) organ, also exhibited by Cavaillé-Coll, was later (1846) installed in the church of Saint-Jean–Saint-François, where César Franck would be *titulaire* from 1853 to 1858 [276, p.15].

Daublaine-Callinet presented its new organ for Saint-Eustache, which was inaugurated on June 18, while the exposition was in progress. The instrument was a reconstruction and enlargement of an organ that had been moved to Saint-Eustache from Saint-Germain-des-Prés, but like many nineteenth-century reconstructions (alternatively termed "restorations"), it was virtually a new instrument with all the latest technology. Charles Spackman Barker had been engaged as technical director, and his experience and inventions were important to the organ's success.

Félix Danjou, artistic director of Daublaine-Callinet, must be credited with masterminding the public inaugural event, an affair of singular importance that was still cited years later. Unlike the chaotic opening of the Saint-Denis

Adolf Hesse (Bibliothèque
Nationale, Paris).

organ, this one boasted a carefully orchestrated selection of five Paris organists, and, for the first time, an imported star: the famous Adolf Hesse, a virtuoso from Breslau. Choral works inserted between organ performances added to the variety of the program. Indeed, it seems that every effort was made to create an occasion that would be attractive to the public and, at the same time, of special artistic significance.

The Paris organists represented the whole spectrum of contemporary taste in organ music, from the colorful, popular improvisations of Lefébure-Wély and Fessy, to the conservative fugues played by Benoist and Boëly (the latter playing a fugue by Albrechtsberger). Séjan, hovering somewhere in the center, seems to have been the least effective of the group.

Hesse played five pieces, including some of his own and the Bach Toccata in F. One can only imagine the effect the toccata had on an audience unaccustomed to organ music with pedals or to any organ works by Bach. Reviewers' opinions were divided about who were the best organists and what kind of organ music was most interesting, but Hesse's playing left an indelible impression on all, even on those who did not like it. They found his pedal technique the most remarkable feature of his performance.

A reviewer who signed his name "Ad. vicomte de Pontecoulant" named Hesse "the king of the pedal":

> He thinks of nothing but power and noise, his playing astonishes, but does not speak to the soul. He always seems to be the minister of an angry God who

wants to punish; I much prefer Misters Lefébure and Fessy, who perceive and interpret our prayers through such gentle thoughts and convey them toward the Eternal in sweet and harmonious chords.

Il est passionné pour la force et le bruit, son jeu étonne, mais ne va pas à l'âme. Il semble toujours être le ministre d'un Dieu en colère qui veut punir; j'aime bien mieux MM. Lefébure et Fessy, qui sentent et traduisent en pensées si suaves nos prières, et les transmettent en accords doux et harmonieux vers l'Eternel. [FM 7, p.197.]

There were two reviews of the inauguration in *Revue et Gazette musicale*. The first, signed "N.," noted "the success obtained by our French organists, in spite of the formidable comparison of Mr. Hesse" [le succès obtenu par nos organistes français, malgré la comparaison redoutable de M. Hesse; RGM 11, p.219]. Two weeks later a long review by Stéphen Morelot appeared. He distinguished between the fashionable style of Lefébure-Wély and Fessy, and "the true traditions of the style of the organ" represented by Boëly and Benoist. Morelot had nothing but praise for Hesse, his technical ability, his impeccable taste, and the German school in general [RGM 11, pp.230-32]. Morelot and Danjou were close allies in the ongoing campaign to improve church music and to interest their compatriots in contrapuntal music, particularly that of Bach. Thus the tenor of his review is not surprising.

The reviewer for *Le Ménestrel* gave his version of the Saint-Eustache in-auguration the entertaining touch then typical of that periodical; he also provides a glimpse of the audience. He reasoned that perhaps Fessy's *musette* gave the greatest pleasure because of its incompatibility with the style of church music. Lefébure-Wély's improvisation was well received, and the audi-ence gave testimony of its satisfaction. Here the reviewer noted that "in the church that satisfaction is shown by a little cough, given out weakly at first, then a little more pronounced, and always *crescendo*. That little coughing is not without charm once it reaches a certain intensity" [à l'église cette satisfac-tion se manifeste par une petite toux d'abord faiblement caractérisée, puis un peu plus prononcée, et toujours *crescendo*. Cette petite toux n'est pas sans charme, quand elle arrive à une certaine intensité; ME 11, no.30, p.2].

In regard to Hesse, the reviewer said that several serious pieces had left the audience cold, and at the moment when Hesse was going to play his most important piece, people were disposed to leave. But the German artist began the Toccata with such extraordinary verve, employing all the resources of his talent, that the listeners quickly resumed their seats, and

the triumph of the artist was complete. However, some mischievous wags attributed this success to the rain, which, falling at that moment in torrents, caused the public to retreat back under the roof of Saint-Eustache. According to them, the audience was thinking less about Mr. Hesse than a shelter.

Le triomphe de l'artiste fut complet. Toutefois, quelques mauvais plaisans attribuèrent ce succès à la pluie qui, tombant en ce moment par torrens, faisait refluer le public sous la voûte de St-Eustache. A les entendre, les assistans songeaient moins à M. Hesse qu'à un abri. [ME 11, no.30, p.2.]

Some days before the Saint-Eustache inauguration Hesse had played for an invited audience on a Daublaine-Callinet organ at the industrial exposition. On June 9 Henri Blanchard informed his readers that the performance included a fantasy in a fugal style, variations on "God Save the King" by Spohr, and a fugue in G minor by Bach. Blanchard, like Morelot, mentioned "the true style of the organ, which recedes more and more every day in this country, where one boasts of loving good music" [le vrai style de l'orgue, qui se perd tous les jours de plus en plus dans ce pays-ci, où l'on se vante d'aimer la bonne musique]. He, too, found Hesse's pedal technique remarkable, concluding that "if the organ of the Daublaine-Callinet firm is perfect from bottom to top, Mr. Hesse is a complete organist from head to feet" [si l'orgue de la maison Daublaine-Callinet est parfait de la base au faîte, M. Hesse est un organiste complet de la tête jusqu'aux pieds; RGM 11, pp.200–201].

National pride and confidence, often at risk when French musicianship was confronted by the self-assured, methodical German approach to artistic questions, was bruised (if not broken) by Hesse's visit to Paris. Thus, when François-Charles Widor (1811–99, father of the more famous Charles-Marie Widor), organist of Saint-François, Lyon, made one of his occasional visits to Paris in the fall of 1844, *Le Ménestrel* announced that he would play at Saint-Eustache, and suggested that he could play the pedals as well as Hesse [ME 11, no.46, pp.3-4]. The same periodical subsequently noted that several of the works Widor played had pedal solos, including a fugue that was quite successful [ME 11, no.47, p.3].

The glory of Daublaine-Callinet's organ at Saint-Eustache was short-lived. Only a few months after the inauguration, on December 16, Barker was making some adjustments to the action when he knocked over a candle. It fell into a part of the instrument that was difficult to reach, and before he could smother the flames, they had spread out of control. The organ was lost, and there was considerable damage to the church. Saint-Eustache would not have another organ until 1854.

Hector Berlioz opined that if the fire had only destroyed those awful mutation stops that cause one to play three notes at a time, and that mix the major mode with the minor, it would have been reason to rejoice. However, he conceded that such an immense loss was indeed too much. Berlioz thought the Alexandre *orgue-melodium* (a type of harmonium) produced an excellent effect in churches and theaters, and had the added advantage of being practical. Those instruments could burn without ruining their owners and would not require years for their reconstruction. Berlioz said that every little church or theater ought to have its *orgue-melodium* [JD, Dec. 29, 1844, p.1].

There were several important inaugurations in 1846: for the Saint-Sulpice organ, rebuilt by Daublaine-Callinet-Ducroquet,[2] and for the new Cavaillé-Coll organs for the Pentemont (sometimes spelled "Penthémont") church and

The Saint-Eustache organ in flames. From *L'Illustration*, 1844 (University of California Library, Berkeley).

the Madeleine. In his review of the Saint-Sulpice inauguration for the *Revue et Gazette musicale,* Henri Blanchard preferred the "severe style" of the Handel fugue Boëly played, and even the frankly modern style of Fessy, to the eclectic mixture of old and new styles in Lefébure-Wély's *offertoire.* He seems to have overlooked the other organist who played: a German immigrant, Georges-Gérard Schmitt (1821–1900) [RGM 13, pp.29-30]. The reviewer in *Le Ménestrel* mentioned his name, but commented only that the Paris organists were superior [ME 13, no.9, p.2]. Nevertheless, Schmitt was to become *titulaire* of Saint-Sulpice, succeeding Louis-Nicolas Séjan in 1849.

An unusually detailed report of the Saint-Sulpice inauguration was written for *La France musicale* by Adolphe Adam, giving us a clearer picture of the organization of a mid-century inauguration. Most of the organ pieces listed below were improvisations, and they were separated by vocal solos and choruses during the two-hour ceremony:

1. Schmitt: a prelude on foundation stops, terminated by a *grand choeur*
2. Fessy: a piece on the *flûte* and *hautbois*
3. Boëly: a piece "in an excellent style and of a charming structure"
4. Lefébure-Wély: an *offertoire* with pedals
5. Boëly: a fugue in F minor by Handel
6. Fessy: two pieces "filled with modulations and extremely elegant delicacies"
7. Lefébure-Wély: a *grand choeur*
8. Schmitt: a *grand choeur*

[FM 9, pp.25-26.]

By the end of summer 1846, Cavaillé-Coll's organ for the Protestant Pentemont church was ready.[3] Simon charmed the audience by exploiting all the possibilities of the organ, but reviewer Blanchard found the organist of the church, Ernest Meumann, a less-effective performer [RGM 13, p.286].

Of more general interest to the public was the October 29 inauguration in the fashionable church La Madeleine. Fessy, Séjan, and Lefébure-Wély played, and the improvisation by the last-named was nothing short of a sensation [ME 13, no.49, p.2]. On November 13 there was a second program on the Madeleine organ, with Lefébure-Wély and Fessy performing, this time for the benefit of victims of a Loire flood. *Le Ménestrel* reported that all aristocratic Paris attended, and that the sumptuous church of La Madeleine royally paid its obligation to the unfortunate [ME 13, no.50, p.2]. Each of the programs included choral music; a children's choir sang at the Pentemont, and there were vocal solos as well as choral numbers at the Madeleine.

The Madeleine inauguration had a curious aftermath. The following spring (1847), Fessy, then organist of La Madeleine, and Lefébure-Wély, organist of Saint-Roch, exchanged jobs. It might appear a defeat for Fessy, but in one way both men profited by the change. At the close of the Easter season Lefébure-Wély received a letter from the administration of La Madeleine inviting him to accept the post as organist for a salary of 3,000 francs, the amount he had required. At the same time, Fessy was offered the Saint-Roch position. Lefé-

The Cavaillé-Coll organ in the church of the Madeleine (Jim Lewis.)

bure-Wély's salary at Saint-Roch had been 2,000 francs, and Fessy's at the Madeleine had been 1,200 francs. Thus, the switch gave both organists substantial raises in salary, but the prestige and visibility of the Madeleine post were added benefits for the performance career of upward-bound 30-year-old Lefébure-Wély [ME 14, no.19, p.3].

The last years of the decade were marred by yet another revolution. On February 22, 1848, workers and students took to the streets of Paris in demonstrations against the government. That was the very date César Franck and Félicité-Saillot Desmousseaux (1824–1918) had chosen for their wedding, and when the ceremony was over the young couple had to clamber over barricades that had been erected in the meantime [66, pp.68–69].[4]

Two days later Louis-Philippe abdicated, and the new republic was proclaimed. In December the nephew of Napoléon I, Prince Louis Napoléon (1808–73), became president. By 1852 he had managed to transform his title into Napoléon III, Emperor.

Once again the political disturbances sent shock waves through the organ world. Cavaillé-Coll experienced serious financial difficulty, for his company was shut down for six months [73, pp.239–42]. His most notable organ toward the end of the decade was not for Paris, but for the cathedral at Saint-Brieuc. The young organist of the cathedral, Charles Collin (1827–1911), was a student of Lefébure-Wély, and no doubt he was proud to welcome his teacher as guest artist for the inauguration in October 1848 [RGM 15, p.339].

Cavaillé-Coll was not alone in suffering because of the 1848 revolution. At Saint-Germain-l'Auxerrois (where Boëly was organist) revisions to the organ had just been authorized. Work was begun, but because of new economies imposed on parishes, it was interrupted for months at a time. More than two years passed before Boëly again had the use of the organ. Meanwhile, his salary had been suspended. The organ revisions were officially received in October 1850, but the organist had only a short time to enjoy them. On October 1, 1851, he was dismissed by church authorities who had no appreciation for Boëly's musicianship [122, pp.152–55].

Louis Séjan was experiencing a replay of the disappointments his father had known. His position at the Royal Chapel had been dissolved in 1830, when the chapel was closed. In the wake of the 1848 revolution his salary at Saint-Sulpice was so drastically reduced that he resigned. He left Paris in March 1849 and died shortly afterward, at age 63 [RGM 16, p.118].

Félix Danjou was a victim of a combination of circumstances. Discouraged by the series of accidents that ultimately ruined the organ company he was associated with, as well as by the general lack of response to his efforts to improve church music, he started to move in other directions even before the revolution. In January 1845 he severed his connection with the Daublaine-Callinet company, and in 1847 he left his organ position at Notre-Dame. The next year, because of the political upheaval, publication of his periodical was suspended, and in 1849 Danjou left both Paris and the music profession [114, vol.2, pp.424–25].[5]

Danjou's post at Notre-Dame was filled by a former student of the Notre-Dame *maîtrise*, Eugène Sergent (1829–1900). He was eighteen when he took the position, and he remained there the rest of his life. Another former student of the Notre-Dame *maîtrise*, Eugène Vast (1833–1911),[6] replaced his teacher, Boëly, at Saint-Germain-l'Auxerrois. He assumed the position in 1851 and remained there until 1909, meanwhile winning first prize in organ at the Conservatory in 1853 [122, p.130; 249, pp.582, 864].

Séjan's position at Saint-Louis-des-Invalides was filled by Pierre-Edmond Hocmelle (1824–95), a blind organist who had won first prize in organ at the Conservatory in 1846. He would become one of the better-known performers at organ inaugurations in the coming decades.[7]

At Saint-Sulpice, Séjan's successor was Georges-Gérard Schmitt. His career was a departure from normal patterns in several respects. Schmitt was German, a native of Trier, where his father had been organist of the cathedral. His first training was with his father, and then he went to Münster, where he attended school and studied organ, harmony, and counterpoint with Joseph Anthony, organist of the cathedral there.

At age fifteen Georges succeeded his father. In addition to his duties as cathedral organist, he began composing works for other media and conducting orchestral music. At the urging of his friends he went to Paris in 1844 to complete his education. He attended Halévy's composition class and also

Georges Schmitt (The British Library, London).

studied with Spontini and Niedermeyer. In about 1846 Schmitt was appointed professor of music in the service of the Queen of Spain, and two years later he was also named *maître de chapelle* in her service. His Paris debut as organ soloist was at the Saint-Sulpice inauguration in 1846. By the time the revolution erupted in 1848, he had been offered an associate organ position (along with Séjan) at Saint-Sulpice, but all things considered, it seemed like a good time to leave France.

Schmitt sailed to America in 1848, became organist at the cathedral in New Orleans, and did some touring as pianist and composer.[8] After the death of Séjan in 1849, Schmitt returned to France to compete for the post of organist at Saint-Sulpice. He was the successful candidate, subsequently serving there as *titulaire* until 1863 [271]. He contributed in various ways to the organ profession—composing, editing collections, writing methods, writing about the organ, and joining the movement to reform church music. He was also involved in activities of the German community in Paris, and for a short time he was a teacher at the Niedermeyer School.

Our account of the 1830s closed with a description of a funeral for which Chopin played the organ. At the close of the 1840s, Lefébure-Wély presided at the organ for Chopin's funeral. It was an elaborate occasion at the Madeleine, with orchestra, choir, and soloists, as well as organ. One journalist observed: "Chopin's preludes, in particular, wonderfully interpreted at the organ by Lefébure-Wély, produced a profound sensation." It was playing, he said, "that went straight to the heart." [Les préludes de Chopin, merveilleusement traduits à l'orgue par Lefébure-Wély, ont surtout produit une profonde sensation . . . qui allaient droit au coeur; ME 16, no.49, p.2.]

VI.
Mid-Century Masters and Their Programs

WHEN the decade of the 1850s opened, Paris received a visitor who would exert a telling influence on the French organ world: Jacques-Nicolas Lemmens. This young virtuoso from Belgium came to Paris armed with the blessing of his mentor, the redoubtable Fétis (director of the Brussels Conservatory), organ studies with Girschner and Hesse, and a recently conferred professorship (1849) at the Brussels Conservatory. Fétis had written a letter of introduction to Cavaillé-Coll, and the latter arranged for Lemmens to see and play various recent organs during his first visit, in May 1850 [73, p.76]. Lemmens returned in August and played some Bach fugues and works of his own on the organ at the Pentemont. Henri Blanchard reviewed the performance and remarked on the purity, elegance, clarity, and expressive quality of the playing. He mentioned Lemmens's legato style and use of finger substitution, which was the prime thrust of the latter's recently published *Journal* (later expanded to form his organ method book) [RGM 17, pp.273–74]. These early visits were valuable introductions to the Paris organ world, and Lemmens was to return from time to time during his career.

The first notable inauguration of the 1850s was at the church of Saint-Vincent-de-Paul. The new Cavaillé-Coll organ was played by Piétro Cavallo for the festival of the patron of the church in July 1851, but it was not complete at that time. Finally, on January 26, 1852 the organ had its public debut. An enthusiastic Maurice Bourges described it as a brilliant occasion, with a large audience of music lovers, artists, writers, and other illustrious members of society. Two organists took turns demonstrating and contrasting the organ's resources: the *titulaire*, Cavallo, and of course, Lefébure-Wély. All the organ pieces were improvised except for a Bach fugue played by Cavallo. Lefébure-Wély's performance included his specialty, a descriptive "storm" piece [RGM 19, pp.37–38].

"Storm" improvisations differed only in details from the earlier battle pieces of the revolutionary period and the "Last Judgment" pieces heard in Te Deum performances. They all began with relative calm; built up to a great roar; subsided to a hymn of praise, victory, thanksgiving, or reflection (depending on the circumstances); and might end there, or return to something like the beginning.

A "storm" improvised by Lefébure-Wély in 1855 and programmed as "a village festival interrupted by a storm," was a typical example. One heard first musettes and hautbois calling the shepherds to the festival. The sounds seemed to come nearer, and a graceful dance began. From time to time the murmur of wind from an approaching storm was heard. It became louder and more threatening; thunder roared. But when the storm subsided for a moment, one could still hear the retreating dancers. Suddenly the full fury of the storm was heard, striking terror in the souls of the listeners (ascending and descending chromatic scales, diminished seventh chords). Gradually the wind became calm, and the storm moved off in the distance. One heard the rain, but as it, too, subsided, the voices of the villagers singing a prayer drifted through. During the prayer the last distant sounds of wind and thunder were heard. The cornemuse and its echoes called the shepherds together again. The happy crowd gathered, and the first motive returned, developing into variations of many kinds: lively, light, brilliant, and culminating in a splendid finale [ME 22, no.41, p.4].

Lemmens and François-Charles Widor both made trips to Paris in 1852, and both played the new Saint-Vincent-de-Paul organ. In February and March, Lemmens reinforced his reputation as a performer of the "severe" type who played written music (including fugues) with great clarity and purity of style. Henri Blanchard regretted, however, that the Belgian musician did not also include improvisations in his performances [RGM 19, pp.66, 77, 84].

When Widor played for an audience invited by Cavaillé-Coll, Blanchard again had reservations: "His melody is in good taste, even distinguished, and his harmony pure and severe, but a little cold." [Sa mélodie est de bon goût, distinguée même, et son harmonie pure et sévère, mais un peu froide; RGM 19, p.330.]

The organ built by Ducroquet to replace one destroyed by fire at Saint-Eustache was finally ready for inauguration in 1854. This event was the first Paris inauguration in which either Lemmens or César Franck participated. Franck, then 32, was organist at Saint-Jean–Saint-François. Others on the program were Cavallo, organist at Saint-Vincent-de-Paul, and Auguste-Ernest Bazille (1828–91) of Sainte-Elisabeth. Organ accompaniments for vocal music were played by Edouard Batiste (1820–76), organist at Saint-Nicolas-des-Champs. Soon after the inauguration Batiste was named organist at Saint-Eustache, and from that time his career as a performer blossomed.

The Saint-Eustache inauguration included fourteen organ pieces, four choral pieces, a vocal duet, and two vocal solos. Nine of the organ pieces were played in sets of three by the star performer, Lemmens. His part of the program included the last movement of Mendelssohn's Sonata No.1, a Bach Prelude and Fugue in E minor, various original pieces, and an improvisation (possibly in answer to earlier criticisms that he did not improvise). Franck played "a *fantaisie* composed with care." Cavallo and Bazille each played two improvisations [RGM 21, pp.174–75].

After the performance Adolphe Adam remained convinced "that Lefébure-Wély is the most skillful artist I know and that Mr. Fessy has much talent" [que Lefébure-Wély est le plus habile artiste que je connaisse et que M. Fessy a beaucoup de talent]. Neither of them had played at the Saint-Eustache inauguration. The thrust of Adam's criticism of Lemmens and Franck was that they had not really demonstrated the organ: "Mr. Franck plays in a very severe style and does not at all use the resources of the modern organ; yet on that day, what one wanted to hear above all was the organ, and he did not apply himself enough in showing it off." [M. Franck joue d'une manière très sévère et n'use nullement des ressources de l'orgue moderne; or, ce jour-là, ce qu'on voulait entendre c'était l'orgue surtout, et il ne s'est pas assez attaché à le faire valoir.] Adam implied that inadequacies in Lemmens's performance were matters more of inexperience than of musicianship, explaining that "The king of the Belgians, who has an excellent organist, does not have a passable organ in his capital. Mr. Lemmens is then a theoretical rather than a practical organist." [Le roi des Belges, qui a un excellent organiste, ne possède pas un orgue passable dans sa capitale. M. Lemmens est donc plutôt un organiste théorique que pratique; ME 21, no.28, p.3.]

The modern organist, taught to venerate the names of Lemmens and Franck, may have difficulty with Adam's criticism. Yet his review goes far toward explaining why Lefébure-Wély's concert career surpassed those of a more profound musician (Franck) and a more polished virtuoso (Lemmens): he knew how to exploit the resources of the contemporary organ, demonstrating its greatest contrasts, its solo colors, its expressive qualities. As Adam pointed out, that was the primary objective of the inaugural program, not the presentation of repertoire, new or old. The builder was concerned that the organ's capabilities be heard, and that is what the public attended an inauguration to hear. Those organists who were more concerned about the music than the instrument were actually at cross-purposes with the idea of the inaugural program, and were not usually well received. Repertoire could not be the primary orientation of an organ performance until recitals independent of inaugurations and demonstrations of new instruments gained a place as an accepted part of the musical fare.

One of Franck's students, J. W. Hinton, wrote:

> Franck's "registration" on the organ was sober, if compared with that of Lefébure-Wély, and in no degree intended to captivate the general public; but while the modern resources of the organ were not neglected by him, it is unquestionable that beauty in the design and combination of ideas, not variety in colour display, was his principal quest. [159, p.13.]

It would be an oversimplification to assume that Lefébure-Wély's success as a performer was based only on his colorful use of the organ, his flashy descriptive pieces, and his appeal to popular taste. There was also a display of musicianship in his improvisations that left an indelible impression on more than one distinguished musician.

Alexandre Guilmant's comparison of Lefébure-Wély and Lemmens is particularly telling, since Guilmant was in other respects a great admirer of his former teacher, Lemmens. When he was interviewed by William George Pearce in the 1890s, Guilmant said: "He [Lefébure-Wély] was the finest extemporaneous player on the organ that France has produced. Extemporaneous players are rare. M. Lemmens could not extemporize at all" [244, p.211]. Saint-Saëns, too, testified: "Lefébure-Wély was a wonderful improviser (I can say this emphatically, for I heard him) but he left only a few unimportant compositions for the organ" [283, p.105].

In spite of his concern for the popularity of his organs, and his long-standing relationship with Lefébure-Wély, Cavaillé-Coll recognized that Lemmens's playing was remarkable, and he tried in various ways to forward the latter's career. When arrangements were being made in 1855 for the inauguration of his organ for the cathedral at Saint-Omer, Cavaillé-Coll wrote to the church suggesting that the organists best acquainted with his instruments were Lefébure-Wély, Simon, Fessy, Cavallo, and Durand. He then noted that Lemmens and Lefébure-Wély were, in his opinion, the best organists, and suggested that both be invited. Both were indeed approached, but their prices were so high that the church invited only one: Lefébure-Wély [73, pp.104–105].

The following year Cavaillé-Coll again suggested both organists for the inauguration of his organ in the church of Saint-Nicolas, Ghent. Again, only Lefébure-Wély played. This time the consequences were far-reaching. Fétis, furious that his protégé had been passed over for an inauguration in Belgium on an organ he (Fétis) had been instrumental in procuring, set about avenging the slight. First he refused to serve as chairman of the organ examining committee [73, pp.105–106]. Then he wrote a stinging article for the *Revue et Gazette musicale*, entitled "The Worldly Organ and Erotic Music in Church" [L'orgue mondaine et la musique érotique à l'église], which lashed out at the decadence of French organists and their descriptive improvisations, and extolled Lemmens and his style [RGM 23, pp.105–106].

The fact that Lemmens never played for the inauguration of a Cavaillé-Coll organ might have been a result of the Ghent affair. Although the builder and performer remained in close contact and Lemmens visited Cavaillé-Coll in Paris, played on new organs in the shop, and sometimes played on newly installed organs, he was never on the official inaugural program for a Cavaillé-Coll organ.

Two students of Lemmens made their first trips to Paris in 1855. The first to arrive was Clément Loret (1833–1909), a member of a family of organists and organ builders. Loret entered the Brussels Conservatory in 1851, where he studied counterpoint and composition with Fétis, and organ with Lemmens, receiving a first prize in organ in 1853. He came to Paris with a letter of introduction to Cavaillé-Coll, who found Loret so unattractive that he did not have the courage to present the newcomer to his friends [79, no.55, p.42].

When Alphonse-Jean-Ernest Mailly arrived, also with a letter of introduction, he appeared "more presentable in all respects" [sous tous les rapports plus présentable]. Cavaillé-Coll took him to Saint-Vincent-de-Paul, where he played for some artists "in a masterly manner with clarity and distinction" [à la manière du magister avec clarté et distingtions (*sic*)]. In a letter to Lemmens dated July 11, 1855, Cavaillé-Coll explained the difference in the welcome he had given the two young organists [79, no.55, p.42]. Mailly had studied organ at the Brussels Conservatory with Girschner, and subsequently with Lemmens. Like Loret, he had won first prize in organ, and he eventually succeeded Lemmens as professor of organ.

In spite of his unauspicious entry into the Paris organ world, Loret remained in the city, where he attained more success than Cavaillé-Coll would have predicted. Initially, Loret had several successive church positions. Then in 1858 he became professor of organ at the school of church music founded in 1853 by Louis Niedermeyer (1802–61), and organist at Saint-Louis-d'Antin, where Niedermeyer was *maître de chapelle*. Loret remained in those positions for the rest of his long career.

At the Exposition universelle in Paris in 1855, Cavaillé-Coll entered his organ at Saint-Vincent-de-Paul, and Cavallo played a series of Wednesday afternoon programs on it. Merklin-Schütze had recently taken over the Ducroquet firm in Paris, but the latter was still represented at the exposition by the recently completed Saint-Eustache organ and a smaller organ. Other French and Belgian pipe-organ builders who participated in the exposition were Claude Frères, Stoltz & Schaaff, Antoine Suret, Charles Gadault, and Merklin-Schütze [RGM 22, pp.349–51, 359–61].

The organ representing Merklin-Schütze was destined for Saint-Eugène, Paris. During the exposition it was played by Batiste of Saint-Eustache, Schmitt of Saint-Sulpice, and Alphonse-Zoé-Charles Renaud de Vilbac (1829–84), called to be organist at Saint-Eugène. Batiste and Renaud de Vilbac became firmly attached to the Merklin-Schütze establishment, one or both appearing on almost every inauguration of that company's organs.

The Saint-Eugène organ had its inauguration in 1856, with Renaud de Vilbac and Schmitt playing. Other interesting events in the organ world of Paris were auditions of Cavaillé-Coll's organ for the cathedral of Carcassonne, played by Piétro Cavallo and César Franck [RGM 23, pp.222–23, 247–48]. In their Brussels manufactory, Merklin-Schütze gave similar presentations on a large organ for the cathedral of Murcia, Spain, with performances by various local and visiting organists [RGM 23, pp.305–306]. The year 1856 also marked the end of the career of a popular and talented organist with the death of Alexandre Fessy. His successor at Saint-Roch was Auguste Durand (1830–1909).

The most interesting inauguration in 1857 was for the Saint-Merry organ, newly rebuilt by Cavaillé-Coll. The organist there was Camille Saint-Saëns (1835–1921), and it was he who played for the opening on December 3. The program was unusual in two respects: Saint-Saëns played all the organ music himself, and most of it was composed music. The whole program, with its initial introduction to the organ stops, its balance between French and German music, and its obvious effort to show different aspects of the organ, represented a new kind of program planning. Cavaillé-Coll sent invitations to his friends and associates, listing the following program:[1]

ORDRE DE LA SEANCE.

1. IMPROVISATIONS sur les différents jeux de l'orgue.
   Par M. Camille Saint-Saëns
2. AVE, MARIA — Miné
   Chanté par le Choeur de Saint-Merri
3. FANTAISIE — C. Saint-Saëns
   Exécutée par M. Camille Saint-Saëns
4. O SALUTARIS — Ch. Gounod
   Chanté par le Choeur de Saint-Merri
5. FRAGMENT D'UNE SONATE — Mendelssohn
6. FUGUE EN *RE* — S. Bach
   Exécutés par M. Camille Saint-Saëns

[Cited in 86, plate 42.]

Saint-Saëns's music was characterized by the reviewer, Henri Blanchard, as "grave, elegant and religious all at the same time." Blanchard appreciated Saint-Saëns's "respect for the old style of sacred music, as great masters of times past understood it" [respect pour le vieux style de la musique sacrée comme l'entendaient les grands maîtres du temps passé; RGM 24, pp.394–95].

From his earliest years his phenomenal talent had placed Saint-Saëns in a class apart. He was playing the piano before he was three, and by the time he was ten he was ready to give his debut recital (May 6, 1846) at the Salle Pleyel. By that time he was studying piano with Camille Stamaty (1811–70) and harmony and composition with Pierre Maleden (1806–?).

Stamaty used the method developed by his teacher Kalkbrenner (1785–1849). Saint-Saëns later wrote that this method was valuable in developing the fingers of young players. The reservations he added to this comment give us some hints about his own playing:

> Unfortunately, this school invented as well continuous *legato,* which is both false and monotonous; the abuse of nuances, and a mania for continual *expressivo* used with no discrimination. All this was opposed to my natural feelings, and I was unable to conform to it. They reproached me by saying that I would never get a really fine effect—to which I was entirely indifferent. [283, p.10.]

On December 29, 1846 Stamaty wrote a long letter to Saint-Saëns's mother from Rome, discussing his young student's education. He suggested that in his absence Saint-Saëns would profit from some lessons from Alexandre Boëly. This musician, he said, had heard the debut recital and was very interested in the young performer. Stamaty mentioned early music, of which Boëly had a large collection, and also original works by Boëly, but did not specify the nature of the lessons [122, p.100]. Nor is it clear how long Saint-Saëns studied

Camille Saint-Saëns at the time of his debut recital, 1846 (Bibliothèque
Nationale, Paris).

with Boëly between early 1847 and his entrance to the Paris Conservatory in
the fall of 1848. Stamaty himself may have had piano lessons in mind.
Certainly Boëly was well prepared to introduce Saint-Saëns to a wide repertoire of little-known keyboard works of various kinds. He also could have
introduced him to the techniques he had developed for playing pedals.
Although Saint-Saëns did not write about his studies with Boëly, he frequently
told his contemporaries and students how much he valued his association with
the old musician [122, p.131].

Saint-Saëns was admitted to Benoist's organ class at the Conservatory at
first as an auditor, but soon after as a regular student; and in 1851 (at age
sixteen) he won first prize in organ. By 1853 he was *titulaire* at Saint-Merry. In
late December 1857, only a short time after the inauguration of the renovated

Alexandre P. F. Boëly (Bibliothèque Nationale, Paris).

organ, the musical press noted that Lefébure-Wély had resigned from the Madeleine and that Saint-Saëns would replace him [RGM 24, p.422]. In less than a decade after entering the Conservatory the brilliant young musician was in one of the best organ positions in Paris. He remained at the Madeleine until 1877. During part of his tenure there he was also teaching at the Niedermeyer School (1861–65).

Meanwhile, the death of Alexandre Boëly in 1858 left a void in the organ profession that at least a few musicians of the time understood and lamented. His friend and former student Camille Saint-Saëns played for the funeral on December 29 in the church of Saint-Philippe-du-Roule [MA 2, no.10, col.156].

Alphonse Mailly made his second trip to Paris in 1858, and this time his program at Saint-Vincent-de-Paul was noted in the press. It was well in line with the Fétis–Brussels Conservatory ideal for organ programs:

Bach—Toccata in F, Fugue in G minor
Mendelssohn—Andante and Final (Sonata in F)
Lemmens—Scherzo
Mailly—Improvisata
Mailly—Prière in A flat

[ME 25, no.15, p.2.]

In the same year, when Lefébure-Wély inaugurated a Cavaillé-Coll organ at the church of Saint-Louis-d'Antin, the program consisted of:

I.

1. Improvisation in F major on the gambes of two manuals, *crescendo,* and on all the stops of the organ, *decrescendo.*
2. Improvisation in E-flat major on the 8' *flûtes harmoniques;* solo on *hautbois* with 4' *flûte.*
3. Vocal solo by Mrs. Lefébure-Wély: "Ave Maria" by Miné, accompanied by a *voix humaine* registration.
4. Fugue in D minor (*Meditaciones Religiosas,* Op.122, No.6), on reeds and foundations of the *récit,* with a *crescendo* leading to a *grand choeur* registration for the end.
5. Improvisation: rustic march in B-flat, detached rhythm, with an *hautbois* solo imitating a bagpipe.

II.

6. Funeral march (*Meditaciones Religiosas,* Op.122, No.9) on foundations, with a solo on *trompette harmonique* and tremblant.
7. Vocal solo by Mrs. Lefébure-Wély: "O Salutaris" by Lefébure-Wély, with a solo on *flûte harmonique.*
8. Improvisation in G major, with harp effects.
9. Improvisation in C: pastoral scene, dance of the villagers, thunder effects.

[ME 25, no.44, p.2.]

It is obvious which of these two programs was tailor-made to demonstrate an organ and which focused on repertoire. No wonder, then, when Cavaillé-Coll finished the new organ for the Sainte-Clotilde church the next year (1859), he arranged for Lefébure-Wély to play it on two occasions before the inauguration: for the Duchess of Albe, and for a wedding. On opening night (December 19) César Franck, organist of Sainte-Clotilde, and Lefébure-Wély shared the program. Franck had been appointed organist and choirmaster of Sainte-Clotilde in 1857. Services were held in a temporary chapel until the new church was opened late in 1857. A small organ was used until the Cavaillé-Coll instrument was ready two years later.

For the inauguration Lefébure-Wély played three improvisations, including a "symphonic improvisation" based on familiar Christmas songs. Franck alternated with his colleague, playing first a piece of "large proportions" in a "forceful style," then a Bach Fugue in E minor, and an original *finale* played on *grand choeur* [RGM 27, pp.4–5]. According to Rollin Smith, the two original pieces played by Franck were both from the *Six Pièces*, one being the *Final*, Op.21, which is dedicated to Lefébure-Wély [303, p.15]. As usual, choral pieces and vocal solos were included in the program. Organ accompaniments were played by Théodore Dubois (1837–1924), the organist-accompanist of Sainte-Clotilde.

The position at Sainte-Clotilde, with its new organ, gave Franck a better professional location than he had had previously. More important for the future, it provided him with an instrument sufficient in size and quality to encourage his work as a composer. Franck's playing in inaugurations and recitals was characteristically reviewed with respect, if not wild enthusiasm. About thirty of his organ performances were noted in French periodicals. They included most of the big inaugurations and some important solo recitals between 1854 and his death in 1890: an achievement not to be underrated (see the list of his performances in the Appendix). But it was Franck's im-

César Franck (Bibliothèque Nationale, Paris).

provisations in church services rather than his public appearances that most inspired his students. They responded to and remembered the quality of the music and the fertility of the composer's imagination, rather than the technical details. J.-Guy Ropartz (1864–1955), Charles Tournemire (1870–1939), Vincent d'Indy (1851–1931), and Louis Vierne (1870–1937) were among those who documented the extraordinary richness of Franck's improvisations. Vierne's recollections are typical:

> I have never heard anything which could compare with Franck's improvisation from the point of view of purely musical invention. At church it took him a certain time to get into the mood—several trials, a little experimenting, then, once started, a lavishness of invention partaking of the miraculous; a polyphony of incomparable richness, in which melody, harmony and structure vied with one another in originality and emotional conception, traversed by flashes of manifest genius. Never any combinations just for their own sake, never any of the feats of skill customary among the acrobats desirous of dazzling the gallery; only a constant concern for the dignity of his art, for the nobility of his mission, for the fervent sincerity of his sermon in sound. Joyous or melancholy, solemn or mystic, powerful or ethereal, Franck knew how to be all those at Sainte Clotilde, and mere technical resources such as contrapuntal artifices, canons, superimposing of themes, etc., etc., would never appear except when justified by the expression of a thought whose criteria were essentially depth and emotion. [324, vol.29, no.11, p.12.]

Although César Franck was thirteen years older than Camille Saint-Saëns, their careers as organists developed about the same time. They had much in common. Both had excellent piano techniques before they began studying organ. Both studied improvisation under Benoist. Both loved to improvise, believing it an essential skill for an organist, and were themselves extraordinarily gifted improvisers. Both were highly respected for their musicianship, but neither was the darling of the general public. Only occasionally did either bridge the distance between personal style and popular taste.

Descriptions of Saint-Saëns's playing, whether on organ or piano, emphasized clarity and brilliance, but reviewers often complained that it was a little cold. Franck's playing (and his music) seemed to puzzle commentators, and they tended to use vague terms like "elevated" or "masterful." Saint-Saëns's mode of expression was essentially Classic rather than Romantic, detached rather than introspective. It was impressive in its craftsmanship, elegance, and proportion. Franck was much more the romantic, using his highly individual style for a distinctly personal expression. Saint-Saëns probably epitomized a fundamental difference between himself and Franck when he wrote: "Franck's religious music, though eminently deserving of respect, calls to mind the austerities of the cloister rather than the perfumed splendours of the sanctuary" [284, p.49].

Yet even with these basic differences, both Saint-Saëns and Franck were

Camille Saint-Saëns (Bibliothèque Nationale, Paris).

classed as "severe" performers by their contemporaries. Counterpoint held no terrors for either of them. They both played and improvised fugues, and counterpoint often pervaded their homophonic music as well. Many (or perhaps most) of their listeners would have preferred an uncomplicated tune on a pretty stop and a bland, unobtrusive accompaniment. Saint-Saëns tells us "there was a tradition that I was a severe, austere musician. The public was led to believe that I played nothing but fugues. So current was this belief that a young woman about to be married begged me to play no fugues at her wedding!" [283, p.107].

Organ performance was not the first priority for either Franck or Saint-Saëns. Neither attempted to build the kind of career Lefébure-Wély had, focused almost exclusively on performance. Both gave composition a higher priority than organ performance. But there was a special satisfaction, fulfillment, and nourishment that each found in playing the organ.

Saint-Saëns left his post at the Madeleine in 1877, but he returned to organ playing time after time. He frequently played services at Saint-Séverin, and in 1897 he was named honorary organist there. In his memoirs he wrote:

> The organ is thought-provoking. As one touches the organ, the imagination is awakened, and the unforeseen rises from the depths of the unconscious. It is a world of its own, ever new, which will never be seen again, and which comes out of the darkness, as an enchanted island comes from the sea. [283, pp.105–106.]

Franck experienced that mystical world as a form of worship. D'Indy tells us that near the end of his life Franck said to the priest of Sainte-Clotilde, " 'Ah! that *Magnificat!* How I loved it! What a number of versicles I have improvised to those beautiful words! I have written down some of them—sixty-three have just been sent to the publisher, but I do want to get up to a hundred. I shall go on with them as soon as I get better—or else,' he added in a lower tone, 'perhaps God will let me finish them—in His eternity to come.' " [171, pp.177–78].

Although Edouard Batiste became one of the most popular recitalists of his time, his career is all but forgotten today. Son of a singer in the Opéra-Comique, Batiste showed an early talent for music. He entered the service of the Royal Chapel as a page and was enrolled in the Paris Conservatory in 1828. From that early time his career centered around the Conservatory. He obtained various honors there, including first prizes in counterpoint and organ in 1839, and second Grand Prix de Rome in 1840. Batiste was already teaching at the Conservatory before his own studies were concluded. His primary teaching areas were solfège, harmony, and vocal ensemble classes; his twelve-volume edition of *Solfèges du Conservatoire* was an important contribution to pedagogy.

From 1841 or 1842 until 1854 Batiste was organist at Saint-Nicolas-des-Champs. Then he became organist at Saint-Eustache, where he remained until his death in 1876. Joseph G. Lennon, an American who had studied organ privately with Batiste, eulogized his playing in 1878:

> Batiste's organ playing was one of the chief attractions for foreign musicians visiting Paris. On his programmes were always found compositions from the greatest masters of this noble instrument. The writer has often heard Batiste play from memory many of the greater organ preludes and fugues of Seb. Bach, organ sonatas of Mendelssohn, also many of the most difficult compositions of the German school of organ playing. His improvisations will never be forgotten by organists who were fortunate enough to hear him extemporize preludes, fugues, fantaisies, offertoires, communions or elevations, while his treatment of the organ in accompanying voices was simply marvellous. [200.]

The fact that Batiste did occasionally program a rather broad repertoire of composed music distinguished him from Lefébure-Wély and, indeed, from many of his colleagues. On the other hand, the style of his own music invites comparison with Lefébure-Wély. In an 1897 article Clarence Eddy (1851–1937) wrote: "Batiste and Wely were effect players. Wely had more technic; he was really a great organist in a charming and unique way. Batiste was a prolific composer, but his compositions are played very little now even in France and are not highly esteemed" [96, p.595]. It would be a mistake to gloss over the mediocrity that typifies much of Batiste's published music; nevertheless, it has some historic significance. His music was exceptionally popular in England and America, and it can probably tell us more about stylistic preference in those countries than in France.[2]

Two English organists, William Spark (1823–97) and Henry Smart (1813–79), visited Batiste at Saint-Eustache. According to Spark, Batiste "was a fat, podgy, round-faced gentleman, full of glib conversation and anecdote. My friend, Henry Smart, spoke French fairly well, and managed to get a word in (edgewise) occasionally" [307, p.300].

Spark had edited all Batiste's organ works in England, but he had mixed feelings about their quality. He praised the andante movements as "not only very melodious, but also very skilfully constructed." A few lines later he concluded: "Batiste's organ music is sometimes noisy, always brilliant, and not so sacred and dignified as English church music is expected to be" [307, pp.301–302].

To his prestigious positions at the Conservatory and at Saint-Eustache, Batiste added the role of organist-of-choice for inaugurations of Merklin-Schütze organs. By the middle of the decade the number of guest-artist performances he gave every year rivaled (and frequently exceeded) the number given by Lefébure-Wély. He was a rising star among French organists, and in the eyes of his contemporaries he was easily among the leading mid-century performers.

Batiste's colleague for many Merklin-Schütze inaugurations was Alphonse-Zoé-Charles Renaud de Vilbac, who had received the first prize in organ at the Paris Conservatory in 1844. For sixteen years (1855–71), he was organist at Saint-Eugène, and during that period he appeared frequently as a featured artist on new or rebuilt Merklin-Schütze organs.

When Renaud de Vilbac left his church position in 1871, his name suddenly vanished from organ programs. However, several collections of his organ compositions appeared later in the 1870s. In addition to original compositions, Renaud de Vilbac made a large number of arrangements of opera extracts for piano and harmonium, piano and violin, and other combinations of instruments.

In 1856 Adrien de La Fage wrote an interesting review of Renaud de Vilbac's playing. The occasion was a demonstration in the builder's shop of the new Merklin-Schütze organ for the cathedral of Murcia, Spain. Renaud de

Vilbac had gone to Brussels for the occasion, and was one of several organists who performed. La Fage noted that many of the pieces Renaud de Vilbac played were improvised, and those that were not belonged to instrumental and theater styles rather than that of the organ. However, they were chosen with taste and transcribed with great ability. This organist, he said, was especially able in displaying the resources of the modern organ, and the possibilities offered by composition pedals and the expression pedal. He concluded that Renaud de Vilbac was a true representative of the current style of the French school [of organ playing]. However one might judge that school itself, La Fage said cautiously, did not diminish the recognition due to the fine talent of this organist [RGM 23, pp.305–306].

Thirteen years later Renaud de Vilbac's "incomparable talent" in displaying all the details and qualities of a new organ could still excite the interest of a critic. On that occasion, though, the organist performed a Bach prelude and fugue and a piece by Lemmens in addition to his own compositions and improvisations [GM 15, no.41, p.3; ME 36, p.382].

Auguste Durand is best known today as the founder of the Durand publishing house, but he began his career as an organist. He studied organ with Benoist at the Paris Conservatory and held several prominent church positions.

After the death of Fessy in 1856, Durand was named organist at Saint-Roch. The announcement of this appointment in *Le Ménestrel* (January 4, 1857) noted that Durand had been organist at Saint-Ambroise for the past seven years and at Sainte-Geneviève for the past four [ME 24, no.5, p.4]. Late in 1863 the musical press announced that he was moving from Saint-Roch to Saint-Vincent-de-Paul, replacing Cavallo, who had been appointed organist at Saint-Germain-des-Prés [RGM 30, p.390]. Durand remained at Saint-Vincent-de-Paul until 1874, but he had meanwhile entered the publishing business, and his interest was increasingly in that direction.[3] Durand's career as a performer was on a much more modest level than those we have just sketched. Nevertheless, one encounters his name as a participant in several of the important organ inaugurations.

Another organist who began carving out an organ career in the 1850s was César Franck's brother Joseph (1825–91). He studied organ at the Conservatory with Benoist, and in 1852 he won first prize in the annual competition. At about that time he became organist and *maître de chapelle* of Saint-François-Xavier (Missions Etrangères), and about three years later he became choir organist at Saint-Thomas-d'Aquin [ME 22, no.16, p.4]. In 1861 he was named organist at Notre-Dame-d'Auteuil. Five years later he became organist at Saint-Jacques-du-Haut-Pas [RMS 7, p.78]. From that time something went wrong with his career. In 1868 he resigned as choir organist at Saint-Sulpice and went to Nancy [RMS 9, p.47].

As children, the two Franck brothers appeared on programs together, César playing piano and Joseph violin. After Joseph completed his studies at the Conservatory, he performed on piano, organ, violin, and harmonium on occasional programs. He also taught harmony, piano, organ, and violin, privately and in several small schools. His published compositions for organ include two sets of preludes and fugues (Op.8 and Op.45), *Sicilienne et orage* (Op.40), *Grand offertoire solennel* (Op.47), and three books of versets, offertoires, and other pieces for organ or harmonium, entitled *Les Feuilles, Les Fleurs,* and *Les Bouquets* (Op.49) [240, col.9–11]. His "storm" piece, *Sicilienne et orage* (c. 1864), is dedicated to his brother César. One wonders if it was ever played in Sainte-Clotilde!

One of the most popular French composers of the third quarter of the nineteenth century, Charles Gounod (1818–93), was also a church organist for a few years early in his career, and for a longer period at the end of his life. He held positions at Missions Etrangères for four and a half years, 1843–48, and at the parish church of Saint-Cloud, 1877–92. Thus, his terms as organist marked "before and after" periods that sandwiched his most productive years as a composer. Gounod's education at the Paris Conservatory was as a composer and pianist, and in 1839 he won the Prix de Rome. During his residence in Italy (1839–42) he became deeply impressed with the music of Palestrina. His musical outlook was further broadened by meeting Mendelssohn's sister Fanny Hensel (1805–47), who introduced him to music of Bach and later German composers.

In the fall of 1842 Gounod left Rome and took the long way home, through Vienna, Berlin, and Leipzig. In Leipzig he was hosted for four days by Mendelssohn himself. Highlights of the visit were a performance by the famous Gewandhaus orchestra (called together even though their season was over, especially for Gounod's benefit) and an organ performance by Mendelssohn, which Gounod described:

> An admirable organist himself, he was anxious I should make acquaintance with some of the numerous and admirable works composed by the mighty Sebastian Bach for the instrument over which he reigned supreme. With this object, he had the old organ at St. Thomas's—the very instrument Bach himself used—examined and repaired, and there for two long hours and more he revealed an unknown world of beauty to my wondering ears. [138, p.125.]

From Leipzig, Gounod made the trip home as quickly as possible: "I left Leipzig on May 18, 1843. I changed carriages seventeen times on the road, and travelled four nights out of six. At length, on May 25, I reached Paris" [138, p.126]. There, his first organ position was already waiting for him. It had been offered to him while he was still in Rome, and he had accepted, provided that he would not be subjected to advice or orders from anyone regarding the church music.

The problems Gounod faced are familiar to many an organist, reminding us that only part of the story of organ playing is linked to the large, famous churches and the glamorous positions: "The means at my disposal were almost *nil*. Besides the organ—a small and very inferior instrument—I had two basses, a tenor, and one choir-boy, without reckoning myself, who was chapel-master, organist, singer, and composer all in one" [138, p.128].

In spite of initial complaints that the musical diet of Palestrina and Bach provided by Gounod was neither cheerful nor entertaining, he was successful in holding his position. Gradually the congregation adjusted to the unfamiliar styles, or at least became resigned to them. It should be remembered that when Gounod arrived home in Paris very few musicians, not to mention average church members, were at all familiar with contrapuntal styles. Hesse had not yet confounded reviewers with his performances of Bach, and the music of Palestrina was practically a closed book.

When Gounod returned to organ playing in 1877, he had a new Cavaillé-Coll organ to play in the Saint-Cloud church, and the organ profession was poised for a remarkable flowering. The days when one could count on the fingers of one hand the French organists who knew any music of Bach were gone forever. Gounod wrote only a few pieces for organ: *Communion, Marche solennelle, Sortie,* and several offertoires.

At Gounod's retirement, Henri Busser (1872–1973) succeeded him as organist at the Saint-Cloud church. He recalled:

> Nearly every Sunday, at the 9 o'clock Mass, Gounod ascended to the tribune and improvised, in preference at the *sortie,* using all the power of the organ, with big, majestic chords, always in the simple keys like G major, F major and especially C major. Didn't he used to say that God was in C?

> Presque tous les dimanches, à la messe de 9 heures, Gounod montait à la tribune et improvisait, de préférence à la sortie, dans toute la force de l'orgue, avec de grands accords majestueux, toujours dans des tons simples comme *sol* majeur, *fa* majeur et surtout *ut* majeur. Ne disait-il pas que Dieu était en *ut?* [40, pp.60–61.]

Théodore Dubois was just beginning his career in the 1850s. He won first prize in organ in 1859, and the Prix de Rome in 1861. From 1855 to 1858 he was organist-accompanist at the chapel of the Invalides. Then Franck chose him to fill the same post at Sainte-Clotilde. The new church had just been opened, and Franck served as *maître de chapelle* until the organ was installed in 1859.

Dubois left for Rome in late 1861, and when he returned to Paris two years later he was named *maître de chapelle* at Sainte-Clotilde. For six years he was Franck's colleague there. Then in 1869 he moved to the Madeleine to be *maître de chapelle* while Saint-Saëns was organist. In 1877 Dubois succeeded Saint-Saëns as organist and stayed in that position until 1896. He was on the faculty at the Paris Conservatory as professor of harmony (1871–90), professor of composition (1890–96), and director (1896–1905).

Dubois appeared on only a few organ inaugural programs. He paid more attention to his extensive and varied catalogue of compositions. Most of his organ works are intended as service music, although some are of a size and quality to warrant a broader use. In addition to organ solos, he wrote a few chamber music pieces with organ. His *Fantaisie Triomphale,* for organ and

Charles Gounod at the 1879 Cavaillé-Coll organ in his studio. From *L'Illustration*, 1893 (New York Public Library).

Théodore Dubois (Bibliothèque Nationale, Paris).

orchestra, was written for the inauguration of the Chicago Auditorium; it was first performed there by Clarence Eddy on December 9, 1889.

The following anecdote about Dubois's organ playing may be a valid reflection, whether it is fact or fiction. After Dubois had succeeded Saint-Saëns at the Madeleine, someone asked an organ pumper there what he thought of the new *titulaire*. He replied, "Oh, sir, he is certainly very capable, very brilliant. . . . But M. Saint-Saëns produced as much effect with less wind." [Oh! Monsieur, il est certainement très habile, très brillant. . . . Mais Monsieur Saint-Saëns faisait autant d'effet avec moins de vent; cited in *L'Orgue* 7, no.24, p.20.]

On the fringes of the organ profession, yet too important to ignore, was Charles-Valentin Alkan (1813–88), one of the most talented musicians in mid-century France. He won first prizes at the Paris Conservatory in solfège at age seven or eight, piano at age eleven, harmony at fourteen, and organ at 21. He was recognized as one of the best piano performers of his time, and he might have been one of the best organists. However, France offered few career opportunities to a Jewish organist.[4]

Alkan became an enthusiastic advocate of the *pédalier* (the pedal piano) and performed various Bach organ works on this instrument in his concerts in the 1870s. For example, his program at the Erard salon on April 30, 1874 concluded with two Bach organ works: *Ich ruf' zu dir* and the Toccata in F [304, p.65]. Vincent d'Indy heard Alkan play the Bach Prelude in E-flat on a pedal piano and described it as "expressive, crystal-clear playing" [cited in 304, p.101].

Alkan's command of the pedal keyboard is documented by his work for pedal solo: *12 Etudes d'orgue, ou de piano à pédales, pour les pieds seulement* (Paris: Richault, c. 1869). In addition to velocity studies, these etudes include a fughetta, an adagio with ornaments and expressive melismatic passages, and a remarkable final set of forty variations on a two-measure theme. The collection is unique in nineteenth-century organ music. Other works by Alkan for organ, or for which organ is one of the instruments listed, are scattered through the catalogue of his works from 1847 to 1872, but most of them are concentrated in the late 1860s.[5]

Paris was the undisputed hub of artistic activity in France, but there were, of course, organists worthy of recognition elsewhere. Unfortunately, their names and accomplishments rarely attracted the attention of the Paris journalists, so information about them is often sketchy.

In provincial France the old tradition of handing down the organ profession (and sometimes an organ position) from father to son still prevailed, although it was rarely practiced in Paris by mid-century. The Widor family is a good example of this tradition. The occasional visits of François-Charles Widor to Paris have been mentioned in previous chapters. He was a teacher at the Collège des Jésuites and organist at Saint-François-de-Sales in Lyon. His father, Jean Widor (1775–1854), had been an organ builder with Callinet, and his son Charles-Marie Widor (1844–1937) became a world-famous organist, composer, and teacher.

Charles-Marie had his first organ instruction from his father, for whom he occasionally substituted. He was named organist of his school when he was eleven. Young Widor finished his general schooling in 1863, studied with Lemmens and Fétis in Brussels, and then returned to live in Lyon (at least nominally, but with increasingly frequent visits to Paris) until he became organist at Saint-Sulpice, Paris in 1870. By then he was already an experienced recitalist. While he had substituted for his father in Lyon and for Saint-Saëns at the Madeleine (1869), he had never before held a church position of his own.

At Boulogne-sur-Mer the Guilmant family traced a surprisingly similar pattern. There were in this case three organ-building great-uncles,[6] the organist father, Jean-Baptiste (1794–1890), and the virtuoso son, Félix-Alexandre

Two views of Charles-Valentin Alkan (Bibliothèque Nationale, Paris).

(1837–1911). Like Widor, Alexandre Guilmant had his early organ studies with his father, studied with Lemmens in Brussels, then remained in Boulogne until he was called to be organist at La Trinité in Paris in 1871. He, too, was by then an experienced recitalist and had appeared in Paris and elsewhere on important inaugural programs. The similarity ends there, for Alexandre Guilmant's professional career was well under way before he moved to Paris, and he was already making a substantial contribution to musical life in his home town. He held positions as organist at Saint-Joseph (1853), then as *maître de chapelle* (1857) and later as organist at his father's church, Saint-Nicolas. He organized and conducted a choral society, taught solfège in the local music school, and participated in various civic music activities.

Members of the Klein family, uncle and nephew, were organists at the cathedral of Rouen. The elder Klein also taught at the cathedral *maîtrise*. In 1855 he sent for his young nephew Aloys and took charge of his musical education. Aloys Klein (1849–89) was born in Romanswiller (Alsace). He was choir organist at Rouen before succeeding his uncle as *titulaire* in 1872. He left the cathedral of Rouen in 1881 to fill the same position at Immaculée Conception, Elbeuf [197].

At Saint-Brieuc, Charles Collin was organist at the cathedral from 1845 to 1909. His son Charles-Augustin Collin (d. 1938) was organist at Notre-Dame, Rennes, from 1884.

Northeastern France was the home of several families of organists. Joseph Wackenthaler (1795–1869) was organist at the cathedral of Strasbourg. His son François-Xavier (1824–56) was organist at Saint-Pierre-le-Jeune, Strasbourg, when he was in his early twenties. In June 1847 he was named organist at Saint-Georges, Haguenau, and he also had a post there as a professor in the municipal music school. In March 1849 the school was dissolved, and Wackenthaler left for Paris. He became organist at Saint-Nicolas-des-Champs, and when the Niedermeyer School was opened in 1853, he was appointed professor of organ. He died three years later, at age 32 [306, p.143]. Another J. Wackenthaler, nephew of the Strasbourg organist, was named *titulaire* at the cathedral of Dijon in 1875.

At Saint-Dié (Vosges) one could hear Jean-Romary Grosjean (1815–88), cathedral organist from 1839. As the son of a poor craftsman in a small Vosges village, his chances of entering a profession were remote. However, he showed an early aptitude for music, and a generous organist provided lessons. By age twelve he could hold a small church position. In gradual stages he progressed to his post at the cathedral.

Not content to stop there, Grosjean took a leave of absence to study organ with Boëly and piano with Stamaty in Paris. He published several collections and a periodical devoted to organ music for church services. He was also interested in research and is credited with the discovery of some important early manuscripts in the Saint-Dié library [239].

Jean-Romary's nephew Ernest Grosjean (1844–1936) followed in his footsteps. He studied organ with his uncle and then with Chauvet. He was organist at the cathedral of Verdun (from 1868) and at Saint-Antoine, Versailles (from 1888) and also wrote and published music suitable for church organists.

At Nancy, members of the Hess family held positions at the cathedral, and for some time father and son were *titulaires* simultaneously. Henri Hess (Georges-Henry-Emile Hess, b. 1841) won first prize in organ at the Paris Conservatory in 1866. He was organist at Saint-Ambroise, Paris, from 1864 to 1868, after which he returned home to become *maître de chapelle* (and later *titulaire*) at the cathedral of Nancy [ME 36, p.31]. The 1872 inauguration of a choir organ at Saint-Epvre, Nancy, included performances by "MM. Hess, father and son, Marteau and Helmer" [ME 38, p.119].

Several members of the Andlauer family received notice in the music periodicals. In 1877 *Le Ménestrel* announced that Andlauer of Andlau (Alsace) had won the competition for the post of organist at the church of Notre-Dame-des-Champs. He had held previous positions at Fontenay-le-Vicomte and Honfleur, and had been a student of Lemmens [ME 43, pp.53–54]. Duclos identified this organist as Auguste Andlauer [76, p.xvii].

When Edouard-Ignace Andlauer (1830–1909) died, a necrology in *Le Ménestrel* observed that he was a native of Andlau, and that he had completed his studies at the Brussels Conservatory in 1849 as a student of Lemmens, Fétis, and Bériot. He then became organist of Saint-Georges, Haguenau, and established a reputation as a distinguished teacher, highly respected in Alsace. His son, who had also attended the Brussels Conservatory, held a position in Schlestadt (Alsace) at the time of his father's death [ME 76, p.16]. One can trace several connections between Edouard Andlauer and the Wackenthaler family. His teachers included Joseph Wackenthaler in Strasbourg; and his predecessor at Saint-Georges, Haguenau, was Xavier Wackenthaler [306, p.144].

One member of the family, Louis-Marie-François Andlauer (1876–1915), attended the Paris Conservatory. By 1900 he had received honorable mention in the annual organ competition, and he held a position as choir organist at Notre-Dame-des-Champs [249, p.686].

Among the better-known musicians in Alsace was Georges-Frédéric-Théophile Stern (1803–86). A native of Strasbourg, he was organist at Saint-Pierre-le-Vieux from 1819, and at Saint-Nicolas from 1824. After a period of study in Germany, he returned to his post at Saint-Nicolas in 1830. In 1841 he was named organist of the Temple-Neuf, and soon after he published the first of several collections of organ music for church use. They contained the music of various composers as well as his own compositions, and were intended to provide organists with more suitable music than they sometimes played in church [298, vol.2, p.827].[7]

In Belgium the organ world was dominated by Fétis, Lemmens, and their circle. A frequent performer on inaugural programs for Merklin-Schütze organs was Charles-Victor Dubois (1832–69), a blind organist and professor of harmonium at the Brussels Conservatory. Other organists given occasional mention in the musical press included Jean-Emmanuel Henskens (1820–59), organist at Saint-Jacques, Antwerp; Charles-F.-J. Delin (1827–53), organist of the cathedral, Antwerp; and Jules Duguet, who succeeded his father as organist of the cathedral of Liège in 1849.

Although women could (and did) study organ at the Paris Conservatory, their names are rare among French organists of the nineteenth century. Out of 60 first prizes awarded from the establishment of the organ class in 1819 until 1900, only six were awarded to women: Geneviève-Louise Rousseau (1827), Jennie Letourneur (1827), Angélique-Elisa Hervy (1836), Marie-Augustine-Aimée-Hippolyte Lorotte (1854), Joséphine-Pauline Boulay (1888), and Marie-Joséphine-Claire Prestat (1890) [249, pp.581–83]. We have noted the brief tenures of Thérèse-Célestine Couperin in the 1820s. For a time during the 1830s a Miss Bigot was *titulaire* of Saint-Gervais. She had succeeded her teacher, Marrigues, in 1834, and she remained in that post until about 1838–40 [122, p.136].

In his 1855 book, *Nouveau Manuel complet de l'organiste,* Georges Schmitt listed women organists active at that time, none of whom held positions in Paris: Mlle Dillon (d. 1854), cathedral of Meaux; Mlle Charpentier, Saint-Pierre, Limoges; Mme Lecourt, at Crespy; Mme Travezini, at Chinon; Mme Blachette, at Loudun; Mme Lévêque, at Nemours; and Mme Warkenthaler [= Wackenthaler], wife of the organist of the cathedral of Strasbourg [289, p.78].

A word of clarification is due Mrs. Wackenthaler. The Strasbourg cathedral, which budgeted 2,400 francs for the two positions of organist and *maître de chapelle,* employed the Wackenthaler husband-and-wife team for 1,650 francs, thus saving 750 francs. Mrs. Wackenthaler, who was reputed to be almost as good as her husband on piano and organ, played the *grand orgue,* and her husband had charge of the choir. She continued to serve as organist after the death of Joseph Wackenthaler in 1869 [101, pp.67–68].

In his account of the Wackenthalers, Erb inserted a curious item concerning performance practice: "It was said that Mr. and Mrs. Wackenthaler played the organ only with gloves, not wanting to spoil the finesse of their pianistic touch." [On racontait que M. et Mme Wackenthaler ne jouaient de l'orgue qu'avec des gants, ne voulant pas gâter la finesse de leur toucher pianistique; 101, p.67.]

One does not find the names of women as organists on nineteenth-century inaugural programs in France. The exception that proves the rule occurred in 1868, when Maria Sannier, young daughter of the organist of Sainte-Catherine, Lille, participated in the inauguration of a Merklin-Schütze organ at Maubeuge. She played a *Méditation* by Lefébure-Wély and an *Offertoire* by Batiste "in a very correct manner," and was well received by the public and the other performers: Bencteux *(titulaire),* Dubois (of Brussels), and Grison (of Reims) [ME 35, p.150].

VII.
New Horizons
The 1860s

THE 1860s were a time of expansion in the French organ world. Many new organs were installed, and old organs were revised and enlarged, not only in Paris but throughout France and Belgium. Leading organists were traveling from one end of the country to another to play for inaugurations, sometimes with the participation of local organists. Most of these occasions followed well-established patterns, but a few merit special attention, because of the importance of the instrument itself or because of the inaugural program. These events include inaugurations of Cavaillé-Coll organs for Saint-Sulpice, Notre-Dame, and La Trinité; Merklin-Schütze organs for the cathedral of Rouen and the Brussels Conservatory; and Barker's organ for Saint-Augustin.

In some ways the 1860s can be seen as a transitional decade. Inaugurations were still the backbone of nonliturgical organ performances, but from time to time the celebration of a new organ was expanded to include a performance by one artist playing composed music. There were even a few organ séances that were independent of inaugurations: they were pilot models for the modern organ recital. Improvisations remained an important feature of organ programs, but composed pieces were included with increasing frequency. Usually they were original pieces by the performer, but sometimes a work by Bach, Handel, Mendelssohn, or Lemmens was also played. Vocal music was still considered an important ingredient in an organ program, to relieve the monotony of too much instrumental music.

The 1860s were also transitional in terms of performers. This decade saw the rise to prominence of a brilliant new generation of organists. The most notable were Guilmant and Chauvet (both born in 1837), and Widor and Gigout (both born in 1844). It saw the decline of an era with the death of Lefébure-Wély in 1869 and the resignation of Lemmens from the Brussels Conservatory the same year.

Both Widor and Guilmant were still living in their home towns, but their Paris debuts and subsequent performances in the capital during the 1860s placed their names high among the most promising young organists.

Unlike their two contemporaries, Chauvet and Gigout both attended music schools in Paris. Charles-Alexis Chauvet (1837–71) received first prize in organ at the Paris Conservatory in 1860. He was organist successively at Saint-Thomas-d'Aquin, Saint-Bernard-de-la-Chapelle, Saint-Merry (from

1864), and La Trinité (from 1868).[1] Highly esteemed by his contemporaries as an improviser and performer, he was well on his way toward a brilliant career when he died at age 34.

Henri Maréchal described Chauvet as "an incomparable master. . . . In regard to technique, Chauvet was an accomplished virtuoso; further, his entirely personal manner of understanding the score was that of a superior intelligence." [Au point de vue du mécanisme, Chauvet était un virtuose accompli; en outre, sa manière toute personnelle de comprendre le texte était celle d'une intelligence supérieure; 217, p.167–68.] Arthur Pougin opined that no one excelled Chauvet in playing the works of Bach with perfection, warmth, loftiness, and grandeur of spirit, displaying all the magnificent beauty of the music [ME 38, p.116].

Eugène Gigout (1844–1925) had his early musical training at the cathedral at Nancy, under Bazile Maurice, *maître de chapelle*, and Hess, the cathedral organist. In 1857 he was sent to Paris to study at the *Ecole de musique religieuse et classique* (the Niedermeyer School) [104, pp.12–13]. His organ teacher there was Loret, but he was more profoundly influenced by Saint-Saëns, who was then teaching piano at the Niedermeyer School. Gigout remained a lifelong friend and disciple of Saint-Saëns.[2]

By 1863 Gigout had received the diplomas *Maître de Chapelle* and *Organiste,* and was already teaching plainchant and solfège at the Niedermeyer School. In that year he was named organist of Saint-Augustin, a post he retained the rest of his life. Gigout soon gained a reputation as an outstanding performer, and his improvisations received particular acclaim.

At the beginning of the 1860s, Lefébure-Wély could probably still claim to be the king of French organists in terms of popularity, but from the end of 1857, when he resigned his church position at La Madeleine, his primary interest was in other areas. He was an artist-performer for the instrument maker Debain, and he played many programs on Debain harmoniums. His specialty, though, was the Debain harmonicorde, an instrument that combined features of the harmonium with those of the piano. It had the sustained quality of the harmonium and the percussive character of stringed keyboard instruments.[3] Later, Lefébure-Wély turned his attention to composing for the musical theater.

Even with these other activities, Lefébure-Wély played for a considerable number of Cavaillé-Coll inaugurations, although he was increasingly selective about the engagements he accepted. He seemed to be making a special effort to keep a low profile in Paris in the first years of the decade. He was again in the spotlight in 1863, when he was appointed *titulaire* of Saint-Sulpice. He remained at that church the rest of his life.

César Franck, Saint-Saëns, Auguste Durand, Schmitt, and Bazille appeared on organ programs occasionally, and Lemmens was always newsworthy whenever he inaugurated an organ or visited the French capital. But the busiest organists, in terms of the sheer number of inaugurations they played, were Batiste and Renaud de Vilbac, sometimes joined by Edmond Hocmelle.

The name of Edouard Batiste appeared with great regularity in the musical press, sometimes for playing inaugurations, sometimes as accompanist for a major choral work performed at Saint-Eustache, sometimes as a composer, choral conductor, or organist for special events. No organist in France was more visible, and Batiste seems to have been unusually successful in bridging the chasm between the "severe" players and their more popular colleagues. One of his most imaginative explorations of organ repertoire occurred in 1860, when some paintings were inaugurated at Saint-Eustache. As a part of the music for that event, Batiste played works of Frescobaldi, Handel, Bach, and Couperin—the composers whose medallions ornamented the organ case [ME 27, p.158]. Such a collection of early organ music had not previously been attempted on a public program in Paris. Batiste was clever enough to link this repertoire to a visual feature of the organ and to the inauguration of visual art in the church building.

An elaborate, two-day inauguration was held in March 1860 to mark the completion of the Merklin-Schütze organ in the cathedral of Rouen. On the first day, organists Batiste, Renaud de Vilbac, Sergent, and Klein played the usual kind of inauguration program, alternating with choral music, and performing original works and improvisations to demonstrate the organ. The next day, Lemmens gave a solo recital for an audience of more than 6,000. He opened with a Handel concerto (arranged for organ solo by Best), followed by a quiet improvisation, his own *Hosanna*, a Bach Prelude and Fugue in D minor, a *Prière en fa*, and an improvised *sortie* [RGM 27, pp.90–91]. While new organs were often given more than one hearing, there was usually only one public event. The idea of having two inaugural programs, one to demonstrate the organ and one to feature an artist and his repertoire, opened the door to many possibilities and was a way to satisfy diverse interests.

The following year (1861) marked another important event for the Merklin-Schütze company: the September inauguration of an organ in the Palais Ducal, the concert hall for the Brussels Conservatory. Actually, only two of the four manuals (34 of the projected 56 stops) were complete at that time, because of a lack of funds. The reviewer for *La France musicale* commented: "Brussels has the honor of being the first city on the continent to have an organ in a concert hall." [Bruxelles a l'honneur d'être la première ville sur le continent qui possède un orgue dans une salle de concert; FM 25, p.307.]

Performers for the inauguration were Lemmens, his students Joseph Callaerts (1838–1901) and Alphonse Mailly, and Jules Duguet, the organist of the cathedral of Liège [RGM 28, p.308]. That the Brussels Conservatory finally had an organ was due to the persistence and determination of Fétis, but he was not satisfied with an incomplete instrument. Finally, in 1866, a second inauguration was held for the four-manual organ, in conjunction with the fiftieth anniversary of the re-establishment of the Académie royale of Belgium. For this occasion Fétis composed his *Fantaisie pour orchestre et orgue*, with Lemmens and the orchestra of the Brussels Conservatory giving the première.

Meanwhile, Cavaillé-Coll completed his monumental organ for Saint-

Sulpice. In April 1862, the organ was ready for preliminary hearings, first at an Easter service (played by Schmitt), and a few days later before French officials and the jury for the exposition then in progress in London. The organ was actually entered in the London exposition, and was represented there by construction plans. For the select audience at Saint-Sulpice, Lefébure-Wély demonstrated the organ's resources by playing four large pieces or improvisations. Reviewing the demonstration, Charles Colin observed that in recent years one rarely had the opportunity to hear Lefébure-Wély [FM 26, pp.130–31].

For the official reception on April 29, Schmitt, the *titulaire,* played an *Offertoire* as the initial organ piece. Franck played "an andante on the foundations," Guilmant played his own *Méditation,* Bazille improvised a pastorale that included a "storm," and Saint-Saëns played a piece "in a broad style and full of originality." The *maîtrise* of the parish sang various pieces, concluding with a chorus from Handel's *Judas Macabbeus.* The theme from this chorus then served as the basis for a final improvisation by Schmitt [FM 26, pp.137–38; RMS 3, col.230–31]. *Le Ménestrel* reported that 6,000 people attended the inaugural program [ME 29, p.182].

On May 2 Guilmant gave a program of his own on the Saint-Sulpice organ, playing a Handel concerto, the Toccata and Fugue in D minor by Bach, *Pastorale* by Kullak, and several works of his own [RGM 29, pp.155–56]. Guilmant had already appeared on inaugural programs elsewhere; the two programs at Saint-Sulpice were his Paris debut.[4]

Adolf Hesse visited Paris in the summer of 1862, on his way back to Germany from the exposition in London. It was the first time he had been in Paris since his long-remembered performance in 1844, and it was destined to be his last, as he died in 1863. Hesse was lavish in his praise for the Saint-Sulpice organ. In an account of his travels in England and France, he wrote that this organ was "the most perfect, the most harmonious, the largest, and truly the masterpiece of modern organ building" [le plus parfait, le plus harmonieux, le plus grand et réellement le chef-d'oeuvre de la facture d'orgue moderne; RMS 3, col.384].

Hesse was urged by his French colleagues to give a program on the Saint-Sulpice organ while he was in Paris. However, he chose to play at Sainte-Clotilde, later explaining that the great distance between his eyes and the music rack at Saint-Sulpice had governed his choice [RMS 3, col.385]. Charles Colin reviewed the performance for *La France musicale* and used the opportunity to scold French artists for being slaves of public taste rather than leaders, looking too often for effects rather than the more profound regions of great music [FM 26, pp.211–12]. Hesse played a sonata, a trio, a Fantasy in E minor, a Fugue in G by Bach, and a Fantasy on *God Save the Queen.*

Georges Schmitt recorded that the audience included Batiste, Saint-Saëns, César Franck and his brother Joseph, Renaud de Vilbac, Chauvet, Durand, Barker, Cavaillé-Coll, critics from the leading music journals, and other prominant musicians. Schmitt remarked about the clarity of Hesse's playing, and the

The Cavaillé-Coll organ in the church of Saint-Sulpice. From *Le Ménestrel*, 1863 (University of California Library, Riverside).

security and ease of his pedal technique, commenting that "he plays the liveliest passages without jolts and without noise, the foot adhering to the key, so to speak" [il exécute les passages les plus vifs sans secousse et sans bruit, le pied adhérant à la touche pour ainsi dire; RMS 3, col.279].

Georges Schmitt himself was soon to get the jolt of his career. He had been *titulaire* at Saint-Sulpice since 1849, but by the spring of 1863 the clergy was seeking to replace him. Hearing that Lefébure-Wély was about to take the organ position at Saint-Germain-des-Prés, the Saint-Sulpice authorities urged him to come there instead. After some negotiations, Lefébure-Wély accepted. The price Saint-Sulpice had to pay suggests the importance of the change. First, Schmitt had to be given severance pay. Then the annual salary had to be doubled to meet the 3,000 francs that Lefébure-Wély required.

In a letter dated April 5, 1863, Cavaillé-Coll wrote to Lemmens: "That nomination astonishes everyone, and the most astonished have been the [organ] builder and the organist himself who at this moment is traveling in the south [of France]." [Cette nommination (*sic*) étonne tout le monde et les plus étonnés ont été le facteur et l'organiste lui-même qui est en ce moment en voyage dans le Midi.] Cavaillé-Coll noted that this change raised the level of organists' salaries in Paris. Now there were two churches paying fixed salaries of 3,000 francs plus 1,000 francs in extra fees: La Madeleine and Saint-Sulpice [79 no.60, pp.85–86]. One can only speculate on the amount of influence Cavaillé-Coll himself exerted in placing Lefébure-Wély at Saint-Sulpice. He may not have been as astonished as he wished Lemmens to believe.

In the summer of 1863 Charles-Marie Widor made his Paris debut on the Saint-Sulpice organ. His program consisted of seven pieces, including works of Handel, Hesse, Bach, and Lemmens. The review that appeared in two periodicals concluded that the young organist interpreted very well the works he performed, particularly those of Lemmens "of whom he is one of the best pupils" [dont il est un des meilleurs élèves; FM 27, p.243; RGM 30, p.246].

The number and variety of organ séances was especially interesting during the middle of the decade. Lemmens came to Paris in the spring of 1864 and gave several programs of works from his *Ecole d'orgue* and *L'Organiste catholique*. Three performances were on an organ in Cavaillé-Coll's hall, and one was at Saint-Sulpice, where he was hosted by his rival, the recently appointed *titulaire*, Lefébure-Wély. Louis Roger commented that Lemmens had changed his style from earlier years, implying that it had now reached a mature balance, with color, variety, grace, and elegance governed by discipline [RMS 5, col.187–88].

Lefébure-Wély, who now included a Bach fugue in his repertoire, had apparently changed somewhat also. At his April program at Saint-Sulpice for the learned societies, where the audience included Rossini, Lefébure-Wély played an original *Offertoire en fa,* a Fugue in E major by Bach, a "storm" piece, and a *grand choeur* for the final piece. Louis Roger reported:

The organ and the organist have had the same success, and the maestro Rossini, on whom all eyes were fixed, appeared satisfied with the one and the other. The great man was going to leave when the storm began. "A storm!" he exclaimed, "That always amuses me; I'll stay." And he did indeed remain.

L'orgue et l'organiste ont eu le même succès, et le maestro Rossini, sur qui tous les regards étaient fixés, a paru satisfait de l'un et de l'autre. Le grand homme allait se retirer lorsque l'orage a commencé. «Un orage! s'est-il écrié, cela m'amuse toujours; je reste.» Et il est resté en effet. [RMS 5, col.188.]

Historically, the most significant organ program of the year was Franck's performance of his *Six Pièces* at Sainte-Clotilde in November. As one reviewer commented:

All these pieces are written in a masterly manner. In the first, one especially noted a *voix humaine* chorus with a most pleasing effect, and in the *grande pièce symphonique*, a most distinguished melody, played first on the clarinet and then repeated on the *voix célestes*.

Tous ces morceaux sont écrits de main de maître. On a surtout remarqué dans le premier un choeur de voix humaine du plus heureux effet, et dans la grande pièce symphonique une mélodie des plus distinguées, jouée d'abord sur la clarinette et reproduite ensuite sur les jeux de voix célestes. [FM 28, p.371.]

On December 5, 1865 Auguste Durand, organist at Saint-Vincent-de-Paul, gave an organ séance that closely resembled a modern recital. Unlike the recent programs by Lemmens and Franck, it did not consist exclusively of his own works, nor was it given for a specific organization or as an organ demonstration. An announcement in *La France musicale* stated that the program would include works by Handel, Mendelssohn, Emanuel Bach, Lemmens, and some new pieces by Durand[5] [FM 29, p.387]. A. Elwart, writing for *Revue et Gazette musicale*, was somewhat disappointed by Durand's innovations: the program had not included improvisations, and there was no vocal music during the intervals between organ pieces. Elwart noted that the pieces particularly well received were a fantasy for four hands by Hesse (played by Durand and Sergent, organist of Notre-Dame), an *Offertoire* of Lefébure-Wély, *Prière en ut* of Lemmens, and an andante by Durand [RGM 32, p.403].

Franz Liszt (1811–86) arrived in Paris in 1866, drawn there by the death of his mother, a resident of Paris for many years. While he was in the French capital he visited Saint-Sulpice, where Lefébure-Wély played for him, and Sainte-Clotilde, where Franck gave a special program in his honor. Lefébure-Wély invited Liszt to take his turn at the Saint-Sulpice organ, but the visitor responded that he only allowed himself to play village organs [qu'il ne se permettait de jouer que les orgues de village; ME 33, p.142]. After the Sainte-Clotilde performance on April 13, Liszt "warmly complimented Mr. Franck on the elevated style of his works and his masterly performance" [a chaleureusement complimenté M. Franck sur le style élevé de ses oeuvres et son exécution magistrale; ME 33, p.166]. The reviewer noted that the audience included J. d'Ortigue, Dubois, Chauvet, Widor, and other distinguished guests.

Théodore Dubois, then *maître de chapelle* at Sainte-Clotilde, had assisted with the registration at that program. Many years later he recalled the occasion: "I will always remember a séance when he had wanted to perform these pieces for a great artist then stopping in Paris. There were only three of us in the tribune: the composer, Liszt, and humble me!" [Je me souviendrai toujours d'une séance où il avait voulu faire entendre ces pièces à un grand artiste de passage à Paris. Nous n'étions que trois à la tribune: l'auteur, Liszt et moi, humble! 74, p.20.]

Alexandre de Bertha, who had been a close friend of Liszt's mother, went with the musician to hear the Paris organists.

> It was thus that I heard César Franck and Lefébure-Wély, the two most renowned organists of that time. Truly, they didn't please us, neither one nor the other, considering the subtilty of the first and the affectation of the second, little in keeping with the grandiose character of their instrument.

> Ce fut ainsi que j'entendis César Frank [*sic*] et Lefèbure-Wély [*sic*], les deux organistes les plus renommés d'alors. A vrai dire, ils ne nous plurent ni l'un, ni l'autre, vu la subtilité du premier et l'afféterie du second, peu en rapport avec le caractère grandiose de leur instrument. [22, p.1163.]

The Paris Exposition universelle of 1867 gave many organists a chance to perform. Saint-Saëns, Chauvet, Durand, Batiste, Renaud de Vilbac, Dubois, Guilmant, d'Etcheverry, Callaerts, and others were all heard on the organs exhibited by Merklin-Schütze, one of ten organ companies participating in the exposition.

In retrospect, of more general interest was Cavaillé-Coll's rebuilding and enlargement of the Notre-Dame organ. It was played by the *titulaire*, Sergent, for the Christmas services, 1867, producing "une grande sensation" [ME 35, p.46]. On February 20, 1868 the commission appointed to examine the organ met. It included well-known musicians, scholars, educators, and representatives of government and church. The organ profession was represented by Benoist. Among the other musicians were Auber, Rossini, and Ambroise Thomas. Several organists presided at the console for the examination: Saint-Saëns, Franck, Sergent, Durand, Widor, Chauvet, and Loret [ME 35, p.102].

The commission's report, written by the *abbé* Lamazou, confirms that the examination was exhaustive. Each stop was tried, pipe by pipe, and then in combinations with other stops. The interior was inspected for its design, materials, and workmanship. Finally the commission gave its unanimous approval, along with highest praise for the builder [ME 35, pp.177, 186].

The official inauguration took place on March 6, 1868, with the following program:

INTRODUCTION.—Prélude sur les jeux de fond
    par M. SERGENT, Organiste titulaire
Chant en faux-bourdon du Psaume *Laudate Dominum*
    Grand Orgue et Choeur
Verset.—Oraison par Mgr. l'Archevêque de Paris

1. Orgue
Prélude et Fugue en mi-mineur   J. S. BACH
    par M. LORET, Organiste à St-Louis d'Antin
Fantaisie en fa   DURAND
    par M. DURAND, Organiste à St-Vincent de Paul

2. Chant
Ave Maria, chanté par le jeune Fél. RENAUD   CHERUBINI

3. Orgue
Introduction et Noël   CHAUVET
    par M. CHAUVET, Organiste à St-Merry
Marche de la Cantate couronnée à l'Exposition
    universelle exécutée par l'auteur   SAINT-SAENS

4. Chant
Paternoster   NIEDERMEYER
    Solo et Choeur, Solo chanté par M. BOLLAERT

5. Orgue
Fantaisie en ut majeur   C. FRANCK
    par M. C. FRANCK ainé, Organiste à Ste-Clotilde
Marche funèbre et Chant séraphique   A. GUILMANT
    par M. GUILMANT, Organiste à Boulogne-sur-Mer

6. Chant
Agnus Dei   HAYDN
    Solo et Choeur, Solo chanté par M. FLORENZY

7. Orgue
Improvisation sur differents jeux de l'orgue   WIDOR
    par M. WIDOR, Organiste à Lyon

8. Chant
Laudate Dominum   Ambr. THOMAS
    Choeur final

SORTIE. par M. SERGENT, Organiste titulaire

[Cited in 157, p.14.]

The inauguration of the Cavaillé-Coll organ in Notre-Dame Cathedral. From *L'Illustration,* 1868 (New York Public Library).

Opinions differed about which organists had been the most impressive. *Revue de musique sacrée* chose Franck, Chauvet, and Saint-Saëns [RMS 9, pp.23–24]; *La France musicale* preferred Chauvet, Saint-Saëns, and Guilmant [FM 32, p.83]; *Revue et Gazette musicale* named Chauvet and Saint-Saëns [RGM 35, p.85]. The last journal was displeased with the noisy, restless audience and the excessive length of the program. *Revue de musique sacrée* concurred, adding to the list of complaints that some of the best organists were not included: Bazille, Batiste, Lefébure-Wély, and G. Schmitt.

Following the inauguration, both public and private hearings of the Notre-Dame organ continued during the spring and summer. A series of half-hour programs was instituted on successive Sundays at 12:30, each given by a different organist. Saint-Saëns initiated the series, followed by Franck and Guilmant, among others [RGM 35, pp.86, 95].

The program played by Saint-Saëns consisted of an improvisation, a march, a transcription of a work by Liszt, and a "storm" piece. The reviewer for *Le Ménestrel* expressed distaste for "storms," especially in church, but he admitted that the atmosphere of the old cathedral combined with cloudy weather contributed to the effectiveness of this one [ME 35, p.135].

In late April Franck and Durand demonstrated the organ for delegates of the learned societies and other officials [RGM 35, p.134]. In July Franck and Sergent played for the members of the scientific association of France, after which Cavaillé-Coll guided the visitors through the instrument [RGM 35, p.222].

Important events were also taking place at Saint-Augustin. The church building was inaugurated on May 28, 1868, and on June 17 the organ was given its blessing and inauguration. The new instrument, built by Barker, was the first organ in Paris with electric action [245, pp.6–7]. Eugène Gigout, who had been appointed organist of Saint-Augustin in 1863, suffered through five years of temporary buildings and services in the crypt with only a harmonium to play, awaiting construction of the church and organ. His patience was finally rewarded, and he remained organist at Saint-Augustin the rest of his life.

By January 1868, the organ was in place, and Gigout played a scherzo by Lemmens, a fugue by Niedermeyer, and a sonata by Mendelssohn for the installation of a clergyman [FM 32, p.36]. Three organists performed for the organ inauguration in June: Gigout, Batiste, and Schmitt. Gigout played an improvised *Entrée,* his own *Prélude* (B minor), part of a Mendelssohn sonata, and the Lemmens *Grand choeur varié.* Schmitt played an original *Grande fantaisie* and an improvisation. Batiste played two of his own works, and as a *sortie,* the final movement of Beethoven's Symphony in C minor. Vocal solos and choruses rounded out the program [178, pp.5–6].

Early in 1869 Merklin-Schütze announced that programs could be heard each Monday and Thursday afternoon at their shop, when they would introduce a new system whereby stops could be transmitted from one manual to another. The great advantage of this system, they said, was that for a moderate price smaller churches and chapels could have a complete organ that required less space [FM 33, p.11]. Batiste and Renaud de Vilbac opened the series of demonstrations.

Cavaillé-Coll was then putting the finishing touches on his organ for La Trinité, and it was inaugurated on March 16. Few such occasions have had as

Eugène Gigout at the Barker organ in the church of Saint-Augustin (Bibliothèque Nationale, Paris).

much press notice as this one. Chauvet, recently named *titulaire* of La Trinité, had announced he would play the *Offertoire* from Rossini's Mass. The famous composer had died in November 1868, but his popularity was never greater. At the last minute the director of the Italian Theater, who held the rights to the Mass, forbade the performance. Rossini fans were irate that anyone could or would prevent their hearing his music, and for weeks after the Trinité inauguration the press continued to fume over the Rossini matter. As added touches of drama, Chauvet refused to substitute another piece for the *Offertoire,* and in a prelude to the *sortie* he used the motif from the forbidden Rossini piece.

Other performers in the Trinité inauguration were Widor, Saint-Saëns, Durand, Franck, and the newly appointed organist of Saint-Merry, Henri Fissot (1843–96) [RGM 36, pp.94, 101]. The reviewer for *La France musicale* gave the honors to Durand, who played a pastorale with a "storm." He did not care as much for the performances of Saint-Saëns or Franck, and it was apparently in their direction that he aimed his pronouncement: "Religious style and tedious style are not synonyms, as the musicians who conceal their creative incapacity under the confusion of a pretentious harmony would like to persuade us." [Style religieux et style ennnuyeux ne sont pas synonymes, comme voudraient nous le persuader les musiciens qui déguisent leur impuissance créatrice sous les fatras d'une harmonie prétentieuse; FM 33, p.91.]

Anton Bruckner (1824–96) visited Paris in May 1869, before returning home from an organ inauguration at Saint-Epvre, Nancy. He and Hocmelle each played in a séance in the Merklin-Schütze shop [RGM 36, p.157]. His most memorable appearance, however, was on the Notre-Dame organ, where he played a program attended by Auber, Gounod, Franck, Saint-Saëns, and other musicians. His success was crowned with a masterful prelude, fugue, and variation improvised on a theme given to him by Chauvet [264, p.93].

Change was in the air. In September 1869, Alphonse-Jean-Ernst Mailly succeeded Lemmens as professor of organ at the Brussels Conservatory. On the final day of the decade Lefébure-Wély died. One could then understand why his public appearances had decreased in number, and why he had not participated in the important inaugurations at Notre-Dame and La Trinité. Ambroise Thomas delivered a final tribute at the funeral service. Recognizing that there were differences of opinion about Lefébure-Wély's art, he reminded those present that this musician was "the first, the most skillful, and the most ardent" [le premier, le plus habile et le plus ardent] to promote the great new developments that had taken place in organ construction.

> I leave to others the task of recalling that marvelous execution, that profound science of registration, that exquisite choice, that happy mixture of such diverse timbres, that inexhaustible variety of effects and sonorities, finally those beautiful improvisations in which charm, elegance, clarity, often grandeur were found united.

> Je laisse à d'autres le soin de rappeler cette exécution merveilleuse, cette science profonde des combinaisons, ce choix exquis, ce mélange heureux de

An organ audition in Cavaillé-Coll's hall. From *L'Illustration*, 1870 (University of California Library, Berkeley).

timbres si divers, cette variété inépuisable d'effets et de sonorités, enfin ces belles improvisations où se trouvaient réunis le charme, l'élégance, la clarté, souvent la grandeur. [ME 37, p.45.]

A few years later, when a monument to Lefébure-Wély was erected in the Père-Lachaise cemetery, the friends and associates who attended the ceremony included few organists and only one instrument maker. Gustave Lafargue identified them: Batiste, Guilmant, Deslandres, and Debain [ME 39, pp.253–54].

In 1868 Cavaillé-Coll moved his business and home to a spacious location on avenue du Maine. There his new organs were set up in a large hall with exceptionally fine acoustics and ample space for audiences. Early in 1870 L'Illustration published a picture of an organ audition in this hall. The large, fashionable audience, the dimensions of the room, and the imposing view of the organ all suggest the importance of the occasion. What we see is perhaps not what one would imagine as the interior of an instrument maker's shop, but rather the setting for a performance in a recital hall. Auditions in builders' shops were, indeed, events of no small significance in establishing the position of the organ as a secular concert instrument.

The organ in the picture, a three-manual organ of 41 stops with two enclosed divisions, was to be installed in the private home of Mr. Hopwood, Bracewell, England [IL 55, no.1411, pp.195–96]. Saint-Saëns and Widor shared the first two performances on this instrument in March 1870. A third program was given soon after by Alexandre Guilmant [ME 37, p.111]. Following its installation in England, the organ was inaugurated by William Spark, on November 7, 1870 [50, p.121].

VIII.
Tragedy to Triumph
The 1870s

THE NEW decade opened with problems that brought artistic life to a stand-still in Paris. The Franco-Prussian War was declared on July 19, 1870. It ended on January 28, 1871, with the capitulation of Paris, which had been under siege since September 19. The plight of the citizens by then was desperate, and their troubles were not over with the end of the war. The internal struggle for control of the French government continued through the spring, creating perhaps as many problems as did the foreign army. It culminated in an armed battle in the streets of Paris between forces of the National Assembly (with headquarters in Versailles) and the national guard (supporting the Paris Commune[1]). To compound the confusion, France was still an occupied country; the last German soldiers did not leave until September 16, 1873.

Everyone who had stayed in Paris had stories to tell about the siege. Cavaillé-Coll had used the planks intended for 32' pipes to board up the façade of his house, as a protection against bombardment. Even his finest lumber eventually had to be used for fuel [50, p.120].

Henri Duparc (1848–1933) recorded an interesting story about César Franck during that time. Duparc's grandmother had left Paris before the siege, but anticipating the difficulties that lay ahead, she had put her supply of charcoal and wood at Franck's disposal. One day at his grandmother's house, Duparc encountered Franck, with a bucket of charcoal in each hand, which he was carrying from 372, rue Saint-Honoré (near the Madeleine) to 95, boulevard Saint-Michel (near the Luxembourg Gardens).

A family related to Franck's wife had been in danger from exploding shells, and Franck had given them refuge in his home. Although the bombardment had recently begun, there was no transportation and food was scarce. One stood in line for hours at the butcher shop to buy a little horsemeat. When Duparc asked how Franck managed to feed all those people, the reply was: "You have surely seen in some chocolate shops enormous boxes of chocolate, 30 to 40 centimeters long and some 15 wide? Well, my wife bought a good supply of them and each morning we make a big tureen of chocolate; we consume a great deal of it . . ." "And then?" asked Duparc. "And then? One waits for the next day however one can." [« Vous avez bien vu chez plusieurs chocolatiers d'énormes boîtes de chocolat, de 30 à 40 centimètres de long sur une quinzaine de large? Eh bien, ma femme en a acheté une bonne provision et nous fait chaque matin une grande soupière de chocolat: nous en mangeons beaucoup . . . » — « Et puis? » — « Et puis? . . . on attend le lendemain comme on peut ».] But, Duparc recalled, it was necessary to cook that chocolate, and that is why Franck and his son George crossed Paris to fetch the charcoal, bucket by bucket [92].

Although the organ profession was overshadowed by political and military events, it still saw some important changes in the early 1870s, setting the stage for the brilliant years toward the end of the decade. Early in 1870 Charles-Marie Widor was appointed organist of Saint-Sulpice, succeeding Lefébure-Wély. The talented young Alexis Chauvet died in 1871 at age 34, and Alexandre Guilmant took his place as organist of La Trinité. The following year Benoist retired, and César Franck took his place as professor of organ at the Paris Conservatory. In 1877 Saint-Saëns resigned from his post as organist at La Madeleine, and he was succeeded by Théodore Dubois. The 1870s saw the demise of some important figures in the organ world: Fétis (1871), Batiste (1876), and Benoist (1878).

At least one talented young American organist visited Paris in 1871. Clarence Eddy stopped there on his way to Berlin to study with Karl August Haupt. He met some of the leading organists during this visit, and would later return as America's best-known organ recitalist [121, p.14].

From the time that order was restored in Paris, the career of Alexandre Guilmant moved quickly to the forefront among French organists. His remarkable capacity for work, his rapport with audiences, his leadership, and his musicianship soon crowned Guilmant the new king of French organists.

Widor was also very successful, but his interests were more divided than Guilmant's. As time went on, Widor tended increasingly to focus on composition and conducting, with organ performance (aside from church services) as an important, but somewhat secondary creative interest. One must realize, however, that Widor's fame as an organist rested to a large extent on his performances during and immediately following services at Saint-Sulpice. While his recitals elsewhere did not approach the number Guilmant gave, organists soon began to make pilgrimages to Saint-Sulpice to hear Widor improvise and perform his own works and those of Bach. Thus a review of secular events reported in the musical press gives a distorted view of Widor's stature as a performer, but it nevertheless reflects the picture as it was seen by most citizens of Paris. The attention of the general public was as infrequently drawn to organ service music in the nineteenth century as it is today.

Aided by the prestige of their new professorial posts, both Mailly (professor of organ at the Brussels Conservatory from 1869) and Franck (professor of organ at the Paris Conservatory from 1872) appeared more frequently in the news as organ performers. Batiste continued to play organ inaugurations for the Merklin firm until shortly before his death. Saint-Saëns, as always, was highly respected, and he continued to appear on occasional programs and inaugurations, even after leaving his church position. Lemmens, too, continued his occasional visits to Paris, and his performances were always well received.

Some other familiar names faded from organ programs after the war: Edmond Hocmelle, Georges Schmitt, and Renaud de Vilbac. On the other hand, Eugène Gigout became increasingly popular; and toward the end of the decade, the organ programs by Jules Stoltz, a member of an organ-building family, were often noted in the musical press. Stoltz had been a student at the Niedermeyer School and subsequently became a member of the faculty there.

Organs at La Trinité and Saint-Eustache were both damaged during the fighting in 1871. The Trinité organ was soon repaired, and it was re-inaugurated by Guilmant in 1872. The Saint-Eustache organ limped along for several years. After Batiste died in 1876 that church remained without an organist until the organ was restored by Merklin in 1879. Henri Dallier (1849–1934), who had received first prize in organ at the Conservatory the year before, was named *titulaire*. Dallier had been choir organist at the cathedral in his home town, Reims, from the time he was sixteen. In 1876 he entered the Paris Conservatory, and during the 1877–78 school year he was enrolled in Franck's organ class. He remained at Saint-Eustache until 1905, when he succeeded Fauré at the Madeleine. Dallier was particularly admired for his fine improvisations [164].

While Paris was still struggling to return to normal, England offered some special opportunities. In 1871 the Willis organ in Royal Albert Hall, London, was inaugurated. W. T. Best, official organist for the Hall, gave the opening program on July 18 and subsequently played three times a week during the International Exhibition then in progress in London. In addition, each foreign country participating in the exhibition was invited to nominate an organist to play a series of programs on the new organ. Belgium's representative was Mailly, and France's was Saint-Saëns.

Somewhat annoyed that other English organists were not included, the reporter for *The Monthly Musical Record* wrote that "many of the performances were characterized by a very respectable mediocrity, and not much beyond" [MMR 1, p.123]. A reviewer for *The Orchestra*, however, singled out Saint-Saëns for special recognition, was favorably impressed by Mailly, and praised Cavaillé-Coll organs so highly that one might interpret parts of the review as indirect criticisms of the new Willis organ [OA 16, pp.329–30].

The Musical Standard noted that each visiting organist was to receive an honorarium of fifty pounds: "an amount calculated, we suppose, to be sufficient to cover the personal expenses of the visit; and as two performances are to be given daily for a week, indicating also the value of each performance as £4 3s. 4d." [MST 14, p.71]

Later in the decade Saint-Saëns was reproached by an English critic for using orchestral effects on the organ and departing from the "true style of the instrument." Saint-Saëns seized the opportunity to present his own thought-provoking view of just what defined the true style of the organ:

> It has been only a short time that the modern organ, an entirely French creation, has penetrated into England. The English, like the Germans, are

The Saint-Eustache organ in 1879, after it was rebuilt by Merklin. From *Le Ménestrel*, 1879 (Bibliothèque Nationale, Paris).

somewhat in the situation of a man who had continued to play the harpsichord and found himself in the presence of a modern pianist equipped with a concert grand piano.

He would assuredly find that that is no longer the *true style* of the harpsichord.

The *true style* of an instrument is not one or another conventional style; it is the one which best uses its resources.

When one plays the organ in the manner of certain mediocre performers who stick with a few little easy and common effects, holding some chords on the *voix humaine* that are supported at long intervals by detached notes on the pedal and ornamented by some flute cooings, one leaves the true style of the organ to confine oneself in a limited genre, without horizon and without egress. On the other hand, the classical organists who disdain the marvelous effects of modern instruments and are content to play some fugues by drawing all the stops of the organ at the same time, are not making music, but a confused noise in which it is often impossible to distinguish anything. If the fugal style with required pedal is the one that best suits the organ, it is with the condition that it can always be heard clearly and intelligibly, which one obtains by varying the timbres [and] by changing from one manual to another according to the circumstances; but then for the lovers of tradition, that is no longer the *true style* of the organ; those are the effects of the orchestra.

Well, it isn't to the organists, it is to the organ builders that the reproach should be addressed. Ever since organs have been made the builders have had no other idea than to imitate the orchestral instruments by their different stops, and all their efforts lead to imitating them as faithfully as possible. . . . In avoiding orchestral effects, one is then going directly against the intention of the builders, and consequently against the nature of the instrument.

The modern organ, such as M. Cavaillé-Coll has created and perfected is a new instrument which requires a new style. At present the *true style* of the organ is that which, taking the old organ as a basis, gives free rein to the effects of the instruments of today, so rich and so marvelous.

Il y a peu de temps que l'orgue moderne, création toute française, a pénétré en Angleterre. Les Anglais, comme les Allemands, sont un peu dans la situation d'un homme qui aurait continué à jouer du clavecin et se trouverait en face d'un pianiste moderne armé d'un grand piano de concert.

Il trouverait assurément que ce n'est plus le *vrai style* du clavecin.

Le *vrai style* d'un instrument n'est pas tel ou tel style de convention, c'est celui qui en utilise le mieux les ressources.

Quand on joue de l'orgue à la façon de certaines médiocrités, qui ne sortent pas de quelques petits effets faciles et vulgaires, tenant sur la voix humaine des accords que soutiennent de loin en loin des notes détachées sur la pédale, et qu'agrémentent quelques roucoulements de flûte, on sort du vrai style de l'orgue pour se renfermer dans un genre borné, sans horizon comme sans issue. En revanche, les organistes classiques qui dédaignent les merveilleux effets des instruments modernes, et se contentent de jouer des fugues en tirant tous les registres de l'orgue à la fois, ne font pas de la musique, mais un bruit confus dans lequel il est souvent impossible de rien distinguer. Si le style fugué, avec pédale obligée, est celui qui convient le mieux à l'orgue, c'est à la condition que l'audition en soit toujours claire et intelligible, ce que l'on obtient en variant les timbres, en passant suivant les circonstances d'un clavier à l'autre; mais alors, pour les amateurs de la tradition, ce n'est plus le *vrai style* de l'orgue, ce sont des effets d'orchestre.

Eh bien, ce n'est pas aux organistes, c'est aux facteurs d'orgue que le reproche doit s'adresser. Depuis qu'on fait des orgues, les constructeurs n'ont pas d'autre idée que d'imiter par leurs différents jeux les instruments de l'orchestre, et tous leurs efforts tendent à les imiter le plus fidèlement possible. . . . En fuyant les effets d'orchestre, on va donc directement contre l'intention des constructeurs, et, par conséquent, contre la nature de l'instrument.

L'orgue moderne, tel que M. Cavaillé-Coll l'a créé et perfectionné, est un instrument nouveau, qui demande un style nouveau. Le *vrai style* de l'orgue, à présent, est celui qui, prenant l'orgue ancien pour base, laisse une libre carrière aux effects des instruments actuels, si riches et si merveilleux. [GM 25, no.43, p.6.]

In 1872 Guilmant performed on the Royal Albert Hall organ in London. His playing was so successful that the College of Organists soon after named him an honorary life member [RGM 40, p.71]. Guilmant had performed in England before; both he and Widor had participated in the inaugural program for Cavaillé-Coll's first organ for England, which was installed in the Carmelite church, Kensington, in 1866 [RGM 33, p.239]. The Royal Albert Hall performance, however, marked the beginning of Guilmant's great popularity in England.

In 1873 Cavaillé-Coll completed a large organ for Albert Hall, Sheffield, England. W. T. Best came to Paris to inspect the organ prior to its removal to Sheffield. He and various French and Belgian organists played the instrument, including Saint-Saëns, Widor, Guilmant, and, later, Mailly. A notice of these programs in the *Revue et Gazette musicale* concluded: "One must go to England to see such masterpieces of workmanship installed elsewhere than in a church. The timid attempts we have made of this type prove how little great religious music has yet entered our artistic habits." [C'est en Angleterre qu'il faut aller pour voir de pareils chefs-d'oeuvre de la facture installés ailleurs qu'à l'église. Les timides essais que nous avons faits dans ce genre prouvent combien peu encore la grande musique religieuse est entrée dans nos moeurs artistiques; RGM 40, p.159.] This theme recurred so persistently in ensuing years, when Guilmant was playing frequently in England, that one might suspect that he, Cavaillé-Coll, the press, or all three were conspiring to see that Paris would have a concert organ.

Guilmant played three times in Sheffield in 1874: early in the year, in the spring (substituting for Lemmens, who was ill), and in the fall. From that time on, Guilmant toured frequently in England, sometimes playing an astonishing number of programs. For example, early in 1876 the *Revue et Gazette musicale* reported that he had played twelve organ concerts in fifteen days [RGM 43, p.22].

Guilmant was not the first French organist to tour. As early as 1839 Lefébure-Wély had traveled through parts of France and Switzerland, playing programs on the organ and poïkilorgue [FM 2, pp.563, 594]. Shorter trips within France to play for inaugurations were routine for the more popular Paris organists; and as we have seen, both Mailly and Saint-Saëns played in London. Widor, too, found a hospitable welcome in England, and he, as well as Guilmant, played in Sheffield in the spring of 1874 [ME 40, p.134].

Although Guilmant's name became ubiquitous by the middle of the decade, other organists also received a measure of attention. An interesting program was given at Saint-Eustache in April 1874, by Batiste, who played for "the principal members of the American colony in Paris." He performed works by Bach, Couperin, Frescobaldi, Handel, Mendelssohn, a transcription of a funeral march by F. Le Couppey, and "several of his compositions, very well known in the New World" [RGM 41, p.143].

Cavaillé-Coll's next large instrument (1875) was again for export, this time to the Amsterdam Palace of Industry. Widor and Guilmant each gave programs on it in Paris, and Guilmant played for the inaugural programs in Amsterdam [ME 41, pp.166, 175]. Guilmant's Paris program included the Bach Toccata in C major, Schumann's Canon No.6, *Gavotte* by Martini, an andante with variations by Lemmens, and several of his own works (notably his Sonata I). Several works for cello and voice were also performed [ME 41, p.182].

In 1876 the Brussels Conservatory installed an organ by Schyven in its new building. The inauguration of the instrument was part of the celebration of the 35th anniversary of the founding of the modern school of organ in Belgium, in October 1840, by Christian Friedrich Johann Girschner (1794–1860). The firm of Pierre Schyven & Co. seemed to be the builder of choice for Mailly, and he frequently appeared on inaugurations of this company's organs. However, when it was a matter of recommending the best organ builder for the Amsterdam Palace of Industry, Mailly did not hesitate to name Cavaillé-Coll the "master of masters" (a choice supported not only by his compatriots Gevaert and Lemmens but also by England's most famous organist, W. T. Best) [ME 41, pp.214–15]. By 1880 Mailly had a Cavaillé-Coll organ to play at the Brussels Conservatory.

In 1877 Jules Stoltz initiated the first series of organ recitals in Paris. He was organist of Saint-Leu, and the series was given in a hall belonging to that parish, on an organ built by his family's firm. The first year the series consisted of six programs, with a repertoire ranging from Bach and Handel to Guilmant. Vocal, violin, and cello pieces were also included on the programs [RGM 44, pp.86, 134].

The following year there were again six programs. A partial list of composers suggests the serious nature of this series: Bach, Handel, Rinck, Mendelssohn, Niedermeyer, Saint-Saëns, Widor, Franck, Gigout, Loret. On the final program of the series there were two concertos, in addition to organ and vocal solos. André Messager (1853–1929) played a Mozart piano concerto, and Stoltz played a Handel organ concerto. They were accompanied by a double quartet of strings, conducted by Gabriel Fauré (1845–1924) [RGM 45, pp.102, 117, 174–75]. As early as 1875 Guilmant had played a Handel concerto on a Conservatory concert [ME 42, p.15], but programming pieces with orchestra on what was essentially an organ concert was an innovation.[2] Stoltz's series was an important, pace-setting model soon to enjoy the compliment of imitation. It continued for several years, at least into the beginning of the next decade.

In February 1877 the musical press announced that Cavaillé-Coll had been selected to build another concert organ for England, this time for the town hall in Manchester [ME 43, p.103]. More than one writer pointed out that fine French organs were going to other countries while Paris itself did not have a comparable instrument in a concert hall. More than one saw the approaching Exposition universelle as an opportunity to correct this embarrassing state of affairs.

It is not altogether surprising, then, that 1878 was truly a banner year. All else that happened in the French organ world was overshadowed by the inauguration of the Cavaillé-Coll organ in the concert hall of the Palais du Trocadéro at the exposition. The concert hall, "La Salle des Fêtes," was a vast room seating some 5,000. The authorities for the exposition waited until the last minute to order the organ, and it was only a matter of luck that Cavaillé-Coll had one ready for an unfinished church in Auteuil. This instrument was enlarged, and it became the famous Trocadéro organ. Paris finally had its concert organ!

The exposition opened in May, but the Trocadéro was not ready, and the organ was not installed.[3] Finally, in early August the star-studded series of organ recitals was initiated by Guilmant. His program was listed in Le Ménestrel:

1. Concerto en *si* bémol de Haendel;
2. Marche funèbre et chant séraphique, d'Alex. Guilmant;
3. I. Fanfare, de Lemmens. II. Allegretto en *si* mineur, d'Alex. Guilmant;
4. *Toccata e Fuga* en *ré* mineur, de J.-S. Bach;
5. I. Marche en *la,* de Chauvet. II. Adagio de la 1re sonate, Mendelssohn. III. Gavotte de la 12e sonate, du père J.-B. Martini;
6. Improvisation;
7. Grand choeur de Haendel, arrangé par Guilmant.

[ME 44, p.287.]

A reviewer observed that the shorter pieces and Guilmant's own pieces were very well received but that the audience was inattentive during the Handel concerto and the Bach work. "So much the worse for the public. Let's console ourselves by thinking that its musical education will improve little by little." [Tant pis pour le public. Consolons-nous en pensant que son éducation musicale se fera peu à peu; ME 44, p.295.]

Subsequent programs, continuing into October, were given by Samuel de Lange, Gigout, Dubois, Widor, Mailly, Victor Nant, Lemaigre, Loret, Stoltz, Scotson Clark, Galimberti, A. Andlauer, Grison, Saint-Saëns, Franck, Locher, and Messager. Some organists shared a recital (Nant and Lemaigre, Clark and Galimberti, Andlauer and Grison) but most of the recitals were given by one artist.

The typical recital, following the plan illustrated by Guilmant's program, included a major Bach work, one or more original compositions by the performer, a movement of a Mendelssohn sonata, an improvisation, and

The Cavaillé-Coll organ in the Salle des Fêtes, Palais du Trocadéro (Jim Lewis).

several pieces by contemporary French composers. However, there were exceptions. Widor's program included the première of his *Symphonie VI*.[4] Saint-Saëns played the Liszt Fantasy on *Ad nos, ad salutarem undam,* his transcription of the Liszt *La prédication aux oiseaux (Saint François d'Assise),* some of his own works, and the Bach Prelude and Fugue in E-flat. Franck played only original works and improvisations, giving the premières of *Fantaisie en la majeur, Cantabile,* and *Pièce heroïque.*[5] A reviewer for *Le Ménestrel* pronounced Franck's program "incontestably one of the most interesting of the series" [sans contredit une des plus intéressantes de la série; ME 44, p.363].

The Trocadéro organ was used in other programs besides the regular series. On August 22 Guilmant played his First Symphony for organ and orchestra on one of the "Official grand concerts." This work, an orchestration of his First Sonata for organ, Op.42, was pronounced the great success of the concert [RGM 45, p.269]. Lemmens and his wife gave a special benefit program in the Trocadéro (September 16, 1878). He played only his own works, including the *Sonate pontificale* and the *Grand Fantasia in E minor (The Storm).* In a review of the program, Eugène Gigout expressed disappointment that the famous performer had not also played some masterpiece of Bach's [ME 44, p.347]. The next day Lemmens gave a private séance on the almost-completed Saint-

Eustache organ that Merklin was restoring. These were Lemmens's last organ performances [76, pp.xxvi–xxvii].

Critics were amazed at the crowds the Trocadéro organ attracted. The *Revue et Gazette musicale* commented that the organ concerts had an advantage in that they were free. Many people came especially to see the great hall and were really only passing through.

> But one also finds there a relatively large nucleus of true music lovers who have come to listen and not to see, and who stay in their seats. The eagerness of these *dilettantes* is something truly new; we would scarcely have believed it possible to bring together in Paris fifteen hundred or two thousand people—that is about the number of the nucleus in question after the approximated deduction of the foreign element—capable of being interested in an organ program, that is, a concert for which there is no staging at all to add to the visual interest, and where everything seems to happen automatically, since one doesn't even see the performer. If that is a true symptom, and not just the result of exceptionally favorable circumstances, we wouldn't be able to rejoice enough.

> Mais on y trouve aussi un noyau relativement considérable de vrais amateurs, qui sont venus pour entendre et non pour voir et ne quittent point la place. L'empressement de ces dilettantes est quelque chose de réellement nouveau; nous n'eussions guère cru possible de réunir à Paris quinze cents ou deux mille personnes,—c'est à peu près la valeur numérique du noyau en question après défalcation approximative de l'élément étranger,—capables de s'intéresser à une séance d'orgue, c'est-à-dire à un concert dont aucune mise en scène ne vient rehausser l'appareil, et où tout semble se passer automatiquement, puisqu'on n'y voit même pas l'exécutant. Si c'est là un véritable symptôme, et non pas seulement le résultat de circonstances exceptionnellement favorables, nous ne saurions assez nous en réjouir. [RGM 45, p.261.]

The spring of 1879 offered various events of interest to the organist. Jules Stoltz opened his series (this time of only four programs) in early March. On March 21 the Saint-Eustache organ, restored and enlarged by Merklin, was inaugurated. Franck, Guilmant, Dubois, Gigout, and Dallier performed. Franck played his *Fantaisie en la;* Dubois played movements from his *Paradis perdu;* Gigout played his *Marche funèbre,* a transcription of a Bach air, and an improvisation on a plainchant melody; Guilmant played his first *Méditation en la,* the Toccata in F of Bach, and an improvisation; and Dallier, the new *titulaire* of Saint-Eustache, played a fantasy on themes of his predecessor, Batiste, and an original symphonic movement [RGM 46, p.101].

Guilmant, meanwhile, had appeared in several programs at the Trocadéro. Encouraged by the success of the organ series during the exposition, he began making plans for a new series. Finally the announcement appeared that he would give four *grands concerts d'orgue* during June. Unlike the organ programs at the exposition, these would have an admission charge ranging from fifty centimes to three francs [ME 45, pp.206, 216].

This series established a pattern Guilmant would follow for some time: a limited number of programs, a varied repertoire, and the inclusion of other media, vocal and instrumental. Guilmant himself usually played all the organ music, including organ accompaniments. Piano accompaniments were played by Fernand de La Tombelle (1854–1928).

The concerts were enormously successful serious programs. Guilmant was very careful not to commit the cardinal sin of boring the audience. Each program in the 1879 series presented music by one or more early composers, including works by Buxtehude, Pachelbel, Clérambault, and Frescobaldi; a Bach work; several Guilmant pieces; an improvisation; and at least one work by another contemporary French composer. There was a good balance of short and long pieces, with considerable variety in the character of the shorter pieces.

When Guilmant's series ended Gigout played two programs at the Trocadéro, following a similar format. Attendance, which had been very good and growing from the beginning, reached capacity. After Gigout's second program, the *Revue et Gazette musicale* noted that the grand festival hall of the Trocadéro was literally packed, and that "several hundred people who had neglected to get their tickets in advance found themselves refused entrance" [plusieurs centaines de personnes, qui avaient négligé de prendre leur billets à l'avance, se sont vu refuser l'entrée; RGM 46, p.230]. The attraction was not only Gigout but also his associates on the program. Paul Viardot (1857–1941) played a movement of the Mendelssohn Violin Concerto, Saint-Saëns played a movement of his Third Piano Concerto (both accompanied by Gigout), and there were some vocal solos and ensembles.

There was one fly in the ointment. Gigout's final organ piece was a Bach fantasy and fugue. The reviewer sighed, "We regret to state that three-fourths of the audience left the place just when he was going to begin" [nous avons le regret de constater que les trois quarts de l'auditoire ont quitté la place au moment où il allait commencer; RGM 46, p.230]. The fault was not Gigout's or Bach's, but a strange custom Paris audiences developed of regarding the last piece (at least on Trocadéro organ programs) as incidental music for their departure. The musical press chided readers from time to time, but this behavior pattern seemed to be chronic; in 1899 H. Barbedette still noted that the final work on Clarence Eddy's Trocadéro program had been scarcely heard, the audience having adopted the bad habit of leaving during the last piece [ME 65, p.175].

This problem was more than counterbalanced by the general enthusiasm for organ concerts. Following Gigout's programs in 1879, Guilmant promptly announced that he would play two more. In addition, the Trocadéro organ was used during the summer and fall for a benefit concert given by Saint-Saëns, Gigout and others, for the annual organ competition of the Niedermeyer School, and for organ performances by Deslandres (1840–1911), Lemaigre (d. 1890), and Widor. In only two years this concert-hall organ, along with Guilmant's leadership, had transformed the public image of the organ in Paris. For the first time French organists could truly explore the organ's potential as a secular concert instrument.

IX.
Renaissance Achieved
The 1880s

ENTHUSIASM for organ recitals was never higher than in Paris in the 1880s. The focal point was Guilmant's series at the Trocadéro, now an annual event with capacity audiences. Beginning in 1880 each program included at least one Handel concerto. Edouard Colonne (1838–1910) conducted the small orchestra—a quintet of strings supplemented by other instruments, as needed. The orchestra opened up many new possibilities in programming; gradually other works for organ and orchestra began to appear on the programs, as well as an occasional piece for the orchestra alone. But the ensemble did not replace the vocal and instrumental solos, which continued to add interest and variety to each program.

As before, Guilmant chose a balanced diet of early music, Bach, and contemporary works for the organ solos. Almost every program contained at least one pre-Bach piece, a large Bach work, and several modern pieces, giving generous attention to the music of his French colleagues. During the four concerts of the 1880 series the composers represented by solo organ works were Frescobaldi, Clérambault, Buxtehude, J. K. Kerl, Muffat, G. Böhm, Bach, Boëly, Mendelssohn, Lefébure-Wély, Lemmens, Salomé, E. Bernard, and Guilmant. The "balanced diet" plan was temporarily interrupted in 1885 when Guilmant observed the double bicentennial by devoting one concert almost entirely to the music of Bach and another to Handel.

The importance of the Trocadéro programs as a valued addition to the musical fare in Paris was noted in the press with gratifying frequency. In June 1880, after the final concert in the series, an amazed journalist reported: "Again it was necessary to turn people away, the festival hall having been filled ahead of time; such today is the attraction of these programs, for which one wouldn't have believed it possible to find an audience, even without admission charge, ten years ago." [On a dû encore refuser de monde, la salle des fêtes s'étant trouvée remplie avant l'heure: telle est aujourd'hui l'attraction de ces séances, pour lesquelles on n'aurait pas cru pouvoir trouver un public, même non payant, il y a dix ans; RGM 47, p.190.]

Three weeks later Ch. Barthélemy commented that the Handel concertos had both astonished and charmed the listeners, and had attracted more-than-capacity crowds to the 5,000-seat hall: "Mr. Guilmant has been justly rewarded for his efforts by success until now without precedent in this branch of the art. His concerts have been more than a pleasant diversion for the crowd; they can lay claim to the status of an artistic initiation." [M. Guilmant a été dignement récompensé de ses efforts par un succès jusqu'ici sans précédent dans cette branche de l'art. Ses concerts ont été plus qu'une agréable récréation pour la foule; ils peuvent revendiquer le caractère d'une initiation artistique; RGM 47, pp.212–13.] Statements of appreciation for the series continued to appear from time to time throughout the decade. *Le Ménestrel* responded to the high interest the 1880 concerts had created by publishing an analysis of the Handel concertos Guilmant had played: "Haendel: ses concertos pour orgue et orchestre" by Maurice Cristal [ME 46, pp.225–26, 233–34].

Other programs augmented the number of public organ recitals. In 1880 Jules Stoltz presented his fourth annual series at Saint-Leu. In the same year Gigout, as before, followed Guilmant's series with two programs of his own; included in the second one were some works sung by the choir of the Niedermeyer School. Commenting on Gigout's organ playing, Eugène de Goyon wrote: "It is indeed difficult to remain indifferent in the presence of the broad and entirely personal style with which he interprets the works he presents to the public." [Il est, en effet, difficile de rester froid devant la manière large et toute personnelle avec laquelle il interprète les oeuvres qu'il présente au public; ME 46, p.247.]

In 1884 a new series of organ programs took place during Lent in Albert-le-Grand hall on the Merklin organ that had been shown in the 1878 exhibition. Gigout and Guilmant alternated programs, with Gigout playing on Tuesdays and Guilmant on Thursdays. The latter performed the six Mendelssohn Sonatas, six Schumann Fugues on B-A-C-H, and a cross section of other works. Gigout reserved an important place on his programs for improvisation [ME 50, p.103].

The best-known Paris organists journeyed one after the other to Angers during the 1888–89 season to participate in an ambitious organ series organized by the Association artistique of Angers. Guilmant opened the series, followed by Franck, Widor, Gigout, and Dubois, among others [ME 54, p.391].

Relatively few new organs appeared in Paris in the 1880s, and the city witnessed no large, spectacular organ inaugurations during the decade. For the time being the most famous and fashionable churches were well equipped with organs. Cavaillé-Coll and Merklin each worked toward developing a foreign market for their instruments. During the 1880s Merklin installed an organ in Rome, and Cavaillé-Coll sent organs to Martinique, Brazil, Spain, and Portugal. Churches in various parts of France and Belgium installed new organs by Cavaillé-Coll, Merklin, Abbey, Ghys, and Puget.

When a new Cavaillé-Coll organ was installed, the guest artist was usually Guilmant or Widor. Widor limited himself almost exclusively to inaugurations of Cavaillé-Coll organs; but Guilmant, with typical eclecticism, also introduced new organs by Merklin, Abbey, and Puget. Gigout played Cavaillé-Coll organs in the builder's shop and at exhibitions, but did not appear in any

Cavaillé-Coll inaugurations in the 1880s. On the other hand, he was frequently the artist for inaugurations of organs by the smaller builders.

Franck's name appeared several times on inaugural programs. In 1881 he
shared with Gigout the program for an organ by Debierre in Saint-Léonard,
Fougères. In 1883 he participated in the reception of a Cavaillé-Coll organ in
the *Institution nationale des jeunes aveugles* (National Institution for Blind
Youth)[1] [ME 49, p.118]. In 1888 a new Merklin choir organ was installed in
Sainte-Clotilde, and subsequently Franck inaugurated two Merklin organs: at
the parish church in Béthune (1888) and at Saint-Jacques-du-Haut-Pas (1889),
where the organ had been damaged during the conflict in 1871 and had been
out of commission ever since, the church lacking the resources to restore or
replace it.

Joseph Merklin began making organs with electro-pneumatic action in
1883, using a system developed by an American firm, Schmoele and Mols of
Philadelphia. His first electro-pneumatic organ, built for the new Protestant
church in Lyon, Temple des Brotteaux, was inaugurated on May 26, 1884.
Subsequently Merklin built at least twenty-five instruments using the Schmoele
and Mols action.[2]

Merklin was quick to exploit the flexibility in placement offered by electricity. In his 1886 three-manual organ for the church of Saint-Nizier, Lyon, the
Positiv was divided in two cases on opposite sides of the choir area, while the
principal part of the organ was installed at the opposite end of the church, over
the west door. At Sainte-Clotilde, Paris, there had not previously been a choir
organ because of placement difficulties. The Merklin electro-pneumatic system
offered a solution, and the reception of the new choir organ took place on
February 20, 1888. Organists who examined and approved the instrument
included Franck, Dubois, Samuel Rousseau (1853–1904), and Verschneider[3]
[ME 54, p.71].

In 1889 Merklin built an organ with two consoles for a theater in Montpellier [ME 55, p.78]. One console was on the stage and the other was in the
orchestra. In the church of Saint-Jacques-du-Haut-Pas, Paris, he used one
console to control more than one organ. *Le Ménestrel* explained: "Thanks to
the electric action, the three organs can be played from the same place,
together or separately, by just one organist." [Grâce à la combinaison électri-
que, les trois orgues peuvent être jouées d'un même point, ensemble ou
alternativement, par un seul organiste; ME 55, p.175.]

Electricity was in the air figuratively as well as literally in the 1880s. By the
fall of 1883, the Trocadéro had electric lights; and in August 1886, *Le
Ménestrel* announced that the installation of electricity was slowly but de-
finitely progressing in the theaters of Paris [ME 52, p.283]. At that stage in its
development, electricity was more successful for lights than for organs, so in
the early 1890s Merklin was ready to return to mechanical action.

Guilmant easily retained first place among French organists in terms of the
number of programs he gave, his popularity, and the scope of his activities as a
concert organist. In addition to his many appearances in France, his reputation

in England flourished, and he received further acclaim for a performance in Rome in 1881 and a tour of Russia in 1884.

Gigout's career continued to grow. In 1885 his organ school was opened, with courses in organ, improvisation, and plainchant (later expanded to include harmony and composition as well). His success as a teacher added further to his professional stature. Gigout made his first tour in England in 1882, and he returned there each year between 1886 and 1890. He played in Barcelona in 1888 and on several later occasions.

Widor's name was often in the musical press, but more frequently as a conductor or composer than as an organist. His highly successful ballet, *La Korrigane,* produced at the Paris Opéra in 1880, tended to overshadow his other activities and accomplishments in the eyes of the general public. When Widor did give an organ recital it often inspired eloquent journalism. In November 1886 he appeared in Amsterdam as composer, conductor, and organist. The critic, identified as "C. P.," was enthusiastic about Widor's success in all roles. In regard to his organ playing he wrote:

> The unshakable security, the finesse and vigor of Mr. Widor's technique never falter; never does he deviate from the most classic correctness, but at the same time he excites, he transports, he knows, in a word, how to captivate by an inexpressible charm. By the choice and blending of sonorities in which nothing clashes, even in the contrasts, where everything connects and fuses in harmonious unity, he arrives at effects of an almost transcendent poetry.

> L'imperturbable sûreté, la finesse et la vigueur du mécanisme de M. Widor ne chancellent jamais; jamais il ne s'écarte de la correction la plus classique, mais en même temps il émeut, il entraîne, il sait, en un mot, captiver par un charme inexprimable. Par le choix et la fusion des sonorités où rien ne se heurte, même dans les contrastes, où tout s'enchaîne et se fond dans une harmonieuse unité, il arrive à des effets d'une poésie presque immatérielle. [ME 53, p.5.]

Saint-Saëns was often reviewed as a conductor, composer, or pianist, but he rarely appeared as an organist during this decade. On May 19, 1886, he conducted the highly acclaimed première of his Third Symphony (with organ), which had been commissioned by the London Philharmonic Society. Later that year it was performed in Paris, where it was also received enthusiastically. Even critics who had previously been somewhat indifferent to the music of Saint-Saëns seemed to like this work. Its success in Paris may have been enhanced by its prior success in London, but the fact that the organ had reached new heights of popularity might have contributed to its reception also.

Franck and Dubois, too, received a measure of attention from the press, but rarely because they were organists. If one reviews the number of large-scale works Franck composed during the 1880s (including his biblical scene, *Rebecca;* the opera *Hulda;* three symphonic poems; the Symphony in D Minor; and various other works), it is not surprising that his appearances as an organ performer were infrequent.

Léon Boëllmann at the Cavaillé-Coll organ in the church of Saint-Vincent-de-Paul (Bibliothèque Nationale, Paris).

The decade of the 1880s saw only a few changes in personnel. Two well-known performers died: Lemmens in 1881, and Renaud de Vilbac in 1884, both in their fifties. The most promising career beginning its ascent during this decade was that of Léon Boëllmann (1862–97). A protégé of Gigout (and related to him by marriage in 1885), Boëllmann was named choir organist at Saint-Vincent-de-Paul in 1881. In 1887 *Le Ménestrel* reported that he had succeeded Henri Fissot as *organiste titulaire* at that church [ME 53, p.207].

Albert-Jacques Périlhou (1846–1936) returned to Paris in 1889 to become organist at Saint-Séverin. He had completed his studies at the Niedermeyer School in 1866, and had then held successive positions in Saint-Etienne and Lyon. His friend and former teacher, Saint-Saëns, persuaded him to return to Paris. Except for a brief period in 1905–1906, Périlhou remained at Saint-Séverin until 1914 [230].

The decade ended on a high note with the 1889 Paris Exposition universelle, which included an extended series of organ programs in the Trocadéro. Henri Dallier opened the series in May with works by Bach, Mendelssohn, Schumann, Saint-Saëns, Franck (his teacher), and some pieces of his own. Among other French performers were Guilmant, Gigout, Widor, Stoltz, Lemaigre, Jules Grison (1842–96), and Henri Deshayes (1838?–1913). There were also organists from other countries, including Charles Locher from Switzerland, Walter Handel Torley from England, and Clarence Eddy from the United States.

Guilmant gave a historical concert, including works by seventeen composers from Gabrieli to Lemmens, which represented a milestone in organ programming. Guilmant not only performed these works but also published them in an anthology (*Concert historique d'orgue,* 1889). In the Trocadéro performance of September 9, 1889, vocal solos by Monteverdi, Cesti, Lully, Scarlatti, Rameau, and Haydn separated the groups. The organ pieces were:

A. Gabrieli—Canzona
Palestrina—Ricercare
C. Merulo—Toccata du 3ᵉ Ton
Wᵐ. Byrd—Pavane: *The Earl of Salisbury*
* * *
Titelouze—Verset de l'hymne: *Exsultet coelum*
S. Scheidt—Choral: *Da Jesus an dem Kreutze standt*
Frescobaldi—Capriccio-Pastorale
* * *
G. Muffat—Toccata en *ut* mineur
* * *
Froberger—Caprice en *fa*
Buxtehude—Choral: *Lobt Gott*
* * *
Pachelbel—Ciacona
Dandrieu—Musette
Clérambault—Prélude

* * *
J. S. Bach—Toccata et Fuga en *ut* majeur
* * *
Boëly—Andante con moto
Mendelssohn—Prélude en *sol*
Lemmens—Scherzo symphonique concertant
* * *

[BN: Vm. Pièce 205.]

Clarence Eddy, the famous Chicago organist, received a cordial welcome when he played at the Trocadéro. As one reviewer noted: "This distinguished organist possesses great virtuosity and a serious style; his program was very artistic; also, the large audience applauded him warmly." [Cet organiste distingué possède une grande virtuosité et un style sérieux; son programme était très artistique; aussi, l'assistance nombreuse l'a-t-elle chaleureusement applaudi; ME 55, p.264.] Eddy played the following program:

Bach—Toccata and Fugue in D Minor
Dudley Buck—Sonata in G Minor, Op.77
Isaac van Vleck Flagler—"Variations on an American Air"
Guilmant—"Concert Piece," Op.21
Widor—"Adagio," Symphony VI
Dubois—"Cantilène Nuptiale"
Thiele—Theme and Variations

[121, p.15.]

Widor had his own ideas about program building. His recital consisted of his Symphonies V and VIII, and a toccata and fugue by Bach.

In addition to the thirteen solo organ programs presented (fifteen were originally planned), Guilmant gave an organ and orchestra concert during the exposition. One can only imagine how enthusiastic the applause was for his performance of Handel's *Largo* with organ, orchestra, and ten harps [ME 55, p.200]!

X.
Years of Fulfillment
The 1890s

THE YEAR 1890 was unusual in several respects. For at least a brief time the main events took place outside Paris. During the spring, Gigout, Guilmant, and Widor successively performed at the Hampstead Conservatory, London, and both Gigout and Guilmant played elsewhere in England. Widor had performed early in the year for the inauguration of a Schyven organ in the Conservatory at Liège. In April he inaugurated the Cavaillé-Coll organ for Saint-Ouen, Rouen. Guilmant, meanwhile, gave four programs in Genoa, Italy.

The annual series of organ programs in the Trocadéro was suspended for a year in 1890, but the most penetrating loss to the organ profession that year was the death of César Franck, on November 8. Gabriel Pierné (1863–1937) was then named organist of Sainte-Clotilde, and Widor became the professor of organ and improvisation at the Paris Conservatory. Pierné, who received both first prize in organ and the Prix de Rome at the Conservatory in 1882, remained at Sainte-Clotilde until 1898. He then concentrated his activities in the areas of conducting and composition.

Organ enthusiasts could hear many fine performers in prominent churches of Paris in 1890. In addition to Pierné at Sainte-Clotilde, there were Boëllmann (Saint-Vincent-de-Paul), Dallier (Saint-Eustache), Dubois (La Madeleine), Gigout (Saint-Augustin), Guilmant (La Trinité), Loret (Saint-Louis-d'Antin), Périlhou (Saint-Séverin), Sergent (Notre-Dame), Vast (Saint-Germain l'Auxerrois), Wachs (Saint-Merry), and Widor (Saint-Sulpice).

By the end of the decade a brilliant parade of young performers was entering the organ profession. Among the more prominent were Adolphe Marty (1865–1942), Albert Mahaut (1867–1943), Charles Tournemire (1870–1939), Henri Libert (1869–1937), and Louis Vierne (1870–1937). All had studied organ with Franck, and the latter three had also been in Widor's organ class. All were first-prize winners in organ at the Paris Conservatory: Marty in 1886, Mahaut in 1889, Tournemire in 1891, Libert and Vierne in 1894. All held important organ positions by 1900. Marty was professor of organ and composition at the *Institution nationale des jeunes aveugles* from 1888, and was organist at Saint-François-Xavier from 1891. Mahaut taught harmony at the *Institution nationale des jeunes aveugles,* and succeeded Boëllmann as organist at Saint-Vincent-de-Paul in 1897. Tournemire replaced Pierné at Sainte-Clotilde in

1898. Libert was *titulaire* at Saint-Denis from 1896. Vierne assisted Widor at Saint-Sulpice and at the Conservatory, and became organist at Notre-Dame in 1900.

The Trocadéro concerts resumed in 1891, with Colonne conducting the orchestra. He was succeeded in 1892 by Gabriel Marie (1852–1928). Guilmant now began to feature contemporary French works for organ and orchestra, including in the 1891 series his own *Sommeil d'Ariane* for organ, orchestra, and harp; Emile Bernard's *Hymn;* and the *Fantaisie triomphale* of Dubois [ME 57, pp.168, 176]. In subsequent years of the decade Guilmant presented several other contemporary French ensemble works with organ, including his own *Marche élégiaque* and *Adoration, Prélude (Christmas Oratorio)* by Saint-Saëns, *Fantaisie* by La Tombelle, *Les Souvenirs de Meylan* by Georges Syme, *Marche hiératique* by Ad. Populus, *Cantabile en la bémol* and *Berceuse* by S. Rousseau, *Hymne Nuptial* by Dubois, and *Berceuse* by Salomé. Other ensemble works, solo pieces for organ, and a sprinkling of music for other media completed the programs.

On April 28, 1898, Albert Mahaut gave a program of Franck works in the Trocadéro, with the participation of a choir, Chanteurs de Saint-Gervais. Mahaut played the *Prière; Grand Pièce symphonique; Prélude, fugue et variation;* and *Fantaisie en ut majeur.* The reviewer in *La Tribune de St. Gervais,* G. de Boisjoslin, praised the program in general, but commented that Mahaut lacked Franck's "incomparable serenity" [TSG 4, no.5, p.119]. This performance was the first one dedicated to Franck's organ works since his death. From that time Mahaut continued to be a leading advocate of Franck's organ music, playing it on tour as well as in Paris. Between 1905 and 1923 he played more than a hundred Franck recitals in various cities of France, Algeria, Switzerland, Belgium, Germany, and England [214, p.13].

In 1899 Guilmant celebrated the twentieth year of the Trocadéro organ concerts with two programs, the first featuring the music of Bach, the second the music of Franck. Organ, orchestra, guest soloists, and the Chanteurs de St. Gervais participated in both concerts. H. Barbedette reviewed the two events, and after the first one he wrote: "A matinee like that one is well fashioned to provide respite from the Wagnerian orgies that have deafened us for so many years." [Une matinée comme celle-là est bien faite pour reposer des orgies wagnériennes dont nous sommes assourdis depuis tant d'années; ME 65, p.140.]

The organ solos on the Bach program were the Prelude and Fugue in E-flat and a movement of Sonata I. For organ and orchestra there was the "concerto" of Cantata 146. The choir sang the cantata *Jesu der du meine Seele,* the last chorus of the St. John Passion, and pieces by Schütz and Palestrina. A Bach aria served as a violin solo, and there were some vocal solos by Handel.

On the Franck program Guilmant played the *Cantabile, Pastorale, Final,* and the second *Choral.* The choir sang the second *Béatitude* and some other choruses. Other composers represented were Sinding, Wagner, and Berlioz. Barbedette opined that Franck could not be compared with Bach, but he was nevertheless *un grand maître* [ME 65, p.149].

The continued popularity of the Trocadéro organ concerts was no doubt a significant factor in the proliferation of organs in other locations outside the church. Dufourcq noted that Cavaillé-Coll, Merklin, and Mutin all built small organs with two manuals and eight to twelve stops for concert halls and private salons [85, p.18]. The limited size of the organs did not discourage leading performers from programming practically anything in the organ repertoire.

In 1893 Merklin installed a new organ in a concert hall known as the Salle d'Harcourt. Eugène d'Harcourt (1859–1918) had been an organ student of Gigout [ME 59, p.120]. Encouraged by the success of a *concert spirituel* given by Gigout, d'Harcourt arranged for him to give an extended series of organ recitals featuring both early and modern music as well as improvisations. The series began late that year and continued into the following spring.

Gigout consistently earned high marks for his performances, and his improvisations were often given special praise. On the other hand, the organ at Salle d'Harcourt may not have been all one could desire. Léon Schlesinger commented: "Mr. Gigout has accomplished that extraordinary feat of extracting some results from a detestable instrument." [M. Gigout a accompli ce tour de force inouï de tirer des effets d'un instrument détestable; ME 60, p.21.] In any case, Paris now had another venue for secular organ recitals and concerts with organ and other instruments. Works for organ and orchestra were included with some frequency on d'Harcourt concerts.

A trend was in motion. By 1893 one could hear organ with orchestra in the concerts at the Palais d'Hiver (Jardin d'Acclimatation). In 1895 works for organ and orchestra were included in the Concerts Lamoureux, Cirque des Champs-Elysées, and in concerts at the Opéra. In fact, on December 8, 1895, one could choose to hear Widor's Third Symphony (conducted by the composer, with Vierne at the organ) at an Opéra concert,[1] or Saint-Saëns's Third Symphony at a d'Harcourt concert, or *Prélude et Choral* for organ and orchestra by Charles Lefebvre on a program conducted by Louis Pister at the Palais d'Hiver [ME 61, p.389]. By the end of the decade the organ-with-orchestra fad had subsided to a more normal level.

Like the d'Harcourt organ, those at the Palais d'Hiver, the Cirque des Champs-Elysées, and the Opéra were criticized as insufficient for the task. On March 10, 1893, a correspondent for Everett Truette's Boston magazine *The Organ* wrote:

> Last Saturday a new building in the Jardin d'Acclimatation, called the Palais d'Hiver was completed. It is a kind of indoor concert garden; the hall itself is about as large as our Music Hall [in Boston], and is designed for popular concerts and various light entertainments. Eventually it is to have a fine organ, but Cavaillé-Coll has set up a small two-manual organ temporarily. At the opening ceremonies last week a concert was given with full orchestra, soloists, and organ. President Carnot was present, and by his special invitation Guilmant played several of his own pieces. . . . Of course the effect was not very striking, as the organ was far too small for the hall; but it could be seen that the acoustics of the building were well adapted for a large organ. [OR 1, pp.283–84.]

On November 8, 1895, Clarence Eddy wrote: "Next Sunday the third Symphony of Saint-Saëns will be played at the Lamoureux orchestral concert. This calls for an organ, and quite recently one has been placed by Cavaillé-Coll in the *Cirque des Champs-Elysée,* where the Lamoureux concerts are given. It is a fair sized organ of two manuals and pedale, but hardly suitable for solo work" [98, p.255].

Meanwhile, other interesting programs were given in Salle d'Harcourt beginning early in 1894. Guilmant and the Chanteurs de Saint-Gervais, conducted by Charles Bordes (1863–1909), performed selected Bach cantatas, some of which received their first hearing in France [ME 59, p.391]. Fannie Edgar Thomas was amazed at the reception these concerts enjoyed. In her column for *The Musical Courier* of February 7, 1894, she wrote:

> The concert of the "Chanteurs de Saint-Gervais" was the most jubilant success. On the way to the dark bare hall where the concert was to be held, filled with sympathy for the earnest musician [i.e., Charles Bordes], one felt like inviting every one on the way to go fill up the seats for his encouragement. Behold, on arriving, there was scarcely room to enter. The house was crowded to the last gallery seat, all in wrapt [*sic*] and expectant attention.

The program consisted of two Bach cantatas; a Bach concerto with piano, two flutes, and orchestra; and some unaccompanied choral pieces by Lassus and Janequin. Thomas concluded:

> If ever any worker received reward for his labor it was M. Bordes this evening. The people did not seem able to express their appreciation. They bravod and cheered, called his praise, thanked him; and the gentle dignity with which he bowed under the storm of applause spoke nothing of the martyr-like endurance that had led up to this point, "For of such is the kingdom of Art!" [311, 28/6:11]

Thomas was referring specifically to the endurance of Bordes in organizing and preparing his concerts, but one can also recall the "martyr-like endurance" of the nineteenth-century musicians who paved the way for his success: Choron, Danjou, Fétis, Boëly, and Niedermeyer, to mention only some of the better-known apostles of early music.

Paris enjoyed a few inaugurations in the 1890s, as the time came for some of the famous organs to be renovated: Saint-Vincent-de-Paul and Notre-Dame in 1894, and Saint-Augustin in 1899. The 1894 inaugurations were old-fashioned in their organization, with several organists displaying the instruments' features. At Saint-Vincent-de-Paul the organists were Boëllmann (the *titulaire*), Dubois, Widor, Gigout, and Guilmant. The restored Notre-Dame organ was played by Sergent (the *titulaire*), Widor, Gigout, and Guilmant.

After the Saint-Augustin organ was reconstructed by the Cavaillé-Coll firm (then under the direction of Charles Mutin), the inaugural program could serve

Aristide Cavaillé-Coll in 1894. From *L'Illustration*, 1894 (University of California Library, Berkeley).

as a measure of the changes that had taken place in organ and choral repertoire, and in attitudes toward the organ as a recital instrument during the century. Gigout played Mendelssohn's Sonata in F, Handel's Concerto in D minor, Bach's Prelude and Fugue in E minor and Toccata in F, an improvisation on two liturgical chants, and three original pieces: *Toccata, Communion,* and *Grand choeur dialogué.* The choir and orchestra, conducted by the *maître de chapelle,* Vivet, performed Bach's Magnificat, and choruses by Handel, Beethoven, Palestrina, and Gluck [ME 65, p.184].

From time to time there were notable organ performances in other parts of France. When the Cavaillé-Coll organ was inaugurated at Saint-Ouen, Rouen, in 1890, Widor promised the *curé,* Panel, that he would write a special work in honor of the church. Thus he played the première of his *Symphonie gothique* on the organ of Saint-Ouen in 1895. A Rouen reviewer commented:

> The acoustics of the immense nave of Saint-Ouen (130 meters long), ordinarily so unfavorable for works in a complex and dense style, proved to be wonderfully transformed Sunday by the crowds that flocked to the celebration. It was between vespers and the salut solennel that the first performance of the *Symphonie gothique* took place, heard in the most religious silence, and of which not a detail, not a note was lost for the listeners. Everything came forth with absolute clarity. The effect was profound.

L'acoustique de l'immense nef de Saint-Ouen (130 mètres de longueur) si
défavorable d'ordinaire aux oeuvres complexes et serrées de style, s'était
trouvée merveilleusement transformée dimanche par les foules accourues à la
fête. C'est entre les vêpres et le salut solennel qu'avait lieu cette première
audition de la « Symphonie gothique » écoutée dans le plus religieux silence, et
dont pas un détail, pas une note n'a été perdue pour l'auditoire. Tout sortait
avec une absolue netteté. L'impression a été profonde. [ME 61, pp.143–44.]

In 1896, when the city of Rouen hosted an exhibition, an organ series was
one of the attractions. Guilmant inaugurated the series. Later Widor played the
organ part in a performance of his Third Symphony for organ and orchestra,
and Vierne gave a solo recital, including the *Symphonie gothique* of Widor, the
Prelude and Fugue in B of Saint-Saëns, and several works of Bach, "played
with a consummate art and a rare virtuosity" [jouées avec un art consommé et
une virtuosité rare; ME 62, p.312]. Vierne had played the first three movements of the new Widor *Symphonie gothique* in Lyon in March 1895, a month
before Widor premiered the complete work.

Guy Ropartz, who became director of the Conservatory at Nancy in 1894,
can be credited with having a Cavaillé-Coll organ installed in that school in
1898. The inaugural celebration included an orchestral concert, with Ropartz
conducting, and an organ recital by Gigout. Later that year Guilmant played
the organ part in a performance at the Conservatory of his First Symphony for
organ and orchestra. The following day he gave a recital of works by Bach,
Schumann, Franck, and Ropartz, along with his own works and an improvisation [ME 64, pp.104, 383].

Foreign tours continued to attract the great French organists. One of the
surprises of the 1890s was that Saint-Saëns, who for years had given little
attention to organ performance, suddenly sprang into action. During 1896 and
1897 he gave organ recitals in Switzerland, Holland, Belgium, and Scandinavia. He was invited to Spain, where the queen particularly requested that he
play an excerpt from *Samson et Dalila* on the organ. Saint-Saëns complied and
also played some other works, including one of his *Rhapsodies bretonnes*. The
lady was apparently pleased, but Spanish critics were incensed that anyone
would play secular music in a church, queen or no queen. They objected to the
Rhapsodie as well as the opera transcription [226, p.113; 177, pp.411–12].

Saint-Saëns often attended services at Saint-Séverin, where his former student Albert Périlhou was organist. He enjoyed taking Périlhou's place from
time to time, for all or part of a service, and in 1897 he was appointed
"honorary organist." Other musicians, too, sometimes congregated in the
tribune of Saint-Séverin. An unidentified witness related:

Périlhou improvises and nods to Fauré. Immediately the latter, without in-
terruption, substitutes for him on the bench and continues to play. In the same
fashion, Saint-Saëns takes a turn. As all three know their craft perfectly, the
transitions are made smoothly and pass unnoticed. But each wants to com-
plicate the task for the next one, modulates in the most remote keys, indulges in

the most complicated counterpoints, leaving it to his successor to resolve the
difficulties.

Périlhou improvise et fait un signe de tête à Fauré. Aussitôt celui-ci, sans
interrompre, se substitue à lui sur le banc et continue à jouer. De la même façon,
Saint-Saëns prend la relève. Comme tous les trois connaissent parfaitement leur
métier, les transitions se font sans heurt et passent inaperçues. Mais chacun veut
compliquer la tâche pour le suivant, module dans les tons les plus éloignés,
s'abandonne aux contrepoints les plus compliqués, s'en remettant au successeur
pour aplanir les difficultés. [Cited in 226, p.112.]

Gigout continued to make annual recital trips to England through 1893. He
traveled to Spain several times for programs in Barcelona (1891, 1892, 1894,
1896, and 1899), and in 1897 he toured in Switzerland. Although he did not
tour as widely as some of his colleagues, he ranked among the greatest of the
French organ performers, and organ recitals remained an important part of his
career to the end of his life.

After 1890 Widor's tours included appearances in England, Switzerland,
Germany, and Russia. Gwilym Beechey has listed two recitals given by Widor
at Newcastle cathedral on May 23, 1891. It is interesting to find that Widor
included token works from a broader repertoire, for he had a reputation for
playing only Bach and his own works.

Afternoon programme:
Toccata and Fugue in D Minor (BWV 565)—J. S. Bach
Symphony No. 5—Widor
Largo (from Sonata, Op.2, No.2)—Beethoven
Allegro in F (from Concerto, Op.4, No. 4)—Handel
Meditation (from Symphony No.1)—Widor
Marche Pontificale (from Symphony No.1)—Widor

Evening programme:
Prelude and Fugue in E Minor (BWV 548)—Bach
Andante cantabile (from Symphony No.4)—Widor
Concerto in A Minor (BWV 592)—Bach
Adagio (from Sonata No.1)—Mendelssohn
Symphony No.6—Widor
Scherzando (from Symphony No. 4?)—Widor
Fugue in D Major (BWV 532)—Bach

[17, p.109.]

In 1894 Widor went to Geneva to conduct his Third Symphony for organ
and orchestra, a work written for the occasion, at the inauguration of Victoria
Hall. Its first Paris performance took place in 1895 in a *Concert de l'Opéra*.
Probably more impressive was a performance at the Trocadéro the following
year, with Widor conducting and Vierne playing the organ part. Widor himself
played the organ part in a performance at Rouen the same year.

In 1896 Widor was engaged by the Imperial Society of Music in Moscow to conduct his Second Symphony (for orchestra) and to give an organ recital. In late 1899 or early 1900 he gave two concerts in Berlin. He conducted some of his own works, including the Third Symphony for organ and orchestra, on an orchestral program. He gave a solo recital at the Gedächtnis Kirche, where he played his new, as yet unpublished *Symphonie romane* and the Bach Fantasy and Fugue in G minor [ME 66, p.14]. Widor had been to Berlin before. In 1895 he was a member of the jury for the Rubinstein competition. The other members prevailed on him to play for them, and he obliged by playing the Sauer organ at the Church of the Apostle Paul [ME 61, p.278].

Characteristically, Guilmant remained the most adventurous of the French organists. In the 1890s he made several recital tours of England and two of his three recital tours in America (1893, 1897–98, 1904). Guilmant was the best of ambassadors, introducing Americans to a comprehensive cross section of the organ repertoire, attracting pupils and disciples, and building transatlantic bridges of friendship and collegiality.

His first trip was prompted by an invitation to represent the French school of organ playing at the World's Columbian Exposition in Chicago. Guilmant played four recitals on the four-manual Farrand & Votey organ. *Le Ménestrel* reported that there had been some problems with the organ during the first recital, but the same accidents had not occurred at the other programs. "Mr. Guilmant writes, however, that he will be happy to see again the organs of Cavaillé-Coll in Paris." [M. Guilmant écrit toutefois qu'il retrouvera avec plaisir à Paris les orgues de M. Cavaillé-Coll; ME 59, p.311.]

However much he might have preferred French organs, Guilmant was diplomat enough to compliment the American builders on their achievements. He named the Chicago Farrand & Votey organ "an instrument of the first order" [cited in 10, p.17]. It was one of many endorsements Guilmant would distribute along the paths of his tours in America. Guilmant's generous encouragement of American organ builders and organists was a matter of significance. No European organist of his stature had come to the United States before, and the self-conscious, insecure American organ profession needed confidence as much as it needed guidance. It was a two-way street, as America offered Guilmant new fields to conquer. His first trip led to another, and on November 27, 1897, he set sail on the ship *La Bretagne* for a series of 75 programs [ME 63, p.391].[2]

One very important result of the second tour was the foundation by William C. Carl (1865–1936) of the Guilmant Organ School in New York. Guilmant himself was named president of the school, and Carl was the director. The school opened on October 9, 1899, with about forty students enrolled [287]. Devoted entirely to the training of church musicians, this school contributed much to elevating standards in church music and organ playing during the first half of the twentieth century.

Clarence Eddy was the first organist of renown to blaze a trail between America and Paris, and he was responsible for inviting Guilmant to Chicago in 1893. In 1896 Eddy and his wife settled in Paris, where they lived for ten years [121, p.16]. During that time Eddy still spent much of his time in the United

States and Canada on extended recital tours, but he found time to serve on the jury for the organ competition of the Paris Conservatory at least once (in 1897) [ME 63, p.230], and he was heard several times in organ recitals at the Trocadéro. A reviewer of his program there on May 12, 1896 wrote: "One has greatly admired the brilliant playing and the technique of Mr. Clarence Eddy, who can justly be classed among the best organists of our time." [On a beaucoup admiré le jeu brillant et le mécanisme de M. Clarence Eddy, qui peut être classé, à juste titre, parmi les meilleurs organistes de notre époque; ME 62, p.159.]

A reviewer identified as "R. D. C." was not as generous following Eddy's 1897 Trocadéro program. He criticized the choice of program because it contained only one Bach piece and none at all by Mendelssohn, Schumann, or Franck. This void was not adequately filled, in his opinion, by the works Eddy did play by Saint-Saëns, Rousseau, and Guilmant, or by the transcriptions of pieces by Schubert and Wagner [GM 43, pp.440–41]. H. Barbedette reviewed his June 1899 recital: "He is a talented artist. His program was not as severe as those of Mr. Guilmant. It was studded with pleasant pieces." [C'est un artiste de talent. Son programme n'avait pas la sévérité de ceux de M. Guilmant. Il était émaillé de pièces aimables; ME 65, p.175.]

Sumner relates an amusing anecdote about Clarence Eddy:

> Vierne told me that as a young man he and Tournemire went to a recital by one Clarence Eddy "from across the sea." Eddy apparently gave out a Bach fugue-subject on the Vox humana! The consciences of the two young French organists were outraged and they promptly stood on their seats and protested vociferously. Having satisfied their feelings, they were immediately thrown out by the porters. It is not known if Eddy continued his performance. [309, p.57.]

In 1895 the vanguard of countless American church music tours arrived in Paris. On July 28 *Le Ménestrel* reported that a large group of American artists had come to Paris with the primary objective of visiting and hearing the great Cavaillé-Coll organs, notably those of the Madeleine, La Trinité, and Notre-Dame. Guilmant gave the visitors a special hearing of the Trocadéro organ. They had hoped to meet Widor, but he was out of town. In his place, Vierne demonstrated the Saint-Sulpice organ [ME 61, pp.240, 248].

Frank Atwater, a columnist for the *Musical Courier,* identified the group as "The Evangelist Church Music Tour, organized under the auspices of the Presbyterian journal of that name in New York . . . whose object it is to hear church music in England and the principal centres on the Continent" [MC 31, no.6, p.9]. The group spent about two weeks seeing churches, organs, and organ factories in various parts of England, and then left for the Continent.

Another *Musical Courier* writer, Fannie Edgar Thomas, recorded in her colorful style some impressions of the tour in Paris:

> Well, there were those ninety-five odd musicians, an association of inquiring souls who were only accidentally as religious as their name denoted, and who represented some sixty cities of the Union. They, with their friends and a

number of congenial French people who were invited to join them, made a fine showing in the grand Palais du Trocadéro, where M. Guilmant for over an hour disclosed to them the beauties, differences, resources and possibilities of the typical Cavaillé-Coll organ, which forms one end of the grand concert hall. Applause was frequent, and no doubt many conclusions were come to that would be pleasant to hear. One of the best artists in the audience was the noble gentleman Cavaillé-Coll himself, to whom the event must have been deeply gratifying.

They visited here, as in England, all the best musical points, and, I believe, drifted homeward after that. [MC 31, no.7, pp.8–9.]

American reviewers in the 1890s tended to prefer Guilmant's playing to that of his compatriots. The Paris correspondent for Truette's *The Organ* (styling himself or herself as "Outre Mer") wrote: "Widor is certainly a most talented and versatile composer, although I do not consider his organ playing as fine as that of Guilmant: he composes in rather higher forms" [OR 2, p.18].

Clarence Eddy's comparisons of leading French organists gave Americans at home some ideas of their performance styles. During the winter season 1896–97 he wrote:

At the head of the organist profession in Paris I place Guilmant, because he is more catholic in his taste, has a broader scope, plays in all schools, and is an organ virtuoso of the first rank. . . .

Widor is a great man, a great organist and a remarkable composer. He plays almost nothing but Bach and Widor; the ill-disposed wickedly say it "Widor and Bach"—for it is, perhaps, true that the compositions of the later master figure more often upon his programs. . . . I sat upon the organ bench with him a number of times at St. Sulpice. On one particular occasion I was in the seventh heaven; his selection was his Toccata in F, which he played wonderfully. He reduces the organ and builds it up again in the most wonderful way; it cannot be done so successfully upon any other organ. . . . He makes a diminuendo which is something extraordinary in that church, and a crescendo which will simply lift you off your feet. He plays with a great deal of nerve, is very rigid in his rhythm, and almost a crank on the subject of rhythm and phrasing. . . .

Next after Guilmant and Widor in rank among the living organists now practically engaged in organ work in Paris I think I would place Eugene Gigout. . . . He is probably forty-five years of age or so and is a delightful improvisor. He has a great technique, contrapuntal knowledge, understands the old scales and all that sort of thing, and introduces many novel effects in his im-provisations. [97, pp.163–67.]

A year later Eddy added some further comparisons:

Without doubt the three greatest organists in Paris are M. Guilmant, M. Widor and M. Gigout. I do not find it altogether easy to characterize the playing of these three artists in a few words, since, when the technic is so masterly as in the case of all three of these, and when all of them are experienced and highly successful composers, the differences in their playing are mainly those

Charles-Marie Widor, Alexandre Guilmant, and Eugène Gigout (Bibliothèque Nationale, Paris).

of personality and temperament, and in this line a multitude of delicate shades will appear in the playing, which it would be impossible to describe in words.

For instance, to begin with their different ways of playing Bach. Guilmant and Gigout both play Bach in a very warm and what I might call human way, not to say humane. That is to say, they use whatever color they think will be most advantageous to the effect of the piece, and they vary the touch, . . . and use whatever expression the sense of the music seems to require. As compared with the German organists, I may say that everything the French organists play they make very clear; all the parts and the form are clearly defined, so that everything they play has a sort of perspective; they do not mass it together the way the Germans do. They accomplish this by special phrasing, and by contrasting staccato with legato touch, which the Germans never have done until quite recently, although they are now getting to do it to some extent.

In many respects M. Widor occupies a peculiarly honorable position in Paris. He plays Bach more in the German manner. He plays everything very slowly, with very strong rhythm, but with no attempt at sentiment. He is what is ordinarily called a cold player; "dry bones" the irreverent call it. For this reason the public cares comparatively little for Widor, but he is admired very much, in fact worshiped, by the fraternity, and by all people who are especially fond of the German classical school of organ playing. . . .

. . . He is a very remarkable player and a great composer. While his technic
lacks the brilliancy of that of M. Guilmant, he has a tremendous command of
the organ. [96, pp.589–90.]

The years 1896–1900 encompassed some important changes in the organ
profession. In 1896 Dubois, who had been professor of composition, counterpoint, and fugue, was named director of the Paris Conservatory. When he
accepted this new responsibility, he resigned from his post as organist at the
Madeleine. This caused a chain reaction. Widor took Dubois's position as
professor of composition, and Guilmant became professor of organ at the
Conservatory. Gabriel Fauré (1845–1924) replaced Dubois as organist at the
Madeleine, and, like Widor, he also became a professor of composition at
the Conservatory in 1896, succeeding Massenet [249, p.533].

Although Fauré had long been involved in church music, he had never before
been *titulaire* in a large Paris church. In 1877 he had succeeded Dubois as
maître de chapelle at the Madeleine, and he continued to follow in Dubois's
footsteps, not only succeeding him as organist at the Madeleine (1896) but also
as director of the Conservatory (1905). Like Dubois, Fauré resigned his church
position when he became director.

The death of Boëllmann at age 35 (1897) and the resignation of Pierné as
organist at Sainte-Clotilde (1898) resulted in further changes. As we have
noted, Boëllmann was succeeded by Mahaut, and Pierné's position was filled
by Tournemire. Joseph Merklin retired in 1898 and left Paris in 1899. His firm
was then in the hands of Joseph Gutschenritter and Philippe Decock.

Cavaillé-Coll died in 1899, followed the next year by Eugène Sergent,
organist of Notre-Dame. Ironically, Sergent was one organist who managed to
retain his position as *titulaire* of a large Cavaillé-Coll organ in spite of the fact
that the influential builder did not like his playing [50, pp.103–104]. Sergent
may not have been a brilliant star among the Paris organists, but it is also
possible that Cavaillé-Coll's attitude was somewhat colored by the fact that
Sergent had been a pupil of his former rival Danjou. One can imagine that the
old builder would have rejoiced in the selection of Louis Vierne as the new
organist of Notre-Dame.

The French renaissance in organ playing did not end with the nineteenth
century. Major players in the late-century drama were still active into the
twentieth century, and such brilliant successors as Marcel Dupré and Joseph
Bonnet sustained the momentum even longer.

The senior generation of organists survived well into the new century.
Guilmant died in 1911 at age 74, Saint-Saëns in 1921 at 86, Dubois in 1924 at
87, Gigout in 1925 at 81, and Widor in 1937 at 93. They were followed soon
after by their younger colleagues (Vierne in 1937 at 67, Tournemire in 1939 at
69). But the years 1900–1940 belong to another story. The apogee had already
been reached at the turn of the century. The organists who rode the crest of the
wave in ensuing decades faced new challenges and dilemmas. One finds a new

stylistic direction in the music of Vierne and Tournemire, and the death of Cavaillé-Coll in 1899 symbolized the end of an era in organ building.

Many other organists active in Paris during the second half of the nineteenth century deserve recognition for their contributions to the music profession. A few who were not mentioned previously or whose positions were not described are now listed here:

Louis Lebel (1831–88). Organist at Saint-Etienne-du-Mont (1853–88); professor of organ at the *Institution nationale des jeunes aveugles.*

Nicolas-Adolphe-Alphonse Populus (1831–1900). Studied organ with Marius Gueit; held positions at Saint-Jacques, Saint-Nicolas-du-Chardonnet, Saint-Pierre-de-Chaillot, returning then to Saint-Jacques as *maître de chapelle,* where he remained many years.

Charles Colin (1836–81). First prize in organ at the Paris Conservatory (1854); organist at Saint-Denis-du-Saint-Sacrement (1869–81); professor of oboe at the Paris Conservatory; uncle of Louis Vierne.

Adolphe-Edouard-Marie Deslandres (1840–1911). First prize in organ at the Paris Conservatory (1858); organist at Sainte-Marie-des-Batignolles.

Emile Bernard (1843–1902). First prize in organ at the Paris Conservatory (1867); held successive positions at Saint-Michel, Saint-Jean–Saint-François, and finally Notre-Dame-des-Champs (1889–1902).

Victor Nant (1850–79). Organist at Saint-Jean-Baptiste; professor at *Institution nationale des jeunes aveugles;* recitalist on the opening series at the Trocadéro.

Paul Wachs (1851–1915). First prize in organ at the Paris Conservatory (1872); organist at Saint-Merry (1874–96).

Raoul Pugno (1852–1914). First prize in organ at the Paris Conservatory (1869); organist (1871–76) and then *maître de chapelle* at Saint-Eugène.

Auguste Chapuis (1858–1933). First prize in organ at the Paris Conservatory (1881); organist at Notre-Dame-des-Champs (1884–88) and Saint-Roch (1888–1906).

Eugène Lacroix (1858–1950). Studied organ with Gigout; organist at Notre-Dame-d'Auteuil (1889–96) and at Saint-Merry (1896–1914); organist for Concerts Lamoureux.

Organists just beginning their careers in Paris in the 1890s included Abel Decaux (1869–1943), Henri Busser (1872–1973), Charles Quef (1873–1931), Georges MacMaster (d. 1898), and Henri Mulet (1878–1947).[3]

In Belgium Alphonse Mailly was the most prominent organist in the latter part of the century. He was professor of organ at the Brussels Conservatory and organist at several churches in Brussels: Saint-Joseph, Notre-Dame-de-Finisterre, and the church of the Carmelites. Prominent organists elsewhere in Belgium included Joseph Callaerts (1838–1901), organist of the cathedral of Antwerp and professor of organ at the Antwerp Conservatory; Philémon

Denefoe (1833–99), organist of Sainte-Waudru, Mons; Joseph Tilborghs (1830–1910), professor of organ at the Conservatory at Ghent; Auguste Wiegand (1849–1904), organist at SS.-Pierre et Paul, Ostende; and Léandre Vilain (1866–1945). Vilain succeeded Wiegand at Ostende when the latter moved to Australia in 1890, and he succeeded Tilborghs at the Ghent Conservatory in 1902 [112a].

PART TWO

The Organist as Church Musician

XI.
Historical Background

CHURCH music was understandably slow to recover from the revolutionary period. The legal status of the Catholic church was restored by an agreement between Napoléon and Pope Pius VII—the Concordat of 1801—which was ratified by the French legislature in 1802 and celebrated that year with a Te Deum in Notre-Dame cathedral. The Concordat was only one step toward some semblance of order in the day-to-day functions of the church. In 1814, the Reverend John Chetwode Eustace described "the treacherous indifference of Napoleon's government" to the plight of churches. Before the Revolution, he said, Paris had had 222 churches, of which 45 were parochial; of those there remained twelve parochial and 27 *succursal,* or minor parish churches [102, pp.27–28].

> The others have either been demolished, or turned into manufactories, schools, or granaries. The greater part of those which remained, were pillaged, stript of all their marble, brass, statues, paintings, and even altars and pulpits. The painted windows were not often spared, and the lead and copper of the roof not unfrequently carried off. Thus they were all reduced to a lamentable state of degradation, nakedness, and gradual decay; and in that state, they remained till the religion of the nation once more became that of the state: and Christianity re-assumed its external honors. The attention of government was then directed to the preservation of the churches; but as Napoleon acted more from political than religious motives, and confined his liberality within the narrowest bounds of strict necessity, the work of restoration proceeded slowly; and many or rather most churches still exhibit the traces of revolutionary profanation. [102, pp.28–29.]

In 1807, 1809, and 1813 Napoléon's officials in charge of churches reported that "people were avoiding the restored church's services because the music was so bad" [72, p.198]. Even the more generous foreign observers of French church music in the first third of the century thought the style of organ music they heard was inappropriate. William Shepherd, an English clergyman visiting Paris in 1802, found high Mass at Notre-Dame to be a curious experience:

> When we arrived at the church, the procession of the host had just begun to move up one of the side-aisles. Penetrating the crowd which was assembled in the nave, we proceeded to the choir, and ascended into a gallery, whence we had a full view of almost the whole extent of the church. Our attention was of

course attracted by the procession, which was preceded by a number of boys, drest in white vestments, and bearing tapers. These were followed by eight or ten priests, who moved on in slow and solemn state, singing as they walked. Then appeared the distributors of the incense, who dispensed the grateful odour from urns of silver, suspended from their waists by a chain of the same metal. The elegance and grace with which they managed these sacred vases would well entitle them to the appellation of clerical Vestris's. In the centre of the procession was borne the canopy which covered the host. This canopy was surrounded by ecclesiastics, and followed by pious votaries, who chaunted the service as they marched along. The chorus which they formed was rendered more deep by the sound of an instrument, similar in tone to a bassoon. The voices of the priests were nicely in tune with this instrument, and the harmony which they produced had a very fine effect. The procession was flanked on each side by a party of soldiers, who I presume attended for the purpose of protecting the ceremony from the insults of those who are dissatisfied with the re-establishment of the Roman Catholic religion. At the elevation of the host, the commanding officer of the military gave the word in a tone of voice, which echoed through the vaulted roofs of the church. At this signal the drums beat; the swell of the organ mingled with the war-like note; the soldiers, kneeling on one knee, fixed the but [sic] end of their muskets on the pavement, and continued in that attitude till, on the cessation of the sound of the drums and organ, the word of command was given, and they arose. After the procession had made the circuit of the inside of the church, the chief priests advanced to the high altar, where they performed the mass, their voices being occasionally assisted by the organ. At various intervals voluntaries were played upon this instrument, some of which were absolutely jiggs. On the whole, our visit to Notre Dame presented to us a strange mixture of religious solemnity, military state, and levity. [297, pp.59–61.]

On a return trip to France in 1814 the Reverend Mr. Shepherd noted the character of the organ music he heard in several church services. At a Mass in Dieppe he found that "the service was more curious than impressive. A bad effect was produced by the lightness of the airs which were occasionally played on the organ; and the perpetual passing of mere gazers tended much to do away the idea of devotion" [297, pp.140–41]. At Louviers there was "a finely toned organ," but again he was annoyed by "the introduction of light, tripping airs on the organ" [297, pp.159–60]. In Paris he once again attended Mass at Notre-Dame, but found the occasion disappointing. "The service was not . . . performed with its usual grandeur; and the singing was totally spoiled by one ambitious youth in the choir, who, wishing to distinguish himself, screamed most unmercifully, and frequently out of tune." Saint-Sulpice, though, was a different story. "The ceremony was august, and the singing excellent and impressive" [297, pp.200–201].

Mendelssohn found nothing good to say about his visit to Saint-Sulpice. On January 21, 1832 he wrote to his sister Fanny:

I have just come from St. Sulpice, where the organist showed off his organ to me; it sounded like a full chorus of old women's voices; but they maintain that it is the finest organ in Europe if it were only put into proper order, which would cost thirty thousand francs. The effect of the *canto fermo,* accompanied by a serpent, those who have not heard it could scarcely conceive, and clumsy bells are ringing all the time. [222, p.335.]

French musicians were well aware of the problems their foreign guests so willingly described, but solutions depended on money to repair organs, an adequate number of well-educated church musicians, and the cooperation of the clergy. All these requirements were in short supply in the early decades of the century.

There was one important exception to the gloomy picture of French church music: the chapel of the Tuileries. Napoléon wanted to establish a chapel at his principal residence (the palace of the Tuileries) similar to the pre-Revolution royal chapel at Versailles. His musical preferences set the course for the new chapel from its organization in July 1802.

The liturgy was treated with great freedom. Works called "Mass" might actually be any kind of religious work. In a typical Sunday service at the Tuileries one might hear one or two sections of the Ordinary sung, along with solos or choruses on other Latin texts. The sung texts did not necessarily correspond with the words recited at the altar by the priest. Jean Mongrédien concluded: "It must be admitted then, while the priest at the altar celebrated the Mass, the music itself gave the listener a text partially or entirely different from that of the office." [Il faut donc admettre que, tandis que le prêtre à l'autel célébrait la messe, la musique, elle, faisait entendre un texte partielle-ment ou entièrement différent de celui de l'office; 225, p.166.]

Criticisms of the music at the Tuileries chapel were more frequently aimed at style than at liturgical usage. Visitors from Germany were characteristically dismayed because the music was not in the "severe" (i.e., contrapuntal) style they associated with church music. However, use of the same style in the theater and the church did not seem inappropriate to Napoléon or, indeed, to most French people. Composers and performers sought to reach their listeners through the heart, to add color and variety to the service, and to capture in music the poetic and dramatic aspects of religious texts. The finest musicians in Paris filled the ranks of singers and instrumentalists, and the chapel at the Tuileries was the showcase of French church music during the first three decades of the nineteenth century.

All came swiftly to a halt in 1830. When Louis-Philippe took the throne he dismissed all chapel musicians, thus eliminating a substantial item from his budget. At that time the keyboard staff included organists Benoist and Séjan, and pianist accompanists Piccinni and Pradher [47, p.224]. The chapel did not function again until the Second Empire.

The changes in the status of the organ profession during the nineteenth century were generally paralleled by changes in church music. From about the 1830s the gradual awakening to a broader repertoire of music of various periods and styles, the new interest in mastery of performance skills, the installation of magnificent new organs, and expanded opportunities for music education transformed the picture of the organist as artist. The same factors contributed to the improvement of music in church services, along with re- forms in the liturgy, concerns about the performance of plainchant, new directions in the composition of church music, and a growing interest in early music.

The gradual replacement of the Parisian rite by the Roman rite (discussed in Chap. XII) required relatively minor adjustments as far as the organist's performance was concerned. Its more important result was the standardization of liturgical practice (at least in theory) throughout France, preparing the way for further reforms.

The Benedictine order had begun work on plainchant reformation at the Solesmes monastery in the 1830s, but the publication of chant editions did not begin until some fifty years later. Discussion of plainchant reform was not limited to Solesmes, however. Concurrent with the work in progress there, other scholars were working on the same problems, and various aspects of plainchant performance were frequent topics of discussion by church musi- cians. Plainchant itself became an increasingly important influence in organ composition in the last quarter of the century, contributing its modal and performance styles as well as its themes to new works for church and concert.

Early music only slowly penetrated the church repertoire. Antoine-Joseph Reicha (1770–1836), a friend of Beethoven's, was one of the most highly respected teachers at the Paris Conservatory. Berlioz, Liszt, and Franck were among his students. In 1833 Reicha spoke for much of the century when he said: "We fancy that the ancient Church music in the style of the celebrated Palestrina is not acceptable in our century. This style, wanting in musical ideas, songfulness, symmetry, grace, variety, can interest us but slightly. It should, therefore, make room for a new style" [cited in 57, p.583].

We have seen how the music of Bach gradually gained a place in the organ recital repertoire. In much the same way, the broader repertoire of early music was introduced to reluctant French listeners by a few persistent pioneers. Some gave concerts or published music; others organized schools for the education of church musicians. But the unfamiliar styles of early music had to gain support from a broad base of performing musicians, critics, and listening public before they could claim a place in the church repertoire. When Charles Bordes began to promote the music of Palestrina in the 1890s, the time was ripe. Musicians in various fields were enthusiastically exploring early music, and audiences at performances of early music were growing.

Young musicians seeking to enter the profession as church organists faced quite different situations in the course of the nineteenth century. In the earlier decades variations of the apprentice system prevailed. The young organist might receive his training from a relative and eventually succeed him. Another route for the aspiring organist was to become a *survivancier* of his teacher or another older organist. That is, he would be designated as the successor of an *organiste titulaire* before the latter's retirement or death. Meanwhile, he could serve as an assistant and substitute. This system gave the young organist some security, and it guaranteed continuity in the music staff for the church. If there was no *survivancier* when a position became vacant, there might be an open competition for the post. During the second half of the century competitions became the more frequent way for a young organist to win a position.

In 1833 the *Revue musicale* announced a competition for the position of organist in the parish church of Gray (Haute-Saône). The candidate was to submit verification of good moral character from his clergyman and mayor. He should know not only organ but at least two other instruments (including a wind instrument) and be capable of giving lessons on them. He should also know the rules of composition. In addition to his duties at the church, the organist would be expected to establish a music school. He would receive a fee of two francs per month (twenty lessons per month) from each student attending. The annual salary for the church position would be 600 to 800 francs plus extra fees [RM 13, p.312].

By the 1860s competitions for organ positions usually required the performance of prepared pieces, improvised pieces, and plainchant accompaniments. Chauvet was the successful candidate for the position at Saint-Merry in 1864. The jury for the competition had been Benoist, Delsarte, Simon, Saint-Saëns, Vervoitte, and Darnault. Competitors were required to play an improvised or prepared piece, a fugue with pedals (chosen by the candidate), an improvisation on a theme given by Saint-Saëns, and a plainchant accompaniment [RMS 5, cols.122–23].

Competitions for prestigious positions late in the century sometimes required memorized performances. In 1896 Widor supervised the competition for the post of organist for the Saint-Denis church. There were four requirements: a plainchant accompaniment, an improvised fugue, an improvised symphonic piece, and a memorized performance of a work by Bach. Eight candidates applied, but only four could meet the requirements. Libert was the winner [ME 62, p.240].

Even more demanding was the competition in 1900, supervised by Dubois, for the position of organist at Notre-Dame cathedral. In addition to the plainchant accompaniment, improvised fugue, and improvised free piece, the candidate had to perform from memory a masterwork chosen by the jury from a list of five submitted by the candidate. Although more organists appeared, only five actually competed. Louis Vierne was selected unanimously by the jury [ME 66, pp.143, 167].

For centuries church musicians have struggled with the problem of defining "appropriate church music." Nineteenth-century musicians were no more successful in resolving that problem than we are today, but it is interesting (and perhaps instructive) to explore their attitudes. In France the problem itself changed character during the century, becoming more refined as successive generations of well-trained musicians began to wear down the more crass expectations of clergy or congregation. There were complaints about jigs and other dances played early in the century. Somewhat later critics tended to focus on excerpts from popular operas. In both periods the goal of reformers in France was to eliminate the most direct allusions to secular entertainment from church music.

Considerable overlapping between sacred and secular music was normal in France both before and after the Revolution. Considering the dance idioms found in French classical organ music, Edward Higginbottom wrote: "An assessment of the penetration of secular elements into liturgical organ music must take into account the extent to which *any* music was then considered to be exclusively sacred or secular. Since an interpenetration of styles was a feature of baroque music, we are bound to experience difficulty in establishing a *unique* set of criteria for 'liturgical' music" [158, pp.32–33].

Looking at the music written for church use by some of the most outspoken mid-nineteenth-century critics of the state of church music, one realizes that they were not advocating an entirely different, separate compositional style for church music. Although Fétis, Danjou, and Niedermeyer urged incorporating more contrapuntal music (especially German contrapuntal music) into the organ repertoire, no one objected to a good songlike melody, a sprightly rhythm, or an energetic march. It was the direct quotation from the opera, the too-obvious hunting song, the excessively dramatic descriptive improvisation that went beyond the limits of the acceptable.

Few nineteenth-century musicians criticized Berlioz, Gounod, or Franck for using the same stylistic ingredients for both church and secular music; their normal musical vocabularies presumably could express or reflect the attitudes appropriate for worship as well as for secular situations. Saint-Saëns wrote that it was impossible to decide what music is most suitable for the church "for the very simple reason that in reality there is no religious art, properly so called, absolutely to be distinguished from secular art. There is good music, and there is bad music; for the rest, it is a matter of fashion, of convention, and nothing else" [282, p.1].

Saint-Saëns's disciple, Gabriel Fauré, agreed. "What music is sacred?" he asked. "What music is not? The attempt to settle the question is hazardous, considering that however profoundly sincere a musician's religious feeling may be, he will express it through his personal impressionability, and not according to laws that cannot be precisely formulated. . . . When we have to do with works truly musical and beautiful, it is fairly impossible to point out the distinction between those that are sacred and those that 'smell of brimstone'" [cited in 57, p.582].

XII.
Organ and Liturgy

LONG before the French Revolution the Catholic church in France had enjoyed more autonomy than Rome might have preferred. In the seventeenth century the nationalistic movement termed Gallicanism had reserved for each French bishop the right to determine the liturgy in his own diocese. Some chose to use the forms prescribed by Rome; others created new liturgies, known as Neo-Gallican.

For organ music, the most important of the Neo-Gallican liturgies was the Parisian rite, adopted not only by the diocese of Paris but also by a number of other areas. Most surviving French liturgical organ music from the late seventeenth century until the middle of the nineteenth was written by Paris organists for this ceremonial. From the beginning there were exceptions. Even within the city of Paris itself, convents and other religious houses could have their own liturgical forms and chants.

The church organist's duties normally required playing for designated celebrations of Mass and Offices. The services involved playing organ versets in alternation with portions of chants sung by the choir. In addition, the organist needed a repertoire of independent pieces of various types for specified parts of the services.

In the Mass, the Offertory was the organist's opportunity to play a movement of substantial size. During the first half of the nineteenth century one might expect to hear a sonata-allegro movement played on a full registration. The Elevation was a quiet piece, sometimes replaced partly or entirely by a sung *O salutaris*. The final verset of the Agnus Dei might serve a dual purpose as a Communion piece. Entrance and exit pieces were optional, depending on whether there was a procession and on local custom.

During the century the *sortie* after the Mass gradually assumed its well-known role as a brilliant virtuostic postlude. On the other hand, the bold character of the Offertory frequently gave way to quieter, more introspective moods toward the end of the century. In Franck's *L'Organiste* (1890) one can find both a *Sortie ou Offertoire* (D major) and an *Offertoire ou Communion* (E minor), illustrating the wide range of character an Offertory might still have. Some years later Guilmant wrote concerning the Offertory: "This moment of the Mass being a prayer, in our time it is considered appropriate to play the organ with less noise, and that stops of a calm character are more suitable to accompany that part of the divine service." [De nos jours, on considère que, ce moment de la messe étant une prière, il convient de toucher l'orgue avec moins de fracas, et que des jeux d'un caractère calme sont plus convenables pour accompagner cette partie du service divin; 145, p.1148.]

Versets were of many different types. In the first half of the nineteenth century they still resembled the varieties found in late seventeenth-century French organ music: duos, trios, fugues, and pieces for traditional French solo and ensemble registrations. Some were stately, some meditative, some sprightly or whimsical. Lively dancelike rhythms and catchy melodies were often part of the mixture of moods and colors that the organist presented to church-goers.

The Parisian rite stipulated that plainchant be employed unaltered in specific versets. While organists did not always comply with all prescriptions of the rite, they usually played a *cantus-firmus* setting for the first verset of each portion of the liturgy in which the organ participated, including the Kyrie, Gloria, Sanctus, and Agnus of the Mass; the Magnificat; and hymns. In addition, the sixth organ verset of the Gloria *(Qui tollis)* was given *cantus-firmus* treatment. There was no restriction on the number of other versets that might use the chant melodies; the second and third Gloria versets were often *cantus-firmus* settings.

In addition to liturgical requirements, the organist also followed some musical traditions. The most ubiquitous was the use of a fugal style for the second verset of a Kyrie, a custom also frequently applied to the second verset of a hymn.

Published examples of liturgical organ music affirm that *cantus-firmus* settings for the Parisian rite typically had the chant melody in the lowest voice in long, equal note values. The accompaniment would consist of two or three upper voices, sometimes providing a simple chordal harmonization of each chant note, and sometimes using a more varied harmonic-contrapuntal style. The *cantus-firmus* versets of Boëly were unusual, both in the quality of the accompaniments and in the location of the *cantus-firmus*. He experimented with placing the chant melody in the soprano, alto, and tenor, in addition to the traditional bass.

An outline of the *Messe des solemnels majeurs* by Guillaume Lasceux, from his 1819 "Annuaire" (pp.14–27), illustrates what was played during a typical organ Mass of the early nineteenth century. Versets designated "C F" are *cantus-firmus* settings with two contrapuntal voices above a chant melody in longer note values. The chant for this Mass is *Cunctipotens Genitor Deus.*[1]

    I. Kyrie
        1. Kyrie [C F]
        2. Fugue [employing the chant melody]
        3. Cromorne avec les fonds
        4. Flûtes
        5. Choeur G^d Jeu
    II. Gloria
        1. Et in terra pax [C F]
        2. Benedicamus te [C F]
        3. Glorificamus te [C F]

        4. Voix humaine
        5. Duo
        6. Qui tollis [C F]
        7. Hautbois et voix humaine
        8. Choeur G^d Jeu
        9. Petit plein Jeu pour l'amen
  III. Offertoire
  IV. Sanctus
        1. Ier Sanctus [C F]
        2. 3e Sanctus [a short free verset]
   V. Elévation. Flûtes
  VI. Agnus Dei
        1. Agnus Dei [C F]
        2. Claironet/ Cromorne/ avec les fonds
 VII. Ite missa est—petit plein jeu

Noël Masses had long been a feature of Christmas celebrations. Like present-day services of carols, their combination of well-known tunes and holiday spirit had a special appeal for the general public. *The New Harvard Dictionary of Music* erroneously states: "With the French Revolution, production of [instrumental] *noëls* stopped, but the genre was revived in the late 19th century" [262, p.541]. Actually, noëls remained a part of the repertoire, and new keyboard arrangements of noëls were written or improvised throughout the century; during the first half of the century they appeared in published collections of Jacques-Marie Beauvarlet-Charpentier, Nicolas Séjan, Jacques-Claude-Adolphe Miné, and Alexandre Boëly.

Noëls were usually published without specific reference to their use in the Mass, but there are exceptions. For example, Boëly's *Messe du jour de Noël,* Op.11 (1842),[2] contains twelve noël settings in a clearly defined order for the Mass. Additional versets were to be supplied by the organist: those using a plainchant *cantus-firmus,* and three brief free versets. Plainchant melodies for the *cantus-firmus* versets were included in the publication, using the Gregorian Mass *Cunctipotens Genitor Deus.* The omission of versets for which noëls would be unsuitable, because of either liturgical requirements or length, leaves a degree of flexibility for use with other rites, as well as the opportunity for the organist to exercise his skill in improvisation.

For vespers the organist played a verset following the first, third, and fifth psalms (or in some parishes, at the conclusion of each psalm). The vesper hymn and the Magnificat were performed in alternation with the choir, and at the end of the service the organist played the Benedicamus. As in the Mass, there might also be a piece for the procession at the beginning of the service and a *sortie* at the end.

In accordance with the Parisian rite, the first verset of a hymn was a *cantus-firmus* setting; the second verset was traditionally fugal. There is no specific pattern for additional versets, and the number required varied from one hymn to another. The Magnificat began with a *cantus-firmus* "intonation." Six versets would seem to be required in all, but composers often supplied a brief verset to follow the choir's final *Sicut érat* verset. In his *Six Magnificats* (c. 1804–14), Beauvarlet-Charpentier confirmed that this final verset is for the *Amen*.

For special festivals and celebrations the organist might play a Te Deum in alternation with the choir. Basically, the Te Deum required sixteen organ versets. During the eighteenth century, as descriptive music gained in popularity, organists recognized a special opportunity in connection with the eleventh organ verset. The text *Judex crederis . . .* ("We believe that thou shalt come to be our judge") inspired elaborate improvised portrayals of the final day of judgment. The more vividly the organist could depict the chaos of the end of the world, the more his skill was appreciated by the general public.

In the early part of the nineteenth century it was customary at many Paris churches to perform a Te Deum on the eve of the patron saint's day. In 1845 the *Revue de la musique religieuse, populaire et classique* noted that Marius Gueit, organist of Saint-Denis-du-Saint-Sacrement, would play for such an occasion but that this custom was gradually being abolished [RMR 1, p.430]. Nevertheless, a few later reports of organ Te Deum performances appeared in music magazines. The last occurrence of this tradition may have been the 1850 performance at Saint-Etienne-du-Mont by the blind organist Gauthier, which was noted by the *Revue et Gazette musicale* [RGM 17, p.273]. The *Judex crederis* continued to have a life of its own for some years; as late as 1861, Edmond Hocmelle improvised a version at the inauguration of the organ in the church of Saint-Philippe-du-Roule [RGM 28, pp.155–56].

The *abbé* Lamazou was one of those who regretted the neglect of the Te Deum tradition. In 1863 he wrote that the organist was given sufficient time in this ceremony to make the instrument heard and develop his musical ideas. Since the Te Deum was a special occasion, it gave organists who were occupied with their own churches on Sundays an opportunity to hear one of their colleagues. Knowing that the congregation would include other organists and visiting music lovers, the performer would make every effort to meet their expectations.

Lamazou said that the ceremony lost none of its religious character, but had all the advantages and none of the disadvantages of an organ concert. Organists and parishes alike profited from the opportunity for organists to hear one another perform the Te Deum. He suggested that organists make an effort to revive this old tradition, but his idea fell on deaf ears [188, col.10–11]. By that time storms were more fashionable than the end of the world as the basis for descriptive pieces.

Since the Te Deum was usually improvised, written examples are rare. Lasceux included a *Judex crederis* piece in his "Essai théorique et pratique" (1809) and a complete organ Te Deum in his "Annuaire" (1819). A later example of a *Judex crederis* is found in the works of Alexandre Boëly (Op.38, No.4, published posthumously, 1859–60).

During the middle decades of the century the Parisian rite was gradually supplanted by the Roman rite. The latter was adopted by the Chapter of Notre-Dame, Paris, in 1855, but its use was not mandatory throughout Paris until 1874 [122, p.431].

In the preface to his *Ecole d'orgue ou méthode complète de cet instrument* (Paris: Richault, 1844), Justin Cadaux (1813–74), then organist of the cathedral of Toulouse, outlined the use of the organ in both the Parisian and the Roman rites. The most significant difference from the standpoint of organ performance was the required use of plainchant in the Parisian rite. For the Roman rite the organist played free versets throughout.

While churches increasingly turned toward the Roman rite, the publication of organ Masses gradually ground to a halt. In mid-century editors and composers moved more and more toward the liturgically neutral area of miscellaneous collections and all-purpose versets. François Benoist's *Bibliothèque de l'organiste*, published in twelve issues, or "suites," over a period of about twenty years (c. 1840–61),[3] spanned this period of transition and illustrates the trend. The first suites contain *Offertoires*, *Grand Choeur* pieces, and *Elévations*. Later suites are devoted to a larger variety, including versets and other small pieces.

Rare examples of late-nineteenth-century French organ Masses are found in the works of Fernand de La Tombelle. Books I and II of his *Interludes dans la tonalité grégorienne et harmonisation des versets pour les messes en usage* (Schola Cantorum, [1897?]) each contain the music for one Mass, including the chant (harmonized for four-voice choir) for the Kyrie, Gloria, Sanctus, Agnus, and Ite Missa Est, as well as organ versets. As the title suggests, the organ versets are modal. They differ further from earlier versets in that they are accompanied by optional intonations of the texts, to be sung by a single voice while the organ versets are being played. The intonations are in free rhythm, independent of the rhythm of the versets.

The collection of pieces for the Magnificat by César Franck, published posthumously as *L'Organiste: Pièces pour orgue-harmonium* (Paris: Enoch, 1892), is another example of late-century music for *alternatim* performance. The pieces are grouped according to key, each group consisting of six versets, a brief *Amen,* and a longer piece (*Offertoire, Sortie,* or *Communion*). The format of six versets plus a concluding *Amen* differs from Magnificats written during the early part of the century only in the substitution of a free verset for the initial *cantus-firmus* intonation of the Parisian rite.[4]

In a general way, too, there remained a strong thread of continuity throughout the nineteenth century in the relationship of organ music to the liturgy. The most significant changes were matters of musical style rather than ritual. In 1895 Guilmant could still state that the *grand orgue* was generally heard in alternation with the choir, "at the Mass, for the Kyrie, Gloria, Sanctus and Agnus Dei; at vespers, after the psalms; for the hymn, for the Magnificat" [à la messe, au *Kyrie, Gloria, Sanctus* et *Agnus Dei;* aux vêpres, après les psaumes; à l'hymne, au *Magnificat;* [147, p.157].[5]

The organist was not ordinarily the choir accompanist in the early part of the century. Van Wye has described the way chant was then performed in Paris:

> According to this method, each note of the liturgical melody—performed by several low male voices doubled by a serpent, or ophicleide, and sometimes even a double bass—was accented and lengthened, regardless of whether or not it was part of a neume, and brought into conformity with major-minor tonality by chromatic alterations in the chant books or introduced by the singers. [318, p.6.]

This manner of performance was frequently criticized, and the standard accompanying instrument, the serpent, was a tempting scapegoat. In 1834 Adolphe Adam wrote: "I find it shameful, when the most insignificant prince of Germany has a chapel, when the smallest church of Belgium has passable music, that in Paris, the center of the arts, one might not enter a church without being pursued by one and sometimes two serpents." [Je trouve qu'il est honteux, quand le plus petit prince d'Allemagne a une chapelle, quand la moindre église de Belgique a une musique passable, qu'à Paris, au centre des arts, on ne puisse entrer dans une église sans être poursuivi par un et quelquefois deux serpents; 1, p.63.]

Similarly, a visitor to Clermont-Ferrand in 1845 reported: "I wanted to attend High Mass here; but the dreadful organ, the organist, the serpent, that terrible animal which still seeks to ruin music, having ruined the first woman, the singers and priests who rival one another as to who will sing the most out of tune, all that forced me to flee." [J'ai voulu assister ici à la grand'messe; mais l'orgue effroyable, l'organiste, le serpent, ce terrible animal, qui cherche encore à perdre la musique après avoir perdu la première femme, les chantres et les prêtres qui rivalisent entre eux à qui chantera le plus faux, tout cela m'a forcé à prendre la fuite; RMR 1, p.214.]

Pistone relates that two serpents and a double bass were used to accompany the singers at Notre-Dame, Paris, in the early decades of the nineteenth century. Serpents were still in use there at the beginning of the twentieth century to accompany processions [253, p.16].

In 1829 Adrien de La Fage (1801–62) was engaged to organize the music program at Saint-Etienne-du-Mont. His first move was to substitute an organ accompaniment (to which double basses could be added) for that of the serpents.[6] The *Agenda musical* of 1837 noted that this system had since been adopted by a number of parishes [256, pp.50–51].

A church that had two organs needed both an *organiste titulaire,* who played the *grand orgue,* and an *organiste accompagnateur,* who accompanied the choir on the *orgue de choeur.* The *maître de chapelle* or *maître de musique* was in charge of the choirs. In 1855 Georges Schmitt wrote that choir organs had been introduced "almost everywhere" [289, p.62]. The three-way division of musical responsibilities by the *titulaire,* the *organiste accompagnateur,* and the *maître de chapelle* became the accepted practice in larger churches. This

DIMANCHE (*dies Dominica*).

Singers accompanied by a serpent. From *L'Illustration*, 1850 (University of California Library, Berkeley).

system was not without problems. According to Schmitt: "Many churches that have a choir leave only two pieces to the *grand orgue* during the Mass: the procession and the offertory, and a prelude for the *Ite missa est*." [Beaucoup d'églises, qui ont une maîtrise, ne laissent au grand orgue que deux morceaux pendant la messe: la procession et l'offertoire, et un prélude pour l' *Ite missa est*; 289, p.63.]

In 1864 L. C. Laurens deplored the way some *maîtres de chapelle* encroached upon the organist's share of the music by reserving the Offertory for a motet and the Elevation for an *O salutaris*. Even more disturbing, he said, was the practice of relocating the choir in the tribune of the *grand orgue* in order to save the cost of an *organiste accompagnateur* [194, col.293].

On the other hand, when both the *titulaire* and the *organiste accompag-nateur* were talented improvisers, the dialogue between the two, across the length of the nave, could add greatly to the musical interest of the service. During the early 1870s the congregation of Saint-Sulpice could hear Widor at the *grand orgue* and Fauré at the *orgue de choeur*, challenging each other with themes and responding in a friendly competition [89, p.198].[7]

Concurrent with the mid-century turn toward the Roman rite and the decline in chant-based organ versets, concern about how the chant should be sung and how it should be accompanied were blossoming as topics of great interest, prompting the publication of various methods and theories. The modal method of accompaniment developed by Louis Niedermeyer was a radical departure from current tonal styles, and it met with strong resistance from Théodore Nisard (1812–88), F.-J. Fétis, and others [241, col.14]. Niedermeyer's method was summarized in his *Traité théorique et pratique de l'accompagnement du plain-chant*, published in collaboration with Joseph d'Ortigue (Paris: E. Repos, 1855). Briefly, that method entailed:

> 1. The exclusive use, in each mode, of notes of the scale. . . .
> 2. The frequent use of the triads of the final and dominant in each mode. . . .
> 3. The use exclusively of the harmonic formulae proper to the cadences of each mode. . . .
> 4. Every chord other than the consonant triads and their first inversions should be barred from plainsong accompaniment. . . .
> 5. The laws which govern plainsong melody must be observed in each of the accompanying voices. . . .
> 6. Since the melody is the essential of plainsong, it should always be placed in the upper voice. . . .
>
> [238, pp.14–16.]

Niedermeyer permitted the use of B-flat to avoid the tritone. The diminished triad could be used, but only in first inversion. All the examples are in four-voice, note-against-note harmony.

Niedermeyer had a powerful means of winning support for his method: it was taught to all the students who attended the *Ecole de musique classique et religieuse,* which he founded in 1853. The influence of both Niedermeyer's school and his method grew as an increasing number of his students assumed important church music positions.

When Wallace Goodrich published his English translation of the Nieder-meyer-Ortigue book in 1905, he inserted the following explanation:

> Nearly half a century has elapsed since this treatise was written. If any excuse for its translation after so long a period were necessary, it would be that since its completion has appeared no better work upon the subject, in point of simplicity and clearness of expression, and faithfulness to the principles of ecclesiastical music instinctively recognized by musicians of the highest authority, and most sensitive appreciation of the element of individuality in music. [238, p.iii.]

Although other methods of chant accompaniment were proposed, none were as influential as Niedermeyer's. In the last quarter of the nineteenth century a few musicians began to make practical use of new ideas about the rhythmic interpretation of Gregorian chant. Then the old habit of accompanying every note of the chant with a chord had to give way to a more flexible treatment; but the modal harmonic style proposed by Niedermeyer was still valid.

XIII.
Notes on the Repertoire

HOWEVER well we might understand the function of organ music in the liturgy, we actually know very little about the way it sounded to the French church-goer in the nineteenth century. Several factors have conspired to obscure or distort our view.

First, and of primary importance, most church organ music was improvised. Published collections were often intended for organists who did not have sufficient training or skill to improvise. Some were the work of one composer, while others were drawn from a variety of sources, including new pieces by contemporary French composers, small pieces extracted from larger works, pieces transcribed from other media, and pieces from other countries (usually Germany). The collections were often published in serial form and were called *journaux*. Some survived for only a few issues, but the *Journal des organistes,* edited and published by Jean-Romary Grosjean and continued by his nephew Ernest Grosjean, appeared regularly from 1859 to 1914.

As greater educational opportunities for organists developed during the century and the supply of well-trained organists grew, the range of difficulty and sophistication in published church organ music also changed. Nevertheless, although some of the most famous organists of the late nineteenth century made major contributions to service music, the published repertoire remained only a partial reflection of the art the best performers could (and did) bring to the console.

Our view is further distorted by nineteenth-century journalism. The most tireless writers on the subject of church music were those who wanted to change it. No one complained more loudly or more frequently than F.-J. Fétis. He established the *Revue musicale* in 1827, and from then on his views on church music and many other topics were given generous space.

While the *Revue musicale* covered a broad range of musical interests, magazines published by Félix Danjou (*Revue de la musique religieuse, populaire et classique,* 1845–48 and 1854) and Louis Niedermeyer and Joseph d'Ortigue (*La Maîtrise,* 1857–61) focused more specifically on church music. Primary objectives were to change the organ and choral repertoires and the manner of singing and accompanying chant. In 1895, when the periodical of the Schola Cantorum (*La Tribune de Saint-Gervais*) was initiated, the thrust was still that of effecting change. Seldom does one find a defense of the status quo.

During much of the century German contrapuntal music, especially that of

Bach, was viewed by some critics as ideal organ music, although it was more often praised than played until the final decades of the century. But the great silent majority of church-goers found contrapuntal music boring and much preferred to hear music that was in a familiar style: melodic, colorful, cheerful, and uncomplicated. Anxious to keep the pews filled and the congregation satisfied, many clergymen supported this view.

As noted earlier, in actual nineteenth-century practice there remained a generous common meeting ground among critics, producers, performers, and consumers of church music. The works praised, published, and sometimes composed by nineteenth-century reformers clearly demonstrate that their view of appropriate church music was less restricted than their words might lead us to believe. Sometimes all the lofty statements about ideals of church music, all the grand ideas about what was or was not appropriate music for worship, had to bend under the weight of public preference. But public taste and artistic integrity also had common meeting grounds. Even the most discriminating organists could treat their congregations to the familiar tune, the colorful setting, and technical display without compromising their standards; nor were they reluctant to do so.

Widor dipped into a French tradition of long standing to please his congregation at Christmas midnight Masses. Paul Landormy tells us the great organist would play an original fantasy on popular noëls that was "a masterpiece of musical imagination and registration, a perpetual surprise, an enchantment. And he would finish the ceremony with his celebrated, his stunning *Toccata*" [un chef-d'oeuvre d'imagination musicale et de registration, une surprise perpétuelle, un enchantement. Et il terminait la cérémonie par sa célèbre, son étourdissante *Toccata;* 189, p.171.]

Gigout regularly played short recitals under the guise of incidental service music. In 1892 Theodore Knauff explained:

> It may be remarked that at St. Augustine, the fashionable Mass is the Low one at the late hour of 1. P.M., and that this important mass may not be without music entirely, for there is none in the service itself. M. Gigout, the organist, is employed to give an organ recital, pure and simple, every Sunday during the whole of this celebration. It lasts from 1. to 1.45 P.M. A regular succession of organ concert numbers is played. [182, p.3.]

Writers in the twentieth century have further contributed to a slanted view of nineteenth-century church organ music. Conditioned by decades of early music and thoroughly steeped in the north European contrapuntal style of the seventeenth and eighteenth centuries, the modern organist or historian has difficulty viewing nineteenth-century French church organ music objectively. Some writers have delighted in locating the most extreme examples in order to shock their readers with the decadence of the period.

It is true that a large percentage of published church organ collections was composed or compiled by well-meaning, sincere organists of mediocre talent (a criticism that could apply to more than one period of history and more than one country). But nineteenth-century France also produced some very gifted organist-composers who wrote or compiled collections specifically for church use.

During the second half of the nineteenth century organ service music was increasingly influenced by new ideas stemming from the church music reform movement. In general the trend was to link organ music more closely to Gregorian chant through use of church modes and chant melodies. Saint-Saëns saw modal organ music as a bonus resulting from Niedermeyer's method of chant accompaniment. In 1916 he wrote that the Niedermeyer system had "made its way throughout France" and had "even overpassed its aim by showing the possibility of introducing the ancient Modes into modern Harmony, thus enriching it in an unexpected manner" [282, p.3].

The possibility of applying modal writing to organ solo music had been grasped quickly by C.-H. Valentin Alkan. His *Petits préludes sur les 8 gammes du plain-chant,* published in *La Maîtrise* (vol.3, 1859–60) in two sets of four pieces, adhered strictly to the modal scales. Although they are among the most interesting easy miniatures of the period, they attracted no imitators at that time. Another group of modal pieces appeared in the posthumous collection *Oeuvres inédites,* vol. 1, by J.-N. Lemmens (Leipzig and Brussels: Breitkopf & Härtel, 1883). Nevertheless, when Eugène Gigout began publishing collections of modal pieces in the late 1880s, they were hailed as innovations.

Early in 1889 L.-A. Bourgault-Ducoudray reviewed Gigout's new *Cent pièces brèves dans la tonalité du plain-chant* (Paris: Heugel, 1888).[1] He praised Gigout for writing outside the usual harmonic patterns, proving that music was not condemned to evolve forever in major and minor [ME 55, p.13]. Later the same year Gigout introduced his modal pieces to a broader public by including some on his recital at the Trocadéro [ME 55, p.200]. However, recital repertoire was not his primary objective; Gigout was concerned about the lack of unity in the church service when modal choral chants and accompaniments alternated with organ pieces in major and minor keys. He continued to write modal pieces the rest of his life. His last big collection, *Cent pièces brèves nouvelles . . .* (London: J. & W. Chester, 1921) contains an assortment of both modal and tonal pieces.

Although *cantus-firmus* versets were not required for the Roman rite, the old church melodies continued to appear occasionally in the 1860s and 1870s in organ pieces for church, teaching, and recitals. Among the publications are Batiste, *Offertoire du saint jour de Paques,* Op.26 (Paris: Richault, c. 1862), based on *O Filii;* Lefébure-Wély, *Verset sur le chant de l'hymne de la Pentecôte* (*L'Organiste Moderne,* No.3) (Paris: Richault, 1867); and Lemmens, *Trois Sonates pour orgue,* Nos.2 and 3 (London: Novello, Ewer & Co., 1874), incorporating respectively *O Filii* and *Victimae Paschali.*

Jacques Lemmens was among the first to urge a greater use of chant melodies in organ music. In 1861 Joseph d'Ortigue wrote: "M. Lemmens has chiefly viewed the organ in its relationship to the Catholic church. His most impressive fugues are written . . . on plainchant motives. He recommends basing preludes and versets on the themes of the hymns and chants that they precede and follow." [M. Lemmens a surtout envisagé l'orgue dans ses rapports avec le culte catholique. Ses fugues les plus imposantes sont écrites, ainsi que nous l'avons vu, sur des motifs du plain-chant. Il recommande d'établir les préludes et les versets sur les thèmes des hymnes et des chants qu'ils précèdent et suivent; 243, p.184.]

One of the most persistent and perhaps the most effective advocate for the use of Gregorian melodies in organ music was Alexandre Guilmant. Like his teacher Lemmens and his colleague Gigout, Guilmant sought a greater unity between organ and choral music in the liturgy. In 1895 he explained:

> In the alternating pieces it is necessary for the organist to play the Gregorian melody or, at least, versets based on these themes. I think that there are very interesting things to be written in the polyphonic style with these old tonalities and on such beautiful chants as these. The German organists have composed pieces based on the melodies of chorales, forming a particularly rich organ literature; shouldn't we do likewise with our Catholic melodies?

> Il est donc nécessaire que dans les pièces alternées, l'organiste joue la mélodie grégorienne, ou au moins, des versets basés sur ces thèmes. Je pense qu'il y a des choses très intéressantes à écrire dans le style polyphonique avec ces tonalités anciennes, et sur ces chants si beaux. Les organistes allemands ont composé des morceaux basés sur le chant des chorals, formant une littérature d'orgue particulièrement riche; que ne faisons-nous de même avec nos mélodies catholiques? [147, p.157.]

Guilmant himself wrote some 130 chant-based organ pieces.

The organ Masses of Fernand de La Tombelle (see above, p.131) illustrate the conscious effort some church musicians were making late in the century to unify the service. Not only are the versets modal but many are based on the chant or on motives derived from it.

Widor was among those influenced by the new direction of church music. Three of his organ symphonies use Gregorian melodies: Symphonie II, Op.13; *Symphonie gothique,* Op.70; and *Symphonie romane,* Op.73.[2] Toward the end of the century he also affirmed that "except for Bach's preludes and fugues, or rather certain preludes and fugues, I can no longer consider any organ music sacred unless it is consecrated by themes from chorales or Gregorian chants" [cited in 293, p.21].

Widor's *Symphonie romane* (published in 1900) marked the peak of nineteenth-century French organ works based on Gregorian chant. Albert Schweitzer recalled hearing Widor play the finale of this work in Saint-Sulpice: "I shared with him the feeling that French organ music had joined sacred art, had experienced that death and resurrection that all organ music must undergo in every individual, if it is to achieve something lasting" [293, p.21].

By the last decade of the century many new ideas about church music were taking root. The Benedictine community at Solesmes had published several volumes of plainchant, restored according to what they considered the most authentic sources; ideas about the nonmetrical interpretation of chant were spreading; leading organists were advocating and demonstrating new directions for church organ music. In 1894–96 the Schola Cantorum was founded. This institution would seek to bring together the various threads of church music reform and transmit them to a new generation of church musicians.

While "progress" is a questionable idea in the arts, there is no doubt that organ music in French churches in 1900 was light-years beyond what it had been in the early 1800s. The Revolution had left church music in shambles: organs damaged or destroyed, music schools closed, and choirs disbanded. By the end of the century French churches bristled with world-famous organs commanded by brilliant performers, and the educational opportunities in Paris for the eager young church musician were without parallel. The church organist had every reason to believe the Golden Age was at hand, or perhaps just around the corner.

PART THREE

Great Schools and Famous Teachers

XIV.
The Paris Conservatory
Organ Class
Séjan to Franck

BEFORE the Revolution music education in France had included private instruction and private schools, but its most important institutions were the *maîtrises:* the choir schools connected to cathedrals or collegiate churches.[1] There, from the age of seven or eight, the student was provided with a general education and instruction in the rudiments of music, plainchant, and singing, advancing then to harmony, counterpoint, and composition. Organ and sometimes other instruments were included in the studies. Mongrédien estimated that there were more than five hundred *maîtrises* on the eve of the Revolution [225 p.11]. When the churches were closed, so were their schools.

The *maîtrises* had been effective in preserving church music traditions and giving boys throughout France an opportunity for at least a basic musical training, even though the quality of instruction and the scope of the repertoire studied varied considerably from one school to another. However, there were some important areas of music education in which the *maîtrises* were inadequate, notably in training singers for careers in opera and instrumentalists for orchestras. Further, the *maîtrises* were restricted to boys, and girls had to receive their musical education through private instruction.

To compensate for some of these deficiencies the *Ecole royale de chant et de déclamation* was founded in 1784, under the direction of Gossec. Its objective was to train singers for the royal service, especially for the opera. It was superceded by the school that now bears the title *Conservatoire national supérieur de musique* (known more familiarly in the English-speaking world as the Paris Conservatory).

The Conservatory owes its foundation to an enterprising, energetic organizer, Bernard Sarrette (1765–1858), who saw opportunities for music and musicians in the service of the revolutionary movement. Through a remarkable series of maneuvers he managed to upgrade a military band to a national conservatory in six years. In 1789 Sarrette organized a band for the newly created National Guard. Three years later it was expanded into the *Ecole de musique militaire,* for the purpose of training instrumental musicians for the military services. The players in Sarrette's band were the teachers, and their students (sons of citizens serving in the National Guard) received instruction in solfège and instrumental music. Gossec was in charge of musical matters and Sarrette was the administrator.

In 1793 Sarrette successfully approached the National Convention with the idea of further expanding the school to an *Institut national de musique,* in order to be able to train large numbers of musicians for participation in the national festivals. Gossec, Méhul, Le Sueur, and Cherubini were appointed directors of studies. It was actually a friend of Sarrette's, Marie-Joseph Chénier (1764–1811), who persuaded the Convention to transform the *Institut* into a national *Conservatoire* in 1795. Its prime objectives were still to provide music for the festivals and musicians for the armed services. Five inspectors of instruction were appointed: Méhul, Grétry, Gossec, Le Sueur, and Cherubini; Sarrette was again the administrator. The curriculum was enlarged to include a broad representation of applied music subjects, and the school was open to students of both sexes.

The restoration of the monarchy in 1814 spelled trouble for the Conservatory, which was suspect because of its origins during the Revolution. In November Sarrette was given notice that his job would cease as of January 1. With Napoléon's return, Sarrette reclaimed his position for a brief time (March 23 to December 28, 1815), but the administration was then taken over by the marquis La Rouzière. The school was reorganized as the *Ecole royale de musique et de déclamation,* with François-Louis Perne (1772–1832) as administrator. Classes resumed in April 1816 [249, pp.xv, 179, 208].

In its new form the school was actually a rebirth of the pre-Revolution *Ecole royale,* with the primary objective of educating singers for the royal theaters and the royal chapel, i.e., for the pleasure of the aristocracy. It was not until 1831 that the title *Conservatoire* was reinstated [225, pp.26–27]. After Perne, the administrators of the school during the nineteenth century were Cherubini (from 1822), Auber (from 1842), Thomas (from 1871), and Dubois (from 1896).

The Conservatory brought a new dimension to French music. It published methods of instruction, collected a comprehensive music library, and set a national standard for music instruction. But it could not be all things to all people. In the early years it was criticized for giving too much attention to instrumental music and not enough to standards of vocal instruction.

It became clear also that the Conservatory was no substitute for the old *maîtrises* in the training of church musicians. The *maîtrises* had also provided music education in cities and towns throughout France, whereas the Conservatory encouraged talented students to seek their musical education in Paris. Since its beginning the Conservatory has centralized musical activity in the capital city to a degree unparalleled in other large countries. Although branches of the Conservatory were established in other cities, almost all French musicians who left a significant mark on music history in the nineteenth century developed their careers in Paris, and most spent at least part of their student years there.[2]

When the Paris Conservatory was first organized in 1795 it had a two-fold purpose: to provide music for national festivals and to educate students in music. It was, of course, the second objective that soon shaped the course of the school. Provision was made in the original plans for 115 professors (including one organ professor) and 600 students of both sexes, chosen proportionately from all the French Départements. Although many details were still not worked out, the Conservatory began to function on October 22, 1796 [249, pp.124–25, 131].

Tuition was free, and the Conservatory was entirely dependent on the government for support. Thus it is not surprising to find references to budget cuts among the early documents. In 1800 the number of professors and administrators was reduced to 82, and the number of students fixed at 400. A more drastic cut was made in 1802, when 35 professors were dismissed, including Nicolas Séjan, the organ professor. Enrollment during the nineteenth century fluctuated between a low of 140 in 1816 and a high of 735 in 1885–86. Throughout the second half of the century the enrollment usually ranged between 550 and 700[3] [249, pp.139, 159, 873]. After Séjan's dismissal, organ instruction was not resumed until 1819. Through the rest of the nineteenth century the position of organ professor was held successively by François Benoist (1819–72), César Franck (1872–90), Charles-Marie Widor (1890–96), and Alexandre Guilmant (1896–1911).

The general educational goals of the Conservatory remained constant throughout the century: to educate students in music performance and composition. Initially there were courses in vocal and instrumental performance, solfège, and composition. The composition course soon spawned separate courses in harmony and counterpoint. In contrast, music history was slow to gain recognition as an essential part of the performer's education. It was not added to the curriculum until 1871[4] [75, p.3447].

The typical keyboard student entering the Conservatory would already have completed his or her general education and acquired considerable proficiency on the piano. To succeed in the organ class one also needed skills in harmony and counterpoint, as improvisation was required. Most students had to provide their own room and board, so it was very difficult to attend the Paris Conservatory unless one happened to live in Paris. César Franck's father solved that problem by moving his whole family from Liège, Belgium, to Paris and becoming a French citizen so that his sons could be enrolled in the Conservatory.

There was no established system for preparing students for admission. Louis-James-Alfred Lefébure-Wély had considerable music instruction from his organist father, capped by a year of piano study with Méreaux and Rigel. By the time he entered the Conservatory at age fifteen (1832), he already held the position of organist at Saint-Roch [120].

Another route to the Conservatory was the preparatory school. For many years Alkan Morhange ran a small boarding school in Paris where elementary music and French grammar were taught. An 1844 advertisement boasted that numerous students from the school had entered the Conservatory in the preceding twenty years [cited in 304, p.40]. Morhange's most talented students were his six children. Ronald Smith speculated that the Morhange household "must have devoured and breathed solfège" [304, p.16]. The most precocious member of the family, who took his father's first name as his last, became famous as Charles-Valentin Alkan. He entered the Conservatory in 1819 at age six and won first prize in solfège at seven-and-a-half.

One can cite still other paths to the Conservatory: the studies Saint-Saëns had with distinguished private teachers; the preparation César Franck received at the Liège Conservatory; and Louis Vierne's student years at the *Institution nationale des jeunes aveugles.*

Once admitted to the Conservatory, the student was evaluated by semester examinations and annual competitions. Only the more able students were eligible for the competitions. They competed for first prize, second prize, first *accessit* (third category, runner-up), second *accessit,* and in some competitions third *accessit.* Performance was measured (at least theoretically) on the basis of Conservatory standards. Thus in some years a first prize in organ might be shared by two students, while in others it might not be awarded at all. The implications of "first prize" were more important than any other material award the student might receive, for it signified that the course had been completed. Those who received a lower rating often remained in the class and competed again the next year. Various other music schools and conservatories in France and Belgium followed the lead of the Paris Conservatory in using annual competitions as a part of the student evaluation system.

Gifted students often managed to collect bouquets of prizes by the time they had completed their studies at the Paris Conservatory. The career of Théodore Dubois, a model of steady, methodical advancement, was anticipated by his school record. He entered the Conservatory in 1854, at seventeen, and made an orderly march toward the coveted composition prize, the Prix de Rome. In 1855 he was awarded first *accessit* in harmony and accompaniment; in 1856, first prize in harmony and accompaniment and third *accessit* in piano; in 1857, first prize in counterpoint and fugue, first *accessit* in organ, and second *accessit* in piano; in 1858, second prize in organ; in 1859, first prize in organ and second in the Prix de Rome competition; and, finally, in 1861, first in the Prix de Rome competition.

There is no convincing evidence that the Paris Conservatory had an organ at the beginning of the nineteenth century. Parts of an old organ are mentioned in a document of 1812, but whether it was ever installed in, or used by, the Conservatory is not clear [82, nos.58–59, pp.56–57]. Although organ was not a part of the Conservatory curriculum between

1802 and 1819, steps were being taken to remedy this situation by 1812. In that year Gabriel-Joseph Grenié signed a contract to build an organ for the Conservatory. It was to contain the following resources:

Manual I (54 notes, C–f³): Montre 8', Bourdon 8', Prestant 4'
Manual II (expressive): five sets of free reeds
Pedal (20 notes, C–g): Bourdon 16', Flûte ouvert 8'

[82, no.60, p.73.]

Work on the organ progressed slowly and with interruptions. It was completed in 1818, and the organ class was opened the next year. Dufourcq has suggested that the finished organ may have included some additions to the original specification: a Flûte 8' on Manual I, and some "expressif" reed stops in the pedal [82, no.60, pp.73–76].

Grenié's organ was finally replaced in 1871. In that year Cavaillé-Coll used part of an old organ by Erard in constructing a "new" study organ. The original organ was a three-manual instrument installed by Pierre Erard in the chapel of the Tuileries in 1855.[5] About half of it was used in the study organ, and the rest was installed in the Conservatory concert hall [82, no.62, pp.16–18].

Vierne described the study organ as "a wretched cuckoo of an organ," and listed its specification:

I. (*Grand-orgue*, 54 notes): Bourdon 8', Flûte 8', Dessus de Montre 8', Prestant 4', Trompette 8'
II. (*Récit*, 54 notes): Flûte 8', Gambe 8', Voix céleste 8', Flûte 4', Hautbois 8' (free reeds), Trompette 8'
Pedal: Soubasse 16', Flûte 8', Flûte 4', Basson 8'.

The entire organ was enclosed in a swell box controlled by a hitch-down pedal with two notches. There were three couplers (II—I, I—Pedal, II—Pedal), and three reversible movements (Manual I Trompette, Manual II Trompette, Pedal Basson). Vierne noted that the Montre and Prestant were worthless [325, pp.21–22].

Alexandre Cellier (1883–1968) later provided some amendments to Vierne's specification. Instead of the Gambe in Manual II, Cellier listed a Diapason 8'. The Hautbois, he said, was "certainly not" a free-reed stop. He further observed that a Plein-Jeu was later added to Manual I under Guilmant's direction. Cellier recalled that the last time this organ was used for the annual competition was the year he was awarded first prize: 1908 [51].

Provision was made for an organ teacher in the original plans of the Conservatory. In the fall of 1795 30 new professors were employed, among them Nicolas Séjan. He was designated professor of the first rank, with a salary of 2,500 francs, effective November 22, 1795 [249, pp.128–29]. Then age 50, Séjan was perhaps the most respected organist in Paris at the time of his appointment. Before the Revolution he had held such distinguished posts as organist at Notre-Dame, Saint-Sulpice, and the Royal Chapel. At another time in history he might have attracted a large class of young organists. In 1795, with churches closed, church music at a standstill, organs in shambles, and a dismal outlook for future careers, the organ profession had little to offer the student musician.

Information about Séjan's work at the Conservatory is sketchy. Lists of professors and courses indicate that Séjan was teaching piano in the years 1796–99, organ in 1800, and solfège in 1801 [249, pp.408–12]. One can conjecture that there were probably neither organ students nor organ at the Conservatory in the early years. Perhaps an organ had been acquired by 1800, and an attempt was made to launch an organ class. Lacking response, Séjan filled in the next year as a solfège teacher. But time was not on his side. In 1802 he was one of 35 professors whose services were terminated as an economy measure [249, p.159]. Apparently there was no effort on the part of the Conservatory administration to reintroduce organ into the curriculum for many years.

In 1817 the Conservatory administration stated that the person filling the post of organ professor should be "an excellent pianist, organist, good harmonist, and good composer" [excellent Pianiste, Organiste, Bon Harmoniste et bon Compositeur; cited in 82, no.61, p.115]. At that time Jean-Louis Adam (1758–1848) was proposed as a candidate. He had been a professor of piano at the Conservatory since 1797, was the author of a well-known piano method, and seemed to satisfy all the requirements for the position.

Ultimately, however, it was François Benoist who was selected. He remained professor of organ for 53 years. By the time he retired in 1872 it was quipped that "three republics and two empires had lived and died under him" [66, p.76]. The generations of students who were in his class included many who made their reputations as composers or pianists, as well as organists. Among the best known were Camille Saint-Saëns, Georges Bizet, Léo Delibes, Jules Massenet, Charles-Valentin Alkan, Félix Danjou, Louis-James-Alfred Lefébure-Wély, Théodore Dubois, and César Franck.

Benoist himself had entered the Conservatory in 1811 and had won a first prize for harmony the same year. Three years later he was awarded first prize for piano, and in 1815 the Prix de Rome. In 1819 he was appointed organist of the Royal Chapel as well as professor of organ at the Conservatory. In 1840 he added *premier chef de chant* at the Opéra to his list of positions.

Benoist was probably not overwhelmed with students in the first years, but a list of organ class applicants from 1819 includes names and qualifications of five boys and five girls ranging in age from twelve-and-a-half to 22. After that initial surge, applicants from 1820 to 1822 totaled six (three boys, three girls). At least one young woman from the initial group persevered. Geneviève-Louise Rousseau, who enrolled in 1819 at age twelve-and-a-half, carried off the second prize in organ in 1826, and (at age twenty) first prize in 1827 [19, no.66, pp.12–13].

The records are more complete beginning in 1843, showing that the size of Benoist's organ class ranged from seven to fifteen until 1863, hovering normally around ten or eleven. In 1863 it suddenly dropped to six, and during the last decade of Benoist's professorship the enrollment stayed between six and nine [AN AJ^{37}, 261–83]. If participation of organ students in the annual competition is an indication, Benoist had an uphill climb pulling his class up to Conservatory standards. Between 1819 and 1832 he had students qualified to compete in only three years: 1825, 1826, and 1827. In 1826 22-year-old Alexandre Fessy had the distinction of being the first organ student to receive a first prize. From 1833 through the rest of the century the organ class was always represented in the competitions. The number of organ students competing rose gradually to highs of ten in 1857 and nine in 1858, and then fluctuated between two and seven for the rest of the century [249, pp.882–84].

It is important to understand the nature of the annual competition because it influenced course content significantly and reflected the official objectives of the course. The success or failure of students in the competition was a matter of serious concern, related to the prestige of professor and course, as well as the success of competitors.

Details of the earliest organ competitions are not defined in available documents, but from 1834 the requirements are clearly specified in Conservatory records.[6] In that year competitors improvised a four-part accompaniment to a chant melody selected by the jury and improvised a fugue in four parts on a subject given by the jury.[7] Those were still the requirements in 1841, when César Franck won second prize in organ. Vallas tells us that one of the judges, Pastou, wrote these notes for his own use: "M. Franck, eighteen years six months; chorale—bass fair, upper parts excellent; fugue—some good points at the beginning, but often poor in the working-out" [cited in 314, p.32]. The themes given to competitors that year are preserved in the Archives nationales [AN AJ^{37}, 200]. The chant to be harmonized is shown in Example 1; and the fugue subject (by Cherubini) appears in the original document with its tonal answer aligned to illustrate a close stretto, as shown in Example 2.[8]

In 1843 a third test was added. In addition to the chant accompaniment and fugue improvisation, competitors were required to improvise a free piece on a given theme. The chant accompaniment requirement was modified in 1851, with a stipulation that the chant be placed successively in the bass and soprano. An important change occurred in 1852 with the addition of a fourth requirement: the memorized performance of a fugue with pedal. For the first time composed repertoire was given official recognition at the Conservatory as a significant element in the organist's education. Through the rest of Benoist's tenure there were only minor modifications to the competition requirements. In 1867 the given theme for the free improvisation was described as a "modern" subject and the memorized fugue was to be one by Bach, chosen by the student with the professor's approval. The following year each student was required to play a different fugue, chosen by the professor.

The semester examinations for the organ class had the same general require-

Example 1

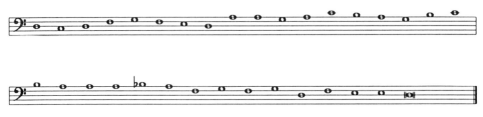

Example 2

ments as the competitions, but students in the earlier stages of study were not expected to participate in all the tests. For example, a first-year student might play only a chant accompaniment, leaving the improvised fugue until he was more advanced. When performance of a memorized fugue with pedal was added to the competition requirements, the semester examinations also included performance of a fugue, but less-advanced students might be assigned a manual fugue from the Bach *Das wohltemperirte Clavier* instead of an organ fugue with pedal.[9] Benoist's report on the June 1852 semester examination shows that for the assigned pieces five of his students played Bach fugues with pedal and three played manual fugues from *Das wohltemperirte Clavier* [AN AJ[37], 271].

Although the official realm of music education was sometimes slow to change, it was not altogether insensitive to contemporary trends and viewpoints. The addition of a memorized fugue to the competition tests in 1852 was perhaps as much a reaction as it was an innovation. Benoist was no doubt aware that performance of composed music was already a requirement in the organ competitions at the Brussels Conservatory, where Jacques Lemmens was professor of organ. Lemmens had made his first visits to Paris in 1850, impressing those who heard him with his performances of composed repertoire, particularly the music of Bach. Lemmens's method of organ playing had been published in periodical form by 1852, and Benoist had been sent copies of at least two issues [80, no.76, pp.88–89].

The great attention given to improvisation in the Conservatory organ class may seem strange today. During the first half of the nineteenth century, when French organists improvised most of the music they played, this emphasis was to be expected. During the second half of the century, as interest in composed repertoire expanded, the required Bach fugues for examinations and competitions were token glances in a new direction, but the main emphasis was still improvisation.

The position that the organ class held in the Conservatory curriculum is the basis of the official view. An 1848 commission on modifications to Conservatory organization defined seven categories of music instruction; piano and harp constituted one, and organ shared a different category with composition and harmony.[10] As the commission report explained: "The study of this instrument [organ], intended principally for improvisation, is essentially connected with those of harmony and composition, indispensable for the organist." [L'étude de cet instrument, destiné principalement à l'improvisation, se rattache essentiellement à celles de l'harmonie et de la composition, indispensables à l'organiste; 249, p.358.] Thus, in the general rules of the Conservatory dated November 22, 1850 [249, p.256], organ was linked with composition and harmony, and there it remained for the rest of the century.[11]

The organ class and its competition were reviewed from time to time in the music periodicals. In some (or perhaps all) earlier years the organ competitions were open to the public, but from 1835 through the rest of the century they were closed. This restriction and the relevance of the course were prime targets for journalists. The Escudier brothers, publishers of *La France musicale,* hit both targets in their detailed review of the 1843 competitions. After objecting that competitions for organ, double bass and trombone were closed, they continued:

> As to the organ, we will particularly insist that the competition be public. According to information that we have reason to believe very exact, here is how one proceeds in the closed competition. First one examines the written lessons of the students, which enters fully into the category of the harmony competition; then the students accompany a plainchant on the organ and improvise a fugue on a given subject. Does anyone imagine that a person who fills these three conditions is or might be an organist? Not in the least; he has the first elements, indispensable elements indeed, but with that he might very well have none of the qualities that constitute a good organist. He can lack imagination, style, taste, make a fugue very properly, accompany plainchant correctly but be incapable of playing a piece in a village. Let us say then for the instruction of the Conservatory gentlemen, who appear to be completely ignorant of it, that in the Catholic rite each office includes twelve to fifteen pieces for the organist; of this number, there are three or four in plainchant, and it is customary to perform

one fugue. One sees that the majority of the pieces to be played arise entirely
from the improviser's imagination. Well! It is the only thing one doesn't teach
them to exercise at the Conservatory! Isn't it a mockery? And should M. Benoit
[sic], the organ professor, of whom we nevertheless recognize all the ability, be
astonished if he never has more than three or four students in a class where only
half of what one comes there to learn is taught. . . ?

Quant à l'orgue, nous insisterons particulièrement pour que ce concours ait lieu en
public. D'après des renseignemens [sic] que nous avons lieu de croire très exacts,
voici comme l'on procède dans le concours à huis-clos. On examine d'abord les
leçons écrites des élèves; ce qui rentre tout-à-fait dans la catégorie du concours
d'harmonie, puis les élèves accompagnent sur l'orgue un plain-chant, et im-
provisent une fugue sur un sujet donné. S'imagine-t-on que celui qui aura rempli
ces trois conditions soit ou puisse être organiste? Pas le moins du monde: il a les
premiers élémens, élémens [sic] indispensables à la vérité, mais il peut fort bien
n'avoir avec cela aucune des qualités qui constituent le bon organiste; il peut
manquer d'imagination, de style, de goût, faire très proprement la fugue, accompagner correctement le plain-chant et être incapable de jouer un morceau dans un
village. Disons donc, pour l'instruction de Messieurs du Conservatoire, qui parais-
sent l'ignorer complètement, que, dans le rite catholique, chaque office comporte,
pour l'organiste, de douze à quinze morceaux; sur ce nombre, il y en a trois ou
quatre en plain-chant, et il est d'usage d'y faire entendre une fugue: on voit que la
majorité des pièces à jouer appartient entièrement à l'imagination de l'improvisateur. Eh bien! c'est la seule chose qu'on ne leur apprenne pas à exercer au
Conservatoire! n'est-ce pas une dérision? et M. Benoit [sic], le professeur d'orgue,
dont au reste nous reconnaissons toute la capacité, doit-il s'étonner s'il ne compte
jamais plus de trois ou quatre élèves dans une classe où l'on n'enseigne que la
moitié de ce qu'on y vient apprendre. . . ? [FM 6, p.261.]

Steps had just been taken to remedy a major deficiency noted in the report. If
the reviewers had been permitted to attend the organ competition in 1843 they
would have found that improvising a free piece was now one of the requirements. Further investigation would have revealed that there were actually eight
students in the organ class that year, two of whom participated in the competition. First prize was not awarded; second prize went to Renaud de Vilbac [249,
pp.581, 883; AN AJ^{37}, 262].

Questions about the relevance of the organ class continued to appear. In
1845 Félix Danjou complained: "One sees again that this part of the official
teaching remains almost sterile, in spite of the vast talent of the professor who
directs it, because it lacks practical application, and moreover, because it is lost
in the middle of a school intended first of all for providing people for the
theater." [On voit une fois de plus que, malgré l'immense talent du professeur
qui la dirige, cette partie de l'enseignement officiel demeure à peu près stérile,
parce qu'elle manque d'application pratique, et qu'elle est d'ailleurs perdue au
milieu d'une école destinée avant tout à fournir des sujets au théâtre; RMR 1,
pp.300–301.]

A decade later the question of relevance was raised by Georges Schmitt, who said that the first prize winners were often incapable of playing a church service. He was also disturbed that the course did not include anything about organ construction [289, p.85].

In his 1863 review of the competitions Oscar Comettant objected vehemently to the practice of closing some events to the public. Open competitions, he said, guaranteed impartial judgments and at the same time provided students with a strong competitive incentive: "I understand very well that one judges scandalous law suits privately; but I can't at all account for the regulation of private sessions when it is a question of harmony, solfège, fugue, organ, keyboard and double bass study, which have nothing contrary to good morals, at least to my knowledge." [Je comprends très-bien qu'on juge à huis clos les procès scandaleux; mais je ne m'explique pas du tout l'ordonnance du huis clos lorsqu'il s'agit de l'harmonie, du solfège, de la fugue, de l'orgue, de l'étude du clavier et de la contrebasse, qui n'ont rien de contraire aux bonnes moeurs, du moins à ma connaissance; ME 30, p.273.] In 1869 Comettant repeated his complaint about the closed competitions, implying further that the students could not learn anything about registration on the terrible old organ they had to play at the Conservatory [58, pp.131–32]. Questioning the course content and the competitions was as close as critics came to the professor. Benoist himself was treated with respect by the musical press.

At semester examination time teachers wrote brief reports on the progress each student in the class had made during the semester. Benoist's reports were often a brief "not bad," or "progresses very well," or "is not progressing." A few students received special notice as "conscientious artist" or "distinguished improviser." The modern frustrated teacher can relate to Benoist's comment: "I rarely see him," and after the next student's name, "like the preceding," or when he notes "This student doesn't know anything; what he needs is a harmony class and not mine" [AN AJ^{37}, 261–82]. But Benoist recognized an outstanding talent when it came his way. In June 1850 he characterized Saint-Saëns as "a born improviser—gifted with the most fortunate nature. From an early age he was nurtured by the study of the great masters" [né improvisateur—doné de l'organisation la plus heureuse. Il s'est nourri de bonne heure de l'étude des grands maîtres; AN AJ^{37}, 269, p.65].

Saint-Saëns entered Benoist's organ class in 1848, won second prize in 1849, and won a first in 1851. He later recorded his respect for Benoist's musicianship:

Benoist was a very ordinary organist, but an admirable teacher. A veritable galaxy of talent came from his class. He had little to say, but as his taste was refined and his judgment sure, nothing he said lacked weight or authority. He collaborated in several ballets for the Opéra and that gave him a good deal of work to do. It sounds incredible, but he used to bring his "work" to class and scribble away on his orchestration while his pupils played the organ. This did not prevent his listening and looking after them. He would leave his work and make appropriate comments as though he had no other thought. [283, p.16.]

In 1866, fifteen years after Saint-Saëns left the organ class, Henri Maréchal (1842–1924) entered it. By then the 72-year-old professor was scarcely going through the motions of teaching. "In reality, it [the organ class] proceeded only by acquired energy and the valor of some remarkable students. . . . The professor intervened only very rarely, and when one questioned him on a difficult case, he would scarcely interrupt reading his newspaper to answer: 'Listen to what the others do!' " [En réalité, elle ne marchait que par la force acquise et par la valeur des remarquables élèves. . . . Le maître n'y intervenait que bien rarement; et lorsqu'on le questionnait sur un cas difficile, c'est à peine s'il interrompait la lecture de son journal pour répondre: «Ecoutez ce que font les autres!» 217, p.162.]

Maréchal assures us that the situation had not always been thus, and that Benoist was regarded at the Conservatory with "a kind of veneration that was merited by his talent as well as the *pléiade* of brilliant students he had shaped" [une sorte de vénération que lui méritaient son talent comme aussi la pléiade de brillants élèves qu'il avait formés; 217, p.148].

Occasionally the students played little pranks. Knowing Benoist had an "almost exclusive" admiration for Haydn, they might harmonize a theme of Haydn in the style of Schumann. "Then he would abandon his paper a moment and, coming to sit on the organ bench, he would reestablish the harmony of the composer with the tips of his thin fingers, saying with a vague smile: 'That is what Haydn wrote.' Of course, we all knew it!" [Alors il abandonnait un moment son journal et, venant s'asseoir sur le banc d'orgue, du bout de ses doigts amaigris il rétablissait l'harmonie de l'auteur, disant avec un vague sourire: «Voila ce qu'a écrit Haydn.» Bien entendu, nous le savions tous! 217, p.163.]

Other times they would say or do something that would prompt Benoist to repeat one of several stories about musicians that they had heard him tell countless times before. Maréchal affirms, though, that they had great respect for their teacher and that their jokes had not the slightest malicious intent. He gives us a rare description of Benoist: "He was a little old man, spruce, well-groomed, with a completely shaved face, hiding blue eyes with a dull gaze behind his glasses. For forty-five years he had met his class three times a week; and that long practice, added to a rather quiet nature, had ended in a scarcely conscious state of indifference." [C'était un petit vieillard propret, soigné, de visage complètement rasé, cachant derrière ses lunettes des yeux bleus au regard éteint. Depuis quarante-cinq ans il faisait sa classe trois fois par se-maine; et cette longue pratique, s'additionnant à une nature plutôt tranquille, avait abouti à un état d'indifférence à peine conscient; 217, p.147.]

César Franck succeeded Benoist as professor of organ on February 1, 1872. The organ world had changed greatly in the three decades since his own student days. The idea of the organ as a concert instrument was taking form, along with a growing interest in composed repertoire. By 1872 one could hear a new breed of organist in some Paris churches: Widor at Saint-Sulpice or Guilmant at La Trinité. One could also hear the older generation of master improvisers from Benoist's class: Saint-Saëns at La Madeleine or Franck himself at Sainte-Clotilde.

During the eighteen years that Franck was professor of organ at the Conservatory, there was only one change in the annual competition tests, but it was a significant one: instead of a fugue by Bach, the student was required to play "a classic piece" by memory [AN AJ^{37}, 251]. This change occurred in 1872, the first year Franck was a professor, and he may have been responsible for initiating it. The other competition tests remained the same: accompaniment of a chant melody in the soprano and bass, an improvised fugue on a given subject, and an improvised free piece on a given theme.

Works of Bach continued to hold a prominent place in the lists of pieces Franck's students played for examinations and competitions, but they now included preludes, toccatas, organ chorales, and other forms, in addition to fugues. One also finds the names of nineteenth-century composers represented for the first time. With a few exceptions organ examination and competition pieces were listed in the Conservatory records during Franck's tenure. They included the following works of Bach:

Preludes, toccatas, fantasies, passacaglia, fugues, performed either as separate movements or as pairs: 46 different works; 152 performances.
Concertos in G major and A minor: fourteen performances of one or more movements.
Sonata I: one performance.
Organ chorales: two works performed three times each.
Harpsichord works (some, or perhaps all, selected from *Das wohltemperirte Clavier*): twelve works, fifteen performances.
Some dozen performances that are not clearly identified.
Five of the so-called little preludes and fugues then attributed to Bach were given eleven performances, separately or paired.

Other composers represented in examination or competition performances were: Mendelssohn, 30 performances of sonata movements; Franck, 22 performances of various works; Lemmens, single performances of three pieces; Handel, Concerto in B-flat, one performance; and Schumann, Canon in A-flat, one performance [AN AJ^{37}, 251–52, 283–92].

In spite of a growing interest in repertoire, most (sometimes all) music an organist performed in church was still improvised, and improvisation was still regarded as the organist's most essential tool. Throughout Franck's tenure at the Conservatory, improvisation remained the primary thrust of his teaching.

This emphasis, as we have seen, was in line with the official Conservatory view of organ instruction, the examination and competition tests, his own student experiences, and doubtless his own pedagogical viewpoint. Accounts of his organ class confirm that most of the six hours a week of class time was devoted to problems of improvisation, and that little time was spent on performance problems. Franck expected a student entering the class to have sufficient technique and experience to prepare the pieces required for the examinations. As Louis Vierne commented:

> Considering the rare lessons devoted to performance, we were in clover, we blind, who in our school [*Institution nationale des jeunes aveugles*] had committed to memory a great amount of organ music. The others necessarily had a very limited repertoire. In the course of the year they scarcely prepared more than the pieces intended for the examinations in January, in June and for the competition. There was no need to worry about manipulation; Franck drew the stops, worked the pedal combinations, managed the swell-box. Everything was simplified, reduced merely to the playing on the keyboards and the observance of style. All of which explains why, except for Dallier, Marty, Mahaut and Letocart, none of the first-prize winners of Franck's class ever had any fame as an instrumental virtuoso. [324, vol.29, no.11, p.12.]

Nevertheless, the place of repertoire should not be entirely discounted. In addition to the pieces he or she prepared for the examinations, each student was at least exposed to the repertoire of other members of the class.

As far as improvisation was concerned, Franck repeatedly urged students to explore new, unexpected ways of treating a theme or expanding a form. He encouraged them to venture off the beaten path and take some risks with their harmonic movement and key relationships. No wonder his organ class attracted young composers and worried their composition teachers!

Albert Mahaut, who entered Franck's organ class in 1888, recalled that "when we would improvise, Franck gave himself completely; his abundant spirit poured out into ours. 'I like it,' he simply said in good passages, 'I like it.' Often he said only that, but he spoke these words with such a variety of inflections that it was sufficient to have us understand his thought and to give life to ours, in order to raise our sights and compel us to take leave of our sorry limitations" [213].

Henri Busser, who joined the class in 1889, added that when a student floundered in his improvisation, Franck would push him back from the keyboard, "and then, under his fingers, all would become clear, marvellous, it was a true enchantment that aroused our enthusiasm" [et alors, sous ses doigts, tout devenait clair, merveilleux, c'était un véritable enchantement qui éveillait notre enthousiasme; 39, p.33].

Louis Vierne concurred that in improvisation, as in composition, Franck's teaching was "truly miraculous" [324, vol.29, no.11, p.12]. His *Memoirs* provide a detailed account of the nature of the plainchant accompaniment and the two forms prescribed for examinations as they were treated by Franck:

> Existing since the foundation of the class in organ, it [the plainchant accompaniment test] consisted in the note-for-note accompaniment of a liturgical chant in the upper part; then the chant became the bass in whole notes, not transposed, accompanied by three upper parts in a sort of classical florid counterpoint; the whole notes then passed into the top part, transposed a fourth higher, and received in their turn the classical florid accompaniment. Nothing was closer to formula than this counterpoint, strict without being exactly so, crammed with retarded fifths, with seventh chords prolonged with the fifth, with sequences—in a word, with all that is forbidden in written counterpoint. It was the "tradition," and Franck could not change it. . . .
>
> The examination program made it necessary for Franck to limit his field to the cultivation of two narrow forms—the classical fugue and the free improvisation on a single theme. Not one of the members of the jury would have tolerated a fugal entry in a distant key; not one would have accepted in the free test an exposition of a second theme in the dominant. So in this straitjacket we had to evolve, and the difficulty, far from disheartening our *maître*, excited his imaginative faculties to give themselves full play in the care of the details. In fugue he was particularly interested in the construction of the episodes, in which he combined, as far as possible, the progression of an ingenious tonal plan with the elegant writing of a counterpoint with imitations in closer and closer stretto. Every now and then he would sit down at the keyboard and give us an example. And what an example! While we poor victims had difficulty working out one correct counter-subject, he, in the same time, had found five or six: "See, you can do this . . . or else this . . . or again. . . ." Then, in the most natural tone: "Come now, choose one and make me a good fugue!" I leave you to imagine the confusion of the student who often—very often—made a lamentable mess of it. Then finally one would manage to get out of it somehow.
>
> For the free subject he found a way of stretching the strict form, either by subtly introducing a new element at the moment of transition to the dominant, an element which could serve later in the development, or by the intensive cultivation in the development of a new theme suggested by a fragment of the given theme. Then there were inversion, cultivated vigorously, and change of rhythm; or an obstinate pattern used with a definite intention and taken from a fragment of the theme; or variety and subtlety of harmonization, etc., etc. All of them were artifices which the *maître* could handle with disconcerting ease. He used few material effects of registration, nor were they really possible on our miserable class instrument. The music itself had to supply everything.[12] [324, vol.29, no.11, p.12.]

The organ class was small during Franck's first years as professor. Beginning with six enrollees in the spring of 1872 (one of whom dropped out), it fell to only four in 1878 and again in 1881. In 1885 the enrollment was only five, but the next year it suddenly jumped to fourteen. One wonders what kind of recruiting methods Franck used to attract eleven new organ students to join his three returning students! Enrollment then ranged from nine to thirteen through 1890. In all, the names of 67 students appear in the records of the organ class during Franck's tenure (see the list of Franck's students in the Appendix).

Franck's reports on his students' work tended to be more detailed than Benoist's. Franck often commented on the degree of talent, application, and accuracy and the areas of particular difficulty. His criticisms were stated in an objective manner, and he did not hesitate to note that Rousseau did not work enough (January 1873), or that Chapuis needed to work more regularly (June 1879), or that Lapuchin was industrious and interesting, but not talented (June 1879), or that Pierné in his first year of organ study (June 1881) was still a little too much of a pianist and not enough of an organist. But in 1882 he could write that Pierné was a student such as one has too rarely: gifted and industrious. Franck had mixed feelings about Bachelet, commenting that he was a very gifted student but as "inexact" as possible (January 1887). When Franck was particularly pleased with a student's work he might write "perfect student." In June 1889 a record three students were given that high praise: Bondon, Mlle Prestat, and Mahaut [AN AJ^{37}, 283–92].

During each year of Franck's professorship, between two and seven students participated in the competition. The results were sometimes discouraging. In the first ten competitions (beginning in 1872), first prize in organ was awarded only four times, and second prize only five times. In two of those years the highest rank awarded was first *accessit* [249, pp.883–84].

In a letter of August 1876, Franck voiced concern. His class had been exceptionally good that year, with seven taking part in the competition.

> I am finding, however, that my pupils are treated with an unusual severity, and I have the feeling that there is a certain opposition against me among the members of the panel, which makes me rather sad since I am quite certain that it comes from people whom I had thought to be my friends. Despite all that, my little group carried off one second prize by unanimous vote (Samuel Rousseau), one *proxime accessit,* also unanimous, and two honourable mentions. These last three awards were all won by girls [Mlles Renaud, Genty, and Papot]. [Cited in 314, p.158.]

If Franck was frustrated by the treatment of his students, he had equal reason to be upset about his own position. Twice he was passed over when there were vacancies in composition [314, pp.259–60]. A position as composition professor would have suited him better in regard to subject matter and would have given him a substantial salary increase and a lighter schedule.

Although Franck may not have been neglected by the official music establishment to the extent some accounts would lead us to believe, he obviously faced some career problems. There were complaints that he was making a composition class out of the organ class [314, pp.256–58]. Actually, the threat he posed to the composition classes lay not only in the organ class (which was simply fulfilling its mission as a branch of composition, in accordance with its official classification in the Conservatory curriculum) but in the fact that he was teaching composition privately, in direct competition with the Conservatory. Such a talented student as Guy Ropartz forfeited the possibility of winning the Prix de Rome because he chose to study composition with Franck rather than at the Conservatory.

Charles Tournemire said that a large number of auditors, "fugitives from harmony, fugue and composition classes," secretly flowed into the organ class at the Conservatory. The private sessions at Franck's home, he said, involved some thirty auditors as well as eight participating students. There is no doubt that Franck's teaching was of a different order than the "fugitives" experienced in some Conservatory classes. For Tournemire it was instruction that gleamed "like the north rose window of the Cathedral of Paris," and the classes were "winged 'lessons,' freed from the heavy chains of formulas" [comme la rosace septentrionale de la Cathédrale de Paris. . . . «leçons» ailées, libérées des lourdes chaînes des formules . . . ; 313, p.141]. Franck had a remarkable rapport with his students. Accounts of his kindness, generosity, and concern for his students abound, and they were not slow to appreciate his great spirit.

John Hinton studied privately with Franck in 1865, 1867, and was an auditor in the organ class in 1873. He found that "Franck's success with his pupils was largely due to his power of eliciting from them earnest and *well digested* work." Hinton quoted some advice Franck often gave his students:

"Don't try to do a great deal, but rather seek to do *well*"; "no matter if only a little can be produced"; "bring me the results of *many* trials, which you can honestly say represent the very best you can do"; "don't think that you will learn from my correction of faults *of which you are aware,* unless you have strained every effort yourself to amend them." [159, p.8.]

Vierne wrote:

What hours! What memories! To recall them all would require an entire volume, and, besides, it would be futile, for no words could give any idea of the sensations felt, of the moods aroused by that apostle's word, by those inspired examples intended not only to make us technicians, but to breathe into us an ardent love of our art. I experienced them forty-five years ago, and they seem like yesterday! [324, vol.29, no.11, pp.12–13.]

But Franck could also be stern, and occasionally the class witnessed a stormy side of his character. Henri Busser recalled that Franck was impatient and "sometimes a little brutal" in dealing with students who were clumsy or untalented [cited in 160, p.35].

Some of Franck's better-known organ students were Auguste Chapuis, Henri Dallier, Vincent d'Indy, Albert Mahaut, Adolphe Marty, and Gabriel

Pierné. Among the students Franck inherited from Benoist were Paul Wachs, Louis Benoît (1847–?), and Samuel Rousseau (1853–1904). Charles Tournemire, Henri Libert, Henri Busser, and Louis Vierne were among those who studied with both Franck and Widor.[13]

XV.
The Brussels Conservatory
Organ Class
Fétis to Mailly

IN THE early nineteenth century music teachers in Belgium faced problems similar to those in France. The church music schools had been closed and the choirs disbanded. Only gradually did avenues of music instruction begin to reappear. Private lessons and music classes in a few private schools were for a time the only choices available for the music student. Then a few music schools were opened, some of which were really only slightly expanded private studios.

In 1813 one such small music school was opened by Jean-Baptiste Roucourt (1780–1849) in Brussels. Unlike most, this little school succeeded, probably far beyond Roucourt's wildest dreams; it was the seed from which the Brussels Conservatory developed. Named *Ecole de chant et d'art dramatique,* it began modestly with only two teachers: Roucourt for voice and Van Helmont for solfège. Its original objective was to train students for the lyric theater [251, p.180].

The school survived the fall of the French empire and into the subsequent United Netherlands period. In 1826 it was subsidized by the Dutch king and authorized to bear the title *Ecole royale de musique.* The school had gradually enlarged its staff and curriculum, and in 1827 it offered eleven classes in music and one in elocution. The music classes included harmony and composition, voice, piano, solfège, and classes for various orchestral instruments, but not for organ [251, p.181].

As a result of Belgium's war for independence in 1830, the school lost its subsidy and was closed. When it was reopened in October 1831 it was in poor condition, lacking facilities, equipment, and direction [285, p.1]. But help was on the way. A decree of February 13, 1832 gave it government support and the title *Conservatoire royal de musique.* This is the school known to many musicians as the Brussels Conservatory.

In April 1833 François-Joseph Fétis was named to the multiple role of director of the Conservatoire royal, professor of composition and harmony, and the king's *maître de chapelle* [329, pp.24–25]. He resigned his post at the Paris Conservatory and moved to Brussels in the summer of 1833.

In addition to his administrative and teaching responsibilities at the Brussels

François-Joseph Fétis (Bibliothèque Nationale, Paris).

Conservatory, Fétis was to direct court concerts, conduct the court orchestra, supervise the music of the Royal Chapel, compose music as required, and act as the king's representative in matters pertaining to music at the Brussels royal theater [16, p.131]. Some of these responsibilities were in name only. In December 1833 Fétis proposed a plan for a royal music establishment with a small permanent orchestra, a choir, and several soloists. The royal treasury was not equal to such an expense, so musicians were employed only as needed, for specific occasions [16, pp.132–33].

Concerts were given at the court from time to time, with Fétis determining the program, organizing the orchestra and choir, choosing the soloists, supervising the rehearsals, and directing the concerts. He and the other musicians who performed for invited court audiences also appeared on the public concerts given by the Conservatory. The Conservatory orchestra played for both types of concert.

Fétis's influence on musical life in Brussels in particular and Belgium in general extended in many directions. In a country just emerging from successive political and military upheavals, much of its musical future depended on his leadership, determination, and energy. Adolphe Samuel (1824–1898), director of the Ghent Conservatory from 1871, affirmed that Fétis greatly affected the destiny of music in Belgium, particularly in the beginning. There was, he said, scarcely anything to be reformed: all had to be created [286, p.124]. Fétis remained in his positions in Brussels the rest of his life. When he died in 1871 his successor as director of the Brussels Conservatory was François-Auguste Gevaert (1828–1908).

The appointment of Fétis as director of the Brussels Conservatory was the first of a chain of events from which the "French Romantic" organ performance style ultimately developed, with its profound influence on organ repertoire and compositional style. Fétis had a many-faceted career as critic, editor, historian, and educator. He was professor of composition at the Paris Conservatory from 1821 to 1833 and librarian of the Conservatory from 1826 to 1830. He founded the *Revue musicale* in 1827 and was almost solely responsible for its contents during its first six years. His eight-volume *Biographie universelle des musiciens,* first published in 1835–44, with a new edition in 1860–65, was a monumental achievement. Fétis was one of the first to affirm that music does not progress: it only changes. Thus he believed that early music still held artistic as well as historic interest for his own time, and he organized early music concerts to prove this theory.

No one ever had to tell Fétis to "think big." He characteristically viewed individual aspects of music in their larger context, and he sketched projects of vast scope. It is not surprising that some remained imperfect or incomplete, but that so much could be achieved in one lifetime. Fétis viewed his roles as director of the Conservatory and *maître de chapelle* to the king in the broadest terms. He believed that his job was not merely to educate the students at the school and organize music for the court but to tend to the musical education and musical standards of all Belgium. To this end he wrote articles and method books, taught extra courses, organized concerts for the public (as well as for the court), and actively participated in cultural organizations, in addition to his official administrative and classroom responsibilities.

The state of church music in Belgium was of particular concern to Fétis. As in France, the *maîtrises* that had formerly educated church musicians had been closed, and by the 1830s churches in Belgium were badly in need of well-trained organists and singers and of adequate instruments.

Fétis's interest in the organ has been overshadowed by his activities in other areas, yet it can be traced through most of his career. François-Joseph Fétis came from a musical family of Mons. His grandfather Simon-Joseph was an organist and organ builder; and his father, Antoine-Joseph, was an organist, violinist, teacher, and conductor [329, pp.8–9]. When he was seven years old François-Joseph entered a *maîtrise,* where he began the customary education for a choir boy, including instruction in plainchant and keyboard. This phase of his education was interrupted when the ecclesiastical institutions were closed in 1794. He later completed his formal education at the Paris Conservatory.

Meanwhile, the organ had already made a lasting impression on him. As a young boy he had often gone with his father to Sainte-Waudru, the church where his father was organist. Sometimes he was permitted to play little preludes on the organ, and by the time he was nine, he could accompany the service [114, vol.3, p.227; 329, p.10]. Late in his life Fétis recalled how interested he had been in watching his grandfather build or repair organs, and how he had always been moved by the sound of simple and pure harmonies on the soft stops of an organ [329, p. 10].

Fétis was organist at Saint-Pierre, Douai, from December 1813 to the summer of 1818. He frequently referred to the experiments he made there regarding organ style and the theories he formulated. In his autobiography in the *Biographie universelle* he wrote:

> The one [i.e., the organ] he was called to play at Douai was an excellent organ of Dallery, composed of fifty-six stops, four manuals and pedal. That instrument offered him immense resources which he set about studying, often locking himself in the church six or eight hours, in order to become familiar with the works of the great organists, ancient and modern, of Italy and Germany, and in the alternative employment of different styles, to look for a diversity that seemed to him to be lacking in the productions of the most celebrated artists; for each of them was fond of certain forms which he reproduced in all his works. One will see the result of his studies in his work entitled *la Science de l'organiste*, one part of which has been engraved a long time, but which is not yet finished.

> Celui sur lequel il était appelé à se faire entendre à Douai, était un excellent orgue de Dallery, composé de cinquante-six jeux, quatre claviers à la main et un clavier de pédales. Cet instrument lui offrait d'immenses ressources qu'il se mit à étudier, se faisant souvent enfermer dans l'église pendant six ou huit heures, pour se rendre familières les oeuvres des grands organistes, anciens et modernes, de l'Italie et de l'Allemagne, et pour chercher, dans l'emploi alternatif des différents styles, une variété qui lui semblait manquer dans les productions des plus célèbres artistes; car chacun d'eux affectionnait de certaines formes qu'il a reproduites dans tous ses ouvrages. On verra le résultat de ses travaux dans son ouvrage intitulé *la Science de l'organiste*, dont une partie est gravée depuis longtemps, mais qui n'est pas encore terminée. [114, vol.3, p. 230.]

In another publication Fétis elaborated on his experiments at the organ. He felt that Bach had brought the fugal style to the height of its development and that nothing remained to be said in that genre. There was another route, he thought, for the Catholic organist: one that would avoid the vulgarity of thought and poverty of harmony he had heard as a child in the music of Balbastre, Charpentier and Miroir; one that would make an artful use of harmonic combinations, choice of timbre, and the resources of the several manuals to form a noble, religious, moving style [RGM 26, p.187].

Fétis's stylistic experiments had already merited the encouragement of some local musicians when Pierre Baillot (1771–1842), the celebrated violinist, stopped in Douai in 1816 on a concert tour. When he was told about Fétis's organ playing, he asked for a demonstration. "I'll play for you," Fétis an-

swered, "but I'll confess to you first that my performance is far from responding to my thoughts, for I have always had clumsy hands." Fétis took Baillot to
Saint-Pierre and played for him for half an hour. Coming down from the
organ, he found Baillot in tears.

> He took my arm in silence. When we were in the street he said to me: "I have
> never heard anything like what you have just played. I sense that there is the
> true style of the church, a style that is moving and that incites devotion. Why
> don't you work on your performance?" "It is too late," I told him; "I have
> another career to pursue."

> Je jouerai pour vous, lui dis-je; mais je vous avouerai d'abord que mon exécu-
> tion est loin de répondre à ma pensée, car j'ai toujours eu les mains maladroites.
> Je conduisis Baillot à Saint-Pierre, et je jouai pendant une demi-heure. Quand je
> descendis, je trouvais Baillot en larmes. Il prit mon bras en silence. Quand nous
> fûmes dans la rue, il me dit:—*Je n'ai jamais rien entendu comme ce que vous
> venez de jouer. Je sens que c'est là le vrai style de l'église, style touchant et qui
> incite à la dévotion. Pourquoi ne travaillez-vous pas votre exécution?—Il est
> trop tard,* lui dis-je; *j'ai une autre carrière à parcourir.* [RGM 26, p.187.]

Fétis tells us that he returned to Paris in 1818 and did not play the organ after
that.[1] However, he remained convinced that a kind of organ music could be
created without breaking away from the grand Bach style, but modifying it to
the Catholic point of view [RGM 26, p.187].

These reminiscences were occasioned by a performance by Lemmens in
1859 on a new Merklin & Schütze organ in Brussels. Fétis recognized with the
greatest satisfaction that Lemmens expressed the same ideas that he himself
had pursued earlier, "but with a superiority of execution which alone can
realize all that is concealed there of beauty and innovation for the art" [mais
avec une supériorité d'exécution qui seule peut réaliser tout ce qui s'y trouve
renfermé de beautés et de nouveauté pour l'art; RGM 26, p.187]. Clearly Fétis
saw in Lemmens a way to fulfill some of the aspirations that he had neither the
time nor the talent to realize. We will return to the relationship between Fétis's
personal agenda and Lemmens's career. It is not clear how much of the new
style that Fétis was looking for was a matter of compositional materials and
techniques, and how much was a matter of performance style. What did Baillot
hear that seemed so different, so moving?

La Science de l'organiste was one of Fétis's incompleted projects. Stemming
from his experiments at Douai, it was to be a comprehensive method of organ
playing. In the prospectus published in *Revue musicale* [RM 6, pp.357–59] the
work is entitled *Le Parfait Organiste, ou traité complet de l'art de jouer de
l'orgue.* Its four parts were to contain "everything the organist needed to
know" [toutes les connaissances necessaires à l'organiste] about the notation
of plainchant, modes, organ construction and maintenance, playing on the
manuals and pedals, combining the stops, and playing for both Catholic and
Protestant church services. Finally, there was to be an annotated anthology of

pieces representing Italian, German, and French organ literature from the sixteenth century to the early nineteenth, and a catalogue of the best theoretical and practical works related to the organ.

The anthology was engraved but never published. Another part of the work was sent to the publisher, but was lost. A third part was never completed. The anthology alone, containing works virtually unknown in mid-century France and Belgium, would have been a major contribution to organ literature. The extant engraved proof is a 200-page collection of works by Merulo, Frescobaldi, Scheidt, Froberger, Buxtehude, Couperin, Bach, Clérambault, and many of their contemporaries [329, pp.88–89].[2]

When Fétis assumed his post of director of the Brussels Conservatory in 1833, he apparently decided to offer the courses he felt were essential, taking the responsibility himself for those that had no teacher. Thus, his autobiographical entry in the first edition of *Biographie universelle* (1835–44) states that he was teaching courses in composition, organ and plainchant, and vocal ensemble, and that he was directing the studies of the orchestra, the rehearsals, and the concerts, in addition to handling the administration of the Conservatory [114, 1st ed., vol.4, p.113].[3]

In connection with his work as organ professor, Fétis published two collections: *6 Messes faciles pour l'orgue* (Paris: Lemoine [1840]), and *Vêpres et saluts des dimanches ordinaires* (Paris: Canaux [1843]). The preface of the first volume, dated December 31, 1840, states that the Masses it contains were "composed for the organ students of the conservatory placed under my direction" [composées pour les élèves organistes du conservatoire placé sous ma direction]. Fétis deplored the "miserable things" habitually played by organists in small towns and rural locations. "Most of them play dance tunes and theater songs in their versets; their preludes and offertories are opera overtures, which are not even appropriate to the nature of the organ." [La plupart exécutent des airs de danse et des chants de théâtre dans leurs versets; leurs préludes et leurs offertoires sont des ouvertures d'Opéras, qui ne sont pas même appropriées à la nature de l'orgue.] Following the preface there is a description and explanation of the stops found in small organs, some typical specifications, a list of stops used in different types of registration, and a discussion of the accompaniment of plainchant.

Vêpres is a sequel to *Messes* and contains organ music and chant accompaniments for the vesper service. Again, there are instructions for performing the service and registrations for all the pieces. By the time this volume was published, Fétis was no longer teaching organ. In 1842 he had engaged Christian Friedrich Johann Girschner as professor of organ, thus bringing to a close his own nine-year term of organ teaching but not his interest in the organ.

By 1850, Fétis had replaced Girschner with Jacques-Nicolas Lemmens and had turned his attention to organ builders. The Brussels Conservatory needed an organ suitable for the development of a strong department, and the quality of organs throughout Belgium left much to be desired. "The present state of organ building in Belgium, compared to the situation in Germany,

France, and England" [Sur l'Etat actuel de la facture des orgues en Belgique, comparé à la situation en Allemagne, en France et en Angleterre] was the title of a report by Fétis, published in the *Bulletin de l'Académie royale de Belgique* in 1850 [116]. Here Fétis displayed his comprehensive grasp of organ construction, stylistic differences from one country to another, important builders, recent developments, and publications related to organ building. He was fearless in his attack on Belgian organ builders, charging that they had failed to keep pace with the rest of the world, that their instruments were mechanically inferior, and that the materials used were of poor quality. It was an irrecusable fact, he said, that "a great organist would not find in all Belgium an instrument on which he could be heard in a manner to give a fair idea of his talent." [Il est un fait irrécusable, c'est qu'un grand organiste ne trouverait pas dans toute la Belgique un instrument sur lequel il pût se faire entendre de manière à donner une juste idée de son talent; 116, p.319.]

To remedy this situation, Fétis proposed the construction of a large instrument by one of the best foreign builders, for example, Cavaillé-Coll, with the condition that workers from Belgium be employed in the construction. Such an organ, he said, could serve as a permanent model, and the training of the workers would contribute toward a progressive future. Anticipating the objection that such a plan would be bad for the domestic industry, he asserted that one does not owe protection to the unworthy [116, pp.319–20].

In his report Fétis acknowledged that organ playing, as well as organ building, was inferior in Belgium. This condition, however, would soon improve, as the organ class at the Conservatory was under the leadership of Lemmens, a fine young artist who had been instructed in Germany in the art of Pachelbel and Bach. Fétis predicted that Lemmens would completely transform organ playing in Belgium [116, pp.309–10].

In 1856, in a new report on the progress of organ building in Belgium [117], Fétis observed that one builder in Belgium, Joseph Merklin (1819–1905), had taken his earlier criticism to heart and had taken all the necessary steps to equal the standards of the most celebrated European builders. Thereafter Fétis was lavish in his praise of Merklin-Schütze organs. Merklin, a German, had opened his shop in Belgium in 1843. He was joined by his brother-in-law, Friedrich Schütze (1808–1894?), in 1847, and they became partners in 1849. They incorporated in 1853, and two years later they bought the Paris firm of Ducroquet [141, p.451].[4]

A four-manual, 54-stop Merklin-Schütze organ for the Brussels Conservatory was placed in the Palais de la rue Ducale (usually called the Palais Ducal) in two installments. Initially, there were funds available for only two manuals and part of the pedal. This part of the organ was finished and examined in 1861. The other two manuals were not installed until 1866 [119].

The completed organ was ready for inauguration at the same time as the 50th anniversary of the reestablishment of the Belgian *Académie royale des sciences, des lettres et des beaux-arts*. For this combined celebration on May 7, 1866, the 82-year-old Fétis wrote the *Fantaisie symphonique pour orgue et orchestre,* his last major contribution to the organ world. He was very proud of his only large-scale organ piece, and in a letter to the *Revue et Gazette musicale,* dated August 17, 1866, he described it as a work for two different but equal "orchestras." It was, he said, an entirely new type of composition for which he had no models, as the concertos of Handel were really only instrumental solos with a small orchestra. His work, on the other hand, was a contest between two large musical forces. Until now, he said, there was no place to perform such a work, as there was (except in England) no concert hall in Europe with a large organ [RGM 33, pp.268–69].

The three-movement *Fantaisie* was heard from time to time on Brussels Conservatory concerts during the nineteenth century, and in 1876 Mailly played it at the Palace of Industry in Amsterdam. Its first performance in America may have been the one given by Stephen Pinel at Round Lake, N.Y., on August 26, 1990.

All his life Fétis was a tireless worker toward his artistic goals. He had the courage and imagination to march on through problems that would immobilize, or at least frustrate, a weaker person. If an obstacle blocked his path in one direction, or if a project failed, he moved along another route. In a letter to Joseph Elsner (1769–1854), dated December 14, 1831, Chopin wrote: "Once again Fétis, whom I know and from whom one can actually learn a lot, has gone to live outside Paris and only comes to town for his lessons—otherwise he would long ago have been locked up for debt in the St-Pélagie prison. He owes more than the *Revue Musicale* brings in. I must tell you that in Paris debtors can only be arrested *à domicile*—so Fétis does not stay at his 'domicile' but goes outside the city where the law cannot touch him at certain times" [54, p.104].

Fétis was viewed with respect by many of his contemporaries, but his focus on larger viewpoints, often at the expense of careful details, and his heavy-handed, manipulative use of the musical press to achieve his goals, invited criticism. A German theorist and composer, Carl Gollmick (1796–1866), challenged Fétis's expertise in theory and counterpoint, his ability as a composer, his effectiveness as a teacher, and his professional ethics. Gollmick's stinging report cited Fétis's extravagant claims regarding the accomplishments of his protégé Lemmens. It then provided illustrations of violations of traditional rules of harmony and counterpoint, other stylistic flaws, and plagiarisms in Lemmens's compositions as well as errors (in Gollmick's opinion) in compositions by Fétis himself. Gollmick suggested that Fétis was striving to create the idea that Lemmens was a great man because he needed that kind of evidence to verify his own effectiveness as the director of the Conservatory. In other words, he was attempting to produce a great name without actually having produced a great musician [135].[5]

A more generous and appreciative view of Fétis appeared in the first edition (1879–89) of the Grove *Dictionary of Music and Musicians* (vol.1, p.517): "In his 'Biographie universelle des Musiciens,' and in his 'Histoire générale de la Musique' errors of detail and mistakes in chronology abound, while many of the opinions he advances are open to question. Easy as it may be however to find fault with these two standard works, it is impossible to do without them." Recently Peter Bloom wrote of Fétis: "It is true that he was a man of many accomplishments; it is unfortunate that he was openly proud of them all" [23, p.61].

Considering his many other responsibilities, Fétis was probably happy to delegate the organ class at the Brussels Conservatory to the German-born Christian Friedrich Johann Girschner. Girschner was a musical jack-of-all-trades. At various times and places he was a piano teacher, music periodical editor, opera composer, civic music director, choral conductor, choral composer, and theater orchestra conductor. Little information is available about his background as an organist. Early in his career, Girschner had an organ position in Berlin for the years 1820–22. After many changes of location and occupation, he arrived in Brussels in 1840 and assumed the position of organist at the Protestant church. In 1842 he was also named organ professor at the Conservatory [FM 5, p.346]. If we accept Fétis's word, Girschner had a drinking problem, which led to his dismissal from the Conservatory in 1848, and soon after he lost his church position [114, vol.4, pp.16–17]. Girschner was succeeded by two of his students: Lemmens and then Mailly. One would like to know more about the years Girschner spent at the Brussels Conservatory and his contribution to the musical development of his two best-known students.

As a young boy, Jacques-Nicolas (or Jaak Niklaas) Lemmens had organ lessons from his father and from an organist in Diest, Van der Broeck. He entered the Brussels Conservatory in 1839 as a piano student of Léopold Godineau but soon left the Conservatory because of his father's illness. Lemmens was then elected organist of Saint-Sulpice in Diest, where he stayed for fifteen months. He returned to Brussels in 1841, and he won first prize in piano (as a student of Michelot) at the close of the 1842–43 school year. He studied counterpoint, fugue, and composition with Fétis, and was awarded first prize in composition in 1845. He received first prize in organ, as a student of Girschner, the same year.

Fétis obtained a government grant for Lemmens to subsidize a year's study in Germany. There he would complete his education as an organist and establish his authority as an expert in the performance of Bach. Provided with a letter of introduction from Fétis, Lemmens went to Breslau in 1846 to study with Adolph Hesse. Whether he gained anything substantial from that experience remains questionable. In any case, Fétis subsequently claimed that Lemmens possessed the true Bach tradition, handed down from Bach's students, and carefully preserved by their successors.

When Lemmens returned to Brussels he competed for the Belgian Prix de Rome, gaining second place in 1847; and he also published a collection of organ pieces, *Dix improvisations* (Mainz: Schott, 1848). Perhaps he was really marking time, waiting for the post of organ professor to become vacant, as it conveniently did soon after.

Lemmens was 26 years old when he became professor of organ at the Brussels Conservatory in 1849. At the end of the 1849–50 school year, *Revue et Gazette musicale* reported that the organ competition at the Brussels Conservatory had been held at the church of the Augustins, and that nine participants had played for the jury and a large audience. There were four requirements: performance of a fugue by Lemmens, *Lauda Sion;* accompaniment of a plainchant selected by the jury; realization at sight of a figured bass; and improvisation of a piece [RGM 17, p.269]. This competition differed from that of the Paris Conservatory for the same year in several respects: it was open to the public, it required the performance of a composed piece of music and the realization of a figured bass, and there was less emphasis on improvisation.

Lemmens remained at the Brussels Conservatory for twenty years, but during the entire time he seemed to try to distance himself from it. He seemed never to be very happy in Brussels. Initially, the general state of organs in Belgium and the lack of an appropriate organ at the Conservatory must have been discouraging to an ambitious young performer. One can imagine, too, that Fétis could be a domineering superior as well as an influential advocate. Perhaps there were other problems. In a letter of February 10, 1863 Lemmens confided to Cavaillé-Coll that Brussels was not artistic enough to suit him [cited in 4, p.39]. For some years after he first joined the Conservatory faculty, Lemmens studied piano at Château de Bierbais, commuting to Brussels only to give his organ lessons [114, vol.5, p.268]. Throughout his life he seemed at least as interested in performing on the piano, and later the harmonium, as on the organ.

In 1857 Lemmens married the English soprano Helen Sherrington, and thereafter he spent considerable time in England, often taking extended leaves of absence from the Brussels Conservatory. Lemmens left his most advanced student, Mailly, in charge of the organ class during his absence in 1856–57 [RGM 24, p.15; RMA 1, p.784]. The periodical *Le Guide musical* had little sympathy for Lemmens and his absences. In 1863 there were comments about the fact that the Palais Ducal organ was not being used [GM 9, nos.25–26, p.4]. The effect of the professor's absence on the performance of the organ class at the year-end competitions was noted various times [GM 9, nos.35–36, pp.4–5; 10, nos.33–34, p.1; 12, nos.31–32, p.2]. In 1866 *Le Guide* reported that Lemmens was listed as professor of harmonium in a new school of music in London; it claimed that this state of affairs should be ended. Lemmens was reported to have given his lessons at the Conservatory during only six weeks of the eight or nine months of the session. *Le Guide* intimated that Lemmens should either fill his post or resign [GM 12, no.35, p.3].

The next year *Le Guide musical* informed its readers that recent rumors of a resignation by Lemmens were unfounded and that he intended to remain in his position at the Brussels Conservatory. An arrangement had been made for lessons to be given through the year by a Lemmens student, Joseph Tilborghs, and the professor himself would come from time to time to survey the studies and prepare the students for the annual competition [GM 13, nos.27–28, p.2].

Lemmens did finally resign in the spring of 1869, and later, in the review of the annual competition, Tilborghs was listed as "Professeur *(ad interim)*" [GM 15, nos.31–32, p.2].

Evidently Lemmens had hoped to retain his position, if in name only. In a letter of May 20, 1868, Xavier van Elewyck (a strong supporter of Lemmens) wrote to Cavaillé-Coll: "They have plotted against him [Lemmens] a great deal in Belgium, but he has poured torrents of light on his obscure blasphemers and has so well beaten them that his position at the Royal Conservatory of Brussels is perhaps stronger than ever." [On a beaucoup intrigué contre lui en Belgique, mais il a versé des torrents de lumière sur ses obscurs blasphémateurs et les a si bien battus que sa position au Conservatoire Royal de Bruxelles est peut-être plus forte que jamais; cited in 4, p.40.]

It was, after all, an important professional position. Lemmens did not have another that was equally visible until he returned to Belgium in 1878 to establish the *Ecole de musique religieuse* (later known as the Lemmens Institute).[6] Instruction in the new school began in January 1879. By then his health was declining, and Lemmens died two years later, on January 30, 1881.

After Lemmens's resignation from the Brussels Conservatory in 1869, Alphonse-Jean-Ernst Mailly was appointed professor of organ. Ten years younger than Lemmens, he was a native of Brussels who had received all his training at the Brussels Conservatory. Although his professional career included appearances in Paris, Amsterdam, and London and organ inaugurations in various locations in or near Belgium, his work was firmly centered in Brussels. He held several church positions there and had been appointed professor of piano at the Brussels Conservatory in 1861.

Mailly, like Lemmens, maintained a strong emphasis on composed repertoire. He made no radical changes in the competition requirements, but inserted a few touches of his own. In 1877 two new tests were added. In addition to the performance of a composed piece, improvisation on a given theme, and accompaniment of a chant with and without figured bass, the student was also required to play a modal "prelude" and a series of modulations in different keys [ME 43, p.294].

Le Guide musical, which had challenged Lemmens for his neglect of the organ class, was enthusiastic about Mailly. One senses here a division into two camps. No doubt it was difficult for Mailly to be continually in the shadow of Lemmens. He was a successful organist in his own right, appearing frequently on inaugural programs and publishing original compositions for organ. When his biography appeared in the 1878–80 Supplement to the Fétis *Biographie universelle,* the fact that Mailly had studied with Lemmens was carefully omitted: "He [Mailly] attributes his taste for the organ and his talent as an organist to the excellent lessons of Christian Girschner, the true founder of the celebrated organ school of the Belgian capital; who counted among his disciples Jacques Lemmens, his student and successor, and Alphonse Mailly, the present head of the school." [Il attribue son goût pour l'orgue et son talent d'organiste aux excellentes leçons de Christian Girschner, le véritable fon-

dateur de la célèbre école d'orgue de la capitale belge, qui a compté parmi ses
disciples Jacques Lemmens, son élève et successeur, et Alphonse Mailly, le chef
actuel de l'école; 114, Supplement, vol.2, p.149.]

The only recognition Girschner received from the Brussels Conservatory
after his dismissal was a tribute arranged by Mailly: a celebration of the 35th
anniversary of the establishment of the organ class by Girschner. Originally the
event was to take place in the fall of 1875, coinciding with the installation of a
new study organ being built for the Conservatory by Schyven. The organ was
not completed on time, so the Girschner celebration actually took place in the
summer of 1876 [GM 21, nos.32–33, p.4; 22, nos.32–33, p.2].

During Mailly's tenure the Brussels Conservatory at long last acquired a
Cavaillé-Coll organ. Installed in the school's new concert hall, it was inaugurated in 1880. Mailly played works of Bach, Mendelssohn, Widor, Martini, and Chauvet, and the choir and orchestra performed under the baton of
Gevaert, director of the Conservatory [ME 46, p.262].

Today the reputation of organ instruction in nineteenth-century Brussels is
linked securely to the fact that Guilmant and Widor went there to study organ
with Lemmens. The impact on later generations of organists resulting from
their dissemination of the Lemmens approach to organ playing can hardly be
overestimated. However, one should not forget that Clément Loret, professor
of organ at the Niedermeyer School in Paris, was also an important disciple of
Lemmens. He could also claim successful students, most notably Eugène
Gigout.

Other Lemmens students who later held prominent positions included
Joseph Tilborghs (who substituted for Lemmens during some of his absences),
professor of organ at the Conservatory of Ghent; Joseph Callaerts, organist at
the cathedral at Antwerp and professor of organ at the *Ecole de musique
flamande* there; and Auguste Andlauer, organist of Notre-Dame-des-Champs,
Paris.

The list of Mailly's students also contains a few internationally recognized
names. Among the best known were Charles Courboin (1884–1973), a native
of Antwerp who emigrated to the United States in 1904; Auguste Wiegand
(from Liège), who became the first organist of the Town Hall in Sidney,
Australia;[7] Louis Maes, organist at the Palace of Industry in Amsterdam; and
Paul Trillat, organist of the cathedral at Lyon, France.

Although the Brussels Conservatory has particular importance in the history
of organ music, it was not the only *Conservatoire royale* in Belgium. By the end
of the nineteenth century there were three others (at Liège, Ghent, and Antwerp) in addition to various other music schools. In 1821 a music school was
established in Liège by Henrard, Jaspar, and Duguet. It was absorbed by a
government-supported *Ecole royale de musique instrumentale et vocale* founded in 1827. After Belgium gained its independence, this school was designated
a *Conservatoire royale* [15].

Dieudonné Duguet (1794–1849), one of the founders of the 1821 music
school, was named professor of solfège in 1827. He became organist of

Saint-Denis in 1829, *maître de chapelle* of the Liège cathedral in 1835, and organist of the cathedral in 1837. Struck by blindness in 1835, he had to retire from the Conservatory the following year, but he continued his work at Saint-Denis and at the cathedral the rest of his life [70]. Duguet had a reputation as a serious, severe musician who did much to raise standards of church music in Liège. Under his influence, music of "German masters and of the school of Cherubini . . . absolutely unknown in the rest of Belgium" were performed frequently and under excellent conditions in Liège [114, Supplement, vol.1, p.286].

Dieudonné Duguet is particularly interesting to modern musicians because he was a teacher of César and Joseph Franck. César was enrolled at the Liège Conservatory in October 1830. He won first prize for solfège in 1832, and for piano in 1834 [303, p.3]. Joseph Franck was enrolled in the Conservatory in May 1833, where he studied violin and solfège, obtaining a first prize in the latter in 1835 [240, col.5–6].

Organ instruction was not offered at the Liège Conservatory while the Franck brothers were enrolled. There is no evidence that César had any organ lessons from his solfège professor, but he was certainly exposed to his influence, and may have heard him play the organ at Saint-Denis. Duguet's son, Jules, later became professor of organ at the Conservatory, and he also succeeded his father at the cathedral [70]. By 1888 the organ professor at the Conservatory was Pierre Danneels [GM 34, p.191].

The Royal Conservatory at Ghent was founded in 1833 [286, p.124]. Organ was added to the curriculum in 1871, when Joseph Tilborghs was named professor of organ. In 1881 *Le Guide musical* noted that Tilborghs had been one of the best students of Lemmens, although he was less brilliant than Mailly. Tilborghs's students, if not virtuosos, were practical organists, well prepared to enter the profession [GM 27, nos.34–35, p.5].[8]

At Antwerp a school of music was organized in 1842, with courses beginning in 1843. Organ was added to the curriculum in 1867 when Lemmens's student Joseph Callaerts joined the faculty [20]. It was not until 1897 that the school was designated a *Conservatoire royale* [221, pp.89–91].

XVI.
Lemmens, a Closer Look

LEMMENS'S organ method initially appeared as a periodical, *Nouveau Journal d'orgue à l'usage des organistes du culte catholique,* published in Brussels by Vanderauwera. Twelve issues were produced during the first year of publication (1850–51) and six in the second year. A final issue, published during the third year, consisted of an easy Mass for three equal voices.

The first seven issues contained descriptions and exercises for finger substitution and other techniques for manual legato, organ pieces by Lemmens (including many short versets and a few longer pieces), chant accompaniments, and an explanation of modes and modal accompaniments for the chant. The eighth issue introduced pedal technique, with two pages of explanation and a series of exercises. More organ pieces followed, along with some vocal motets with organ accompaniments and (in the eleventh issue) modulations. The first twelve issues contained a total of 150 pages; the following six, 72 pages. Except for some exercises in modulation and one piece by Joseph Tilborghs, the latter were devoted to pieces by Lemmens.

Lemmens's approach to organ pedagogy attracted considerable attention from the first. In the spring of 1850, Lemmens made his first trip to Paris, bearing a letter of introduction from Fétis to Cavaillé-Coll. The organ builder was very impressed with Lemmens's playing, and from that time he was influential in promoting Lemmens's career. Through Cavaillé-Coll Lemmens met and played for leading organists, critics, and other musicians when he returned to Paris in 1852; and it was Cavaillé-Coll who actively promoted sales of the *Nouveau Journal* and later Lemmens's *Ecole,* not only in Paris but also during his business trips. No other organ method of the time had such a prestigious agent.[1] But the most convincing advertisement for Lemmens's method was his own playing. Even those who preferred a lighter, more entertaining style were impressed with his pedal virtuosity and over-all technical control. His performances in Paris in 1850 and 1852 undoubtedly did much to promote his *Nouveau Journal* there and to enhance his image back home in Brussels.

Fétis wrote a review of the *Nouveau Journal* after eight issues had appeared. He explained that organ playing in France had long been inferior to that in Germany, where the traditions had flourished since the sixteenth century. Bach's works and his style of playing were handed down, said Fétis, by successive generations of students; and the Bach tradition was now preserved by Schneider of Dresden, Hesse of Breslau, and Haupt of Berlin.

According to Fétis, France's great traditions from the time of Titelouze to Couperin had been lost, primarily because French organists gave all their attention to improvisation and rarely played written music. Thus artists of real talent left almost no music for the future, and neither organ composition nor technique progressed.

Fétis noted that legato playing was the basic style for organ playing and that substitution was essential to produce legato. These techniques, as well as pedaling, were virtually ignored by French organists. He called for reform in both France and Belgium: The time was at hand; young Lemmens had been to Breslau to study with Hesse. On his return, Fétis wrote, Lemmens had brought a letter from Hesse that stated "I have nothing more to teach Mr. Lemmens." [Je n'ai plus rien à apprendre à M. Lemmens; RGM 18, pp.29–30.] Fétis did not state in so many words that Lemmens now knew the authentic Bach tradition and that this tradition included legato style, finger substitution, and a comprehensive pedal technique, but he clearly implied as much.

Shortly after eighteen issues of the *Nouveau Journal* had appeared, Maurice Bourges wrote a review of the Lemmens method. He described the manual studies as progressive daily exercises designed to foster the habit of legato playing, "which is of the very essence of the organ, and to which the ingenious process of the substitution of one finger for another on just one key contributes singularly" [qui est de l'essence même de l'orgue, et auquel contribue singulièrement l'ingénieux procédé de la substitution d'un doigt à un autre sur une seule touche].

Bourges noted that the pedal exercises would give the feet the same facility and precision as the hands. He described the pedal method as the most complete and best arranged that had ever been published. Lemmens himself, he said, was "the living proof of the excellence of that method" [la preuve vivante de l'excellence de cette méthode; RGM 19, pp.179–81].

In 1862 Lemmens published his *Ecole d'orgue, basée sur le plain-chant romain* (Brussels: Chez l'Auteur [Preface dated August 1, 1862]),[2] which is essentially a revised edition of the earlier *Nouveau Journal*. It is divided in two parts: the first without pedal, the second with pedal. Some of the repertoire is different, but the only substantial change is that the *Ecole* omits the material on plainchant accompaniment and the use of modes.

The title page states that the *Ecole* had been adopted by the conservatories of Brussels, Paris, and Madrid, the *Ecole de musique religieuse* (the Niedermeyer School) in Paris, normal schools, and others. One might question just what "adoption" meant. Surely Loret was by then using his own material (some of which was published in 1858) at the Niedermeyer School. Benoist, at the Paris Conservatory, wrote to Cavaillé-Coll to thank him for a copy of the *Nouveau Journal,* but there is no evidence he actually used it in his organ classes [letter cited in 80, no.76, p.88].

Lemmens assumed that the organ student using his method would already have a good command of basic keyboard techniques. In the Preface to the *Ecole* he stressed the importance of prior piano study for the young person wanting to learn to play the organ. Accordingly, he limited the manual exercises almost entirely to techniques that were either unique or especially important for the organ: those that would make it possible to maintain a legato line in each voice part. These exercises included substitution, sliding a finger from one key to another, using the base and tip of the thumb to play two keys successively, and crossing fingers.

Although all these techniques were necessary components of the method, substitution attracted the most attention and became the symbol or watchword for the entire system of fingering for legato playing. In his introduction to the manual exercises, Lemmens explained that piano fingering is insufficient for playing organ music in four parts correctly. He also noted that the legato style is characteristic of organ playing, and that substitution is especially important in playing legato.

Lemmens did not make any specific connection between legato style and a particular historic period, compositional style, or national school. He regarded it as the normal touch for organ playing in general. Nor is there a specific connection between the *Ecole* and performance of the music of Bach. Quite the contrary! In the Preface Lemmens states that his objective was to create a method for Catholic organists, for music of Protestant composers could be used only with the greatest caution for Catholic services. While he acknowledged the great talent to be found among Protestant composers, much of their music was based on Protestant chorales and was therefore, he felt, unsuitable for Catholic use. Lemmens himself did not claim (at least in writing) to be the transmitter of the Bach tradition. This notion was publicized originally by Fétis and later by students of Lemmens—most vehemently and persistently by Widor (who had also studied with Fétis).

Fétis linked substitution directly with the Bach tradition. In the article on Bach in the second edition of *Biographie universelle* (1860–65), he wrote:

> Bach was not only a man of genius and the greatest musician of his time; he also had, with an indisputable superiority, the talent for teaching composition and the art of playing the harpsichord and the organ. The complicated nature of the works for these two instruments, always written in three, four or five parts, had obliged him to invent a special fingering, which was known for a long time in Germany by the name *fingering of Bach*, but which one can designate in a more significant manner by the name *fingering of substitution*.

> Bach ne fut pas seulement un homme de génie et le plus grand musicien de son temps; il eut aussi le talent d'enseigner, avec une incontestable supériorité, la composition et l'art de jouer du clavecin et de l'orgue. La nature compliquée des ouvrages pour ces deux instruments, toujours écrits à trois, quatre ou cinq parties, l'avait obligé à inventer un doigter particulier, qui fut connu longtemps en Allemagne sous le nom de *doigter de Bach*, mais qu'on peut désigner d'une manière plus significative par le nom de *doigter de substitution*. [114, vol.1, p.194.]

It is interesting to note that Fétis made no reference to substitution in the first edition of *Biographie universelle* (1837–44). Its publication was already in progress in 1838 when he paid a visit to Christian Heinrich Rinck (1770–1846), who had studied with Bach's own student Kittel [114, vol.7, p.270]. Could Rinck have been the source of Fétis's theories about the Bach style? Did Lemmens learn from Hesse his techniques for playing legato, and that legato was the basis for organ style? Was Fétis himself the source of this stylistic idea, having perhaps derived it from his extensive knowledge of early organ music and his own experiments as an organist?[3]

Neither finger substitution nor legato were new ideas in 1800, but during the nineteenth century there was an unmistakable trend toward greater preference for legato, not only in organ music but in general.[4] Lemmens's method was in step with the times, and today it is usually regarded as a product of nineteenth-century performance tendencies. However, it is still not clear where Lemmens and Fétis got their ideas.

Pedal technique was given a more comprehensive treatment than manual technique in the Lemmens publications. As Bourges observed, it was indeed the most complete pedal method then available. In the *Ecole* there are pedal exercises for alternate toes, major and minor scales, sliding from one key to another, sliding the heel forward or back on a white key to position it for the next move, substitution of one foot for the other, substitution between heel and toe of the same foot, arpeggios, trills, intervals and chords, the chromatic scale, octaves, and combinations of techniques.

At a time when most methods included only a few pedal exercises and advocated alternate toes as the basic technique, with toe-heel pedaling as an alternative, Lemmens had devised a new approach. No method before his showed evidence of such careful and detailed analysis of the motions involved in pedal playing. He applied principles of virtuoso manual playing to the pedals, streamlining movement, and eliminating (through increased ankle motion and increased use of the heels) much of the foot crossing typical of alternate-toe pedaling. With its thorough, systematic approach, this method went well beyond the needs of the average church organist. Lemmens was addressing the talented student who could master the entire repertoire—Catholic, Protestant, or secular.

As with the manual techniques, the method of pedal playing raises questions about the source of Lemmens's ideas. One point is clear: these ideas must have been well formulated even before his teaching career began, as publication of the *Nouveau Journal* began the year after Lemmens assumed the organ post at the Brussels Conservatory. One can determine that some material was derived from Fétis, who had proclaimed early in his career that there should be a distinct difference between Catholic and Protestant organ music, and both he and Lemmens reiterated this idea frequently.[5]

Lemmens himself acknowledged that the system for plainchant accompaniment he had followed in the *Nouveau Journal* was Fétis's. When Lemmens actually began using it with his students he soon found that it was unsatisfactory. Therefore he omitted all the material related to chant accompaniment when he published the *Ecole*.[6] That he would accept and publish as his own these ideas of Fétis's suggests that other aspects of the Lemmens method might also have come from Fétis.

Accounts of Lemmens's studies with Hesse contain so many contradictions that one cannot tell how much influence the German organist had on Lemmens. The latter arrived in Breslau in the fall of 1846 and may have left in mid-December. In an arrogant letter of November 9, 1846, the 23-year-old Lemmens informed his parents that he had been told initially that he played too fast, but that Hesse knew nothing more to teach him about organ playing. Lemmens felt he already knew more than Hesse about fugue writing and improvisation, and he was by far the better pianist [cited in 330, pp.16–18].

A letter written by Hesse on December 16, 1846 affirms that Lemmens had studied with him since September, that this talented musician had worked very hard and could now play the most difficult organ pieces with ease, that he had a thorough education in serious music, and that he was now prepared for a position of professor of organ playing at the Conservatory[7] [cited in 330, p.16]. It may have been this letter (combined, perhaps, with reports from Lemmens) that prompted Fétis to write that Hesse had no more to teach Lemmens. In 1852 Hesse read about Fétis's claim in an article by Carl Gollmick, published in the *Neue Zeitschrift für Musik* [135]. Hesse lost no time in publishing a denial, saying he had never given Lemmens such a letter. Further, he rated Lemmens's talent as average at best. In a way, he said, it was true that he could not teach Lemmens anything more, as Lemmens had left Breslau without saying goodbye or even inquiring about his obligations to his teacher [156].

Fétis, not one to be easily distracted, stuck to his story. The second edition of *Biographie universelle* contains the following quotation attributed to Hesse: "I have nothing more to teach Mr. Lemmens: he plays the most difficult music of Bach as well as I can." [Je n'ai plus rien à apprendre à M. Lemmens: il joue la musique la plus difficile de Bach aussi bien que je puis le faire; 114, vol.5, p.267.]

This collection of letters and articles poses some intriguing questions. Was the letter of December 16, 1846 really written by Hesse? Had the German organist forgotten about writing this letter of recommendation by 1852, or did he consider Fétis's claim too outrageous a paraphrase of his 1846 letter? What relationships can be found between Hesse's playing as it was described by his contemporaries and the ideas espoused by Lemmens in his *Nouveau Journal?*[8]

Whatever Lemmens may have learned from Fétis and Hesse, one must assume that some ideas were his own. The physical aspects of the pedal method seem particularly likely candidates, but one cannot rule out other possibilities. In any case, he himself composed the large collection of pieces included in his publications. While the skills and style of playing fostered by the technical exercises had an especially telling effect on future generations of organ students, the importance of the collection of pieces should not be overlooked. Some of the pieces explored unusual techniques, such as playing on two manuals with one hand. The pedal played a more demanding role than most French and Belgian music required. A wide variety of textures and timbres were demonstrated. At a time when plainchant had all but disappeared from composed organ music, Lemmens incorporated it in several pieces. However one might assess their musical quality, the Lemmens pieces opened new doors and expanded the view for future organ composers.

No one understood the Lemmens method better than Charles-Marie Widor. In 1863 he had gone to Brussels, where he had followed a rigorous "total emersion" program, with daily organ lessons from Lemmens and daily counterpoint, fugue, and composition lessons from Fétis.[9] Widor was convinced that what he and the other students learned from Lemmens was the true, traditional style of organ playing, handed down from Bach himself to his students and eventually transmitted to Adolph Hesse.[10] In 1899 Widor wrote:

> It is from him [Lemmens] that we have the Bach tradition: tradition that in his youth he had gone to acquire at the school of the venerable Hesse of Breslau, and that he piously preserved in order to transmit it in all its integrity to his students. "Now it is up to you to uphold it!" he told us, at the time of his last visit to Paris.

> C'est de lui que nous tenons la tradition de Bach, tradition qu'il était allé chercher dans sa jeunesse à l'école du vénérable Hesse, de Breslau, et qu'il conservait pieusement pour la transmettre dans toute son intégrité à ses élèves: «A vous maintenant de la défendre!» nous disait-il, lors de son dernier séjour à Paris. [332, p.132.]

Widor also said that in his counterpoint lessons Fétis told him about Rinck (with whom he had associated), Rinck's musical father, Kittel, and the great ancestor of both, Sebastian Bach [337, p.ix].

Widor published a new edition of the Lemmens *Ecole* in 1924. In the Preface he explained other aspects of Lemmens's teaching that were not defined in the original edition. Phrasing, articulation, and the careful control of all aspects of rhythm in shaping the musical interpretation were of prime concern. Widor noted the remarkable authority, clarity, and flexibility with which Lemmens played. He said that the elimination of all unnecessary motion was important for precision in playing. Hands and feet should be kept as close to the manual and pedal keys as possible, and the knees and heels should be kept together (the knees up to the interval of an octave, and the heels to the interval of a fifth). When Lemmens played, he said, it was as if his knees and heels were tied together.

Widor added that these ideas were not personal: he owed them to Lemmens and considered it his duty to publish them here. The seriousness with which he regarded his obligation to preserve Lemmens's teaching is underlined at the close of the Preface: "Moreover, the present edition reproduces that Method faithfully, text and music, without any kind of modification, with the religious respect it deserves, and with which no one is permitted to tamper." [La présente édition reproduit d'ailleurs cette Méthode, texte et musique, intégralement, sans modification d'aucune sorte, avec le religieux respect auquel elle a droit et qu'il n'est pas permis à personne de tripatouiller.]

By the time Widor's edition was published, Lemmens's method had already appeared in several other versions. The earliest was the collection of manual and pedal exercises published by Loret in *La Maîtrise* in 1858; it was followed by Loret's four-volume *Cours d'orgue* published during the 1860s and 1870s. Loret's method was derived from his studies with Lemmens and is obviously indebted to the *Nouveau Journal,* but it also contains much that is different, including a substantial collection of original compositions by Loret.

In the mid-1880s W. T. Best, the famous English organist, published an edition of the Lemmens *Ecole* entitled *Organ-School,* with English translations, fingering, and registrations (London: Schott & Co. [1884]). In view of the freedom editors often exercised in the nineteenth century, Best remained remarkably faithful to the original *Ecole*. Aside from adding a few dynamic and phrase marks, the only changes he made were those necessary to make the *Ecole* intelligible and useful for English organists.

In 1920 Eugène Gigout brought out a revised version of the *Ecole* (Paris: Durand). He omitted one paragraph from Lemmens's Preface and a number of pieces. He added two movements from sonatas by Lemmens: *Adoration (Sonate pascale)* and *Fugue-Fanfare (Sonate pontificale).*

It is interesting to note that in revising the repertoire of the *Ecole,* Gigout retained contrapuntal pieces and those related to plainchant. He tended to eliminate melody-and-accompaniment pieces, marchlike pieces, those with considerable chromaticism, and some small pieces that he may have considered redundant. Among those to go was an old-fashioned *Andante avec variations,* featuring harplike arpeggio figures and rolled chords. In all other respects, Gigout reproduced the content of the *Ecole* as it was in the original edition. All the exercises and explanations remained intact.

Many organists today would see Gigout's edition as an improvement over the original. To 76-year-old Widor it no doubt seemed an intrusion and a violation. His own 1924 edition, reproducing text and music "without any kind of modification," responded to Gigout's presumptuous tampering. Widor was still the valiant defender of every aspect of the Lemmens tradition.[11] Ironically, it is Gigout's edition that can more readily be found in music libraries today.

Lemmens was proud of his accomplishment as an educator. By 1877 four of his former students were in prominent positions in Paris: Loret at the Niedermeyer School and church of Saint-Louis-d'Antin, Widor at Saint-Sulpice, Guilmant at La Trinité, and Andlauer at Notre-Dame-des-Champs.[12]

In a letter to Cavaillé-Coll dated January 13, 1877, Lemmens wrote: "I believe that it was my visits to Paris in 1850, '51, '52, etc., that started the regeneration of the art of organ playing in France. The adoption of my *Ecole d'orgue* by the Conservatory of Paris, and later the successive placement of four of my students in as many important positions in Paris are proof of the soundness of my method." [Je crois que ce sont mes visites à Paris en 1850, 51, 52, etc., qui ont commencé la régénération de l'art de jouer de l'orgue en France. L'adoption de mon école d'orgue par le Conservatoire de Paris et plus tard le placement successif de quatre de mes élèves dans autant de positions importantes de Paris, sont la preuve de la solidité de mon école; cited in 79, no.65, p.112.]

Interest in Lemmens himself has been regenerated in recent years. In an article published in 1981, Christian Ahrens credited Lemmens and his students with "the development of a new, in the full sense of the word 'romantic,' organ music" [die Entwicklung einer neuen, im vollen Sinne des Wortes "romantis-chen" Orgelmusik; 3]. Subsequent studies by Lowell Lacey, William Peterson, and Carol Weitner [330] have clarified various aspects of Lemmens's life, work, and influence.

Certainly, through both his teaching and his performance Lemmens fostered a new respect for written repertoire and a new standard for organ perfor-mance. He developed a systematic approach to organ playing that offered solutions to the most difficult technical problems in the repertoire. He insisted on attention to all details of performance: not only precision and accuracy but also the refined control of rhythm to produce accents, clarify form, and give character to a performance.

But Lemmens gave his students more than a set of sophisticated tools to work with: he gave them a sense of mission, and they considered themselves the torchbearers of a great historic tradition. No crusaders ever responded to a call with greater confidence in the validity of their cause, greater determination to fulfill their commission, greater enthusiasm for victory than did Lemmens's most gifted disciples, Widor and Guilmant.

During the latter part of his career Lemmens devoted considerable study to Gregorian chant. In the Preface to his *Du Chant grégorien* (1886) he explains that he found a twelfth century manuscript of chant in the British Museum Library in August 1876. On the basis of this manuscript he developed theories about the rhythmic interpretation of chant and about chant accompaniment. Later viewed as an interesting but unsuccessful endeavor [212, p.1837], Lem-mens's theory of chant rhythm nevertheless acted as a springboard for the concentrated involvement in church music that characterized his final years.

In 1878 Lemmens campaigned like a politician in election year. In early March he was in Paris lecturing in the Erard hall about his new system of plainchant accompaniment [GM 24, no.10, p.5]. In June he was in Belgium discussing a plan for a school of sacred music with the Archbishop of Mechelen. By July 30 he had the solid endorsement of the Belgian clergy for the establishment of his school; and less than a month later a prospectus announc-ing the objectives and curriculum of the *Ecole de musique religieuse* (the Lemmens Institute) was ready for circulation [76, p.xxxi].

In mid-September Lemmens was again in Paris, where he gave a concert with his wife at the Trocadéro and a private hearing at Saint-Eustache. Later in the fall he went to Rome to discuss the restoration of Gregorian chant and the plans for his school with Pope Leo XIII. He returned to Paris in December and gave a lecture about chant and chant accompaniment in Cavaillé-Coll's hall.

With what seems like a rather callous disregard for his host, Cavaillé-Coll, Lemmens reproached organ builders in his December 2 lecture, blaming them in part for the "present degeneration" of the art. He thought young musicians were too easily distracted from more important objectives by the many timbres and combinations provided by builders on modern organs.

Reviewing the presentation, Eugène Gigout was quick to observe that Lemmens was the master "who has contributed the most through these [Lemmens's] compositions, very modern indeed, to the complete success of organ building of our time, and who only very recently made liberal use of the innumerable resources amassed in Mr. Cavaillé-Coll's splendid instrument at the Trocadéro" [qui a le plus contribué, par ces compositions, certes très-modernes, au plein succès de la facture d'orgue de notre époque et qui, tout récemment encore, a usé largement, au Trocadéro, des innombrables ressources accumulées dans le splendide instrument de M. Cavaillé-Coll; GM 24, no.50, pp.6–7; ME 45, p.15].

Classes in Lemmens's *Ecole de musique religieuse* began in early 1879. Courses were offered in religion, liturgy, and church Latin; plainchant; organ; piano; harmony; counterpoint and fugue; and composition of sacred music, vocal and instrumental. The course in religion, liturgy, and Latin was assigned to the school chaplain; all other courses were taught by Lemmens himself. In a letter to Cavaillé-Coll dated February 8, 1879, Lemmens reported that sixteen students were enrolled. By December 31 that number had increased to 29 [79, no.68].

Still not content, Lemmens wanted to expand his work to include clergy and all those involved in church music. In September 1880 he convened a conference at Mechelen to form a society analogous to the Cecilian societies in Germany. The new organization adopted the name *Société de Saint-Grégoire.* During the same period Lemmens was composing pieces which were to appear in annual publications with the title *L'Organiste catholique.* They were later published in the posthumous collections of Lemmens's compositions [76, pp.xxxviii–xxxix].

Lemmens died on January 30, 1881. His successor as director of the *Ecole de musique religieuse* was Edgar Tinel (1854–1912).

XVII.
Widor as Teacher

CESAR Franck died the morning of November 8, 1890. The great sense of loss his students experienced was mixed with questions about the future. Who could possibly take his place? What was to become of the Paris Conservatory organ class? One can imagine that more than one Paris organist speculated on those questions. High on the list of eligible candidates were Alexandre Guilmant, Eugène Gigout, and Charles-Marie Widor, all of whom would eventually hold the position of professor of organ at the Conservatory.

Widor was first. He lost no time in launching his campaign. On November 9 he wrote Ambroise Thomas, director of the Paris Conservatory, that he would be available to fill the vacancy if he were called on to do so [209, p.106]. He also asked other influential friends and colleagues to support his candidacy [233b, p.53]. One letter concludes: "It appears that one must fear furious assaults from 'the blind man,' as you say, alias Guilmant!" [il paraît qu'il faut craindre les furieux assauts de «l'aveugle», comme vous dites, alias Guilmant! cited in 111, p.46].

On November 17 Ambroise Thomas sent his recommendations to the Minister of Public Instruction and Fine Arts with three distinguished candidates listed in order: Widor, Guilmant, and Gigout. He commented that since the organ class included improvisation as well as execution, it was essential that the professor be a composer as well as a virtuoso. He indicated that Widor, whose works had been well received by colleagues and public alike, best met these qualifications [160, p.58]. Organ was still classified with harmony and composition at the Conservatory in 1890, and improvisation was still the most decisive part of the organ examinations and competitions.

On November 25 Widor was appointed professor of organ, and he met his class for the first time on December 11. He was 46 years old, and his career was already well established. He had been organist at Saint-Sulpice for almost 21 years; his successful ballet, *La Korrigane* (produced in 1880), had earned him an important place among contemporary composers; he had written eight organ symphonies; and his elite social orbit included writers, artists, and prominent social figures, as well as other musicians. It was no timid soul that faced the organ class that afternoon; although Widor had little (if any) previous experience as a teacher, he knew exactly what he was going to do.

The new organ professor did not have much respect for Franck's organ teaching. In 1921 he was still scoffing: "The class indeed had little success. As organist, the technique of the instrument troubled him little; he was satisfied to

Charles-Marie Widor (Bibliothèque Nationale, Paris).

give instruction in free improvisation on an immutable plan of andante." [La classe en effet avait peu de succès. Organiste, la technique de l'instrument l'inquiétait peu: il se contentait de faire un cours d'improvisation libre sur un plan immuable d'andante; 331, p.238.]

Widor prefaced the first meeting of his organ class with the general observation that improvisation had previously been over-emphasized at the expense of performance and repertoire. Feigning reluctance to be there, he announced the revolution. Vierne recalled his saying:

> I hesitated a long time before accepting the position which falls to me today. I finally decided to do it with the determination to restore organistic performance in general, and in particular to revive the authentic tradition in the interpretation of the works of Bach. It was bequeathed to me by my teacher, Lemmens, who had it from Hesse of Breslau, who had received it from Forkel, pupil and biographer of the old cantor. [Cited in 324, vol.29, no.12, p.10.]

A student was then selected to play. The detail with which Widor dissected his playing, note by note, and measure by measure, for an hour and a half, left the rest of the class stunned, including Vierne and his classmate Charles Tournemire. "Well, old chap," Tournemire said to Vierne, "one thing is clear; we don't know anything. If we have to do everything all over we'll be having a weird sort of competition. The prize is done for!" Vierne recalled:

> I was of the same opinion and profoundly discouraged. It meant that I should have to verify, note by note, everything I had learned for three years, for I could not dream of relying upon the hazard of my memory. It would be dog's work, and seemed to me absurd. Happily for the clearness of my later judgment, I had a devilish pride and, cost what it might, I resolved to come out of this difficulty victorious. "Better die than give up," I replied to Tournemire, who also felt that this was the only attitude to adopt. He was stubborn, too. [324, vol.29, no.12, p.10.]

The students gradually overcame their initial shock and grew to appreciate the new perspective Widor brought to the organ class. For Tournemire, the appreciation was selective and guarded. Years later he wrote of the great care Widor gave to every detail of playing, leaving nothing to chance. Through those who experienced this instruction, he said, the "true technique of the organ, in all its purity" was manifested [313, p.141]. Certainly this "extraordinarily brilliant disciple of Lemmens" deserved a measure of praise, but Tournemire carefully avoided reference to artistic qualities. The contrast with his description of Franck's teaching—replete with such expressions as "one of the greatest inspired persons of all time," "*maître grandiose,*" "*père spirituel,*" "*séraphique artiste,*"—leaves no doubt about where Tournemire's allegiance remained [313, p.141].

Resistance in other quarters posed problems of a different type. Widor fared no better than Franck in the annual competitions. While Widor was professor of organ, first prize was given in only three years: 1891 to Tournemire, 1894 to Vierne and Libert, and 1895 to Galand [249, p.583]. All but Galand had been pupils of Franck. Vierne suggests that the unimpressive showing was the result of a conspiracy among some members of the jury [324, vol.30, no.2, p.8].

Ten students were enrolled in the 1890–91 organ class that Widor inherited from Franck. Ternisien and Runner were then in their third year; Libert, Burgat, Bouval, Busser, Guiraud, and Tournemire in their second year; and Vierne and Berger in their first.[1] In subsequent years while Widor was professor, enrollment in the organ class ranged between six and eight, and the following new students were enrolled: Quef in 1892; Galand in 1893; Marichelle, Mulet, Charles Michel, Harnisch, and Rottembourg in 1894; Gabriel Dupont, Coedes, and Alphonse Schmitt in 1895 [160, pp.59–63].

Beginning in October 1891 Vierne assisted Widor with the organ class. His task initially was to prepare students who were auditing the class and were seeking admission, by instructing them in plainchant (according to the Conservatory requirements) and technique. He was officially appointed Widor's assistant by the director, Ambroise Thomas, in 1894, after he won his first prize in organ. From that time Vierne's job was to prepare students for all the competition tests, leaving Widor more class time for improvisation in other forms and a broader study of repertoire and interpretation.

Much of what happened during the first months of Widor's professorship may have been a replay of his own student experiences under Lemmens at Brussels. First, there was intensive technical training. Probably for the first time in the history of the Conservatory the organ students were assigned studies in an organ method book. They had to work their way through the manual and pedal studies in the Lemmens *Ecole*. Particular attention was given to the pedal scales, which had to be memorized and mastered [324, vol.29, no.12, p.11].

Widor insisted on attention to every detail of technique, including position and types of movement. All unnecessary motion was to be avoided, small movements as well as grandiose gestures. When there was a choice of fingering or pedaling, the one requiring the least motion was to be selected. Similar care was given to note values. Precision in attack and release was a prime requirement. Legato notes were connected exactly, without gaps or overlapping. Staccato notes were measured and uniform. Repeated notes were separated by a specific rest whose value was determined by the length of the note and the tempo of the piece. As a general rule the rest was equal to the length of the smallest note value found frequently in the piece.

Phrasing, registration, changes of manual, and use of the swell box were all planned along long lines, related to the architecture of the piece. Widor did not like frequent changes of registration or special effects of any kind. The basis of expression in organ playing was a matter of rhythm: subtle adjustments in note length to emphasize important notes and subtle delays in the entry of a note to give it an accent.

Widor insisted on slow tempos. Maintaining that the essential character of the organ is grandeur, he said: "Bach used two principal tempos, one not very fast, corresponding to our andante; one rather slow, which was the present-day adagio" [cited in 324, vol.29, no.12, p.11].

Widor's own account of how the organ should be played, which was published while he was professor of organ at the Conservatory, can be found in his preface to a study of Bach by André Pirro.[2] A few extracts from this source, translated by Wallace Goodrich (1871–1952), confirm his pedagogical position.

> He [Bach] played with the body inclined slightly forward, and motionless; with an admirable sense of rhythm, with an absolutely perfect polyphonic ensemble, with extraordinary clearness, avoiding extremely rapid *tempi*; in short, master of himself, and, so to speak, of the beat, producing an effect of incomparable grandeur. . . .
>
> A serious organist will never avail himself of these means of expression [changes of intensity], unless *architecturally*; that is to say, by *straight lines* and by *designs*. By *lines*, when he passes slowly from *piano* into *forte*, by a gradient

almost imperceptible, and in constant progression, without break or jolt. By *designs,* when he takes advantage of a second of silence to close the swell-box abruptly between a *forte* and a *piano.*

Seek to reproduce the expressive quality of an E-string, or of the human voice, and we shall no longer hear an organ; it will have become an accordeon.

The most striking characteristic of the organ is grandeur; that is to say, determination and power. Every illogical variation in the intensity of the sound, every nuance which, graphically, cannot be represented by a right line, is a crime, the offence of artistic *lèse-majesté.*

In fact, we should declare to be criminals, and hold up to the contempt of the public, those who make an accordeon of the organ; those who arpeggiate, who do not play legato, whose rhythm is but passable.

With the organ, as in the orchestra, precision must rule; the perfect ensemble of feet and hands is absolutely necessary, whether in attacking or leaving the keyboard. . . .

Culpable are the organists who do not play the four parts of the polyphony with a rigorous *legato,* tenor as well as soprano, the alto like the bass. . . .

. . . with the organ, that we may clearly hear the repetitions of a note in a quick movement, or even in moderate tempo, there must intervene between the repetitions periods of silence equal to the duration of the sound; from which we may formulate this law: *every repeated note loses one-half of its value.* The periods of silence have a time-value exactly equal to that of the sixteenth-notes.

With regard to notes of larger value, in slow movements, it is clear that the spirit rather than the letter of our law is to be regarded. . . .

What is rhythm?

The constant manifestation of determination, or will, upon the periodical recurrence of the accented beats. It is only by rhythm that one wins attention. Particularly with the organ, all accents, all effects are dependent upon it. You may bear upon the keyboard with the weight of pounds, with all the strength of your shoulders—you will gain nothing by it. But delay by a tenth of a second the attack of a chord, or prolong this same chord the very least, and judge of the effect produced! Upon a manual not provided with a swell-box one may obtain a crescendo without the aid of a mechanism of any kind: by the simple augmentation of the duration allowed successive chords or detached phrases.

To play upon an organ is to deal with chronometric values.

Woe be unto you if your tempo is not absolutely regular, if your will does not manifest itself at every breathing-point of the phrase, at every "lift"; if you unconsciously permit yourself to "hurry"! . . .

To be master of one's self it is necessary to abstain from every superfluous movement, from any displacement of the body. A good organist sits firmly, well-balanced upon his bench, inclining slightly towards the manuals, never permitting his feet to rest upon the frame which surrounds the pedals, but letting them glide lightly along over the keys; heels and knees riveted, so to speak, together.

Nature has vouchsafed us two guides of the greatest value; with the heels pressed one against the other, the maximum separation of the other extremities of the feet gives us a *fifth;* with the knees held similarly together, the maximum interval obtainable should be an *octave.*

Precision and confidence will never be obtained except by adopting this method; holding the two limbs as if bound together, the two feet unceasingly in contact with each other. . . .

The organ is a wind instrument; it requires opportunity to take breath. Like the literary sentence, the musical phrase has its commas, its periods, its paragraphs. As a speaker changes his intonation, so must the organ vary its "designs." [337, pp.x-xviii.]

Widor frequently referred to the importance of the "will" in organ playing. When he was a student, Lemmens told him virtuosity was worthless without "will." He did not understand until later that what Lemmens meant was analogous to the art of the orator:

his authority which asserts itself by the composure, order, and precise proportions of his speech. For us musicians, the will manifests itself above all through rhythm. A mechanical piano doesn't interest us longer than the ticktock of a clock; one doesn't hear it; whereas the mastery of a Liszt or a Rubinstein, "who did not play fast," moved the world.

Such, at the organ, [was] the authority of Lemmens.

son autorité qui s'impose par le calme, l'ordre et les justes proportions du discours. Chez nous musiciens, la volonté se manifeste avant tout par le rythme. Un piano mécanique ne nous intéresse pas plus longtemps que le tic-tac d'une pendule, on ne l'écoute pas; tandis que la maestria d'un Liszt ou d'un Rubinstein, «qui ne jouaient pas vite», a remué le monde.

Telle, à l'orgue, l'autorité de Lemmens. [335, p.12.]

But Widor also expanded the idea of "will" in organ playing well beyond rhythm in explaining his view of its spiritual and philosophical aspects. In 1906 Albert Schweitzer (1875–1965) quoted Widor's revealing statement on the meaning of organ playing and the objectives of organ teaching:

To play the organ is to reveal a will that is full of the vision of eternity. All organ instruction, whether technical or artistic, has as its only purpose to educate a human being to that pure, higher manifestation of the will. The player must objectify his will in the organ, so as to overpower the listener. The organist must concentrate his great will in the theme of a Bach fugue so that even a distracted listener cannot tear himself away, but must notice and comprehend by the second measure, and see the entire fugue as well as hearing it. If the player doesn't have that concentrated, communicative, serene will, he may be a great artist, but he is not a born organist. He has simply chosen the wrong instrument, for the organ represents the objective transfiguration of a human spirit into the eternal, unending spirit. The organ is alienated from its place and its essence the moment it is reduced to being only the expression of a subjective spirit. [Cited in 293, p.20.]

The repertoire Widor used in the Conservatory class was drawn primarily from the works of Bach, with a few other composers represented. Criticized for not including works of Franck in the 1891 competition repertoire, Widor assigned three to Vierne: *Prélude, fugue et variation* for the January 1892 examination, *Pièce héroïque* for the June examination, and *Grande Pièce symphonique* for the competition [324, vol.30, no.2, p.8]. According to Vierne, after the reorganization of the organ class was effected, Widor "was also able to broaden the repertoire, adding the Mendelssohn sonatas, a few pieces by Boëly and Saint-Saëns, and some of his own works. In this way he opened new horizons of interpretation while retaining Bach as the intangible foundation" [324, vol.30, no.2, p.9].

It is interesting to note that Widor was a rigid disciple of Lemmens in all aspects of Bach performance except one. Lemmens and Fétis both felt strongly that there was a fundamental difference between Catholic and Protestant music, and that Bach's music was generally not well suited for use in Catholic services. Widor was of a different opinion. He took credit for having introduced the Bach organ chorales into the Conservatory repertoire, and he seemed not to have understood that their previous neglect might have had some relationship to their specific connection with the Protestant church. Vierne related:

> At the reopening of the class at the beginning of October 1892, there occurred an event of considerable importance to our artistic development. I mean the discovery of Bach's chorales. I say "discovery," and this is not an exaggeration, as you may judge for yourselves. At the first class in performance Widor remarked with some surprise that since his arrival at the Conservatoire not one of us had brought in one of the celebrated chorales. For my part I was acquainted with three of them, published in Braille in the edition that Franck had prepared for our school. They had seemed to me to have no technical difficulties and I had paid no further attention to them. My classmates did not even know that they existed. On looking through the music cabinet where there were several books in the Richault edition we discovered three volumes, two of preludes and fugues and one of chorales, the latter completely untouched, its leaves uncut. The *Maître* spent the entire class time playing these pieces to us, and we were bowled over. The most overwhelming part of the giant's organ works was suddenly revealed to us. We all set to work on them at once, and for three months nothing else was heard in class. We all played chorales at the examination in January, and the surprise of the jury was no less great than our own had been. Upon leaving the hall I heard Ambroise Thomas say to Widor:
> "What music! Why didn't I know about that forty years ago? It ought to be the Bible of all musicians, and especially of organists." [324, vol.30, no.2, p.8.]

Actually, if Thomas had listened to the examinations of Franck's organ students, he would have heard *O Mensch, bewein dein' Sünde gross* (BWV 622) performed in January 1876, 1884, and 1885, and *O Lamm Gottes, unschuldig* (BWV 656) performed in June 1876 and 1886, and January 1889 [AN AJ[37], 283–92].

Widor himself did not realize until later that there was an intrinsic relationship between the music of the organ chorales and the chorale texts. Even then, he saw no reason to restrict their use. In 1907 he wrote: "What speaks through his [Bach's] works is pure religious emotion; and this is one and the same in all men, in spite of the national and religious partitions in which we are born and bred" [336, p.x].

Widor's distribution of class time was much the same as Franck's. According to Vierne, there were three class meetings per week, and Widor devoted two to improvisation and one to plainchant and execution [324, vol.29, no.12, p.10]. There was, however, a decided difference in what a student was to prepare. Widor required a new piece each week: perhaps a Bach prelude one week and the fugue the next, thus placing a much greater emphasis on repertoire than had previously been the case. Meanwhile, the requirements for the annual competition remained the same, and the decisions of the jury were still based primarily on improvisation. Although Widor found the prescribed forms artificial, he had to conform to them.

Vierne compared Franck's teaching of improvisation with Widor's. Franck, he said, "was interested above all in detail—melodic invention, harmonic discoveries, subtle modulations, elegance of pattern—in a word, everything that touches upon the domain of purely musical expression." Widor, on the other hand, "gave his principal effort to construction, logical development, the formal side." Franck was much more severe in his requirements for the fugue than Widor: "He permitted licences, to be sure, but they had to be strictly justified by the logic of the lines. The examples that Widor gave us often departed from strict counterpoint and constantly surprised us. He imposed nothing upon us, moreover, and his criticisms remained absolutely objective; we were to make of them what we would" [324, vol.29, no.12, p.10]. Vierne observed that Franck had learned his fugue technique from Reicha. Widor's counterpoint and fugue teacher was Fétis.

Among the visitors to Widor's organ class at the Conservatory were two Americans, Clarence Eddy and Fannie Edgar Thomas. Eddy wrote: "He gives Bach a great deal in teaching at the conservatory and founds everything upon this greatest of masters. Every theme must be given out with dignity and purpose. It is very impressive. This is the strongest characteristic of his teaching" [97, p.165]. On another occasion Eddy reported:

> I heard him give a lesson at the Conservatoire to an organ class, but all the pupils were playing Bach solely. He is most strenuous with regard to the rhythm. Rhythm is the strongest thing. He wants every theme to weigh a ton, and every measure to be just as solid as it is possible to be. No emotion, no nuance, no special phrasing, but very strong rhythm and the tempo very strict. As he was illustrating this on an ineffective two manual organ, of course, something had to be left to the imagination. [96, p.590.]

Fannie Edgar Thomas, columnist for *The Musical Courier,* observed a session of Widor's class in 1893. She recorded that the two-and-a-half-hour class contained performances of Bach, improvisations on a Beethoven theme, work on aspects of service playing, analyses of some Bach chorales, discussion of registration problems, and a critique of an original piece by one of the students. It is possible that Widor included a sampling of everything in his course for the benefit of the American journalist.

Thomas noted that the class was attended by some fifteen men between the ages of eighteen and 35. Throughout the class Widor emphasized "Go slow!" "The last word as the first was 'trop vite!'" She was impressed with his thoughtful consideration of the direction and form of a piece, "'breathing' with the organ as a means of phrasing," careful attention to the approach to a climax, and insistence on exactness and precision in all aspects of performance [311, vol.27, no.26, pp.11–12].

In a subsequent issue Thomas gave her readers some cold, hard facts about professorships at the Conservatory: "The teachers are divided into four classes, the incumbents receiving from $300 to $480 a year; the deputy professors from $120 to $240 a year. Professors of composition receive $600 a year each. The latter give two lessons a week; the former three of two hours each. . . . Although the professorship emolument is ridiculously small in our eyes, the honor with which it endows the incumbent gives him the power to become rich through private class prices" [311, vol.28, no.6, p.12]. Widor's annual salary at Saint-Sulpice was reported to be 2,400 francs ($480) [97, p.167].

After Widor became professor of organ at the Paris Conservatory, his reputation as a teacher, coupled with his renown as a performer and composer, soon attracted students from America and other foreign countries. Most of them were not eligible for the Conservatory class. Fannie Edgar Thomas explained that at the Conservatory only two foreigners were admitted to each class, "leaving a long line of grumbling aspirants aging before the very door, for those in [i.e., admitted] remain an indefinite time according to requirement" [311, vol.28, no.6, p.12]. Not all who came to study with Widor were interested in attending the Conservatory. Some were professional organists who could spend only their vacations in Paris; others probably thought just a few lessons would cover all they really needed to know.

In 1892 Widor ordered a small organ from Aristide Cavaillé-Coll's son Gabriel (1864–1913), and it was on this organ that he gave private lessons, individually or in classes. The organ itself was built by Gabriel, but the case was made by his brother, Emmanuel (1860–1922) [56]. The original stop-list was:

> *Grand-Orgue expressif* (56 notes): Principal 8', Flûte harmonique 8', Prestant 4'.
> *Récit expressif* (56 notes): Bourdon 8', Gambe 8', Voix céleste 8', Flûte octaviante 4', Trompette 8'*, Basson-hautbois 8'.
> *Pédale* (30 notes): Soubasse 16'.
> *Pédales de combinaison:* Appel Soubasse 16; Appel Basson-Hautbois Récit; Tirasse G.-O.; Tirasse Récit; Copula; Octaves graves du Récit sur le G.-O.; Expression Récit; Expression Grand-Orgue.
> *Trompette replaced by Plein-Jeu III around 1900.

[160, pp.54–55.]

As Widor did not speak English, he would ask a bilingual student to act as interpreter for British and American students. Albert Riemenschneider (1878–1950), an American organist and Bach scholar, served for a time in that capacity. In a 1930 tribute to Widor he wrote:

> He has untiring patience, as the following anecdote will show. The writer was leaving the Institute de France after taking a lesson when another student, an organist from Sweden, began his lesson. It was the E flat Prelude of Bach. A number of requests to repeat the opening measure drew the writer's closer attention to the episode and before the organist went on there were seventeen repetitions by actual count of the opening measure until it was considered satisfactory. On the other hand, the one thing which he cannot tolerate is indifferent and mediocre work. He once instructed the writer, whom he had called to interpret a lesson for a poorly trained pupil who could not talk French, to tell that pupil "that I am gone, gone to England"—"no," he said, "tell him that I am dead and cannot give him any more lessons." [269.]

Archibald Henderson, organist at the University of Glasgow and conductor of the Glasgow Bach Choir, was another prominent musician who studied with Widor. Like Riemenschneider, he sometimes served as interpreter for English-speaking students. Regarding Widor's classes of private students in the summers of 1908, 1909 and 1912, he wrote:

> It will interest and perhaps amuse readers to know that in the thirty class lessons I attended . . . Widor taught the organ works of only two composers: Bach and Widor! From my conversations with other Widor students of the same time, such as Marcel Dupré and Nadia Boulanger, I believe this was Widor's usual practice. Widor greatly admired Guilmant as an organist, and Saint-Saëns and César Franck as composers, but I never heard him play or teach anything by any of these masters. [154, p.341.]

Other talented musicians who made positive contributions to the organ profession found their way to Widor's doorstep, but none was more gifted, or ultimately more influential, than Albert Schweitzer, who studied with Widor from time to time, beginning in 1893. Their relationship eventually became that of colleagues rather than master and pupil, and their shared interest in the music of Bach resulted in the Widor-Schweitzer edition of his organ works.

In writing about his first studies with Widor, Schweitzer emphasized the ideas of plasticity and architecture. These terms, identifying a style of playing and a basis for interpretation, reappear several times in his memoirs:[3] "This instruction was for me an event of decisive importance. Widor led me on to a fundamental improvement of my technique, and made me strive to attain perfect plasticity in playing. At the same time there dawned on me, thanks to him, the meaning of the architectonic in music" [292, p.4].

Schweitzer spent the summer of 1899 in Berlin and cited some interesting comparisons. With the exception of Egidi, he found the Berlin organists somewhat disappointing, "because they aimed more at outward virtuosity than at the true plasticity of style to which Widor attached so much importance. And how dull and dry was the sound of the new Berlin organs compared with that of Cavaillé-Coll's instruments in St. Sulpice and Notre Dame" [292, pp.21–22].

It was from Schweitzer that Widor gained a new understanding of the Bach organ chorales. In 1899 he told Schweitzer that he found much in those works that was enigmatic. Schweitzer explained that many things in the chorales were only explicable by the texts. Widor recalled:

> I showed him the movements that had puzzled me the most; he translated the poems into French for me from memory. The mysteries were all solved. During the next few afternoons we played through the whole of the chorale preludes. While Schweitzer . . . explained them to me one after the other, I made the acquaintance of a Bach of whose existence I had previously had only the dimmest suspicion. [336, p.vi.]

After this experience Widor urged Schweitzer to "write a little essay upon the chorale preludes for the benefit of French organists" [336, p.vii]. Not one to take an assignment lightly, Schweitzer wrote a 455-page French study of Bach: *J. S. Bach, le musicien-poète* (1905), and then an 844-page, more complete German study: *J. S. Bach* (1908).

Overall, the Widor-Schweitzer relationship was one of considerable consequence for the organ profession, particularly because of the publications and the ideas they fostered. There is also another lesson to be learned from this model of cooperative scholarship and intellectual sharing: it was fruitful not only in spite of, but sometimes because of, their differences.

This lesson can also be applied to an assessment of Widor's stature as a teacher. The modern organist, having survived various changes in concept about the way Bach's music should be performed, may be inclined to underestimate the importance of the Lemmens tradition as it was documented by Widor. This tradition obviously differs from modern ideas about the performance of Bach, but if we accept this difference and agree to disagree with Widor about the Bach style, we can discover Widor's lasting contributions to organ pedagogy.

Widor's teaching techniques (as well as organ techniques) were derived from Lemmens, but it was Widor himself who most vigorously insisted on their preservation and dissemination through his own teaching, his influence, his highly visible positions, his writings, and his perseverance. The standards Widor required from his pupils, both at the Conservatory and in his studio, firmly established a new day in organ pedagogy, based on principles as valid, demanding, and humbling today as they were in 1890:

1. Every detail of organ playing can, and should be, subjected to critical analysis, including physical motions, use of the instrument, and expressive performance of the score.

2. Every detail contributes to the musical result and should therefore be planned, practiced, and ultimately controlled by the performer.

3. Expression in organ playing is not produced by whim, special effects, or bizarre exaggerations, but by correlating rhythm, phrasing, touch, and use of the instrument with the musical content and structure of the piece.

4. The organist is not exempt from the professional standards required in other branches of music.

5. Organists must learn to listen to what they play.

Doubtless the best performers have always been able to control the physical elements of music making in order to produce artistic results, whether the approach was intellectual, intuitive, or both. But it required a Widor to demonstrate in the classroom how the serious organ student can be taught to solve performance problems through logical procedures. Modern organ pedagogy has relied so long on this model that one tends to forget it had a beginning.

XVIII.
Guilmant as Teacher

WIDOR left the position of organ professor at the Paris Conservatory in 1896 to become professor of composition. He recommended Guilmant as his successor, with the provision that Vierne remain as assistant [324, vol.30, no.2, p.9]. Guilmant apparently thought this arrangement satisfactory, and, indeed, one can imagine that he found it convenient to have a talented, experienced assistant who could substitute for him when he was on tour and who could tutor students both for admission to the class and for examinations. If Guilmant in any way resented the lack of confidence in his ability this condition suggested, he never openly gave evidence of it.

One can list many similarities between professors Widor and Guilmant. Both set examples for their students of commitment to the art of music; both insisted on precise control of all details of organ technique in their own playing and in that of their students; and both held the objective of creating in France a school of organ playing of the highest order. Both were great performers who had studied with Lemmens and continued to follow his method in their teaching; both were remembered by their students for their kindness, generosity, and personal concern; and both made significant contributions to the music community through their leadership in professional organizations.

When Guilmant took over the organ class from Widor, there was no sudden change in method or procedure, no wave of troubled mutterings among the students. Unlike Widor, he announced no revolution at his first class meeting. One might have the impression that Guilmant simply imitated Widor's example, carefully monitored by the latter's disciple and acknowledged informant, Vierne.[1] But Guilmant, too, had his own style and his own agenda, which he set about putting in place without fanfare but with great authority.

Alexandre Guilmant met his first Conservatory class when he was 59 years old. He was perhaps the best-known organist in the world. He had been organist at La Trinité for 25 years; his series of concerts at the Trocadéro had attracted record crowds for eighteen years; he had played for Queen Victoria at Windsor Castle (1890), and had made his first tour to the United States (1893). Unlike Widor, he was already an experienced teacher with a well-established private studio; he was president of the Schola Cantorum society, and the new school by that name was just opening its doors. Guilmant had written a large number of organ compositions, including five sonatas, the eighteen books of *Pièces dans différents styles,* and the twelve books of

L'Organiste pratique; and he was actively engaged in collecting and editing works of early composers.

There were two special areas in which Guilmant reigned supreme: repertoire and registration. No other French organist approached his comprehensive knowledge of organ repertoire of all periods. Widor focused his teaching on the music of Bach, to which he added a sampling of works of the best-known nineteenth-century composers; Guilmant, too, centered his teaching around Bach, but from there he sought to expand his students' repertoire to include a broad choice of styles, both early and contemporary. This expanded repertoire did not indicate a diluted or less-rigorous insistence on the importance of Bach's music. In an 1898 article Guilmant wrote:

> Organ music reached its climax with Bach: it may, perhaps, be said that all music did. At any rate, one thing is certain: viz., if there has been any progress in music since the day of Bach, it has been due to him. . . .
> For pure organ music, Bach still is, and probably will always remain, the greatest of all composers. . . .
> My admiration for Bach is unbounded. I consider that Bach is music. Everything else in music has come from him; and if all music, excepting Bach's, were to be destroyed, music would still be preserved. [146, p.xxvi.]

The artistry of Guilmant in choosing registration was legendary. He understood organ timbre both in its historic context and in its modern manipulations. Neither Widor nor Guilmant tolerated frequent, irrelevant stop changes, but while Widor taught his students general principles of registration, Guilmant could (and did) explain the character and use of each stop. In repertoire and registration Widor tended to become ever more conservative, while Guilmant tended to become more comprehensive and eclectic.

Widor's concerns about leaving the organ class to Guilmant may have been related to the latter's harmonic style. In tutoring the organ students in improvisation on the free subject, Vierne felt it necessary to go beyond what Guilmant would have preferred:

> I set myself the role of maintaining the Francko-Widorian tradition, and the pupils chimed in with me enthusiastically. It is true that Père Guilmant made a slight grimace on first hearing of some of the combinations, which were more or less raw at the beginning, and he balked a bit, too, at certain fanciful rhythms, but at bottom he was liberal and, provided that a thing was logical, he tolerated tendencies which were not his own. [324, vol.30, no.2, p.9.]

One of the changes Guilmant achieved at the Conservatory was in the examination requirements. After his first year as professor he approached Dubois (then director) with a plan to substitute a more valid test for the outmoded plainchant harmonization and make some modifications in the structure of improvised fugues. The plainchant accompaniment would no longer be note-for-note, "but in a broader style, admitting melodic ornaments, such as embellishments and passing notes, with chords falling only on the principal notes" [324, vol.30, no.3, p.8]. The commentary on the plainchant would be either a free prelude on one or more chant fragments or an embellished organ chorale on the chant. In either case it was to be modal. Dubois agreed to the changes, but he was apprehensive about the reaction of the examination jury. As it turned out, there was no cause for concern.

Characteristically, Guilmant did not worry about what the reactions might be when he was certain of his course of action. He planned carefully and acted with determination. He was as clear and precise in his goals and relationships as he was in his playing. He had infinite patience with his students, but none with the petty intrigues and jealousies that swarmed around professional activities. Both Franck and Widor had experienced problems with the Conservatory jury discriminating against their students. When Guilmant faced the same problem, he took the matter up with the director and warned that he would complain to the minister, if necessary [324, vol.30, no.3, p.8].

While Guilmant did not write an organ method *per se,* his article "La Musique d'orgue," in the *Encyclopédie de la musique et dictionnaire du Conservatoire* [145] indicates the scope of the information and the viewpoint he brought to the classroom. He refers to an impressive array of sources from the sixteenth through the nineteenth centuries. Guilmant was familiar with the most recent studies as well as original sources related to the development of forms, repertoire, performance practice, and organ design.

Guilmant cited the Lemmens *Ecole* frequently, and he obviously regarded the Lemmens method as authoritative for the performance of Bach. He traced the performance tradition from Bach through J. C. Kittel, J. C. H. Rinck, and A. Hesse to Lemmens. Legato, he said, was the true organ style: the goal toward which systems of fingering had always progressed. Like Widor, he advocated keeping knees and heels together, eliminating all unnecessary movement, and strictly controlling all attacks and releases. Separations between repeated notes, staccato notes, and other articulated notes were to be measured precisely. Guilmant, too, noted that modern tempos were sometimes too fast to permit the listener to hear the music clearly [145, pp.1155–60, 1171].

Regarding both touch and tempo, Guilmant cautioned that performers must take into account the situation in which they are playing. A large church or concert hall requires a less legato touch than a smaller place; choice of tempo should be influenced by the size of the room and the dimensions and resources of the organ [145, pp.1157, 1171].

Guilmant argued strongly for authenticity in registration. He quite emphatically stated that one could not perform the music of Bach or his contemporaries well if one did not have the timbres those masters used [145, p.1172]. He especially regretted that modern organs did not include the stops needed for the registration of early French music, and he concluded that "it is as ridiculous to play a composition with stops for which it has not been written, as to play an orchestral work replacing the clarinets by oboes or the violins by trumpets." [Il est aussi ridicule de jouer une composition avec des jeux pour

lesquels elle n'a pas été faite, que d'exécuter une oeuvre d'orchestre en rempla-
çant les clarinettes par des hautbois, ou des violons par des trompettes; 145,
p.1173.]

Students of Guilmant who were awarded first prize in organ during his
tenure at the Conservatory included Louis Andlauer, Emile Avine, Augustin
Barié, Ermend Bonnal, Joseph Bonnet, Roger Boucher, Nadia Boulanger,
Joseph Boulnois, Alexandre Cellier, Marcel Dupré, Paul Fauchet, Félix Four-
drain, Georges Jacob, Georges Krieger, Emile Poillot, Charles Quef, Alphonse
Schmitt, Juliette Toutain, and René Vierne.[2]

Marcel Dupré (1886–1971) started studying privately with Guilmant when
he was twelve years old. In 1905 he began auditing the Conservatory organ
class. The following year he was enrolled in the class, and he was awarded first
prize in organ in 1907. He recalled his early studies with Guilmant:

> Guilmant was the strictest of teachers. He would stop me almost at each bar
> for the slightest detail and I had to repeat my bar until he considered every little
> point was right. But he was always patient and gentle: Had I skipped a sharp or
> a flat or a silence, he would just say: "put on your glasses, Marcel"; and, with a
> blush, I quickly corrected my oversight. One can imagine the benefit of such
> discipline applied to a child.
>
> Later, when I entered the organ class at the Conservatory where Guilmant
> taught for 17 years, I found him just as strict with grownup students. Nothing
> passed unnoticed; "You cannot obtain perfect clarity," he would repeat to us,
> "unless you get absolute precision, that is, if you give each note its exact value.
> Always remember this which is of supreme importance: it is as imperative to
> release a note exactly in time as it is to strike it on the beat. All depends on this."
> [93, p.8.]

Dupré noted further that Guilmant's own playing was "a magnificent illustration of his teaching. The perfection of his technique, his brilliant virtuosity
which never exceeded the speed of the right tempo, his smooth legato and
marvelous clarity thanks to which all the inner parts of the most complex
polyphony were brought out, his splendid musical phrasing soon made him
famous" [93, p.8]. Dupré's testimony was confirmed by another of Guilmant's
famous pupils, Joseph Bonnet (1884–1944). Guilmant's uncompromising
standards applied to every aspect of performance, he said. Nothing escaped
him [28, p.9]. Far from being discouraged by Guilmant's exacting requirements, Bonnet and his peers responded with an enthusiasm for their work and
a warm affection for "Père Guilmant."

Praise for Guilmant's teaching at the Conservatory was not limited to his
own students. In 1906 Albert Schweitzer affirmed that "Guilmant is not only
one of the foremost performers, but also one of the most universal teachers of
the present day, possessing outstanding pedagogical talent and music-
historical background. It was he who made the French acquainted with the
old, pre-Bach organ music" [293, p.21]. Even Vierne, for all his allegiance to
Widor and his nickname, "Widor junior" [157, p.55], ranked Guilmant at the

top of the teaching profession. Under Guilmant, he said, the year-end Conservatory competitions were artistic manifestations of an unprecedented level. Guilmant, the "marvellous educator," produced "the most impressive generation of organists" France had ever known [321, p.31].

Guilmant had established his reputation in Paris as an organ teacher long before he became organ professor at the Conservatory. On October 8, 1871, *Revue et Gazette musicale* announced that Alexandre Guilmant, organist from Boulogne-sur-Mer, would succeed Chauvet as *titulaire* at La Trinité [RGM 38, p.282]. Guilmant moved to Paris and took up residence near the church, at 62, rue de Clichy, where he opened a private studio. Notices in the music journals in late October and early November 1872 announced the opening of elementary and advanced courses in organ offered by Guilmant [RGM 39, p.343; ME 38, p.399].

Some years earlier, Guilmant was given a small organ. It had one manual of 54 notes, a coupled pedal of 30 notes, and four stops: Principal 8', Prestant 4', Flûte 8', Flûte 4' [94, p.74n]. This little instrument had been made with great care, and it served Guilmant well for practice and teaching in his new location. He liked to tell the story of a young man from Leipzig who came to apply for lessons. He began to play a Bach fugue, but he became excited, and his playing became so vigorous that Guilmant laid a hand on his shoulder. "Please don't break the organ," he said, "my father built it" [cited in 42].

Later Guilmant moved to Meudon, a few miles outside Paris, but he retained his private studio on rue de Clichy for a time. A description of the studio and some interesting details about Guilmant's private teaching appeared in *The Musical Courier* in 1893, while Guilmant himself was on his first American tour. The article was written by William C. Carl, who had gone to Paris in 1890 to study with Guilmant. He was among the first of an army of Americans who became Guilmant pupils, and he remained one of the French master's most devoted and influential disciples.

> On leaving the church [La Trinité], a few steps up the Rue de Clichy, brings one to No. 62, the town residence and studio of Mr. Guilmant, consisting of a suite of rooms, "au premier étage," with a salon, containing an Erard grand [,] Mustel harmonium, a portion of his large library, a signed portrait of M. Cavaillé-Coll, a pen portrait of himself when quite a young man, and several laurel wreaths, as prominent among the furnishings. The music room adjoining is devoted to the organ, built for him by his father, who was a prominent organist in Boulogne, and who died recently at the age of ninety-seven years. It is upon this instrument, with its single manual and pedal board of twenty-seven notes, and not over a dozen stops, that Mr. Guilmant gives all his lessons, except in rare instances, when he will go to the organ factory of Mr. Cavaillé Coll.
>
> Strange as it may seem the test is much greater than on a larger or more modern organ, and much can be accomplished.
>
> The Lemmens "Organ School" is strongly recommended and used. The scales are pedaled, as indicated in this work, and Mr. Guilmant always speaks

in the highest praise of his former master, Mr. Jacques Lemmens, with whom he was a favorite pupil in Brussels.

At the lesson Guilmant rigidly insists on exact tempo and rhythm. He will not permit the smallest detail to pass unnoticed until correctly played.

In harmony, he teaches the "Traité d'Harmonie de Reber," and with it the "Notes et Etudes d'Harmonie" of Dubois, interspersed with exercises by Bazzin, Fennroli, Durand, &c.

After this the "Traité du Contrepoint de Fétis."

In teaching these subjects, his "Comprenez-vous?" after each explanation shows how particular he is that nothing shall pass until thoroughly understood. I well remember this interrogative having been asked at least twenty times in the course of a single lesson in harmony.

Another room, in which his publications are kept, completes the suite.

Mr. Guilmant returns to his villa at Meudon each day after the duties in Paris are completed, where his life, surrounded by his family, has been a peculiarly happy one. [43, p.10.]

A few more interesting remarks about Guilmant's private teaching in the early 1890s are furnished by Theodore Knauff: "His pupils learn to love and revere him. His high prices do not deter any, though for the sake of their pockets, he will take none unless they are advanced pupils, able to profit by his work. All who are not, have to study under another master first, until prepared for his moulding hand" [182, p.7].

In 1899 the Cavaillé-Coll-Mutin company built a three-manual, 28-stop organ for the music room at Villa Guilmant, Meudon. The little four-stop organ was placed in an adjoining room. Thereafter, Guilmant's private students had their lessons in Meudon. Guilmant had designed the new organ himself, specifying many of its technical details. He also supervised its tonal finishing. Its original specification was:

Grand-orgue: Bourdon 16', Montre 8', Flûte harmonique 8', Salicional 8', Prestant 4'.

Récit expressif: Diapason 8', Flûte traversière 8', Dulciane 8', Voix céleste 8', Flûte octaviante 4', Doublette 2', Plein-jeu III, Basson-Hautbois 8', Trompette harmonique 8'.

Positif expressif: Flûte creuse 8', Viole de Gambe 8', Cor de nuit 8', Flûte douce 4', Nasard 2 2/3', Quarte de Nasard 2', Tierce 1 3/5', Cromorne 8'.

Pédale: Soubasse 16', Contrebasse 16', Flûte 8', Violoncelle 8', Bourdon 8', Basson 16'.

Pédales de Combinaisons: Fonds Pédale, Tirasse du Grand Orgue, Tirasse Positif, Tirasse Récit, Anches Pédale, Piano Grand Orgue, Forte Grand Orgue, Anches Récit, Expression du Positif, Expression du Récit, Fonds Grand Orgue, Octaves aiguë du Grand Orgue, Copula Positif sur Grand Orgue, Copula Récit sur Grand Orgue, Récit sur Grand Orgue à l'octave grave, Récit sur Positif, Tremolo du Récit. [203, p.xi.]

Alexandre Guilmant at his Cavaillé-Coll-Mutin organ in Meudon (Bibliothèque Nationale, Paris).

After the new organ was installed, Meudon became a center of organ activity. Here Guilmant, his wife, and children shared their family circle with countless students, visiting musicians, friends, and neighbors. In the evening guests might be treated to an organ program by their host.

Archibald Henderson, the organist and choirmaster of the University of Glasgow, visited an organ class at Meudon in 1908. He commented on

Guilmant's meticulous care regarding all aspects of performance. Then he related an incident that illustrates why Guilmant was loved, as well as respected, by his students:

> As a critic Guilmant was kindly and constructive. An enthusiastic and talented American student once disturbed him by his exaggerated movements at the console. Guilmant corrected him gently by saying, "Let me play the movement as you play it, and see if you like it so." He then imitated the student faithfully, the pupil being the first to laugh heartily at the sight. As Guilmant remarked afterward, "such exaggeration is to be avoided; first, because it is unnecessary and disturbing, not to say ridiculous, and, second, because it is wasting a great deal of energy." [151.]

Guilmant's three tours to America (1893, 1897–98, and 1904) opened a whole new world for many American organists, and they were soon flocking to Paris to study. As Joseph Bonnet commented: "Formerly, the American organists scarcely went across Paris to go to study in Leipzig, Berlin, or Munich. Since 1893, date of Guilmant's first tour to the United States, it's to Paris that their successors come to pitch their tent and receive our instruction." [Jadis, les organistes américains ne faisaient guère que traverser Paris pour aller étudier à Leipzig, Berlin ou Munich. Depuis 1893, date de la première tournée de Guilmant aux Etats-Unis, c'est à Paris que leurs successeurs viennent planter leur tente et recevoir nos enseignements; 27 p.82.]

Agnes Armstrong estimated that "several hundred Americans travelled to France to study with Guilmant as private students" [10, p.23]. Among the early arrivals—those who made the pilgrimage to Paris before the turn of the century—were Philip Paul Bliss, William C. Carl, Percy B. Eversden, Charles Henry Galloway, Philip Hale, James Alfred Pennington, Charles Albert Riemenschneider, Samuel Tudor Strang, and William C. Gustin Wright.[3] Other prominent American musicians who studied with Guilmant included Seth Bingham, Clarence Dickinson, Harvey B. Gaul, Edwin Arthur Kraft, James H. Rogers, Frederick B. Stiven, and Everett E. Truette.

In 1911, shortly after the death of Guilmant, *The Musician* printed a list of 114 Americans who had been his pupils [MU 16, p.418]. But his influence in America went far beyond those students. In 1912 William C. Carl wrote that "the great advance in organ playing made here can easily be traced to the date of his first tour when he was summoned to play the great organ at the World's Fair in Chicago. The succeeding visits did much to confirm this, and now in no country of the world is organ music more appreciated than here" [44].

One cannot even venture a guess at how many organists studied with pupils of Guilmant. New York's Guilmant Organ School, founded by William C. Carl in 1899, offered instruction based on Guilmant's methods as well as practical training in church music. While this school, by virtue of its name and Guilmant's personal involvement, testified visibly to his influence in America, it was only one of countless means through which the Lemmens-Guilmant-Widor tradition reached and gradually dominated American organ playing. How pleased old Fétis and his pupil Lemmens would have been to see what a mighty oak their acorn became, with its branches spreading from Paris to the Pacific!

XIX.
The Niedermeyer School

THE Niedermeyer School, unlike the Paris Conservatory, was organized specifically for the education of church musicians. When it was founded in 1853, no other institution in France was adequately serving this purpose. However, there had been earlier institutions and endeavors with similar or related objectives.

With its secular orientation, the Paris Conservatory had never been a satisfactory substitute for the traditional choir schools, or *maîtrises*, so far as training church musicians was concerned. In the early decades of the nineteenth century some musicians wanted to revive the network of *maîtrises* that had provided musical training in communities throughout France before the Revolution. But money was scarce, and the government (which controlled the church purse strings) had priorities it deemed more pressing than the funding of choir schools.[1] Even in so prominent a location as Notre-Dame Cathedral, Paris, the *maîtrise* (resuscitated soon after the Revolution) limped along with fluctuating fortunes.

In spite of financial difficulties, churches that wanted choral music had to institute some kind of program for recruiting and training boys. Gradually church music schools were revived in cathedrals and larger parishes in various parts of France. The nineteenth-century *maîtrise* did not have the prestige of its predecessors as a route to a professional career in music, but it sometimes still served as an effective first step in that direction.

Through the century musicians sought additional ways to improve the quality of church music through education. The first of several notable church-music schools in nineteenth-century Paris was organized by Etienne-Alexandre Choron. Beginning in 1817 with some experimental classes in singing, Choron's school expanded to become the *Institution royale de musique religieuse* in 1825.

Choral music of earlier periods received particular attention, and Choron's students performed works by Palestrina and other early masters in services of the church of the Sorbonne from 1825,[2] in concerts at the Institution from 1827, and on tours in other parts of France. Funded by the government, Choron's school had some 150 students by 1830, when its financial support was discontinued by Louis-Philippe [225, p.28]. Choron continued his educational efforts as best he could with dwindling means and failing health until his death in 1834 [45].

While early choral music was a novel feature in Choron's school, and his choral performances attracted special attention, organ playing was not entirely neglected. Choron himself edited German organ methods by Johann Christian Heinrich Rinck (1770–1846) and Johann Gottlob Werner (1777–1822) specifically for use by the students at his Institution. The Rinck method, translated as *L'Ecole pratique d'orgue.* . . . (Paris: Richault [1828]), contained manual and pedal exercises, and pieces of progressive difficulty. The Werner method, translated by Hellert and edited by Choron, was published some five years later with the title *Méthode élémentaire pour l'orgue.* . . . (Paris: Richault [1833]). It was designed as an introduction to organ playing, preparing the student for the Rinck method. The sequence of material was similar, but on a more elementary level.

The link Choron forged between early music and the training of church musicians was later embraced by other educators. While there was no successor to Choron's school for some twenty years, various musicians applied themselves to the task of educating the listening public to appreciate the unfamiliar styles of earlier periods. Soon after Choron's school concerts, a series of historical concerts was presented by François-Joseph Fétis. These events were actually lecture-concerts, each devoted to a specific area of music history, with Fétis himself commenting on the works performed. The topics were the history of the opera (April 8, 1832), music of the sixteenth century (December 16, 1832), music of the seventeenth century (March 24, 1833), and another program on the history of opera (April 2, 1833). The first two concerts created considerable interest and were well received, the third was less popular, and the fourth was a disaster. In 1833 Fétis moved to Belgium to become director of the Brussels Conservatory. From time to time he organized historical concerts in Brussels (1835, 1839, four in 1855, 1858). He made an unsuccessful attempt to revive them in Paris in 1835, and he presented one more there in 1855 [329, pp.266–71].

In 1843 the *Société de musique vocale religieuse et classique* was created in Paris to perform choral works written before the nineteenth century. The works programmed were then published. The organization was founded by Joseph-Napoléon Ney (1803–57), who was usually referred to by his title, *le prince de la Moskowa*. The eldest son of Marshal Ney, Duke of Elchingen, he was a statesman, musician, and scholar.

Louis Niedermeyer, a Swiss-born musician, was associated with Ney in the activities of the choral society. Convinced that the music of earlier centuries held the key to the improvement of church music, as both model and repertoire, Niedermeyer founded a new school that incorporated the study and performance of early music within its larger objective of training church musicians.

Niedermeyer had an impressive musical background, having studied in Vienna, Rome, and Naples. Like many of his contemporaries, he aspired to a career as an opera composer. Through the friendship and support of Rossini, several of his operatic works were actually mounted. He met with some success, but in general his works failed to capture the interest of the public. It

Louis Niedermeyer (Bibliothèque Nationale, Paris).

was after one final disappointment in 1853 that he turned his attention to the education of church musicians, and he devoted his remaining years entirely to this objective.

As a composer Niedermeyer merits some attention for his secular songs and sacred choral music. His 28 organ pieces include short versets and more extended *offertoires,* preludes, fugues, marches, and communions. In general they are well-crafted church pieces in a dignified (if not highly original) style. The organ pieces all appeared in the periodical published by Niedermeyer and Joseph d'Ortigue (1802–66), *La Maîtrise* (1857–61). These two men also collaborated in the publication of a treatise, *Traité théorique et pratique de l'accompagnement du plain-chant* (1855).

Niedermeyer's school has sometimes been viewed as a revival of Choron's school. Actually, it had no connection with the earlier institution, although the two shared the objective of improving church music, and both emphasized the study of early music. Unlike its predecessor, the Niedermeyer School was started at a time when interest in church music was beginning to accelerate, when new organs were appearing in the churches, and when there were more incentives for a young person to study church music. It was originally called *Ecole de musique classique et religieuse* and was established under the Ministry of Public Instruction, with the participation of the Bishops of Paris [229, p.365]. The government subsidized 36 scholarships, and some twenty students enrolled when the school opened in 1853 [5, p.304; 127, p.32].

Pierre-Louis-Philippe Dietsch (1808–1865) was the first superintendent of studies at the Niedermeyer School, and the school continued under his direction after Niedermeyer's death in 1861. When Dietsch died in 1865, the leadership went to Victor-Gustave Lefèvre (1831–1910), Niedermeyer's son-in-law [127, pp.35–40]. Family ties within the Niedermeyer School were further represented by another son-in-law, Eugène Gigout, a teacher at the school from 1863. In 1869 Gigout married the younger of Louis Niedermeyer's two daughters, Mathilde.

In 1885 the school passed from the authority of Public Instruction and Churches to that of Fine Arts. Its name was shortened to *Ecole de musique classique,* a change that reflected a somewhat modified policy: the Niedermeyer School no longer limited its primary objective to the training of church musicians. The diplomas *Maître de Chapelle* and *Organiste* were discontinued, as were the church-funded organ and composition prizes. The director, Lefèvre, felt that the change of emphasis was necessary for the future of the school [220, p.60]. Indeed, as a church-music school, it was periodically in danger of losing its scholarship subsidy as sentiment for the separation of church and state became increasingly aggressive in France. Although organ and church music remained important parts of the curriculum, the Niedermeyer School gradually lost its position on the cutting edge of church-music reform. At the end of the century progressive education in this area fell to the Schola Cantorum.

Nevertheless, the changes effected by Lefèvre seem to have been more cosmetic than essential, and the Niedermeyer School still retained its image as a school of church music. In 1894 Fannie Edgar Thomas described the origins of the school for her American readers, and then continued:

> With little modification the Niedermeyer school of sacred music exists to-day as then. . . .
> Nothing but the ancient classic and ecclesiastical music is considered. Indeed some consider the régime too severe. Yet the lesson which created the school was severe. No doubt the authorities consider that a standard cannot be too inflexible, human nature is so wavering. [311, vol.28, no.18, p.13.]

In 1896 Clarence Eddy, too, still described the Niedermeyer School as a "school of church music": "This school, which is well known in France, is after the general design of the school of church music at Regensburg, in Germany" [97, p.168].

Among twentieth-century writers, Martin Cooper concluded that the Niedermeyer School "provided an excellent musical education, in many ways superior to that of the Conservatoire" [60, p.78]. Arthur Hutchings surmised that the most valuable contribution of both the Niedermeyer School and the

Schola Cantorum was "among the mass of local musicians and fine teachers of sterling worth who do not achieve international distinction but are the backbone of musical life in church and nation" [166, p.93].

The Niedermeyer School offered instruction in general musicianship and church music, including solfège, harmony, counterpoint, fugue, composition, orchestration, improvisation, organ, piano, plainchant and plainchant accompaniment, voice, and choir. In addition, students pursued a normal selection of basic general education subjects, such as reading, writing, and history [127, p.29]. The focus of the musical studies was defined by Niedermeyer: "For plainchant, we say: Saint Gregory; for sacred music: Palestrina; for the organ: J. S. Bach." [Pour le plain-chant, déclarait Niedermeyer, nous disons: Saint-Grégoire; pour la musique sacrée: Palestrina; pour l'orgue: J.-S. Bach; cited in 206, p.73.]

The Niedermeyer School did not seek to compete with the Conservatory, as there were major differences in their organization and objectives. A report of 1907 noted that from its beginning the Niedermeyer School had been a boarding school that accepted without examination young people who wanted to follow all the courses required for a thorough musical education. The Conservatory, on the other hand, admitted only a selection of students, and their education was more specialized in the areas of performance and composition. While instruction was free at the Conservatory, one almost always needed to pay for private lessons as well as for room and board. At the Niedermeyer School everything was provided, and a student could obtain government grants to cover almost all the costs of his musical education. The report observed that the Niedermeyer School was the only one in France in which a young person without money could get a musical education. It was also unique in the assistance it gave its students in finding employment when they had completed their studies [cited in 260, p.65]. In 1908, its name was changed again, to *Ecole Niedermeyer.*

Unlike the Conservatory, the Niedermeyer School gave its organ students at least occasional opportunities to gain public performance experience. There were student programs of organ, piano, and vocal music, and more elaborate concerts in which faculty as well as students participated. In July 1880, for example, a concert given by the Niedermeyer School at the Trocadéro included organ performances by two students, Walter and Boëllmann, and a professor, Gigout [ME 46, p.264]. The organ students' experience was further enriched by participation in the school chorus, which from time to time gave performances of works by Palestrina, Lassus, and other early masters.

Niedermeyer believed in a liberal admission policy: there was no entrance examination or age requirement. However, the prospective student had to present a birth certificate and proof of baptism to verify that he was French and Christian [127, p.37]. These requirements were later dropped, and foreign students as well as non-Christians were admitted [260, p.64]. In 1914 Arthur de Guichard could assure prospective American students that they would be welcomed on an equal basis with French, and that the cost of attending the Niedermeyer school would not be prohibitive:

> At the Ecole Niedermeyer it costs $274 for the entire scholastic year of ten months. For this amount the pupil has board, lodging, instruction in the full curriculum, bedding, and the doctor's care. The only extras are paper, books, music, and piano hire, and extra special classes for violin and for pedagogy. Thus it need not cost more than $400 for a year's study, including the steamer ticket there and back (second cabin). [143, p.370.]

In 1875 the staff of the school consisted of the director, the chaplain, four music professors (including the director), two resident teachers of general subjects, two supervisors (or guardians), and four student tutors. A committee of studies consisted of the director, the professors, and six other members (including Guilmant and Saint-Saëns). All the students were residents of the school. At that time Clément Loret taught organ; Alexandre Georges taught lower-division piano; Eugène Gigout taught upper-division piano, plainchant, harmony, counterpoint, and fugue; and the director, Gustave Lefèvre, had classes in solfège, applied harmony, accompaniment, music history, and vocal ensemble. Soon after, Jules Stoltz joined the staff as professor of solfège [6, vol.1, pp.25–26; vol.3, pp.27–28].

Students entered the school at about age ten to thirteen. Those who remained until the completion of their studies were eligible for diplomas: *Maître de Chapelle* and *Organiste*. Gifted students could qualify for one or both diplomas by age eighteen or nineteen.

Gabriel Fauré (1845–1924), who entered the school at age ten, found that the boarding-school environment conserved time and energy and eliminated many of the contradictory, confusing, and undesirable influences a young student might otherwise encounter. He benefited also from the fact that humanities were taught on an equal basis with music. As for music itself, he said: "Music? we were impregnated with it; we lived in it as in a bath; it penetrated us through all the pores." [La musique? nous en étions imprégnés, nous y vivions comme dans un bain, elle nous pénétrait par tous les pores; 105, p.6].

Fauré listed the composers whose music constituted the students' repertoire. The school chorus sang works of Palestrina, Vittoria, Orlando Lasso, Bach, and Handel. In piano one studied the clavecin composers as well as Bach, Haydn, Mozart, Beethoven, Weber, and Mendelssohn. In organ one learned music of Bach, Handel, Boëly, Mendelssohn, and the eighteenth-century French composers. Fauré observed that this repertoire was anything but usual in 1853. Bach was the daily bread at the Niedermeyer School, but his music had not yet penetrated the organ class of the Paris Conservatory[3] [105, p.7].

XX.
Organ Study at the Niedermeyer and Gigout Schools

FRANÇOIS-XAVIER Wackenthaler was the first professor of organ at the Niedermeyer School. His death at age 32 left the post vacant in October 1856. By December of that year Georges Schmitt had been named organ professor [RGM 23, p.402], but he left the school after two years, because of a difference of opinion with Niedermeyer on a pedagogical question [271, col.11].

Schmitt was succeeded by Clément Loret, who had been a student of Lemmens at the Brussels Conservatory. In a letter to Lemmens dated February 21, 1858, Loret told his teacher the good news about his two new positions: as professor of organ, and also as organist at Saint-Louis-d'Antin, where Niedermeyer was *maître de chapelle*. He was very happy to be associated with Niedermeyer at the church, as the music there would be on a higher level than in some Paris churches. He also looked forward to a new Cavaillé-Coll organ, which was to be ready by Easter. Loret asked Lemmens for a list of "all the organ pieces," both old and modern, as Niedermeyer wanted to publish them in *La Maîtrise*. He also wanted a copy of Lemmens's *Journal*. His students were using copies they had made, none too accurately, and Loret himself no longer had a copy of his own [cited in 80, p.89]. No wonder he was soon to publish his own teaching material!

The first sets of exercises for manuals and pedals by Loret appeared in *La Maîtrise* in 1858.[1] His major contribution to organ pedagogy was his *Cours d'orgue*, Op.19, a four-volume organ method. The first two volumes were in use at the Niedermeyer School by the mid–1860s. The third volume appeared in 1879, by which time the final volume was in preparation [RGM 46, p.383]. The contents, by volume, are: 1. manual exercises and etudes; 2. pedal exercises and etudes for manuals and pedals; 3. an explanation of the organ and a collection of pieces by Loret; 4. explanations and exercises for transposition, improvisation, and plainchant accompaniment.

Loret's approach to organ technique followed the path already defined by Lemmens. Like his teacher, Loret wrote exercises for substitution, finger and thumb glissando, legato playing, combinations of legato and detached playing, and studies for the pedal that involve the oblique movement of one foot behind the other after a black note. His original compositions consist of etudes, music for church services, and longer concert pieces (including a sonata). Loret also wrote recreational parlor music with organ or harmonium, and he made transcriptions of Handel organ concertos for organ solo.

Henri Letocart (1866–1945) remarked that Loret's organ pupils studied works of Bach, Mendelssohn, Rinck, Lemmens, Boëly, and others, but the most essential was Bach. "From my entrance in the school [1879], I owned, like many of my comrades, the eight volumes of organ of J. S. Bach (Peters edition). (The ninth would not appear until some years later.)" [Dès mon entrée à l'Ecole, je possédais, comme beaucoup de mes camarades, les huit cahiers d'orgue de J.-S. Bach (Edit. Peters). (Le neuvième ne devait paraître que quelques années plus tard); 202, no.36, p.6.]

In the annual competitions for the organ prize, Loret's students played a required piece and one of their choice. In 1858, his first year at the Niedermeyer School, the organ competition was held on the new Cavaillé-Coll organ at Saint-Louis-d'Antin, where Loret was organist. The required piece was the Bach Passacaglia and the second a Bach fugue of choice[2] [RGM 25, p.243].

By 1879 the organ students were competing in three divisions. The required piece for the first division was Handel's Concerto in B-flat; for the second, Mendelssohn's Sixth Sonata; for the third, Bach's Canzona. As before, each competitor also played a second piece of choice. That year the competition was held in the Trocadéro [ME 45, p.248]. It is important to note that Lemmens's techniques and his emphases on the performance of composed music and on Bach as the cornerstone of organ repertoire were the bases of organ instruction at the Niedermeyer School long before Widor promoted the same ideas at the Paris Conservatory in 1890.

Loret seems to have had a rather colorless personality. His former students generally remembered him with respect, but not with the affection that signals a special teacher-pupil relationship. Henri Letocart wrote: "Clément Loret was an unassuming person, perhaps little susceptible to grand emotions. His teaching was clear and correct. One recognized him as a pupil of Lemmens by his concern for articulation." [Clément Loret était un modeste, peut-être peu sensible aux grandes émotions. Son enseignement était clair et correct. On retrouvait en lui l'élève de Lemmens par son souci de l'articulation; 202, no.36, p.6.]

Désire Walter, a classmate of Boëllmann, had a somewhat warmer view of Loret: "This good papa Loret, our organ professor, brilliant student of Lemmens, gave us precious advice for the interpretation of the works of J. S. Bach. I have even encountered again, in the advice of Vierne (*Bulletin des Amis de l'orgue* 1934–36), the same recommendations given earlier by Loret." [Ce bon papa Loret, notre professeur d'orgue, brillant élève de Lemmens, nous donnait de précieux conseils pour l'interprétation des oeuvres de J. S. Bach. J'ai même retrouvé, dans les conseils de Vierne (Bulletin des «Amis de l'orgue» 1934–1936), les mêmes recommandations données jadis par Loret; cited in 220, p.51.]

Henri Busser was less generous. In his four years at the Niedermeyer School he found Gustave Lefèvre and Alexandre Georges to be excellent educators, but Loret's teaching, he said, seemed very rudimentary [40, pp.31–32]. Jean Huré commented that Loret played with much precision and moderation and that "Cl. Loret really worshiped Lemmens. On the other hand Saint-Saëns couldn't endure the great Belgian master." [Cl. Loret avait pour Lemmens un véritable culte. Par contre Saint-Saëns ne pouvait pas souffrir le grand maître belge; 162, p.6.]

While his list of publications is considerable, Loret gave relatively little attention to performance aside from church services, and his name rarely appeared on organ programs. He participated in the inauguration of the Cavaillé-Coll organ at Notre-Dame in 1868 and was one of the organists who played on a series of Sunday programs after the primary inaugural event. Ten years later he played one of the programs in the initial series at the Trocadéro. Only a few other performances were noted in the musical press.

At the Notre-Dame inauguration Loret played a Bach prelude and fugue, while all the other organists played their own works [RGM 35, p.85]. At the Trocadéro he played several of his own works, part of a Handel concerto, and a Bach fugue. A reviewer commented that Loret's compositions were in an agreeable melodic style that quite suited the public taste. They were well received, especially the *Variations sur des noëls*. He found the style of Loret's improvisation "perhaps a little dull," but it did use certain stops of the organ advantageously. The Bach and Handel pieces, he said, were played very well [RGM 45, p.297].

A clue that Loret was somewhat on the fringe of organ circles may be implied from his reaction to the acclaim Guilmant received when the latter included Handel organ concertos (with orchestra) in his 1880 series of programs at the Trocadéro. Loret wrote a letter to the editor of *Revue et Gazette musicale* reminding readers that the Handel concertos were not entirely unknown in France before the Guilmant programs; Loret himself had transcribed twelve of them for organ solo [published in 1872–74] and had played two movements from one concerto at his 1878 Trocadéro program [RGM 47, p.223; ME 46, p.264].

Guilmant responded that his intention had not been to introduce the Handel concertos for the first time, as they had long been available in arrangements, but to present them in their original form. He had begun doing this as early as 1875, when he performed the tenth concerto at a Conservatory concert. This and other performances had led to the Trocadéro series of Handel performances [RGM 47, p.238; ME 46, p.272]. It is interesting to note that Clément Loret's son, Victor, married Guilmant's youngest daughter, Marie-Louise.[3]

In the early years of the school, Louis Niedermeyer himself taught piano and composition. When he died, on March 14, 1861, Camille Saint-Saëns was called to teach piano. Only 26 at the time, Saint-Saëns applied the full force of his formidable talent and enthusiasm for the art to his teaching, and he added a genuine personal interest in his students. It is no wonder that many of them soon became his disciples. Saint-Saëns did not limit himself to teaching piano but invaded other areas as well. He had a particularly strong influence on the careers of four young students: Eugène Gigout, Gabriel Fauré, André Messager, and Albert Périlhou (1845–1936).[4] Only about a decade younger than their teacher, they became his lifelong friends and colleagues.

When Niedermeyer died, the teaching of composition had fallen to the new director of the school, Louis Dietsch. Fauré later described him as "*maître de chapelle* at the Madeleine, *chef d'orchestre* at the Opéra, but a musician of small scope" [maître de chapelle de la Madeleine, chef d'orchestre de l'Opéra, mais musicien de petite envergure; 103, p.97].

Much of what the students learned about composition came instead from their piano teacher. Saint-Saëns prolonged his classes, and, seated at the piano, introduced his students to music that was entirely new to them: works of Schumann, Liszt, and Wagner—composers too modern for the classical program of studies at the Niedermeyer School. Saint-Saëns did not just demonstrate; he also examined the students' compositions and offered both criticism and encouragement [103, pp.97–98]. Archibald Henderson wrote: "Gigout often told me of the excellent lessons they had from Saint-Saëns; of his enthusiasm, of his wonderful piano playing, of his encyclopedic knowledge of the classics, of his breadth of view and pioneer work in the cause of Liszt and Wagner" [152].

During the time he was at the Niedermeyer School, Saint-Saëns was also organist at the Madeleine. His students were often with him at the organ during services, and they substituted for him on occasion. There can be no doubt that he greatly influenced their organ playing, both by example and by instruction, although he did not officially hold the position of organ professor.

Saint-Saëns loved to play the organ. Even after he left his church position in 1877 he never lost interest in the instrument, and took great pleasure in an occasional return to it. Improvisation was his particular joy, and his skill at it was legendary. Ermend Bonnal related that one could not distinguish his improvisations from written works and that Saint-Saëns could reproduce several times, note-for-note, an improvisation that particularly pleased him [25, p.7]. It was more than coincidence that both Fauré and Périlhou became noted for their very personal and original styles of improvisation, and that Gigout became the most renowned improviser and teacher of improvisation of his generation.

Saint-Saëns left the Niedermeyer School in 1865, when Gustave Lefèvre became director. His four years there had a lasting effect on the school and the students, as well as on Saint-Saëns. His former students became, in a sense, his family. Messager, Périlhou, Gigout, and Fauré all shared in that family, but Fauré was closest of all. After Saint-Saëns died, Fauré wrote: "I was then fifteen or sixteen years old, and from that period date the almost filial affection (in spite of the few years that separated my age from his), the immense admiration, the boundless gratitude that I have retained for him all my life and that will only be extinguished with me." [J'avais alors quinze à seize ans et de cette époque datent l'attachement presque filial—malgré le peu d'années qui séparait mon âge du sien,—l'immense admiration, l'infinie reconnaissance que je lui ai gardés toute ma vie et qui ne s'éteindront qu'avec moi; 103, p.98.]

Saint-Saëns's influence as a teacher spread far beyond the immediate circle. Three of his young organist friends eventually held important church organ positions in Paris, and all three gained prominent positions as music educators. In 1910 Albert Périlhou succeeded Lefèvre as director of the Niedermeyer School, remaining there until 1914; Fauré was director of the Paris Conservatory from 1905 to 1920; Gigout had his own school of organ playing from 1885 to 1911, and was then professor of organ at the Paris Conservatory until 1925. André Messager, meanwhile, pursued a distinguished career as conductor and composer.

Eugène Gigout completed his studies at the Niedermeyer School in 1863. He remained there until 1885, first as professor of plainchant and solfège, then adding successively harmony, counterpoint, fugue, and piano to his schedule.[5] Henri Letocart described Gigout's teaching as strict, thorough, and conscientious. Gigout examined harmony and counterpoint homework, armed with a well-sharpened pencil, and nothing escaped him. Although somewhat reserved, he was a very kind man who earned the love and respect of his students [202, no.36, p.5].

Like Saint-Saëns, Gigout was influential well beyond his assigned subjects. His reputation as one of France's finest organists did not escape the notice of the Niedermeyer students, and they had ample opportunity to hear his performances. Gigout's special protégé, the gifted young Léon Boëllmann, attended the Niedermeyer School from 1874 to 1881. He became choir organist and then *titulaire* at Saint-Vincent-de-Paul. Later, he was also assistant to Gigout in the latter's organ school.

Letocart gives us a vivid picture of life at the Niedermeyer School in 1879, including particularly interesting descriptions of the study room and organ room:

> The former [the study room] consisted of a large rectangular room in the center of which were three rows of study tables. Some twenty pianos were arranged side-by-side around that room, against the walls. Since some forty students shared the keyboards in turn, the twenty pianos were always in use—*together, of course*—. The musical disorder that resulted was an indescribable cacophony. What has always remained an enigma for me, is that each kneader of ivory succeeded in isolating himself and hearing what he was doing; but the most surprising is that at the same time the other students at the tables prepared their homework in harmony or counterpoint, and even composed—. It is evident that this hullaballu created a sonorous environment, a kind of constant *flou musical* very much like factory noise. Bad boys that we were, we took pleasure in waking the supervisor; for there was a supervisor who succeeded in sleeping in this hubub?! To accomplish that, nothing was easier: at an agreed-upon signal, all the pianists suddenly stopped playing. The effect was infallible and sudden. The contrary also had its charm. Here is how it worked: the first

piano played at the unison the characteristic theme of the *Mouvement perpétuel* of Weber, and progressively, with crescendo, the other pianos, one after the other, joined the performance; when the twenty pianos were sounding, the occupants of the study tables came to help out and the intensity of sound was at its height. This furious outburst of sound almost certainly had the effect of making the director appear. Everything then returned to calm.

These little innocent jokes were not customary and certainly didn't prevent the students from applying themselves to serious and sustained work.

The organ room presented another aspect. It was quiet here. The organ that furnished that room was a small instrument of six stops without character, distributed on two manuals, and a pedal of . . . 27 keys without a Soubasse, which functioned with a simple coupler to the *grand-orgue*. However, it was on this hybrid instrument that several generations of talented organists were formed.

For practice outside the class, the use of the organ was divided among the students by the hour. Two of them took possession of the instrument together; one occupied the keyboards for half an hour while the other acted as pumper; the roles changed for the second half hour. This procedure had the advantage of giving future organists the ability to appreciate at their just value the precious assistants who were pumpers.

La première consistait en une grande pièce rectangulaire au milieu de laquelle se trouvaient trois rangées de tables scolaires. Autour de cette salle, adossés au mur, étaient placés, côte à côte, une vingtaine de pianos. Etant donné qu'une quarantaine d'élèves se partageaient les claviers à tour de rôle, les vingt pianos étaient toujours en fonction . . . *ensemble*, bien entendu . . . Le chahut . . . musical ainsi obtenu formait une indescriptible cacophonie. Ce qui est toujours resté pour moi une énigme, c'est que chaque pétrisseur d'ivoire arrivait à s'isoler et à entendre ce qu'il faisait; mais, le plus surprenant, c'est que sur les tables pendant ce temps-là, les autres élèves préparaient leurs devoirs d'harmonie ou de contrepoint et même composaient . . . Il est évident que ce tohu-bohu créait une ambiance sonore, une sorte de *flou musical* constant, assez semblable à un bruit d'usine. L'expérience à laquelle les méchants garçons que nous étions prenaient plaisir à se livrer, était de réveiller le surveillant; car il y avait un surveillant qui arrivait à dormir dans ce vacarme?! Pour ce faire, rien n'était plus simple: sur un signe convenu, tous les pianistes cessaient brusquement de jouer. L'effet était immanquable et subit. Le contraire avait aussi son charme. Voici comment on opérait: le premier piano prenait à l'unisson le thème caractéristique du Mouvement perpétuel de Weber et progressivement, en crescendo, les autres pianos, l'un après l'autre, entraient en jeu; lorsque les vingt pianos résonnaient, les occupants des tables arrivaient à la rescousse et l'intensité sonore était alors à son comble. Ce furieux déchaînement sonore avait pour effet à peu près certain de faire surgir le Directeur. Tout alors rentrait dans le calme.

Ces petites plaisanteries bien innocentes n'étaient pas une coutume et surtout n'empêchaient pas les élèves de se livrer à un travail sérieux et soutenu.

La salle d'orgue présentait un autre aspect. Ici c'était le calme. L'orgue qui meublait cette pièce était un petit instrument de six jeux sans caractère, répartis sur deux claviers et un pédalier de . . . 27 notes sans soubasse, qui fonctionnait par une simple tirasse sur le clavier du grand-orgue. C'est pourtant sur cet instrument hybride que se sont formées plusieurs générations d'organistes de talent.

Pour le travail en dehors des cours, l'usage de l'orgue était partagé par heure entre les élèves. Deux d'entre eux prenaient ensemble possession de l'instrument; l'un occupait les claviers pendant une demi-heure tandis que l'autre remplissait les fonctions de souffleur; les rôles changeaient pour la seconde demi-heure. Ce procédé avait l'avantage de donner aux futurs organistes le pouvoir d'apprécier à leur juste valeur les précieux auxiliaires qu'étaient les souffleurs. [202, no.36, p.4.]

The first organ at the Niedermeyer School was built by Moser, originally for a private estate. Gustave Lefèvre decided to let the beginning classes use it and to get a new one from Merklin for the advanced classes, but the old organ was soon completely out of service [127, p.45]. The organ Letocart describes above was the Merklin organ, but the students' competitive examinations were usually played on more important instruments: at the Trocadéro, the churches of Saint-Louis-d'Antin and Saint-Augustin, or in Cavaillé-Coll's hall [202, no.36, p.4]. In 1896, when the school moved to a new location in Auteuil, a new organ was installed by P. Mader, Arnaud et Cie, of Marseilles. It was a two-manual, twelve stop organ, described as "electro-pneumatic, Hope-Jones system" [ME 62, pp.48, 55]. It malfunctioned soon and often, and in 1911 it was replaced by an organ from the Cavaillé-Coll firm [127, p.45].

Perhaps no one at the Niedermeyer School was more devoted to the founder's objectives than Eugène Gigout. He became an authority in plainchant accompaniment following Niedermeyer's principles, and he was among the late-century leaders in advocating the use of chant in organ composition. Throughout his career Gigout specialized in training church musicians. It is not surprising that he was opposed to the changes that Lefèvre, his brother-in-law, instituted in 1885: moving the Niedermeyer School in a more secular direction and deleting the reference to religion from the school's official title [220, p.60].

Perhaps as a result of these changes, and no doubt also because he longed for the opportunity to teach organ (after more than twenty years of piano and theory courses), Gigout left the Niedermeyer School in 1885 and established his own school of organ playing: *Ecole d'orgue, d'improvisation et de plainchant*. As the title suggests, it emphasized the skills particularly necessary for the church organist—improvisation and plainchant accompaniment—but it also gave considerable attention to the performance of composed repertoire.

At first Gigout met his classes at the Albert-le-Grand hall. In 1887 he began supplementing the course of studies with instruction in harmony and composition [ME 53, p.335]. He had recently moved to a large home (63 bis rue Jouffroy) that included both living quarters and studio space, with room for a variety of *soirées* and student programs. Here he installed a ten-stop Cavaillé-Coll organ.

The house on rue Jouffroy also became the residence of Léon Boëllmann and his wife, Louise (daughter of the director of the Niedermeyer School, Gustave

Lefèvre). One can only speculate on the challenges this young couple may have had in smoothing over any strained relations there may have been between Boëllmann's mentor, Gigout, and his bride's father, Lefèvre. Whatever may have been going on beneath the surface, as far as the public eye was concerned, Gigout's leaving the Niedermeyer School caused no rift in the complicated family connections of the Niedermeyer-Lefèvre-Gigout-Boëllmann clan.

In 1890 Boëllmann was appointed assistant professor of the Gigout organ school [ME 56, p.327]. For most of the next decade Gigout (whose wife died in 1890), the Boëllmann family, and the organ school shared the house on rue Jouffroy. Gigout was immersed in teaching, programs, and composing. Then tragedy entered, with the deaths of Léon Boëllmann in 1897 and of his wife in 1898. The next year Gigout moved to 113 avenue de Villiers. He continued his *Ecole d'orgue* until 1911, when he succeeded Alexandre Guilmant as professor of organ at the Paris Conservatory.

During a part of its 26-year existence the Gigout school was subsidized. The 36 scholarships that were originally granted to the Niedermeyer School were continued for a time by the Fine Arts administration, but after Gigout's school became firmly established, they were divided equally between Lefèvre's school and Gigout's [220, p.61].

In the Bibliothèque nationale, Paris, there is a hand-written memo, presumably by Gigout, dated 1897. It is the draft of a letter to M. Roujon requesting that the Fine Arts administration continue to support the organ school. The memo reveals that Gigout had had this support since 1888 and describes some of the school's contributions to the artistic environment: programs had been given at the school; and Gigout not only instructed the students and let them use his organ but also found positions for them. Ten Gigout students in church positions in Paris were listed, including Eugène Lacroix, then organist of Saint-Merry and of the Lamoureux concerts, and Georges MacMaster, *maître de chapelle* of Saint-Ambroise [BN Rés. Vm. dos 18 (7)].

Students at Gigout's school were given frequent opportunities to perform. In contrast to the Conservatory, where there were no student organ recitals, Gigout presented his students in several highly visible programs each year. They were announced in the musical press and were frequently reviewed. Dufourcq listed the composers usually found on the programs of Gigout's students: Bach, Lemmens, Mendelssohn, Schumann, Boëly, Saint-Saëns, Gigout, Boëllmann, and sometimes Franck and Guilmant. Works of Liszt, Widor, and later Vierne and Dupré were regularly omitted [85, p.4].

In the late 1890s Clarence Eddy made some observations about Gigout's organ school:

> M. Gigout has in his house a very charming two-manual organ which he uses for his own pupils, and he has what he calls an organ school, and his pupils practice there when there is an opportunity. He frequently gives recitals with his pupils at his studio, which other teachers cannot do for lack of the opportunity. In Paris you are not allowed to give recitals in a church, and the only private

organ I know of in Paris is that of M. Widor, which is in his studio and is never
used for anything else than lessons. [96, p.593.]

Jean Huré noted that Gigout emphasized clarity and moderation in his
teaching. Where technique was concerned, he followed the Lemmens method.
However, in pedal playing he favored more crossing and less use of the heel
[162, pp.25–26]. His own playing was distinguished by clarity and precision.
Huré described Gigout as an "anti-romantic" who disliked excessively slow
tempos, affectation, mannerisms, and sentimentality [162, p.16].

Archibald M. Henderson, a pupil of Widor, visited Gigout's Conservatory
organ class and noted the emphasis on improvisation and plainchant
accompaniment. He described Gigout's approach to the teaching of improvisation, an approach that was no doubt refined and perfected during his many
years of teaching in his own school.

> The class-training in improvising . . . was original, and being carefully graded,
> proved encouraging, even to the youngest students. It was conceived much more
> [on] contrapuntal than on harmonic lines. In the early stages it consisted in
> adding a single part, note against note, to a simple diatonic melody. This being
> added in the bass, the melody would then be given to a lower voice, the
> counterpoint being added above. When two-part counterpoint could be im-
> provised easily, three- and four-part work was then considered. When note-
> against-note harmony had been mastered, the student passed on to free counter-
> point. Later, examples were given for canonic treatment; and lastly, the exposi-
> tion of a fugue was demanded. It was a rigorous but stimulating course. [152.]

According to Paul Locard, Gigout sacrificed the satisfaction of success in
other areas to his teaching. He was, Locard said, an "incomparable professor,"
above all through his eclecticism, the lucidity resulting from his erudition and
experience, the diversity of his methods, his power of abstraction, and his
intuition about other people. Locard saw Gigout's "unrivaled private school"
as a particular high point in Gigout's teaching career: an institution through
which Gigout was especially effective in training "missionaries" capable of
disseminating his message [206, p.73].

XXI.
The Schola Cantorum

THE Schola Cantorum represents a culmination of nineteenth-century efforts to improve church music and interest the public in historical styles. The ideals shared by Choron and Niedermeyer once more fueled a new institution and revitalized the crusade against mediocrity in liturgical music. The driving force behind the establishment of the Schola was a young early-music enthusiast, Charles Bordes. He had studied piano with Marmontel and composition with Franck, but he first gained recognition as an authority on Basque folk music. His special interests fanned out to cover a broad range of early vocal music, including Gregorian chant, the sixteenth-century polyphonic choral repertoire, and the choral music of Bach.

In March 1890, 27-year-old Bordes became choir master at Saint-Gervais, Paris, the famous old church where generations of the Couperin family had served as organists. Encouraged by a sympathetic clergyman, Bordes soon initiated performances of choral works still rarely heard in France, notwithstanding the efforts of Choron, Ney, Niedermeyer, and a few others earlier in the century. When Bordes conducted the Palestrina *Stabat* for two choirs and the Allegri *Miserere* on March 26, 1891, he opened a new period in the performance and appreciation of early choral music. Largely through his persistence during the remaining eighteen years of his life, this important category of music gained a firm foothold in the contemporary French musical scene, both in the church and in the concert hall.

It does not detract from Bordes's achievement to note that by 1891 an early-music renaissance was waiting to happen. Guilmant had been performing organ works by Frescobaldi, Buxtehude, and other early composers for many years; Trocadéro audiences were well accustomed to hearing major Bach works on organ programs; Guilmant and Gigout had both published modern organ music based on modes; and Joseph Pothier's edition of the *Liber gradualis* had been published in 1883, the first in a series of editions representing a half century of work on the restoration of Gregorian chant by the Benedictine scholars at Solesmes.

Like some of his predecessors, Bordes launched a multifaceted campaign, channeled through publications and educational programs as well as public performances. His first step was to organize a chorus dedicated to the performance of early music, the *Chanteurs de Saint-Gervais*. At first this group concentrated on polyphonic music of the fifteenth and sixteenth centuries. Then in 1894 it initiated a series of performances of Bach cantatas in cooperation with Alexandre Guilmant.

On June 6, 1894 Bordes convened a meeting of Guilmant, Vincent d'Indy, and others who were especially interested in furthering the performance and dissemination of early music. A society named *Schola Cantorum* was formed, with Guilmant as president. It had four objectives: the return to the Gregorian tradition for the performance of plainchant; the restoration of the Palestrina style to a position of honor as a model for polyphonic church music; the creation of a modern church music repertoire inspired by Gregorian and Palestrinian traditions, and respectful of the text and liturgy; and the improvement of organ repertoire from the standpoint of its union with Gregorian melodies and its suitability for use in church services [46, p.7].

The society began working toward its goals immediately. Bordes had already moved into the field of publications with the edition of an anthology of early choral music. Now publication of a magazine became a primary objective. A sample issue of the new magazine, *La Tribune de Saint-Gervais*, appeared in the same month the society was founded. Regular publication commenced in January 1895 with Vol. I, no.1, which contained articles on Palestrina, the history of the motet, and Gregorian chant. There were also reports on activities of the Schola Cantorum and other current events of interest to church musicians. Articles about early organ music appeared from time to time in subsequent issues. Furthering the third and fourth goals of the society, competitions for choral and organ works were announced in the first two issues of the *Tribune,* the latter to be organ versets for the hymn *Ave Maris Stella*.

The goals of the Schola Cantorum did not meet with unanimous approval. In February 1897 *Le Guide musical* published critical observations by Anatole Loquin, soon followed by a rebuttal by Charles Bordes [GM 43, pp.103–104, 143–46], and a stream of letters to the editor, pro and con, that extended the debate through the spring. Bordes may have welcomed this opportunity to air his views in another periodical.

Meanwhile, the Schola Cantorum had begun its most ambitious project: a school of church music. Bordes was fearless. He rented a building on rue Stanislas that could serve as a school and headquarters for the publications and other activities of the society, confident that somehow the 37 francs 50 centimes then in the treasury would multiply like the biblical loaves and fishes [172, p.3622]. With the title *Schola Cantorum, Ecole de chant liturgique et de musique religieuse,* the new school accepted its first students on October 15, 1896. By then benefactors had contributed 3,545 francs for the new school, including a gift of 1,000 francs from the archbishop of Paris [46, p.9].

While Bordes spear-headed this and other new projects of the Schola Cantorum, his two collaborators, Guilmant and d'Indy, also assumed important responsibilities. Guilmant remained president of the society, and d'Indy became director of the school. The three co-founders were also the professors for major areas of the curriculum: Bordes in choral music, d'Indy in counterpoint and composition, and Guilmant in organ.

October 1896 marked the beginning of Guilmant's professorship at the Paris Conservatory as well as the start of instruction at the new Schola Cantorum. Vierne tells us, however, that Guilmant was not apprehensive about his responsibilities in two schools at the same time. In Guilmant's words, "one will never train enough talented organists" [on ne formera jamais assez d'organistes de talent; cited in 321, p.30].

Originally the Schola Cantorum had two types of courses: elementary classes offered without charge, and more advanced courses that required a tuition fee. As listed by d'Indy, the free classes offered solfège, Gregorian chant, keyboard, and vocal ensemble, and were taught by de Boisjoslin, Vigourel, Pirro, and Bordes. By paying a fee, one could study history and paleography, organ, harmony, counterpoint, and composition; the professors for these classes were Pirro, Guilmant, La Tombelle, and d'Indy [172, p.3622].

The free courses proved to be a disappointment. The founders had hoped that they would attract singers from the churches and would thus serve to improve the performance of liturgical music. As it turned out, professional church singers were apparently not interested, and the level of talent found in the classes was too unpromising to justify the time and effort of the professors. The courses requiring tuition fees, on the other hand, soon prospered. From an initial enrollment of ten,[1] the number of students increased to 65 by 1899, 157 in 1902, 292 in 1904, and some 600 by 1929 [172, pp.3623, 3625]. As the school grew, new courses and teachers were gradually added, and some courses were offered at more than one level of proficiency.

The first years of the new school were characterized by experimentation, as the founders searched for innovative ways to attack age-old problems. For a time the school maintained a model choir school. Ten young boys were selected by competition to participate. About the same time there was an apprenticeship program in music engraving [46, pp.11–13]. Among the more successful experiments were field trips to Solesmes for intensive training in the performance of Gregorian chant.

From the beginning the founders wanted to emphasize the position of music as an art rather than as a craft or profession. For this reason the annual competitions that so dominated course structure and content at the Paris Conservatory were not instituted at the Schola Cantorum. Such competitions, they felt, placed undue stress on virtuosity, vanity, and rivalry, as opposed to the attitudes they wanted to foster. D'Indy said that the objective was to train "artists conscious of their mission of absolute devotion to the work of art that they have the honor of interpreting, and placing above all things the unselfish love of music" [des artistes conscients de leur mission de dévouement absolu à l'oeuvre d'art qu'ils ont l'honneur d'interpréter, et plaçant au-dessus de toutes choses l'amour désintéressé de la musique; 172, p.3624].

Meanwhile, Bordes toured throughout France with his Chanteurs de Saint-Gervais, seeking to stimulate interest in early music and organize Schola

Cantorum societies in other parts of the country. These efforts eventually met with some success, but at a discouragingly slow pace. Among the first provincial early music societies founded as a result of Bordes's tours were those at Saint-Jean-de-Luz (1897) and Avignon (1899).

With the beginning of the new century, a new era opened for the Schola Cantorum. It had outgrown its original building, and in his typical style, Bordes acquired a new location, trusting that somehow the practical problems would be solved, and somehow they were. In the fall of 1900, classes convened in the Saint-Jacques street site that still houses the school: a former English Benedictine monastery built in the seventeenth century.

With the change in place came also a change in name. Instead of *Schola Cantorum, Ecole de chant liturgique et de musique religieuse,* the new subtitle was *Ecole supérieure de musique.* Although the study of church music was still an important part of the curriculum, a much broader range of studies was offered, including orchestral instruments and instrumental ensembles. This trend toward a more comprehensive curriculum rather than a specialized concentration on church music, echoed changes that had taken place in the Niedermeyer School some fifteen years earlier.

Guilmant remained the professor of the advanced course in organ from the opening of the school until his death in 1911, when he was succeeded by Louis Vierne. As the number of students increased, additional organ teachers were engaged to instruct students at elementary and intermediate levels. The first was Abel Decaux. According to Eliane Lejeune-Bonnier, he attended the Paris Conservatory from 1890 to 1895. His studies there included organ with Widor, and he subsequently studied organ privately with Guilmant[2] [199, p.4]. In 1896 Decaux enrolled in the first class of the Schola Cantorum, and the following year he was selected to instruct the newly created elementary organ class[3] [46, pp.9–10]. He remained on the Schola Cantorum faculty until 1923. In that year he left both his teaching post and the organ position he had held since 1903 as *titulaire* at Sacré-Coeur, in order to join the organ faculty of the Eastman School of Music, in Rochester, New York.

It is not clear what organ Guilmant used for his classes in 1896–98, but during the Advent season of 1898 a small organ by the Cavaillé-Coll-Mutin company was inaugurated. Two programs given by Guilmant, La Tombelle, Tournemire, and Decaux marked the event. *La Tribune de Saint-Gervais* listed its stops:

> *Récit:* Cor de nuit, Salicional, Nazard, Doublette, Flûte harmonique, Trompette, Basson Hautbois
> *Grand Orgue:* Bourdon 8', Montre 8', Prestant
> *Pédale:* Bourdon 16'

Pedal movements included three couplers (G.O.-P, R-P, G.O.-R), five reversibles (Montre, Prestant, Nazard, Basson, Trompette), and an expression pedal [TSG 5, no.1, p.21]. Soon after the school moved to its new quarters on rue Saint-Jacques, plans were under way for a larger instrument suitable for concerts as well as teaching. On February 20, 1902 a 30-stop Cavaillé-Coll-Mutin organ was inaugurated. That organ, modified, continues to serve the school today.

XXII.
Postlude

WHAT were the determining features of the nineteenth-century French-Belgian school of organ playing? There were many strands in the fabric, but in retrospect a few can be singled out as particularly decisive. During the final decades of the century these strands became ever more closely interwoven and interdependent. In any historical period, musical performance is evaluated in terms of four variables: what is played, how it is played, how it sounds, and how it is heard. Let us view briefly the dominant strands in our story as they are linked to composition, interpretation, performance medium, and audience.

The most pervasive strand throughout the century bound organ playing to contemporary composition, with the performer in the role of creative musician. The American organist Wallace Goodrich observed the French-Belgian school in full bloom when he went to Paris in the 1890s to study with Widor. He later wrote:

> In no other country has the organ achieved so high a position of honor among musicians, or have so many of the greatest contemporary composers interested themselves in the organ, both as executants and as writers of organ music. I refer particularly to composers of established reputation and recognized pre-eminence in all forms of music: orchestral, instrumental, and choral. [136, p.xi.]

The link between composition and organ playing that Goodrich found remarkable was at least as strong early in the century. In 1819, when Benoist was appointed professor of organ at the Paris Conservatory, one qualification for the position was that the candidate had to be a good composer. Benoist's 1815 Prix de Rome was a strong mark in his favor. Benoist's class attracted not only composers whom we also recognize as leading organists (most notably Saint-Saëns and Franck) but also some whose connection with the organ world was marginal. Georges Bizet, for example, studied organ in 1852–55 and won first prize in organ in 1855; Léo Delibes was enrolled in Benoist's class for a semester in 1854; and Jules Massenet was enrolled in organ in 1861–63.

The fact that organ was in the same classification as composition in the Conservatory curriculum was not due to some whim of the Conservatory administration. It resulted rather from a prevailing, long-accepted view of the nature of organ playing and the skills that were most essential for an organist. The idea persisted that an organ class was primarily about music making, and that the objective of organ students was to learn to speak their musical language fluently at the keyboard (i.e., to create music), observing principles of musical grammar, style, and formal organization.

their musical language fluently at the keyboard (i.e., to create music), observing principles of musical grammar, style, and formal organization. No wonder composition students were interested! All the organists in our saga were composers.

The role of the organist only gradually shifted to include that of interpreter in addition to that of improviser-composer. Most organ music published in France between 1800 and 1840 was instructional or utilitarian, intended for those not capable of improvising their own music for church services. A gradually rising quantity of published organ music was accompanied by modest gains in over-all quality and occasional publications of more enduring interest. The collections of organ music by Boëly published in the 1840s and 1850s constitute the first substantial French contribution to the repertoire of nineteenth-century organ music.

It is not surprising that only a few French musicians had seen any of Bach's organ works before mid-century. In Germany itself only a limited selection of his organ works was available before the Griepenkerl-Roitzch (Peters) edition began to appear in 1844. German publications were slow to trickle in to Paris, and the first French edition of the Bach organ works (published by Richault) was issued in 1855–65.

In spite of tradition and practical limitations, it was inevitable that French organists would finally become interpreters as well as improviser-composers. That they became world leaders for the authority and virtuosity of their playing can be traced to the Fétis-Lemmens influence from Brussels. If Clara Wieck Schumann (1819–96) set a high standard for other pianists as interpreters, exerting meticulous care in following the composers' indications, Lemmens set a new standard for organists, furnishing them not only with a model but also a method.

In retrospect the year 1833 was a turning point for organ playing. In that year Fétis became director of the Brussels Conservatory, initiating the chain of events that influenced to some extent *what* French and Belgian organists played and changed decisively *how* it was played.

The same year witnessed the arrival in Paris of Cavaillé-Coll. His instruments, more than any others, determined how nineteenth-century French organ music *sounded*. After the long, difficult post-Revolution period, he gave the organ a new voice eminently suited for the music of his age, and it remained a consistent voice for the rest of the century, changing in details but not in direction or objectives. When Cavaillé-Coll rebuilt an old organ he did so in his own style, assuming his responsibility was to the present day rather than to the preservation of the past. The idea of the historically faithful organ restoration belongs to the twentieth century.

As we have seen, Cavaillé-Coll contributed in many ways to the organ profession, encouraging talented performers, providing opportunities for them to be heard, and inviting leading musicians in other fields to hear them. But his greatest influence was still as a builder of organs that inspired those who composed and played, and thrilled those who listened.

No wonder composition students were interested! All the organists in our saga were composers.

The role of the organist only gradually shifted to include that of interpreter in addition to that of improviser-composer. Most organ music published in France between 1800 and 1840 was instructional or utilitarian, intended for those not capable of improvising their own music for church services. A gradually rising quantity of published organ music was accompanied by modest gains in over-all quality and occasional publications of more enduring interest. The collections of organ music by Boëly published in the 1840s and 1850s constitute the first substantial French contribution to the repertoire of nineteenth-century organ music.

It is not surprising that only a few French musicians had seen any of Bach's organ works before mid-century. In Germany itself only a limited selection of his organ works was available before the Griepenkerl-Roitzch (Peters) edition began to appear in 1844. German publications were slow to trickle in to Paris, and the first French edition of the Bach organ works (published by Richault) was issued in 1855–65.

In spite of tradition and practical limitations, it was inevitable that French organists would finally become interpreters as well as improviser-composers. That they became world leaders for the authority and virtuosity of their playing can be traced to the Fétis-Lemmens influence from Brussels. If Clara Wieck Schumann (1819–96) set a high standard for other pianists as interpreters, exerting meticulous care in following the composers' indications, Lemmens set a new standard for organists, furnishing them not only with a model but also a method.

In retrospect the year 1833 was a turning point for organ playing. In that year Fétis became director of the Brussels Conservatory, initiating the chain of events that influenced to some extent *what* French and Belgian organists played and changed decisively *how* it was played.

The same year witnessed the arrival in Paris of Cavaillé-Coll. His instruments, more than any others, determined how nineteenth-century French organ music *sounded*. After the long, difficult post-Revolution period, he gave the organ a new voice eminently suited for the music of his age, and it remained a consistent voice for the rest of the century, changing in details but not in direction or objectives. When Cavaillé-Coll rebuilt an old organ he did so in his own style, assuming his responsibility was to the present day rather than to the preservation of the past. The idea of the historically faithful organ restoration belongs to the twentieth century.

As we have seen, Cavaillé-Coll contributed in many ways to the organ profession, encouraging talented performers, providing opportunities for them to be heard, and inviting leading musicians in other fields to hear them. But his greatest influence was still as a builder of organs that inspired those who composed and played, and thrilled those who listened.

How the music was *heard* depended on the instrument, the performer, and the repertoire, but also on the relationship of these factors to the audience. Popular taste has not changed much. The average concert audience still prefers a familiar harmonic style and loves a memorable tune that can be hummed or whistled. It accepts new patterns only gradually and tends to reject music that is too challenging or confusing. The audience overdosed with unfamiliar styles is just as bored today as was its counterpart a century ago.

Performers who have enjoyed public acclaim have characteristically been mindful of these conditions. In nineteenth-century France most of the music played by fine musicians who were successful as organ performers was contemporary: expressions of their own time and place, whether written or improvised. And the instruments they played were expressly designed for that purpose. The musical style they applied to the organ was not a watered-down compromise, but was the same one they used in their compositions for orchestra, choir, or any other media. It was the contemporary style of art music one might expect to hear in the concert hall. While it changed greatly during the century and separated itself with increasing determination from the lower common denominators of musical taste, it never lost contact with its public. One does not find here a radical group of composers that viewed the audience as the enemy, or that chose to speak in unknown tongues.

In a remarkable achievement, French organists in the final quarter of the century succeeded in expanding their repertoire to include masterworks of other countries and other periods without losing those essential bonds with their audiences and the music of their own day. The popularity of their programs actually increased as the repertoire became more adventurous, more demanding. But with rare exceptions, works of Bach, Handel, Mendelssohn, Buxtehude, and Frescobaldi were introduced one piece at a time—frequently one movement at a time. Contemporary music remained an essential ingredient in most organ programs. In a tabulation of the works played at the ten official organ concerts at the Exposition universelle of 1900, Kurt Lueders counted 94 works by 36 different composers. Bach tops the list with fourteen pieces, but more than 60 pieces (almost two-thirds of the works played) were by French composer-organists of the nineteenth century [210, p.78].

The final strand in our fabric is the relationship of the artists to their profession. A study of programs and methods reveals how the renaissance in organ playing was achieved, but one must consider the organists themselves to understand why it happened. This story is not just about winners. Some of the most enduring contributions were coupled with personal frustrations and professional failures. Some musicians saw their instruments ruined, some lost their jobs, some were never given the positions they deserved, some saw their projects fail from lack of funds or apathy, and the efforts of some never gained public recognition.

In spite of personal setbacks, there remained a conviction that organ playing had something vital to offer society, both in the preservation of treasured traditions and as an indispensable type of expression, relevant to contemporary taste, forms of worship, and artistic aspirations.

Le remplissage des réservoirs : les souffleurs.

Behind the scenes: Organ-pumpers at work. From *L'Illustration,* 1894 (University of California Library, Berkeley).

Today, as funds for art are eroding and the outlook for music education is bleak, the example of that firm conviction could be our most inspiring (perhaps our most important) lesson from the French-Belgian organ school. Through the nineteenth century it survived political bungling, barricades in the streets, and empty shelves in the markets, in addition to prosperous times.

Ultimately, a novelist could not invent a happier ending. Musicians had never faced greater problems than did Séjan, Lasceux, and their organist-colleagues in 1800; never could musicians view their profession with greater pride and confidence than could Gigout, Widor, and Guilmant in 1900.

APPENDIX A
Organ Performances by César Franck

1841: Won second prize in organ in the Conservatory competition [RGM 8, p.353].

1854: With Bazille, Cavallo, and Lemmens, inaugurated Ducroquet organ at Saint-Eustache [ME 21, no. 28, p.3; RGM 21, pp.174–75].

1856: Played organ for the cathedral of Carcassonne in Cavaillé-Coll's hall [RGM 23, pp.247–48].

1857: Played organ for the cathedral of Luçon in Cavaillé-Coll's hall; Waitzennecker, a student at the Niedermeyer School, also performed [MA 1, no. 2, col. 31].

1859: With Lefébure-Wély, inaugurated Cavaillé-Coll organ at Sainte-Clotilde [FM 23, pp.506–507; FM 24, pp.3–4; RGM 27, pp.4–5].

1862: With Bazille, Guilmant, Saint-Saëns, and Schmitt, inaugurated Cavaillé-Coll organ at Saint-Sulpice [FM 26, pp.137–38; RGM 29, pp.155–56; RMS 3, cols.230–31]; with Chauvet and Scola, inaugurated Loret organ in the "chapelle des Jésuites, rue de Sèvres" [RMS 4, col.20].

1863: With Durand, J. C. Hess, and Lebel, inaugurated organ reconstructed by Cavaillé-Coll at Saint-Etienne-du-Mont [ME 30, pp.166,175; RGM 30, p.143].

1864: Recital at Sainte-Clotilde [FM 28, p. 371; ME 31, p.408; RGM 31, p.375].

1866: Recital at Sainte-Clotilde [ME 33, p.166; RGM 33, p.126].

1867: With Chauvet, Durand, and Serrier, inaugurated organ reconstructed by Cavaillé-Coll at Saint-Denis-du-Saint-Sacrement [FM 31, p.331; ME 34, p.367; RGM 34, p.331; RMS 8, p.72].

1868: With Chauvet, Durand, Guilmant, Loret, Saint-Saëns, Sergent, and Widor, inaugurated Cavaillé-Coll organ at Notre-Dame [FM 32, p.83; RGM 35, p.85; RMS 9, pp.23–24]; played a half-hour program at Notre-Dame [ME 35, p.135; RGM 35, pp.86, 95]; with Widor, played in Cavaillé-Coll's hall [RGM 35, p.94]; with Durand, played for delegates of learned societies at Notre-Dame [RGM 35, p.134]; with Sergent, played for members of the scientific association at Notre-Dame [FM 32, p.219; ME 35, p.264; RGM 35, p.222].

1869: With Chauvet, Durand, Fissot, Saint-Saëns, and Widor, inaugurated Cavaillé-Coll organ at La Trinité [FM 33, p.91; ME 36, p.126; RGM 36, p.101].

1871: With Darnault, Dubois, Minard, and Rivet, participated in reception of Martin organ at Saint-Paul–Saint-Louis [264, p.217].

1872: Conservatory concert [RGM 39, p.414; RGM 40, p.5].

1873: Program at the Conservatory [RGM 40, p.85].

1877: With Emile Renaud, played in the chapel of the palace of Versailles [RGM 44, p.126].

1878: Recital at the Trocadéro [RGM 45, p.321]; with Gigout and Wachs, inaugurated organ renovated by Cavaillé-Coll at Saint-Merry [ME 44, p.405; RGM 45, p.366–67].

1879: With Gigout, Albert Renaud, and Widor, inaugurated Fermis et Persil organ at Saint-François-Xavier [ME 45, p.118; RGM 46, p.78]; with Dallier, Dubois, Gigout, and Guilmant, inaugurated organ renovated by Merklin at Saint-Eustache [ME 45, p.133; RGM 46, p.101].

1881: With Gigout, inaugurated Debierre organ at Saint-Léonard, Fougères [ME 48, p.30].

1883: With Fissot, Guilmant, and Lebel, received Cavaillé-Coll organ at *Institution nationale des jeunes aveugles* [ME 49, p.118].

1887: Conducted a performance of his Mass and played an improvised organ offertory at Bordeaux [187, p.109].

1888: With Dubois, Rousseau, and Verschneider, received Merklin choir organ at Sainte-Clotilde [ME 54, p.71]; with Paul de Vreed, inaugurated Merklin organ at parish church, Béthune [ME 54, p.103]; recital for the Association artistique, Angers [ME 54, p.391; GM 34, pp.319–20, 337].

1889: Inaugurated organ reconstructed by Merklin at Saint-Jacques-du-Haut-Pas [ME 55, pp.160, 175]; played some improvisations in connection with a performance of his Mass at Saint-Bonaventure, Lyon [276, p.18].

APPENDIX B
Students in Franck's
Organ Class
Paris Conservatory, 1872–1890

Key to symbols:
- A: Year student enrolled in the organ class.
- B: Prizes in organ, and date each was received. 1 = first prize; 2 = second prize; 3 = first *accessit;* 4 = second *accessit;* 5 = third *accessit.*

Arnal de Serres, Marie-François-Louis (1864–?). A: 1885.

Aubry, Georges (1868–?). A: 1885; B: 4 (1888).

Bachelet, Alfred-Georges (1864–1944). A: 1885.

Benoit, Louis-Françis Bazile (1847–?). A: 1868; B: 5 (1870), 4 (1872).

Benoit, (1852–?). A: 1875.

Berger, Georges-Arthur-Alfred (1871–?). A: 1890 (see below, chap. XIV, note 13); B: 3 (1891).

Billault, Adèle-Alexandrine-Désirée (1848–?). A: 1872.

Bondon, Georges-Paul (1867–?). A: 1885; B: 2 (1887), 1 (1889).

Bopp, (1866–?). A: 1887.

Boulay, Joséphine-Pauline (1869–?). A: 1887; B: 1 (1888).

Bouval, Jules-Henri (1867–?). A: 1889; B: 4 (1891).

Broutin, Clément-Jules (1851–89). A: 1876.

Burgat, André-Paul (1865–?). A: 1889.

Busser, Paul-Henri (1872–1973). A: 1889.

Chapuis, Auguste-Paul-Jean-Baptiste (1858–1933). A: 1878; B: 3 (1879), 2 (1880), 1 (1881).

Chrétien, Hedwige-Louise-Marie (1859–?). A: 1886.

Dallier, Henri-Edouard (1849–1943). A: 1877; B: 1 (1878).

Deslandres, Georges-Philippe (1849–1875). A: 1868; B: 4 (1869), 3 (1870).

Duplessis, Frédéric-Alexandre-Norbert (1858–?). A: 1881.

Dutacq, Amédée-Jean (1848–?). A: 1874.

Féry, Aimé (1862–?). A: 1885.

Fournier, Emile-Eugène-Alix (1864–97). A: 1885.

Frémaux, Louis-André (1867–?). A: 1885.

Fumet, (1867–?). A: 1885.

Gaillard, Marie-Antoinette (1850–?). A: 1872.

Galeotti, Césarino (1872–?). A: 1885; B: 1 (1887).

Ganne, Gustave-Louis (1862–1923). A: 1880; B: 3 (1882).

Genty, Marie-Mathilde-Louise (1850–?). A: 1875; B: 4 (1876).

Grand-Jany, Anatole-Léon (1862–91). A: 1881; B: 2 (1882), 1 (1883).

Guintrange, Léonie (1858–?) [married E. Rouher, 1885]. A: 1883.

Guiraud, (1868–?). A: 1889.
Hillemacher, Lucien-Joseph-Edouard (1860–1909). A: 1878.
Honnoré, Léon-Antoine-Anatole (1859–?). A: 1882.
Hue, Georges-Adolphe (1858–1948). A: 1878.
Humblot, Joseph-Paul (1845–?). A: 1872; B: 3 (1873), 2 (1874).
D'Indy, Vincent (1851–1931). A: 1874; B: 4 (1874), 3 (1875).
Jeannin, Paul-Marie-Joseph (1858–87). A: 1881; B: 3 (1882).
Jemain, Jean-Joseph-Jacques (1864–?). A: 1884; B: 4 (1886), 3 (1887).
Kaiser, Henri-Charles (1861–?). A: 1881; B: 4 (1882), 2 (1883), 1 (1884).
Landry, Louis (1867–?). A: 1882; B: 3 (1884).
Lapuchin, Jean-Louis-Frédéric (1850–?). A: 1878.
Letocart, Victor-Jean-Félix-Henri (1866–1945). A: 1885; B: 4 (1887).
Libert, Jules-Victor-Henri (1869–1937). A: 1889; B: 4 (1893), 1 (1894).
Mahaut, Jean-Baptiste-Albert (1867–1943). A: 1888; B: 1 (1889).
Marty, Adolphe-Alexandre-Silvain (1865–1942). A: 1885; B: 1 (1886).
Marty, Eugène-Georges (1860–1908). A: 1878.
Maurel, Bruno-Marius (1867–?). A: 1887.
Mesquita, Carlos (1864–?). A: 1883; B: 4 (1884), 3 (1885).
Papot, Marie-Anna (1855–96). A: 1876; B: 4 (1876), 3 (1878), 2 (1879).
Pierné, Henry-Constant-Gabriel (1863–1937). A: 1880; B: 2 (1881), 1 (1882).
Pillard, Marie-Paul-Albert (1867–?). A: 1886.
Pinot, François-Gabriel-Henry (1865–?). A: 1884; B: 1 (1885).
Prestat, Marie-Joséphine-Claire (1862–?). A: 1887; B: 4 (1888), 3 (1889), 1 (1890).
Renaud, Marie-Léonie (1852–?). A: 1874; B: 4 (1875), 3 (1876).
Rigaud, (1859–?). A: 1879.
Rouher, Edouard-Marcel-Victor (1857–?). A: 1882.
Rousseau, Samuel-Alexandre (1853–1904). A: 1871; B: 4 (1872), 3 (1875), 2 (1876), 1 (1877).
Runner, Joseph-Achille (1870–?). A: 1888; B: 4 (1892), 2 (1893).
Schneider, Jean-Ferdinand (1864–?). A: 1887.
Sourilas, Pierre-Théophile (1859–?). A: 1879; B: 3 (1880).
Ternisien, Paul-Louis-Auguste (1870–?). A: 1888.
Thomé, François-Luc-Joseph (1850–?). A: 1871.
Tolbecque, Jean (1857–90). A: 1872; B: 3 (1873).
Tournemire, Charles-Arnould (1870–1939). A: 1889; B: 3 (1890), 1 (1891).
Verschneider, Georges-Marie-Antoine (1854–95). A: 1872; B: 4 (1874), 3 (1875).
Vierne, Louis-Victor-Jules (1870–1937). A: 1890 (see below, chap. XIV, note 13); B: 4 (1891), 2 (1892), 1 (1894).
Wachs, Etienne-Victor-Paul (1851–1915). A: 1869 or 1870; B: 2 (1870), 1 (1872).

[249, pp.684–872; AN AJ^{37}, 283–292.]

APPENDIX C
Organ Performances by Camille Saint-Saëns

1849: Won second prize in organ in the Conservatory competition [FM 12, p.227; RGM 16, p.228].

1851: Won first prize in organ in the Conservatory competition [RGM 18, p.254].

1857: Inaugurated an organ refurbished by Cavaillé-Coll at Saint-Martin, L'Isle-Adam [302, p.30]; inaugurated organ reconstructed by Cavaillé-Coll at Saint-Merry [MA 1, no.9, cols.141–43].

1862: With Bazille, Franck, Guilmant, and Schmitt, inaugurated Cavaillé-Coll organ at Saint-Sulpice [FM 26, pp.137–38; RGM 29, pp.155–56; RMS 3, cols.230–31]; inaugurated Cavaillé-Coll organ at Notre-Dame, Saint-Dizier [ME 29, p.390; RGM 29, p.358]; inaugurated organ reconstructed by Cavaillé-Coll at Saint-Thomas-d'Aquin [226, p.109; RMS 3, col.260–61].

1866: Participated in inauguration of organ reconstructed by Merklin-Schütze at Saint-Maclou, Rouen [226, p.109]; participated in inauguration of the Athénée, a new hall in Paris with a Merklin-Schütze organ [ME 33, pp.399, 414].

1867: Played Merklin-Schütze organs at the exposition in Paris [FM 31, p.282; ME 34, p.183].

1868: With Chauvet, Durand, Franck, Guilmant, Loret, Sergent, and Widor, inaugurated Cavaillé-Coll organ at Notre-Dame, Paris [FM 32, p.83; RGM 35, p.85; RMS 9, pp.23–24]; half-hour program at Notre-Dame [ME 35, p.135; RGM 35, pp.86, 95]; inaugurated Cavaillé-Coll organ at Saint-Pierre, Dreux [ME 35, p.311; RGM 35, p.263].

1869: With Chauvet, Durand, Fissot, Franck, and Widor, inaugurated Cavaillé-Coll organ at La Trinité [FM 33, p.91; ME 36, p.126; RGM 36, p.101]; played a Merklin-Schütze organ at the Cirque de l'Impératrice for a benefit given by the Société Académique de Musique [302, pp.95–96].

1871: Played daily programs for a week during inaugural series of Willis organ, Royal Albert Hall, London [OA 16, pp.329–30]; played organ solos and a piano concerto at the Cercle Philharmonique, Bordeaux [302, p.101].

1873: With Lambert, Renaud, and Widor, inaugurated organ reconstructed by Cavaillé-Coll in palace of Versailles [ME 39, p.102; RGM 40, p.62]; with Widor, played organ for Sheffield, England, in Cavaillé-Coll's hall [ME 39, p.183; RGM 40, p.150].

1874: With Grillé, Lavocat, and Martin, inaugurated Abbey organ in a church in Neuilly [RGM 41, p.223].

1878: Organ performance in Brescia, Italy [ME 44, p.332]; recital at the Trocadéro [ME 44, p.363; RGM 45, p.321]; one of several organists playing the restored Saint-Eustache organ for invited audiences, prior to the inauguration [ME 44, p.355].

1879: Played a Bach prelude and fugue in Saint James's Hall, London [302, p.120]; program with Gigout at the Trocadéro [RGM 46, p.239].

1880: Played a *Rhapsodie Bretonne* on a church concert in Baden-Baden [302, p.120].

1882: Played two organ pieces on a Brussels Conservatory concert [GM 28, no.14, pp.2–3]; played for Liszt in Brussels [GM 28, nos.18–19, p.3]; recital at Saint-Etienne, Mulhouse [226, p.110]; played a piece by Liszt at the cathedral, Zurich [302, p.121].

1884: Appeared in Bordeaux as composer, pianist, and organist [ME 51, p.32].

1896: Toured in Switzerland, giving organ and voice concerts with Miss Baldo [ME 62, p.312]; several organ programs in the south of France [226, p.113]; played the organ part of his Third Symphony at an exposition in Switzerland [226, p.113].

1897: Organ programs in Holland, Scandinavia, and at the exposition in Brussels; played in Spain for the king and queen at the San Francisco church, Madrid [26, p.166; ME 63, pp.176, 182, 271, 333].

1904: Played the organ part in his Third Symphony and two organ solos at the Salle Pleyel [302, p.147].

1906: Played excerpts from his Third Symphony and two organ solos at the Saint Cecilia academy, Rome [226, p.113]; played two organ pieces at the Mozart Festival, Salzburg [302, p.149]; played the organ parts in his Third Symphony and *Sérénade* (Op.15) at Carnegie Hall, New York [302, p.162].

1910: Participated in a program at the cathedral of Lausanne, Switzerland [26, p.190; 226, p.113].

1913: Played organ and piano in the Salle Gaveau, Paris [26, p.199; 226, p.113]; appeared as composer, conductor, pianist, and organist in a festival in his honor at Vevey, Switzerland [26, p.196; 226, p.113].

1917: Played his *Improvisations,* Op.150, on concerts in Marseilles, Nice, and Lyon [26, p.210].

1920: At age 84 played the organ at a wedding [26, p.214]. This may have been his last organ performance. He died on December 16, 1921.

BIBLIOGRAPHY

Abbreviations: Manuscript Collections

AN   Archives nationales, Paris
BN   Bibliothèque nationale, Paris

Abbreviations: Periodicals

FM	*La France musicale*	OR	*The Organ* [ed. Truette]
GM	*Le Guide musicale*	RGM	*Revue et Gazette musicale*
IL	*L'Illustration*		*de Paris*
JD	*Journal des débats politiques*	RM	*Revue musicale*
	et littéraires	RMA	*Revue de musique ancienne*
MA	*La Maîtrise*		*et moderne*
MC	*The Musical Courier*	RMR	*Revue de la musique religieuse,*
ME	*Le Ménestrel*		*populaire et classique*
MMR	*The Monthly Musical Record*	RMS	*Revue de musique sacrée,*
MST	*The Musical Standard*		*ancienne et moderne*
MU	*The Musician*	TSG	*La Tribune de Saint-Gervais*
OA	*The Orchestra*		

Books, Articles, and Dissertations

1. Adam, Adolphe. *Souvenirs d'un musicien*. Paris: Calmann Lévy, 1884.
2. Adam, Louis. *Méthode de piano du Conservatoire*. 1804. Reprint. Geneva: Minkoff, 1974.
3. Ahrens, Christian. "Deutscher Einfluss auf die französische Orgelmusik der Romantik?" *Die Musikforschung* 34 (1981):311–12.
4. Alexis, Georges L. J. "Aristide Cavaillé-Coll et ses amis belges." In *Mélanges Ernest Closson: recueil d'articles musicologiques offert à Ernest Closson à l'occasion de son soixante-quinzième anniversaire,* edited by Charles van den Borren and Albert van der Linden, pp.30–47. Brussels: Société Belge de Musicologie, 1948.
5. d'Angers, J. Martin. "L'Ecole Choron ressuscitée." *La France musicale* 17 (1853):303–305.
6. *Annuaire musical et orphéonique de France*. Paris: Coyon et Bettinger, 1875, 1876, 1877–78.
7. Anthony, Jimmy Jess. "Charles-Marie Widor's *Symphonies Pour Orgue:* Their Artistic Context and Cultural Antecedents." DMA diss., Eastman School of Music, 1986.
8. Archbold, Lawrence. "Franck's Organ Music and Its Legacy." *19th Century Music* 12/1 (Summer 1988):54–63.
9. d'Argoeuves, Michel. "Alexandre Guilmant." *L'Orgue* 114 (April–June 1965):60–68.
10. Armstrong, Agnes. "Alexandre Guilmant: American Tours and American Organs." *The Tracker* 32/3 (1989):15–23.

11. Arnold, Corliss. *Organ Literature: A Comprehensive Survey*. 2d ed. 2 vols. Metuchen, N.J.: The Scarecrow Press, 1984.
12. Bailey, Mark David. "Eugène Gigout (1844–1925): Performer and Pedagogue." DMA diss., Cincinnati College-Conservatory of Music, 1988.
13. Barlow, Andrew Hallam. "French Organ Music: 1770–1850." Master of Philosophy thesis, University of Nottingham, England, 1980.
14. Barzun, Jacques. "Paris in 1830." In *Music in Paris in the Eighteen-Thirties*, edited by Peter Bloom, pp.1–22. Stuyvesant, N.Y.: Pendragon Press, 1987.
15. Becker, G. "Le Conservatoire de musique de Liège." *Le Guide musical* 23/28–29 (July 12 and 19, 1877):1–3.
16. Becquart-Robyns, Godelieve. "François-Joseph Fétis: maître de chapelle de Léopold Ier." *Revue belge de musicologie* 26–27 (1972–73):130–42.
17. Beechey, Gwilym. "Organ recitals by French organists in England." *The Organ* 49 (1969–70):108–17.
18. Benoit, Marcelle. "César Franck et ses élèves." *L'Orgue* 83 (April–September 1957):76–78.
19. ———. "La Classe d'orgue du Conservatoire de Paris." *L'Orgue* 66 (January–March 1953):12–17; 67 (April–June 1953):54–56.
20. Bergmans, Paul. "L'enseignement musical à Anvers (1835–1884)." *Le Guide musical* 31 (1885):333–34.
21. Bertha, A[lexandre] de. "Ch. Valentin Alkan aîné: étude psycho-musicale." *Bulletin français de la S.I.M.* 5 (1909):135–47.
22. ———. "Franz Liszt: étude musico-psychologique." Part 3. *Mercure musical et Bulletin français de la S.I.M.* 3 (1907):1160–84.
23. Bloom, Peter. "A Review of Fétis's *Revue Musicale*." In *Music in Paris in the Eighteen-Thirties*, edited by Peter Bloom, pp.55–79. Stuyvesant, N.Y.: Pendragon Press, 1987.
24. Boëllmann-Gigout, Marie-Louise. "Quelques Souvenirs sur Eugène Gigout." *L'Orgue* 25 (March 1936):14–16.
25. Bonnal, Ermend. "Saint-Saëns à Saint-Séverin." *L'Orgue* 24 (December 1935): 6–8.
26. Bonnerot, Jean. *C. Saint-Saëns*. 2d ed. Paris: Durand et Cie., 1923.
27. Bonnet, Joseph. "Alexandre Guilmant." *La Revue musicale* 18 (1937):82.
28. ———. "Quelques Souvenirs personnels sur Alexandre Guilmant suivis d'une notice biographique à propos du centenaire de sa naissance." *L'Orgue* 29 (March 1937):8–13.
29. Bordes, Charles. "Le Sentiment religieux dans la musique d'église de César Franck." *Le Courrier musical* 7 (1904):577–78.
30. Borren, Charles van den. *César Franck*. Brussels: La Renaissance du Livre, 1950.
31. Boschot, Adolphe. *Notice sur la vie et les oeuvres de M. Charles-Marie Widor*. Paris: Institut de France, Académie des Beaux-Arts, 1937.
32. Bourligueux, Guy. "François Lacodre, dit Blin (1757–1834), organiste de l'église métropolitaine Notre-Dame de Paris." *Recherches sur la musique française classique* 16 (1976):71–113.
33. ———. "Les Organistes de Notre-Dame de Paris au XIXe siècle (Desprez, Blin & Pollet)." *Revue internationale de musique française* 16 (February 1985):51–74.
34. Bouvet, Charles. *Les Couperin: une dynastie de musiciens français*. 1919. Reprint. Hildesheim: Georg Olms, 1977.
35. ———. "La Fin d'une dynastie d'artistes." *Revue de musicologie* 10 (1926):134–48.
36. ———. *Nouveaux Documents sur les Couperin*. Paris: Pierre Bossuet, [1933].
37. Brunold, Paul. *Le Grand Orgue de Sᵗ Gervais à Paris*. Paris: Editions de l'Oiseau Lyre, 1934.

38. Buenzod, Emmanuel. *César Franck.* Paris: Editions Seghers, 1966.
39. Busser, Henri. "La Classe d'orgue de César Franck en 1889–1890." *L'Orgue* 102 (April–June 1962):33–34.
40. ———. *De Pelléas aux Indes galantes.* Paris: Librairie Arthème Fayard, 1955.
41. Carl, William C. "Alexandre Guilmant as a Composer; His Recital Tours in U.S." *The Diapason* 27/8 (July 1936):8.
42. ———. "Alexandre Guilmant; Noted Figure Viewed 25 Years After Death." *The Diapason* 27/7 (June 1936):4.
43. ———. "All about Guilmant." *The Musical Courier* 27/15 (October 11, 1893):9–10.
44. ———. "Guilmant's Contribution to Organ Music and Organ Playing." *The Musician* 17 (1912):202.
45. Carlez, Jules. *Choron: sa vie et ses travaux.* Caen: F. le Blanc-Hardel, 1882.
46. Castéra, René de. "La Fondation de la Schola Cantorum." In *La Schola Cantorum: son histoire depuis sa fondation jusqu'en 1925,* edited by Vincent d'Indy, pp.4–18. Paris: Bloud et Gay, 1927.
47. Castil-Blaze [François-Henri-Joseph Blaze]. *Chapelle-Musique des rois de France.* Paris: Paulin, 1832.
48. Cavaillé-Coll, Cécile. "Aristide Cavaillé-Coll en 1870–71." *L'Orgue* 40–41 (December–March 1939–40):5–6.
49. ———. "Lemmens: 1823–1881; quelques souvenirs." *Bulletin de l'Association des anciens élèves de l'Ecole de musique classique* 17/44–45 (July–October 1923):1–4.
50. Cavaillé-Coll, Cécile et Emmanuel. *Aristide Cavaillé-Coll.* Paris: Librairie Fischbacher, 1929.
51. Cellier, Alexandre. "L'Orgue de la salle d'examen de l'ancien Conservatoire." *L'Orgue* 62 (January–March 1952):20–21.
52. ———. "Une heure avec Camille Saint-Saëns." *L'Orgue* 73 (October–December 1954):122–24.
53. Chantavoine, Jean. *Camille Saint-Saëns.* Paris: Richard-Masse, 1947.
54. Chopin, Fryderyk. *Selected Correspondence of Fryderyk Chopin.* Translated and edited by Arthur Hedley. London: Heinemann, 1962.
55. Choron, Alexandre Etienne, and François Joseph Fayolle. *Dictionnaire historique des musiciens.* 2 vols. 1810. Reprint. New York and Hildesheim: Georg Olms, 1971.
56. Clerc, Maurice. "L'Orgue G. et E. Cavaillé-Coll de Charles-Marie Widor et sa récente installation à Selongey (Côte-d'Or)." *La Flûte harmonique* 37 (1986):11–25.
57. Coeuroy, André. "Present Tendencies of Sacred Music in France." *Musical Quarterly* 13 (1927):582–604.
58. Comettant, Oscar. "Le Conservatoire de Paris tel qu'il est." *Le Ménestrel* 36 (1869):100–101, 108–109, 123–24, 131–33.
59. Cooper, Jeffrey. *The Rise of Instrumental Music and Concert Series in Paris 1828–1871.* Ann Arbor: UMI Research Press, 1983.
60. Cooper, Martin. *French Music From the death of Berlioz to the death of Fauré.* London: Oxford University Press, 1951.
61. Cramer, Craig Jay. "The Published Organ Works of A. P. F. Boëly (1785–1858)." DMA diss., Eastman School of Music, 1983.
62. Crauzat, Claude Noisette de. *L'Orgue dans la société française.* Paris: Honoré Champion, 1979.
63. ———. "L'Orgue romantique." *La Revue musicale* 295–96 (1977):83–95.
64. Dandelot, Arthur. *La Vie et l'oeuvre de Saint-Saëns.* Paris: Editions Dandelot, 1930.

65. Danjou, Félix. "Quelques Mots aux anciens abonnés de la *Revue de la musique religieuse*." *Revue de la musique religieuse, populaire et classique* 4, part 2 (1854):v–xvi.

66. Davies, Laurence. *César Franck and His Circle.* Boston: Houghton Mifflin Co., 1970.

67. Debay, Victor, and Paul Locard. "Ecole romantique française de 1815 à 1837." In *Encyclopédie de la musique et dictionnaire du Conservatoire*, edited by Albert Lavignac and Lionel de La Laurencie, part 1, pp.1661–97. Paris: Librairie Delagrave, 1913–31.

68. Delosme, René. "L'Orgue français de transition." *La Revue musicale* 295–96 (1977):57–82.

69. Demuth, Norman. *César Franck.* New York: Philosophical Library, 1949.

70. Dewalque, G. "Duguet *(Dieudonné)*." In *Biographie nationale*, vol. 6, p.258. Brussels: Bruylant-Christophe, 1878.

71. *Dictionnaire biographique de musiciens.* Lachine, Québec, Canada: Mont Sainte-Anne, 1922.

72. Donakowski, Conrad L. *A Muse for the Masses.* Chicago: University of Chicago Press, 1977.

73. Douglass, Fenner. *Cavaillé-Coll and the Musicians.* 2 vols. Raleigh: Sunbury, 1980.

74. Dubois, Théodore. "Discours de M. Théodore Dubois." In *A César Franck: ses disciples, ses amis, ses admirateurs; souvenir du 22 Octobre 1904*, pp.19–21. Paris, n.p. [1904].

75. ———. "L'Enseignement musical." In *Encyclopédie de la musique et dictionnaire du Conservatoire*, edited by Albert Lavignac and Lionel de La Laurencie, part 2, pp.3437–71. Paris: Librairie Delagrave, 1913–31.

76. Duclos, Joseph Désiré. "Essai sur la vie et les travaux de l'auteur." Preface to *Du Chant grégorien: sa mélodie, son rhythme, son harmonisation*, by Jacques-Nicolas Lemmens, xiii–xlix. Ghent: Annoot-Braeckman, 1886.

77. Dufourcq, Norbert. *Alexis Chauvet.* Cahiers et mémoires de l'orgue. Paris: Les Amis de l'Orgue, 1991.

78. ———. "A propos de César Franck." *L'Orgue* 201–204 (Special issue, 1987):71–77.

79. ———. "A propos du Cinquantenaire de la mort de Cavaillé-Coll (1899–1949)." *L'Orgue* 53 (October–December 1949):114–17; 54 (January–March 1950):21–22; 55 (April–June 1950):42–44; 57 (October–December 1950):111–12; 58–59 (January–June 1951):58–60; 60 (July–September 1951):85–87; 62 (January–March 1952):22–25; 63 (April–June 1952):57–58; 64 (July–September 1952):87–88; 65 (October–December 1952):111–13; 67 (April–June 1953):59–61; 68 (July–September 1953):84–85.

80. ———. "Autour de l'Ecole d'orgue française (1850–1890)." *L'Orgue* 76 (July–September 1955):88–90; 78 (January–March 1956):20–22.

81. ———. "Autour des Boëly." *Recherches sur la musique française classique* 5 (1965):51–69.

82. ———. "Autour des Orgues du Conservatoire national et de la chapelle des Tuileries." *L'Orgue* 58–59 (January–June 1951):56–57; 60 (July–September 1951):72–78; 61 (October–December 1951):115–23; 62 (January–March 1952):13–20.

83. ———. *César Franck.* Paris: La Colombe, 1949.

84. ———. "L'Enseignement de l'orgue au Conservatoire national avant la nomination de César Franck (1872)." *L'Orgue* 144 (October–December 1972):121–25.

85. ———. *Eugène Gigout.* Cahiers et mémoires de l'orgue. Paris: Les Amis de l'Orgue, 1982.

86. ———. *Le Grand Orgue et les organistes de Saint-Merry de Paris.* Paris: Librairie Floury, 1947.
87. ———. *La Musique d'orgue française de Jehan Titelouze à Jehan Alain.* 2d ed. Paris: Librairie Floury, 1949.
88. Dumesnil, Maurice. "Charles Marie Widor, the Grand Old Man of French Music." *The Etude* 53 (1935):143–44, 192.
89. Dumesnil, René. *Portraits de musiciens français.* Paris: Librairie Plon, 1938.
90. Dumoulin, J.-B. *Biographie de Prosper-Charles Simon.* Paris: Chez l'Auteur, 1866.
91. Dunan, Elisabeth. *Inventaire de la série AJ³⁷.* Vol. 1. Paris: S.E.V.P.E.N., 1971.
92. Duparc, Henri. "César Franck pendant le siège de Paris." *La Revue musicale* 4 (1922):139–41.
93. Dupré, Marcel. "Alexandre Guilmant." *The Diapason* 53/4 (March 1962):8, 38–39.
94. ———. "Alexandre Guilmant." *La Revue musicale* 18 (1937):73–81.
95. ———. *Recollections.* Translated and edited by Ralph Kneeream. Melville, N.Y.: Belwin-Mills, 1975.
96. Eddy, Clarence. "Clarence Eddy on French Organists." *Music* 13 (November 1897–April 1898):589–95.
97. ———. "Leading Organists of France and Italy." *Music* 11 (November 1896– April 1897):163–70.
98. ———. "Recent Glimpses of Saint-Saens." *Music* 9 (October 1895–April 1896):251–56.
99. Einstein, Alfred. *Music in the Romantic Era.* New York: W. W. Norton & Co., 1947.
100. Emmanuel, Maurice. *César Franck.* Paris: Librairie Renouard, 1930.
101. Erb, J. "Episodes de la vie d'un musicien d'Alsace (II)." *L'Orgue* 39 (September 1939):65–71.
102. Eustace, John Chetwode. *Letter from Paris, to George Petre, Esq.* 3d ed. London: J. Mawman, 1814.
103. Fauré, Gabriel. "Camille Saint-Saëns." *La Revue musicale* 3 (1922):97–100.
104. ———. *Hommage à Eugène Gigout.* Paris: H. Floury, 1923.
105. ———. "Souvenirs." *La Revue musicale* 22 (October 1922):3–9.
106. Favre, Georges. "A Propos de l'organiste rouennais: Charles Broche." *Revue de musicologie* 20 (1939):25–26.
107. ———. *Compositeurs français méconnus.* Paris: La Pensée Universelle, 1983.
108. ———. "Les Organistes parisiens de la fin du XVIIIᵉ siècle: Guillaume Lasceux." *Revue de musicologie* 34 (1952):38–45.
109. ———. "Les Créateurs de l'école française de piano: Nicolas Séjan." *Revue de musicologie* 17 (1936):70–78.
110. ———. "Un Organiste de la cathédrale de Rouen: Charles Broche (1752-1803)." *Revue de musicologie* 18 (1937):84–96.
111. ———. *Silhouettes du Conservatoire.* Paris: La Pensée Universelle, 1986.
112. Félix, Jean-Pierre. "Etat de l'orgue à Bruxelles dans le dernier quart du XVIII° s." *L'Organiste* 16 (1984):87–103.
112a. ———. "Léandre Vilain (1866–1945)." *L'Organiste* 22 (1990):141–49.
113. Ferchault, Guy. "La Musique religieuse française de la mort de Franck a nos jours." *La Revue musicale* 222 (1953–54):121–37.
114. Fétis, François-Joseph. *Biographie universelle des musiciens et bibliographie générale de la musique.* 8 vols. Brussels: Leroux, 1835–44. 2d ed., 1860–65. *Supplément et complément,* 2 vols., edited by Arthur Pougin, 1878–80. Reprint (1873 impression). Brussels: Culture et Civilisation, 1963. [Unless otherwise indicated the reprint edition is the source of references in the text.]

115. ———. "De la Musique religieuse." *Le Guide musical* 14/17 (April 23, 1868): 1–2.
116. ———. "Sur l'Etat actuel de la facture des orgues en Belgique, comparé à sa situation en Allemagne, en France et en Angleterre." *Bulletins Académie royale de Belgique* 17 (1850):309–20.
117. ———. "Sur les Progrès de la facture des orgues en Belgique dans les dernières années." *Bulletins Académie royale de Belgique* 23 (1856):234–42.
118. Fétis, François-Joseph, and Ignaz Moscheles. *Méthode des méthodes de piano.* 1840. Reprint. Geneva: Minkoff, 1973.
119. Fétis, François-Joseph; Thé. Fallon; X. Van Elewyck; V. Bender; and Alphonse Mailly. *Rapport adressé à M. le Ministre de l'Intérieur, sur le grand orgue construit pour le Conservatoire royal de musique, dans le palais de la rue Ducale.* Brussels: Imprimerie de Deltombe, 1866.
120. Fisquet, H. "Lefébure-Wély." *Revue de musique sacrée ancienne et moderne* 10 (1869):100.
121. Fox, Ronald L. "The International Concert Career of Clarence Eddy." *The Tracker* 33/4 (1990):14–18.
122. François-Sappey, Brigitte. *Alexandre P. F. Boëly, 1785-1858: ses ancêtres, sa vie, son oeuvre, son temps.* Paris: Aux Amateurs de Livres, 1989.
123. ———. "A l'Occasion du bicentenaire de sa naissance, un versaillais à redécouvrir: A.-P.-F. Boëly (1785–1858)." In *A.-P.-F. Boëly 1785–1985,* pp.3–15. Special issue of *Les Goûts-Réünis,* 1985.
124. ———. "La Vie musicale à Paris à travers les *Mémoires* d'Eugène Sauzay (1809–1901)." *Revue de musicologie* 60 (1974):159–210.
125. Fromageot, P. "Un Disciple de Bach: Pierre-François Boëly." *Revue de l'histoire de Versailles et de Seine-et-oise* 11 (1909):193–203.
126. Fuller, David. "Zenith and Nadir: The Organ versus Its Music in Late 18th Century France." In *L'Orgue à notre époque,* edited by Donald Mackey, pp.129–48. Montreal: McGill University, 1981.
127. Galerne, Maurice. *L'Ecole Niedermeyer: sa création, son but, son développement.* Paris: Editions Margueritat, [1928].
128. Gallois, Jean. *Franck.* Paris: Editions du Seuil, 1966.
129. Ganvert, Gérard. "Alkan, musicien français de religion juive." In *Charles Valentin Alkan,* edited by Brigitte François-Sappey, 263–81. Paris: Fayard, 1991.
130. Gastoué, Amédée. "A Great French Organist, Alexandre Boëly, and His Works." *Musical Quarterly* 30 (1944):336–44.
131. ———. "Nécrologie: F. de La Tombelle." *La Tribune de Saint Gervais* 25 (1928):170–72.
132. Georgeot, Jean-M. "Note sur Nicolas Séjan." *L'Orgue* 141 (January–March 1972):14–17.
133. Gérard, Bernadette. "La condition du musicien d'église à Paris en 1826." *L'Orgue* 136 (October–December 1970):119–22.
134. Gigout, Eugène. "Musique liturgique et religieuse catholique." In *Encyclopédie de la musique et dictionnaire du Conservatoire,* edited by Albert Lavignac and Lionel de La Laurencie, part 2, pp.2315–30. Paris: Librairie Delagrave, 1913–31.
135. Gollmick, Carl. "Herr Fétis, Vorstand des Brüsseler Conservatoriums, als Mensch, Kritiker, Theoretiker und Componist." *Neue Zeitschrift für Musik* 36 (1852):16–17, 31–32, 44–45, 51–53.
136. Goodrich, Wallace. *The Organ in France.* Boston: The Boston Music Co., 1917.
137. Gorenstein, Nicolas. "L'Orgue post-classique français: du concert spirituel à Cavaillé-Coll." *La Tribune de l'orgue* 39 (1987)/1:9–10; 2:1–9; 3:1–3; 4:5–9; 40 (1988)/1:1–5; 2:1–6; 3:1–6; 4:11–14; 41 (1989)/1:1–7; 2:1–5; 4:1–10; 42 (1990)/1:14–19.

138. Gounod, Charles. *Autobiographical Reminiscences.* Translated by W. Hely Hutchinson. London: William Heinemann, 1896.
139. Grace, Harvey. *French Organ Music Past and Present.* New York: H. W. Gray Co., 1919.
140. Grout, Donald Jay. *A History of Western Music.* 3d ed. New York: W. W. Norton, 1980.
141. Guédon, Joseph. "L'Orgue modern." In *Nouveau Manuel Complet du Facteur d'Orgues,* 2d ed., pp.357–508. Paris: L. Mulo, 1903.
142. Guenther, Eileen Morris. "French Keyboard Noël Variations of the 17th and 18th Centuries." M.A. thesis, Catholic University of America, 1973.
143. Guichard, Arthur de. "Ecole Niedermeyer: a Music School which makes musicians." *The Musician* 19 (1914):369–71.
144. Guillard, Georges. "Adolphe Hesse à Paris en 1844." *L'Orgue* 206 (April–June 1988):8–10.
145. Guilmant, Alexandre. "La Musique d'orgue." *Encyclopédie de la musique et dictionnaire du Conservatoire,* edited by Albert Lavignac and Lionel de La Laurencie, part 2, pp.1125–80. Paris: Librairie Delagrave, 1913–31.
146. ———. "Organ Music and Organ Playing." *The Forum* 25 (March 1898):83–89. Reprint in Preface to *The Organ Works of Alexandre Guilmant,* edited by Wayne Leupold, xxv–xxviii. Melville, N.Y.: McAfee, 1984.
147. ———. "Du Role de l'orgue dans les offices liturgiques." In *Congrès diocésain de musique religieuse et de plain-chant,* pp.157–59. Rodez: E. Carrère, 1895.
148. Harding, James. *Saint-Saëns and his Circle.* London: Chapman & Hall, 1965.
149. Hardouin, Pierre J. *Le Grand Orgue de Notre-Dame de Paris.* Kassel: Bärenreiter, 1973.
150. ———. "Les Orgues de Paris en l'an III." *Renaissance de l'orgue* 7 (1970, part 3):19–22; 8 (1970, part 4):21–24.
151. Henderson, A. M. "Alexandre Guilmant: Memories of Great Organist of France." *The Diapason* 42/9 (August 1951):20.
152. ———. "Personal Memories of Gigout." *Musical Opinion* 80 (1956–57):359–61. Also published as "Memories of Gigout, 60 Years at Church of St. Augustin in Paris." *The Diapason* 42/5 (April 1951):8.
153. ———. "Personal Memories of Saint-Saëns." *Musical Opinion* 78 (1954–55):531–33.
154. ———. "Widor and His Organ Class." *The Musical Times* 78 (1937):341–45. Also published (with slight alterations) as "Widor and His Organ Class are Recalled by Friend and Pupil," *The Diapason* 41/10 (September 1950):16; and as "Memories of Widor and his Teaching," *Musical Opinion* 78 (1954–55):657–59.
155. Hervey, Arthur. *Saint-Saëns.* 1922. Reprint. Freeport, N.Y.: Books for Libraries Press, 1969.
156. Hesse, Adolph. "Kleine Zeitung." *Neue Zeitschrift für Musik* 36 (1852):163.
157. Hielscher, Hans Uwe. *Alexandre Guilmant (1837–1911): Leben und Werk.* Bielefeld: Robert Bechauf Druckerei und Verlag, 1987.
158. Higginbottom, Edward. "Ecclesiastical Prescription and Musical Style in French Classical Organ Music." *The Organ Yearbook* 12 (1981):31–54.
159. Hinton, J. W. *César Franck. Some Personal Reminiscences.* London: William Reeves, n.d.
160. Hobbs, Alain. *Charles-Marie Widor.* Cahiers et memoires de l'orgue. Paris: Les Amis de l'Orgue, 1988.
161. Horton, John. *César Franck.* London: Oxford University Press, 1948.
162. Huré, Jean. "Eugène Gigout." *L'Orgue et les organistes* 2/21 (December 1925):2–35.

163. ———. "The French School of Organ Playing in its Own Land." *Musical Quarterly* 6 (1920):272–75.
164. ———. "Henri Dallier." *Le Monde musical* 38 (1927):369.
165. ———. "La Tradition de J.-S. Bach." *L'Orgue et les organists* 3/33 (December 1926):15–17. Continued in *Le Monde musical* 38 (1927):183–86, 233, 265–66; 39 (1928):10–11. [The last two installments are entitled "Lemmens et la tradition de J.-S. Bach."]
166. Hutchings, Arthur. *Church Music in the Nineteenth Century*. New York: Oxford University Press, 1967.
167. Imbert, Hugues. "Maîtres contemporains: Emile Bernard." *Le Guide musical*, 39 (1893):204–205.
168. ———. *Médaillons contemporains*. Paris: Librairie Fischbacher, 1903.
169. ———. *Nouveaux profils de musiciens*. Paris: Librairie Fischbacher, 1892.
170. ———. *Portraits et études*. Paris: Librairie Fischbacher, 1894.
171. D'Indy, Vincent. *César Franck*. Translated by Rosa Newmarch. London: John Lane the Bodley Head, 1909.
172. ———. "La Schola Cantorum." In *Encyclopédie de la musique et dictionnaire du Conservatoire*, edited by Albert Lavignac and Lionel de La Laurencie, part 2, pp. 3622–25. Paris: Librairie Delagrave, 1913–31.
173. D'Indy, Vincent, ed. *La Schola Cantorum: son histoire depuis sa fondation jusqu'en 1925*. Paris: Bloud et Gay, 1927.
174. Jaquet-Langlais, Marie-Louise. "Une Curiosité: l'oeuvre d'orgue de Jean-Sébastien Bach doigtée par César Franck." *L'Orgue* 207 (1988):1–6.
175. ———. "L'Oeuvre d'orgue de César Franck et notre temps." *L'Orgue* 167 (July–September 1978):5–41.
176. Jemain, Adine. "Quelques souvenirs de la classe d'orgue d'Eugène Gigout." *L'Orgue* 155 (July–September 1975):73–74.
177. Jimeno de Lerma, D. Ildefonso. *Estudios sobre Música Religiosa: El Canto Litúrgico, El Órgano*. Madrid: La España Editorial, [c. 1899].
178. Jouin, Mgr. *Les Noces de diamant de l'organiste de St. Augustin M. Eugène Gigout*. Paris: Association paroissiale de Saint-Augustin, 1923.
179. Jouve, Esprit-Gustave. "Lettres au rédacteur en chef de La Maîtrise sur le mouvement liturgico-romain en France, durant le XIXᵉ siècle." *La Maîtrise* 1 (1857–58), cols.26–29, 53–58, 65–69, 114–18, 129–34.
180. Joy, Charles R. *Music in the Life of Albert Schweitzer*. New York: Harper & Bros., 1951.
181. Klaus, Kenneth B. *The Romantic Period in Music*. Boston: Allyn and Bacon, 1970.
182. Knauff, Theodore C. *Three Great Organists*. n.p., 1892.
183. Kooiman, Ewald. "Jacques Lemmens, Charles-Marie Widor und die französische 'Bach-Tradition'." Translated by Ute Gremmel-Geuchen. *Ars Organi* 37 (1989): 198–206; 38 (1990):3–14.
184. Kremer, Rudolph. "The Organ Sonata Since 1845." Ph.D. diss., Washington University, 1963.
185. Kreps, Joseph. "Bach et l'orgue catholique; Lemmens à l'école de Fétis." *Musica sacra* 53 (1952):73–96.
186. Kunel, Maurice. *César Franck: l'homme et son oeuvre*. Paris: Editions Bernard Grasset, 1947.
187. ———. *César Franck inconnu*. Brussels: La Renaissance du Livre, 1958.
188. Lamazou, l'Abbé [Pierre]. "Biographie de Lefébure-Wély." *L'Illustration musicale* 1/2 (1863).
189. Landormy, Paul. *La Musique française de Franck à Debussy*. Paris: Gallimard, 1943.

190. La Salle, Geneviève de. "L'Orgue symphonique en France." *La Revue musicale* 324–26 (1979):173–87.
191. Lasceux, Guillaume and Traversier. "Essai théorique et pratique sur l'art de l'orgue . . . par Mr. Lasceux. . . . La partie littéraire a été rédigée par Mr. Traversier. . . ." Paris: Ms., 1809.
192. Launay, Paul de. "Widor as I Knew Him." *The American Organist* 20 (1937):202–203.
193. Laurens, J.-B. "Conseils pour se former une bibliothèque de musique religieuse et de musique d'orgue en particular." *Revue de la musique religieuse, populaire et classique* 2 (1846):433–40; 3 (1847):103–11, 202–208.
194. Laurens, L.-C. "Des Fonctions du grand orgue pendant les offices." *Revue de musique sacrée ancienne et moderne* 5 (1864), cols.289–96.
195. Lavignac, Albert, and Lionel de La Laurencie, eds. *Encyclopédie de la musique et dictionnaire du Conservatoire.* 2 parts in 11 vols. Paris: Librairie Delagrave, 1913–31.
196. LeClère, Marcel. "Un brillant élève des frères Haydn: Sigismond Neukomm organiste et compositeur (1778–1858)." *L'Orgue* 150 (April–June 1974): 56–64.
197. Ledru, Emilien. Preface to *Marche religieuse pour orgue,* Op.14, by Aloys Klein. Rouen: E. Ledru, [1912].
198. Lefèvre, Gustave, and Mme. Henri Heurtel. "L'Ecole de musique classique Niedermeyer." In *Encyclopédie de la musique et dictionnaire du Conservatoire,* edited by Albert Lavignac and Lionel de La Laurencie, part 2, pp. 3617–21. Paris: Librairie Delagrave, 1913–31.
199. Lejeune-Bonnier, Eliane. "Abel Decaux." *L'Orgue* 210 (1989):4–10.
200. Lennon, Joseph G. Preface to *Batiste's Last Series of Voluntaries for the Organ.* Edited by Joseph G. Lennon. Boston: Oliver Ditson, 1878.
201. Lesure, François. "L'Affaire Fétis." *Revue belge de musicologie* 28–30 (1974–76):214–21.
202. Letocart, Henri. "Quelques Souvenirs." *L'Orgue* 36 (December 1938):2–7; 37 (March 1939):4–6.
203. Leupold, Wayne. Preface to *The Organ Works of Alexandre Guilmant.* 6 vols. Edited by Wayne Leupold. Melville, N.Y.: McAfee, 1984.
204. Locard, Paul. *Léon Boëllmann.* Extract from *La Revue alsacienne illustrée* 3/3 (1901). Strasbourg: J. Noiriel, n.d.
205. ———. *Les maîtres contemporains de l'orgue.* Paris: Librairie Fischbacher, [1901].
206. ———. "Souvenirs sur Gigout et Boëllman [*sic*]." *L'Orgue* 30–31 (Special issue, *Bulletin trimestriel des Amis de l'Orgue,* 1937):71–74.
207. Loesser, Arthur. *Men, Women and Pianos.* New York: Simon and Schuster, 1954.
208. Longyear, Rey M. *Nineteenth-Century Romanticism in Music.* Englewood Cliffs, N.J.: Prentice-Hall, 1969.
209. Louchart, Jean-Michel. "Charles-Marie Widor (1844–1937)." *L'Orgue* 201–204 (Special issue, 1987):103–107.
210. Lueders, Kurt. "L'Orgue à Paris en 1900." *Revue internationale de musique française* 4/12 (November 1983):75–78.
211. Lyle, Watson. *Camille Saint-Saëns: His Life and Art.* London: Kegan Paul, Trench, Trubner & Co., 1923.
212. Lyr, René, and Paul Gilson. "Histoire de la musique et des musiciens belges." In *Encyclopédie de la musique et dictionnaire du Conservatoire,* edited by Albert Lavignac and Lionel de La Laurencie, part 1, pp. 1815–61. Paris: Librairie Delagrave, 1913-31.

213. Mahaut, Albert. "César Franck, Professor of Organ." Translated by Beverly
     Scheibert. *The American Organist* 16/10 (October 1982), p.54.
214. ———. *L'Oeuvre d'orgue de César Franck*. 3d ed. Paris: Chez l'Auteur, 1923.
215. Mailly, Edouard. *Les Origines du Conservatoire royal de musique de Bruxelles*.
     Brussels: Hayez, 1879.
216. Mangold, C. N. "A Winter in Paris, 1837–8." *The Musical World* 13 (January–
     June 1840):348–50.
217. Maréchal, Henri. *Paris: souvenirs d'un musicien*. Paris: Librairie Hachette et Cie,
     1907.
218. Marmontel, Antoine-François. *Silhouettes et médaillons: les pianistes célèbres*
     Paris: A. Chaix et Cie, 1878.
219. ———. *Silhouettes et médaillons: symphonistes et virtuoses*. Paris: Heugel et Fils,
     1880.
220. Mathias, Franz X. *Leo Boellmann (1862–1897), sein Leben und Werk; seine
     Beziehungen zur Niedermeyer-Schule*. Reprint from *Jahrbuch der Elsass-
     Lothringischen Wissenschaftlichen Gesellschaft zu Strassburg* 10 (1937):76–
     137. Strassburg: Elsass-Lothringischen Wissenschaftlichen Gesellschaft, 1937.
221. McDowell, G. D. "Belgian Music." In *Belgium: Comparative Culture and Gov-
     ernment*, edited by O. Westervelt, 80–94. Skokie, Ill.: National Textbook Co.,
     1970.
222. Mendelssohn-Bartholdy, Felix. *Letters from Italy and Switzerland*. Translated by
     Lady Wallace. Boston: Oliver Ditson Co., n.d.
223. Mercier, Louis-Sébastien. *Tableau de Paris*. 12 vols., 1782–88. Abridged version
     edited by Lucien Roy. Paris: Louis-Michaud, n.d. See also English translation by
     Helen Simpson, published as *The Waiting City: Paris 1782–88*, Philadelphia: J.
     B. Lippincott Co., 1933.
224. Mongrédien, Jean. "Boëly et son temps." In *A.-P.-F. Boëly 1785–1985*, pp.16–
     20. Special issue of *Les Goûts-Réünis*, 1985.
225. ———. *La Musique en France des lumières au romantisme (1789–1830)*. Paris:
     Flammarion, 1986.
226. Morel, Fritz. "Camille Saint-Saëns organiste." *L'Orgue* 160–61 (October 1976–
     March 1977):103–16.
227. Morelot, Stéphen. "Artistes contemporains. A.-P.-F. Boely, pianiste-composi-
     teur." *Revue de la musique religieuse, populaire et classique* 2 (1846): 23–33.
228. Morin, Michel. "Eug. Gigout: compositeur-organiste." *Bulletin de l'Association
     des anciens élèves de l'Ecole de musique classique* 3/10 (October–December
     1908):2–5.
229. Moskowa, Prince de la [Joseph Napoléon Ney]. "De L'Ecole de musique de M.
     Niedermeyer." *La France musicale* 17 (1853):365–67.
230. Moulis, Adelin. "Un grand musicien ariégeois méconnu: Albert Perilhou [*sic*]."
     L'Orgue 159 (July–September 1976):89–96. First published as "Un grand musi-
     cien méconnu: Albert Périlhou." *Société ariégeoise: sciences, lettres et arts* 19
     (1960–61):46–51.
231. Muess, Claude Rémi. "L'orgue du temple de Penthemont à Paris." *Connaissance
     de l'orgue* 41 (Winter 1981):19–27; 42 (Spring 1981):9–15, 18.
232. Mutin, Charles. "Alexandre Guilmant." *S.I.M. revue musicale mensuelle* 7/5
     (May 1911):37–40.
233a. Near, John Richard. "Charles-Marie Widor." *La Flûte harmonique* 59–60
     (1991):44–50.
233b. ———. "Charles-Marie Widor: The Organ Works and Saint-Sulpice." *The
     American Organist* 27/2 (February 1993):46–59.
233. ———. "The Life and Work of Charles-Marie Widor." DMA diss., Boston
     University, 1985.

234. Nectoux, Jean-Michel. "Fauré, Gabriel (Urbain)." In *The New Grove Dictionary of Music and Musicians,* edited by Stanley Sadie, vol.6, pp.417–28. London: Macmillan, 1980.
235. Neukomm, Sigismond. "Esquisse biographique de Sigismond Neukomm." *La Maîtrise* 2 (1858–59), cols.125–28, 141–44, 188–96.
236. Newman, William S. *The Sonata Since Beethoven.* 3d ed. New York: W. W. Norton, 1983.
237. Niedermeyer, [Louis Alfred]. *Vie d'un compositeur moderne.* Paris: Librairie Fischbacher, 1893.
238. Niedermeyer, Louis, and Joseph d'Ortigue. *Traité théorique et pratique de l'accompagnement du plain-chant.* 1855. Revised and translated by Wallace Goodrich as *Gregorian Accompaniment.* New York, London, Chicago: Novello, Ewer & Co., 1905.
239. Nisard, Théodore [Théodore Elzéar Xavier Normand Torfs]. "Jean-Romary Grosjean." Part 8 of *Biographies par T. Nisard.* Paris: E. Repos, [1866].
240. ———. "Joseph Franck." Part 5 of *Biographies par T. Nisard.* Paris: E. Repos, [1866].
241. ———. "Louis Niedermeyer." Part 13 of *Biographies par T. Nisard.* Paris: E. Repos, [1866].
242. d'Ortigue, Joseph. *Dictionnaire liturgique, historique et théorique de plain-chant et de musique d'église.* Vol.29 of *Nouvelle Encyclopédie théologique,* edited by l'Abbé Migne. Paris: J. P. Migne, 1853.
243. ———. *La Musique à l'église.* Paris: Didier et Cie 1861.
244. Pearce, William George. "Through Canada with Alex. Guilmant." *The Organ* [ed. Truette] 2 (1893–94):211–12.
245. Peschard, Albert. *Les Premières applications de l'électricité aux grandes orgues.* Paris: Larousse, 1890.
246. Philipp, Isidor. "Charles-Marie Widor: A Portrait." Translated by Gustave Reese. *Musical Quarterly* 30 (1944):125–32.
247. ———. "Paris in the 'Golden Days.' " *Musical Courier* 144/7 (November 15, 1951):8–9.
248. Piccand, Jean. "Trois organistes français." *Schweizerische Musikzeitung* 105 (1965):87–93.
249. Pierre, Constant. *Le Conservatoire national de musique et de déclamation: documents historiques et administratifs.* Paris: Imprimerie National, 1900.
250. ———. *Sujets de fugue et thêmes d'improvisation donnés aux concours et examens (années 1804 à 1900).* Paris: Au Ménestrel, 1900.
251. Pinsart, Gérard. "Aspects de l'enseignement musical à Bruxelles sous le régime hollandais (1815–1830)." *Revue belge de musicologie* 34–35 (1980–81): 164–97.
252. Pirro, André. "L'Art des organistes." In *Encyclopédie de la musique et dictionnaire du Conservatoire,* edited by Albert Lavignac and Lionel de La Laurencie, part 2, pp. 1181–1374. Paris: Librairie Delagrave, 1913–31.
253. Pistone, Danièle. "La Musique à Notre-Dame de Paris de la Révolution à 1914." *Revue internationale de musique française* 6/16 (February 1985):7–38.
254. ———. "Paris et la musique 1890–1900." *Revue internationale de musique française* 28 (February 1989):7–55.
255. Planchet, D.-C. "L'Art du maître de chapelle." In *Encyclopédie de la musique et dictionnaire du Conservatoire,* edited by Albert Lavignac and Lionel de La Laurencie, part 2, pp.2337–54. Paris: Librairie Delagrave, 1913–31.
256. Planque. *Agenda musical, ou indicateur des amateurs, artistes et commercans en musique . . . par Planque, musicien et accordeur de pianos.* Vol.3, 1837. Reprint. Geneva: Minkoff, 1981.

257. Plantinga, Leon. *Romantic Music: a History of Style in Nineteenth-Century Europe.* New York: W. W. Norton, 1984.
258. Pressensé, Edmond Déhault de. *Religion and the Reign of Terror; or, the Church during the French Revolution.* Translated by John P. Lacroix. New York: Carlton & Lanahan, 1869.
259. Prod'homme, J.-G. "Camille Saint-Saëns." *Musical Quarterly* 8 (1922):469–86.
260. Prunières, Henry. "Il faut sauver l'Ecole Niedermeyer." *Revue musicale S.I.M.* 8/3 (March 1912):64–65.
261. Radiguer, Henri. "La Musique française de 1789 à 1815." In *Encyclopédie de la musique et dictionnaire du Conservatoire,* edited by Albert Lavignac and Lionel de La Laurencie, part 1, pp. 1562–1660. Paris: Librairie Delagrave, 1913–31.
262. Randel, Don, ed. *The New Harvard Dictionary of Music.* Cambridge: Harvard University Press, 1986.
263. Raugel, Félix. "Former Organs of the Abbey Church of Saint-Denis." *The Organ* 5 (1925–26):41–44.
264. ———. *Les Grandes Orgues des églises de Paris et du département de la Seine.* Paris: Librairie Fischbacher, 1927.
265. ———. "La Musique religieuse française de l'époque révolutionnaire a la mort de César Franck." *La Revue musicale* 222 (1953–54):111–20.
266. ———. *Les Organistes.* 2d ed. Paris: Librairie Renouard, 1962.
267. ———. "The Organs of Saint-Merry and Saint-Nicolas-des-Champs, Paris." *The Organ* 2 (1922–23):230–36.
268. Raynor, Henry. *A Social History of Music.* New York: Schocken Books, 1972.
269. Riemenschneider, Albert. "Tribute to Widor as He Completes Sixty Years at St. Sulpice." *The Diapason* 21/7 (June 1930):26.
270. Roger, Louis. "Biographie de L'Abbé Jouve." *L'Illustration musicale* 1/[12? (1863)].
271. ———. "Biographie de Georges Schmitt." *L'Illustration musicale* 1/[3? (1863)].
272. Ropartz, Guy de. "César Franck." Translated by Miss Milman. In *Studies in Music by Various Authors reprinted from 'The Musician',* edited by Robin Grey, 79–109. London: Simpkin, Marshall, Hamilton, Kent and Co., 1901.
273. Rupp, J. F. Emil. *Charles Marie Widor und sein Werk.* Bremen: Schweers & Haake, 1912.
274. Russell, Alexander. "Widor: As Recalled by Pupil and Friend." *Musical America* 57/8 (April 25, 1937):13, 65.
275. Russell, Carlton T. "Franck's l'Organiste Reconsidered." *The American Organist* 53/2 (February, 1970):9–12. See also "Addendum." *The American Organist* 53/6 (November 1970):3.
276. Sabatier, François. *César Franck et l'orgue.* Paris: Presses Universitaires de France, 1982.
277. ———. "L'oeuvre d'orgue et de piano-pédalier." In *Charles Valentin Alkan,* edited by Brigitte François-Sappey, 227-52. Paris: Fayard, 1991.
278. ———. "Les Orgues en France pendant la Révolution." *L'Orgue* 143 (July–September 1972):76–79.
279. ———. *Pour une Approche d'Alexandre Guilmant.* Cahiers et mémoires de l'orgue. Paris: Les Amis de l'Orgue, 1986.
280. ———. *Pour une Histoire des orgues de France pendant la Révolution (1789–1802).* L'Orgue, dossier 4. Paris: Les Amis de l'Orgue, 1989.
281. Sadie, Stanley, ed. *The New Grove Dictionary of Music and Musicians.* 20 vols. London: Macmillan, 1980.
282. Saint-Saëns, Camille. "Music in the Church." Translated by Theodore Baker. *Musical Quarterly* 2 (1916):1–8.
283. ———. *Musical Memories.* Translated by Edwin Gile Rich. Boston: Small, May-

nard & Co., 1919. Originally published as *Portraits et Souvenirs*. Paris: Société d'édition artistique, 1899.

284. ———. *Outspoken Essays on Music*. Translated by Fred Rothwell. 1922. Reprint. Freeport, N.Y.: Books for Libraries Press, 1969.

285. Samuel, Adolph. "Le Conservatoire royal de musique." *Le Guide musical* 4/34 (October 21, 1858):1–2.

286. ———. "Histoire de la musique en Belgique." *Le Ménestrel* 42 (1876):100–101, 115–16, 124, 131–32.

287. Schanck, Robert E. *"A History of the Guilmant Organ School 1899–1953."* MSM thesis, Union Theological Seminary (New York), 1953.

288. Scherers, Bernd. *Studien zur Orgelmusik der Schüler César Francks*. Regensburg: Gustav Bosse, 1984.

289. Schmitt, Georges. *Nouveau Manuel complet de l'organiste*. Vol.1. Paris: Roret, 1855.

290. Schonberg, Harold C. *The Great Pianists*. New York: Simon and Schuster, 1963.

291. Schwarz, Boris. *French Instrumental Music Between the Revolutions (1789– 1830)*. New York: Da Capo Press, 1987.

292. Schweitzer, Albert. *Aus Meinem Leben und Denken*. 1933. Translated by C. T. Campion as *Out of My Life and Thought*. New York: Henry Holt & Co., 1949.

293. ———. *Deutsche und französische Orgelbaukunst und Orgelkunst*. 1906. Translated by Charles Ferguson as "Organ Music and Organ Design in Germany and France." *The Tracker* 36/1 (1992):13–22.

294. ———. *J. S. Bach*. 2 vols. Translated by Ernest Newman. 1911. Reprint. New York: Dover, 1966.

295. Servières, Georges. *Documents inédits sur les organistes français des xviie et xviiie siècles*. Paris: Schola Cantorum, [1924].

296. ———. *Saint-Saëns*. Paris: Librairie Félix Alcan, 1923.

297. Shepherd, William. *Paris, in 1802 and 1814*. 3d ed. London: Longman, Hurst, Rees, Orme & Brown, 1814.

298. Sitzmann, Edouard. *Dictionnaire de biographie des hommes célèbres de l'Alsace*. 2 vols. 1909–1910. Reprint. Paris: Editions du Palais Royal, 1973.

299. Smith, Rollin. "Alexandre Guilmant, Commemorating the 150th Anniversary of His Birth." *The American Organist* 21/3 (March 1987):50–58.

300. ———. "Camille Saint-Saëns." *Music/A.G.O.* 5/12 (December 1971):24–26.

301. ———. "Gabriel Fauré, Organist." *The American Organist* 13/6 (June 1979):41– 42.

302. ———. *Saint-Saëns and the Organ*. Stuyvesant, N.Y.: Pendragon Press, 1992.

303. ———. *Toward an Authentic Interpretation of the Organ Works of César Franck*. New York: Pendragon Press, 1983.

304. Smith, Ronald. *Alkan: The Enigma*. London: Kahn & Averill, 1976.

305. ———. *Alkan: The Music*. London: Kahn & Averill, 1987.

306. Société savant d'Alsace. *La Musique en Alsace*. Publications de la Société savante d'Alsace, vol.10. Strasbourg: Librairie Istra, 1970.

307. Spark, William. *Musical Memories*. 3d ed. London: W. Reeves, [1909].

308. Spelle, Thierry G. "The Organ of Transition in France (1785–1835)." *The American Organist* 21/4 (April 1987):68–70.

309. Sumner, William Leslie. "Paris Organs and Organists in the 'Twenties'—Some Reminiscences." *The Organ Yearbook* 2 (1971):51–57.

310. Thistlethwaite, Nicholas. *The Making of the Victorian Organ*. Cambridge: Cambridge University Press, 1990.

311. Thomas, Fannie Edgar. "Organ Loft Whisperings." *The Musical Courier*. [A weekly feature in this magazine, 1892–94. Columns related to this study appeared regularly from 27/20 (November 15, 1893) through 28/24 (June 13, 1894).]

312. Tournemire, Charles. *César Franck*. Paris: Librairie Delagrave, 1931.
313. ———. "La Classe d'orgue du Conservatoire de Paris." *Le Monde musical* 41 (1930):141–42.
314. Vallas, Léon. *César Franck*. Translated by Hubert Foss. New York: Oxford University Press, 1951.
315. Vander Linden, Albert. "Le Conservatoire royal de Bruxelles en 1835." *Revue belge de musicologie* 26–27 (1972–73):143–45.
316. Van Hulse, Camil. "Jaak Lemmens, Who Founded the Belgian School of Playing." *The Diapason* 46/3 (February 1955):4.
317. Vanmackelberg, Maurice. "Les Guilmant et la facture d'orgues." *L'Orgue* 100 (October–December 1961):152–80.
318. Van Wye, Benjamin. "Gregorian Influences in French Organ Music before the *Motu proprio*." *Journal of the American Musicological Society* 27 (1974):1–24.
319. ———. "The Influence of the Plainsong Restoration on the Growth and Development of the Modern French Liturgical Organ School." DMA diss., University of Illinois, 1970.
320. ———. "Marcel Dupré's Marian Vespers and the French *alternatim* Tradition." *The Music Review* 43 (1982):192–224.
321. Vierne, Louis. "Alexandre Guilmant." In *La Schola Cantorum: son histoire depuis sa fondation jusqu'en 1925*, edited by Vincent d'Indy, pp. 27–38. Paris: Bloud et Gay, 1927.
322. ———. "Ch.-M. Widor (1844–1937)." *L'Orgue* 30–31 (Special issue, *Bulletin trimestriel des Amis de l'Orgue*, June–September 1937):75–76.
323. ———. *Journal (fragments)*. Cahiers et mémoires de l'orgue. Paris: Les Amis de l'Orgue, 1970.
324. ———. "Memoirs of Louis Vierne; His Life and Contacts with Famous Men." Translated by Esther E. Jones. *The Diapason* 29/10 (September 1938):6–7, 11 (October 1938):12–13, 12 (November 1938):10–11; 30/1 (December 1938):6–7, 2 (January 1939):8–9, 3 (February 1939):8–9, 4 (March 1939):8–9, 5 (April 1939):8–9; 6 (May 1939):8; 7 (June 1939):8–9, 8 (July 1939):8–9, 9 (August 1939):8–9, 10 (September 1939):8–9.
325. ———. "Mes Souvenirs." *L'Orgue*, 1934–37, reissued as special issue 134bis. Cahiers et mémoires de l'orgue. Paris: Les Amis de l'Orgue, 1970.
326. Viret, Jacques. "César Franck vu par ses élèves." *La Tribune de l'orgue* 39/4 (December 1987):9–14; 40/1 (March 1988):5–7, 2 (June 1988):6–14; 3 (September 1988):7–14; 41/1 (March 1989):21–27, 2 (June 1989):6–11.
327. Wachs, Paul. *L'Organiste improvisateur: traité d'improvisation*. Paris: Schott, [1878].
328. Wangermée, Robert. "François-Joseph Fétis, la musique et son histoire." In *François-Joseph Fétis et la vie musicale de son temps 1784–1871*, pp.xi–xx. Catalog of the Exposition on the 100th Anniversary of the acquisition of the Fétis collection. Brussels: Bibliothèque Royale Albert 1er, 1972.
329. ———. *François-Joseph Fétis, musicologue et compositeur*. Brussels: Palais des Académies, 1951.
330. Weitner, Carol. "Jacques Nicolas Lemmens: Organist, Pedagogue, Composer." DMA essay, Eastman School of Music, 1991.
331. Widor, Charles-Marie. "La Classe d'orgue du Conservatoire." *Le Ménestrel* 83 (1921):237–38.
332. ———. "L'Ecole d'orgue en France." *Le Ménestrel* 65 (1899):131–32.
333. ———. "John Sebastian Bach and the Organ." Translated by B. L. O'Donnell. In *Studies in Music by Various Authors reprinted from "The Musician,"* edited by Robin Grey, pp.52–68. London: Simpkin, Marshall, Hamilton, Kent and Co., 1901.
334. ———. *Notice sur la vie et les travaux de M. Théodore Dubois*. Paris: Institut de France, Académie des Beaux-Arts, 1924.

335. ———. *L'Orgue moderne.* Paris: Durand & Cie., 1928.
336. ———. Preface to *J. S. Bach,* by Albert Schweitzer. 2 vols. Translated by Ernest Newman. 1911. Reprint. New York: Dover, 1966.
337. ———. Preface to *L'Orgue de Jean-Sébastien Bach,* by A. Pirro. 1895. Translated by Wallace Goodrich as *Johann Sebastian Bach: The Organist and his Works for the Organ,* pp.v–xx. New York: G. Schirmer, 1902.
338. Winn, Edith Lynwood. "Memories of César Franck." *The American Organist* 10/7 (July 1927):170–71.

NOTES

I. Prelude: Music for a Revolution

1. The Protestant churches were state controlled and supported from 1802; Jewish religious institutions were state controlled from 1808 and received state support from 1831. Separation of church and state was effected in 1905.

2. Specifically *opéra comique*, distinguished from *tragédie lyrique* (the official opera of the French crown) by use of spoken dialogue instead of recitative, and by its more liberal, progressive, and popular character.

3. For a detailed account of the church in France during the Revolution see bibliography [258]. In regard to the three cults named, see especially pp.226–33, 243–47, 276.

4. Several generations of the Somer family built and serviced organs in Paris in the late eighteenth and early nineteenth centuries. Bouvet mentions Nicolas Somer (d. 1771) and his sons Joseph, Louis, and Antoine Etienne [36, pp.138–39, n.1]. According to Raugel, Antoine was still active in 1800 [264, p.165]. Another member of this family, Jean Somer (d. 1830), was associated with Louis Callinet (1786–1846) from about 1821 to 1829. It is not clear which member of the Somer family was in charge of organs for the festivals.

5. The organ of Saint-Denis was heard for the last time on March 30, 1794. Then it was left to decay. An effort was made to salvage what remained of the instrument in 1800, but much was already ruined, and the rest, transported to Saint-Martin-des-Champs for storage, disappeared [264, pp.164–65].

Part One: Performers and Programs

1. Planchet gives the following explanation of the salut:

Vespers are followed, on Sundays and feast days, with a ceremony that is called *Salut du Saint Sacrement* in France. This ceremony is of recent origin, at least in its present form. The *Cérémonial des Evéques* anticipates only the chant of the *Tantum ergo* followed by the verset *Panem de caelo*. For all the rest the usages vary according to the dioceses, often even according to the churches.

Les vêpres sont suivies, les dimanches et les jours de fête, d'une cérémonie qu'on nomme en France «Salut du Saint Sacrement». Cette cérémonie est d'origine récente, du moins dans sa forme actuelle. Le *Cérémonial des Evéques* ne prévoit que le chant du *Tantum ergo* suivi du verset *Panem de caelo*. Pour tout le reste, les usages varient selon les diocèses, souvent même selon les églises. [255, p.2353.]

2. In the early part of the century the title was usually *maître de musique*. *Maître de chapelle* was the name usually given to this position from about 1829 [253, p.9, n.10].

II. In the Wake of the Storm: 1800–1809

1. In 1795 Claude-Pierre Molard (1759–1837) was appointed by the *Commission temporaire des arts* to make a survey of the organs in Paris, in consultation with a committee of prominent organists and organ builders. Molard's notes concerning thirty-two organs include the names of the organists as well as detailed information about the organs themselves.

Notre-Dame, he said, had had four organists: Balbastre, Séjan, Charpentier, and Desprez. Desprez held additional positions at Saint-Merry and Saint-Nicolas-des-Champs, and Séjan was also at Saint-Sulpice. Other organists named by Molard included Miroir at Saint-Germain-des-Prés, Lacodre-Blin at Saint-Germain-l'Auxerrois and Saint-Philippe-du-Roule, Couperin at Saint-Gervais, Lasceux at Saint-Etienne-du-Mont, Beauvarlet-Charpentier at Saint-Paul and at Saint-Victor, and Gautier at Saint-Leu [cited in 150].

By the time the Concordat of 1801 was ratified, Notre-Dame had lost two of the four organists named by Molard: Jean-Jacques Beauvarlet-Charpentier (1734–94) and Claude Balbastre (1727–99). During the nineteenth century the cathedral had only one *titulaire* at a time, and the post went first to its senior surviving organist, Antoine Desprez, then in his late seventies.

From 1802 Miroir was at Saint-Eustache as well as Saint-Germain-des-Prés. The same year Marrigues became organist at Saint-Thomas-d'Aquin, and Antoine Lefébure-Wély at Saint-Jacques-du-Haut-Pas [264, pp.131, 136, 195]. Gervais-François Couperin was then at Saint-Pierre de Charonne as well as at Saint-Gervais [137, vol.42, no.1, p.17].

In 1804 Ferdinand-Albert Gautier left the post he had held at Saint-Leu since about 1770 to take charge of the recently restored organ at the cathedral of Soissons [295, p.29; 264, p.70]. The next year Antoine Lefébure-Wély moved to the organ position at Saint-Roch, and in 1806 Lacodre-Blin succeeded Desprez at Notre-Dame [264, pp.91, 111]. However, Lacodre-Blin still retained his position at Saint-Germain-l'Auxerrois until 1831. It was in 1806 that Séjan added the position of organist at Saint-Louis-des-Invalides to the one he had long held at Saint-Sulpice [295, p.40]. Miroir and Marrigues were both named organist at Saint-Nicolas-des-Champs in 1808, following a brief tenure of Pierre Lecourt (1806–1808) [264, p.41].

Meanwhile, Beauvarlet-Charpentier followed the organ he had played at Saint-Victor to its new home at Saint-Germain-des-Prés. The re-installation was not completed until 1810. According to Raugel, Miroir was still actually *titulaire* until 1811, and he was succeeded by Beauvarlet-Charpentier, *titulaire* from 1815 to 1833 [264, p.50].

2. Fétis knew the situation in Paris from first-hand experience. He had gone there in October 1800, to enter the Paris Conservatory, and (except for a period during 1803–1804) remained until 1811. He again lived in Paris 1818–33. On at least one occasion he played the organ at Saint-Sulpice, where Séjan was *titulaire* [114, vol.3, pp.227–35].

3. Possibly Louis-Charles Bordier (1700–64).

4. According to Choron and Fétis, Séjan was named organist to the king in 1789 [55, vol.2, p.310; 114, vol.8, p.10]. According to Favre the date was 1790 [109, p.71].

III. Years of Rebuilding: 1810–1829

1. The original letter, in Paris, Archives nationales, F^{19} 3947, no.231, also exists in a printed edition [32, pp.109–10]. Bourligueux estimates that the letter was written "around 1807" [32, p.109].

2. The Bibliothèque Nationale, Paris, contains the following manuscripts of organ

music by Isaac-François-Antoine Lefébure-Wély: MS 13356, 12 Messes pour orgue; MS 13357, 7 Recueils d'antiennes; MS 13358, 14 Suites de pièces d'orgue; MS 13766, Recueil de Magnificats pour l'orgue; MS 13767, Pièces d'orgue; MS 14754, Messe Solemnelle majeure; MS 14755, Messe Solemnelle majeure pour le jeudi saint; MS 14756, Deux Messes des doubles majeures; MS 14757, Rentrée de la procession; MS 14758, Benedictus; MS 14759, Antiennes à la Ste Vierge; MS 14760, Saluts; MS 14762, Magnificat du 6me ton.

3. Biographers differ somewhat on the number of years Antoine Lefébure-Wély suffered from paralysis [218, p.263; 188, col.9; 114, vol.5, p.251]. Alfred probably substituted for his father with gradually increasing frequency from 1826.

IV. The Romantic Dawn: The 1830s

1. The remains of the Tuileries organ were put in storage. Years later Pierre Erard (nephew of Sébastien) used what he could salvage from it in constructing a new organ for the chapel. It was completed in 1854 and installed the next year. This instrument was used until the burning of the château in May 1871 [82, no.62, pp.16–18].

2. For a detailed exploration of this subject, see [137].

3. This firm was organized in 1838 as Daublaine et Cie. In December of that year Louis Callinet joined the company, and the name was then changed to Daublaine et Callinet.

4. With the final issue—vol.4, part 2, 1854—Danjou fulfilled his obligation to the subscribers. In an introductory article he described his discouragement with the state of church music and organ playing [65].

5. For a more detailed review of the Danjou–Cavaillé-Coll debate, see [73, pp.53–62]. The debate appeared in the pages of RMR, vol.2, pp.377–91, and vol.3, pp.35–40.

6. Examples of Boëly's pedal markings in organ works of Bach are included in Georges Guillard, "J.-S. Bach—A.P.F. Boëly: le maître recopié par le disciple," *L'Orgue* 216 (1990):1–10.

7. François-Sappey [122, pp.148–52] documented five events between 1838 and 1846 in which Boëly performed on the organ:
May 7, 1838, at Notre-Dame, for the reception of work completed by Dallery
January 24, 1839, played music of Bach and Couperin in the shop of Daublaine et Callinet
June 18, 1844, played a fugue by Albrechtsberger at the inauguration of the Daublaine et Callinet organ at Saint-Eustache
October 27, 1845, played for the inauguration of the Daublaine et Callinet choir organ at Saint-Gervais
January 22, 1846, played a fugue by Handel and another piece at the reception of the work by Daublaine et Callinet at Saint-Sulpice.

8. An 1833 biography of Nicolas Séjan in the *Revue musicale* verifies that after his death, his son made a collection of several of his organ pieces and noël variations, and that they had been engraved. The biography is signed "F. D." [Félix Danjou?] [RM 13, p.237].

9. At the time that Fessy and Miné published *Le Guide de l'organiste*, Fessy was organist at the Madeleine and Miné was choir organist at Saint-Roch. This periodical was described in *Revue musicale* in 1835 [RM 15, p.176]. At that time eight volumes had already appeared, and subscriptions were invited. In 1847 Fessy became organist at Saint-Roch, but by then Miné was in Chartres.

V. Contrasts, Conflicts, and Conquests: The 1840s

1. In his autobiography, Neukomm describes organ concerts he gave in the British Isles. He played only improvisations on these programs, never wishing to play either his

own compositions or those of other composers [235, col.189]. When he played the new Birmingham Town Hall organ, his improvisation was a "storm" piece, which was viewed by a writer for the *Morning Post* (October 11, 1834) as "unfortunate" [cited in 310, p.130]. He apparently held to the idea of playing only improvisations in France, too, but storms are not mentioned in the reviews [see FM: 2, p.375; 5, pp.178, 203; 6, p.219. RGM: 9, p.238; 12, p.247. RMR: 1, p.303].

Neukomm was one of the designers of the Birmingham Town Hall organ, which was built by Hill. Neukomm called his Birmingham performance the inauguration and gave the date as October 7, 1833 [235, col.189]; but according to Thistlethwaite, the official opening was August 29, 1834 and Neukomm's performance was for "the ensuing Festival (October 1834)" [310, p.130].

2. The Daublaine-Callinet firm had been visited by disaster even before the Saint-Eustache fire. In a fit of temper or madness, Louis Callinet smashed much of the work that had been completed for a restoration of the Saint-Sulpice organ. Callinet was dismissed, but the firm had to repair the damage. This setback and the Saint-Eustache fire were ruinous, and the Daublaine-Callinet firm was liquidated. It was sold in 1845 to Pierre Ducroquet, and continued thus until 1855 [73, pp.39, 41, 62]. For more on the history of the Saint-Sulpice organ, see the collection of articles on this subject in *La Flûte harmonique* 59–60 (1991).

3. Formerly a convent of the Bernardines de Penthémont, this building was designated as a Protestant church in 1802. However, it was not actually made available for this purpose until 1846 [231, no.41, pp.19–20].

4. A slightly different version of this story was related by Tournemire, who said the couple had to climb the barricades to reach the church [312, p.67].

5. In 1863 Danjou returned at least briefly to the organ. He was one of several musicians who examined and played a new choir organ installed in Notre-Dame cathedral by the Merklin-Schütze firm [ME 30, pp.252–53].

6. Vast's date of birth is cited as 1833 by Pierre and as 1835 by François-Sappey [122, p.130; 249, p.864].

7. Hocmelle held positions as organist at Saint-Thomas-d'Aquin (from 1851) and Saint-Philippe-du-Roule (from 1861).

8. Schmitt tells us that he was responsible for the three-manual, 36-stop organ built for the cathedral of New Orleans by Schwab of Cincinnati in 1848 and 1849 [289, p.312]. For a romanticized biography of Schmitt, see Maria Schröder-Schiffhauer, *Der Vergessene Lorbeer: Die Geschichte der Domorganister Johann Georg Gerhard Schmitt aus Trier,* 2 vols. (St. Michael: J. G. Bläschke Verlag, 1980).

VI. Mid-Century Masters and Their Programs

1. In a review of the inauguration, Joseph d'Ortigue adds the information that the Mendelssohn movement was in D minor, and that the Bach fugue was the one in D major in which the pedal plays an important role [MA 1, no.9, col.141].

2. The most successful of Batiste's compositions was the *Andante in G.* Its enormous popularity in England can be judged by the fact that the British Library catalogue carries entries for fifty different editions of this piece, under various titles: "The Pilgrim's Song of Hope," "Favorite Andante in G," "Batiste's celebrated Andante," "Voix céleste." In vocal settings it bears the titles "In the Cathedral," "Wake, Morn of Splendour!" and "Rest of the Weary." It was arranged for piano, flute and piano, one or two mandolins with piano accompaniment, violin and piano, violoncello and piano, vocal solo, and vocal duet. It was also "choralized" for four voices. The earliest copy in the British Library dates from 1876 and is edited by W. Spark. Most of the versions were published before the end of the century, but a few appeared later—as recently as 1943.

Familiarity bred contempt; Harvey Grace snarled: "It is not easy to say which is the worst of all Batiste's pieces, but one may safely back the 'Song of Hope' for a 'place' " [139, p.52]. Most organists today would be embarrassed to perform the *Andante in G* because of its excessive sweetness and sentimentality.

3. In 1870 Durand entered music publishing as a partner in the firm Durand & Schönewerk. His son replaced Schönewerk in 1891, and the firm became Durand & Fils. Later it became Durand & Cie.

4. The use of an organ in religious ceremonies of the Jewish community in Paris dates from 1844, when a harmonium was introduced. In 1852 a Cavaillé-Coll organ was installed in the reconstructed temple. Alkan was named organist in 1851, before the organ was completed. He resigned almost immediately, thus ending his career as a professional organist before it began. For further information on this topic see [129].

5. César Franck chose ten pieces from three collections by Alkan and edited them for organ, making only minor adjustments. These pieces were published in 1889 (the year after Alkan's death) with the title *Préludes et Prières de C. V. Alkan choisis et arrangés pour l'orgue par César Franck*. It is instructive as well as interesting to see which pieces Franck chose and what changes he thought appropriate. For more on the Alkan works for organ and pedal-piano see [277].

6. See [317] for a detailed study of these organ builders.

7. Other organists active in France in mid-century included Jacques Masson (1791–1878), organist at the cathedral of Reims for 30 years; Etienne-Paul Charbonnier (1797–1872), organist at the cathedral of Aix; Alphons-Augustin Dupuis (1801–69), organist at the cathedral of Orléans for 38 years; J.-B. Labat (1802–75), organist at the cathedral of Montauban and former student of Benoist; Ignace-Xavier-Joseph Leybach (1817–91), organist at the cathedral of Toulouse; Edouard Mangeon (1818–67), organist and *maître de chapelle* at the cathedral of Angers; Jacques-Louis Battmann (1818–86), organist at Belfort and Vesoul; Louis Sannier (1821–87), organist at the church of Sainte-Catherine, Lille, for 43 years; d'Aubigny (d. 1877), organist at the cathedral of Poitiers; Charles Herzog (1827–76), organist at Saint-Cyr, Issoudun; Louis-Etienne Bignon (1828–74), organist at Notre-Dame-du-Mont, Marseille, professor of harmony at the conservatory of Marseille, and former student of Danjou at the *maîtrise* of Saint-Eustache, Paris. See also the list of organists in chap. X, note 3.

VII. New Horizons: The 1860s

1. According to Dufourcq, Chauvet held the post at Saint-Merry from 1866 [77, p.6]. However, contemporary periodicals confirm that he was organist at Saint-Merry from 1864 [RGM 31, p.38; RMS 5, col.120; FM 28, p.35].

2. Jean Huré named both Loret and Saint-Saëns as Gigout's organ teachers. Through Loret, he said, Gigout learned the techniques of the Lemmens school, but in matters of style, registration, and improvisation he was influenced above all by Saint-Saëns [162, pp.6–7].

3. The harmonicorde had been demonstrated during the exposition of 1855. It was described by Adrien de La Fage in *Revue et Gazette musicale* 22 (1855):266.

4. Guilmant had visited Cavaillé-Coll in 1859, and the latter had taken him to see and play his new organ in Saint-Louis-d'Antin. Cavaillé-Coll was very impressed with the young man's playing, and in a letter to Guilmant's father dated February 16, 1859 he wrote: "While at St.-Louis-d'Antin, I had the opportunity to speak with Mr. Leuilleux [*vicaire* of Saint-Nicolas, Boulogne] about your son's talent and the way in which he played our organ. I told him, and this is not false flattery, that no one in my opinion had demonstrated the instrument's resources as well as he" [cited in 73, p.384].

Between that time and the Saint-Sulpice performances Guilmant had studied with Lemmens in Brussels.

5. For more details about this program see ME 33, p.15. Durand had been organist at Saint-Vincent-de-Paul since 1863. He had previously been organist at Saint-Roch [ME 31, p.7].

VIII. Tragedy to Triumph: The 1870s

1. The Paris Commune was formed by a coalition of radical and moderate socialist and republican groups that opposed the policies of the monarchist majority in the National Assembly. The Commune gained control of Paris in March 1871, but was overthrown in late May.

2. Guilmant played the Handel Concerto No.10 in D minor with orchestra at the Conservatory concert of December 5, 1875 and again on April 19, 1878. In September 1879 he played another Handel concerto at the Trocadéro, first at a concert given by M. Félix Clément and then at one given by M. Vizentini. He had also played his own arrangement of Concerto No.2 on the inaugural program of the Trocadéro organ, August 7, 1878 [ME 46, p.272].

3. Preliminary hearings of the organ were given in Cavaillé-Coll's hall in April [ME 44, pp.164, 166].

4. It was programmed as *Symphonie V*, but its number was later changed to VI. For more on this subject see [233, pp.119, 122; and 160, p.30].

5. An autograph manuscript of these pieces in the Bibliothèque nationale, Paris, is apparently the copy Franck used for this performance, as it contains registrations for the Trocadéro organ (MS 20153 [1–3]). For more on this subject, see Wayne Leupold, "The Organ Manuscripts of César Franck," *The American Organist* 24/12 (December 1990):109–11.

IX. Renaissance Achieved: The 1880s

1. Franck took a great interest in the *Institution nationale des jeunes aveugles*. From 1876 he participated in the jury for final examinations in organ. Albert Mahaut recalled: "Each year we had a visit from César Franck; he came to preside over our competitive examinations, taking an interest in everyone and noticing certain ones among us" [213]. His *Psalm 150* was written for the inaugural program of the new Cavaillé-Coll organ, and in 1887, at the request of the school administration, Franck wrote fingerings for the Braille edition of thirty Bach organ works [174, p.1].

2. For further details concerning Merklin's use of electro-pneumatic action, see Pierre-Marie Guéritey, "Introduction à l'étude des transmissions électropneumatiques dans l'orgue au xixe siècle," *L'Orgue* 213 (1990):1–50.

3. The first name of this organist is not given. It was probably Georges Verschneider (1854–95), who had been a classmate of Rousseau's in the 1870s in Franck's organ class. Georges Verschneider was the son of Charles Verschneider, Barker's partner in organ building [159, pp.6–7].

X. Years of Fulfillment: The 1890s

1. This symphony, Op. 69, is an original work for organ and orchestra, not to be confused with Widor's symphonies for organ solo. See also p.111.

2. The number of programs he actually played may have been less than the projected 75. Some fifty have been documented by Agnes Armstrong [information furnished by Agnes Armstrong].

3. Among the organists active in other cities of France during the second half of the century were MM. Chareire, father and son, organists at the cathedral of Limoges; Desse, organist at Saint-Nicolas, Blois; Albert Duhaupas, organist and *maître de chapelle* of the cathedral of Arras; Ernest Duval, organist of Saint-Jacques, Reims; Duvois, organist of the cathedral of Moulins; E.-A. d'Etcheverry, organist of Saint-Paul, Bordeaux; Jules Grison (1842–96), organist of the cathedral of Reims (1864–96); Aloÿs Kunc (1832–95), successively organist at Lombez and the cathedral of Auch, then in Toulouse as *maître de chapelle* at the Feuillants, at Saint-Aubin, and finally at the cathedral (Saint-Etienne) [40, p.18]; Laurent, organist at the cathedral of Autun; Ernest LeGrand, organist at the cathedral of Nantes; Edmond Lemaigre (d. 1890), organist at the cathedral of Clermont-Ferrand; Moreau, organist at the cathedral of Blois; Permann, organist of Saint-Michel-des-Lions, Limoges; Querm, organist of the cathedral of Cambrai; Emile Renaud, organist of the palace chapel, Versailles; Scheurer, organist at the cathedral of Carcassonne; Henri Tournaillon (1832–87), organist at the cathedral of Orléans; Paul Trillat, organist of the Primatiale, Lyon; Charles Verschneider (d. 1865), organist at the cathedral of Besançon, and for a time associated with the organ builder Charles S. Barker; Mlle Vincent, organist at the cathedral of Senlis.

XII. Organ and Liturgy

1. A similar plan is found in the *Trois Messes* by Jacques-Marie Beauvarlet-Charpentier (Paris: chez l'auteur [c. 1814–22]). See also descriptions of the organ Mass in Alexandre-Charles Fessy, *Manuel d'orgue* (Paris: Troupenas [1845], pp.25–26), and [194 (1864), cols.292–93].

2. An earlier example of a nineteenth-century Noël Mass is found in Fessy and Miné, *Le Guide de l'organiste*, vol. 5 (Paris: Troupenas, c. 1835). From a musical standpoint, however, the Boëly Mass of 1842 is more noteworthy.

3. According to Barlow, Benoist's *Bibliothèque* was published in two groups: the first six volumes between November 1840 and October 1842, and the other six between 1859 and 1861 [13, pp.260–71].

4. There is no reference to "Magnificat" in the original publication, but Franck himself referred to his collection of Magnificat versets (see p.60). Perhaps the publisher or Franck (or both) preferred to leave the impression that these were all-purpose versets.

5. *Alternatim* practice was continued in France well into the twentieth century. For more on this subject see [320].

6. At Saint-Sulpice double basses were regularly used to reinforce the choir accompaniment. In 1892 Theodore Knauff wrote: "The lusty monkish bass players, particularly in the Glorias, add greatly to the body of tone" [182, p.15]. For important festivals the choir accompaniment was augmented by a small string orchestra of some dozen players [189, p.171].

7. Fauré was at Saint-Sulpice from October 1871 to January 1874 [234, p.418].

XIII. Notes on the Repertoire

1. At least part of this collection must have been written over a decade earlier. In 1876 *Le Ménestrel* announced that Gigout's *Pièces brèves* following the laws of modal harmony would soon appear [ME 42, pp.263, 383]. Examples of Gigout's modal pieces had been published in the *Journal* of Romary Grosjean by 1878 [ME 44, p.255].

2. In its original version, Widor's Symphonie II did not use plainsong. In the 1900–1901 edition the composer replaced the fourth movement, Scherzo, with a

chorale fantasy on the antiphon *Salve Regina*. For more on this subject, see the Introduction to *The Symphonies for Organ: Symphonie II,* edited by John R. Near (Madison: A-R Editions, 1991).

XIV. The Paris Conservatory Organ Class: Séjan to Franck

1. The term *maîtrise* is sometimes used to refer to the church choir rather than to the choir school.

2. Branches of the Conservatory were established in Lille and Toulouse in 1826, in Marseille and Metz in 1841, in Dijon in 1845, Nantes in 1846, Lyon in 1874, and Avignon in 1884. Still others were added later [75, p.3452].

3. Enrollment was limited, and there were large numbers of candidates for each opening. Pistone records that in 1900, 210 singers applied for 21 places, 195 pianists for 27 places, and 131 violinists for fourteen places [254, p.24n].

4. A course in music history was proposed in a reorganization plan of 1848, but was not instituted at that time. However, a course in the history of dramatic literature was authorized in 1854.

5. For the earlier history of this organ, see p.22, 24 and Chap. IV, note 1.

6. Official reports of professors and juries and other documents related to the Paris Conservatory are in the Archives nationales, Paris, in the collection AJ[37]. The following items relate to the organ class during the nineteenth century: AJ[37] 261–302: semester reports written by the organ professors; AJ[37] 249–254: official reports of organ competition juries; AJ[37] 237, 238, 240: notes taken by Dubois, Fissot, and Salomé when they served on organ examination committees, 1879–96; AJ[37] 200: themes for improvisations and chants for accompaniments; AJ[37] 84 (#7n): miscellaneous documents.

7. The chant melody was called a "choral" in the requirements until 1872; thereafter it was called "plainchant."

8. When d'Indy wrote about Franck's organ competition he seems to have indulged in some free improvisations of his own. His well-known story, quoted below, is marred by the fact that neither improvisation of a piece in sonata form nor performance of a composed organ piece was included in the competition in 1841.

> The tests for this [the organ] examination were—and still are—four in number: the accompaniment of a plainchant chosen for the occasion, the performance of an organ piece with pedal, the improvisation of a fugue, and the improvisation of a piece in sonata form, both these improvisations being upon themes set by the examiners. Franck, with his wonderful instinct for counterpoint, observed that the subject given for the fugue lent itself to combination with that of the free composition, and treated them simultaneously, in such a way that one set off the other.
>
> He tells us that he was "very successful in combining the two subjects," but the developments which grew out of this unusual method of treating the free composition ran to such unaccustomed lengths that the examiners (Cherubini was absent through illness), bewildered by such a technical feat, awarded nothing to this tiresome person. It was not until Benoist, the master of this too ingenious pupil, had explained the situation that they went back upon their first decision and decided to give the young man a *second* prize for organ! [171, pp.33–34.]

9. All enrolled students were normally expected to participate in semester examinations, but only the most advanced were eligible to enter the competitions. They were

selected on the basis of the second-semester examinations and were expected to learn a different composed piece for the competition, which was held later in the summer.

10. The other five categories of music instruction were elementary studies, voice, lyric declamation, stringed instruments, and wind instruments.

11. An 1892 commission proposed that the courses at the Conservatory be classified under four major divisions: Solfège, Voice, Instruments, and Composition. Organ was to be in the "Instruments" category, but this recommendation was not accepted, and it remained in the classification encompassing harmony, counterpoint and fugue, and composition [249, pp.265, 354, 374–75].

12. Tournemire recalled the improvisation on a free theme differently. In Franck's time, he said, it was based on the sonata-allegro form with two themes: "I don't know why that has been changed, and I don't comprehend why Guilmant substituted for so liberal a plan that of the Andante, [which is] much less favorable for improvisation." [Je ne sais pourquoi cela a été changé, et je ne saisis pas la raison pour laquelle Guilmant substitua à ce plan si généreux celui de l'Andante, beaucoup moins favorable à l'improvisation; 313, p.142].

Perhaps Franck encouraged such a gifted student as Tournemire to improvise sonata-allegro movements for class, but in the competitions and examinations only one theme was given to the candidates for the free form. Vierne's description of the competition corresponds with Conservatory records.

13. Vierne became a student of Franck's even before he completed his studies at the *Institution nationale des jeunes aveugles.* In 1888 Franck admitted him to the organ class at the Conservatory as an auditor, and also gave him private lessons in counterpoint, fugue, and composition. Vierne said he was admitted to the organ class as a regular student on October 4, 1890 [323, p.162; 324, vol.29, no.11, p.13].

Franck died during the fall 1890 semester, and Widor became professor of organ. In his semester examination reports, dated January 24, 1891, Widor wrote that Vierne had been admitted eight days earlier [AN AJ[37], 292, p.403]. Perhaps there was some delay in processing his official enrollment; perhaps Franck in his final illness had neglected some paperwork. Vierne was evidently under the impression that he was officially enrolled for the entire semester. Widor noted that another student, Berger, had also been admitted eight days earlier. It seems reasonable to assume that he, too, had actually been in the class all semester.

XV. The Brussels Conservatory Organ Class: Fétis to Mailly

1. Fétis neglects to mention that he competed unsuccessfully for the position of organist of the Royal Chapel on March 31, 1819 [82, no.62, p.14].

2. In a catalogue of his works, Fétis lists among the unpublished manuscripts "a large number of organ pieces of all types" and "sixty fugues and fugal preludes for the same instrument. A choice of these pieces [i.e., the preludes and fugues] forms a part of *la Science de l'organiste,* a work not yet completed" [114, vol.3, p.236].

Fétis's organ method was to have been published by Pleyel. On the extant engraved anthology Fétis wrote that two parts of the manuscript had been sent to the publisher for engraving. By mistake only the second part (the anthology) was actually given to the engraver. Some time later, when the Pleyel publishing business was being sold, it was learned that the first part had not been engraved. The manuscript could not be found, and the plates for the second part were melted down. Thus the proofs and the manuscript of the anthology were all that remained. Pleyel ceased publication in 1834 [328, pp.25–26].

3. By the time the second edition was published (1860–65), vocal ensemble, organ, and plainchant were no longer on Fétis's schedule [114, 2d ed., vol.3, p.235].

4. In 1870 Merklin separated from the firm, went to Paris, and started a new

company. He was in Switzerland during the war of 1870, but returned to France in 1872. He settled in Lyon, but maintained shops in both Paris and Lyon. In 1894 he left Lyon and this firm, and organized a new company in Paris. Meanwhile, the firm in Belgium remained in business until 1873 under the direction of Jacques Verreyt and Pierre Schyven (1827–?). Schyven, who had worked in the Merklin shop since it first opened in Belgium in 1843, then formed his own company, in partnership with Jacques Verreyt's son, Armand. For more information about Merklin and his associates, see Michel Jurine, *Joseph Merklin, facteur d'orgues européen*, 3 vols. (Paris: Aux Amateurs de livres, 1991).

5. Similar criticism of Fétis and Lemmens is found in an 1854 article by Kulack, "M. Fétis; nouveau journal d'orgue de M. Lemmens" [FM 18, pp.293–95]. Fétis was also accused of appropriating books from the Paris Conservatory library for his own library. For more on this subject see [201].

6. According to the 1878–80 Supplement to Fétis's *Biographie universelle*, Lemmens held a position as organist at the Jesuit church in London [114, Supplement, vol.2, p.97]. In a letter to Cavaillé-Coll dated June 1864, Lemmens said he had accepted a position as organist in a Catholic church in London, on the condition that the church would have a new organ [79, no.63, p.57]. There has not yet been a thorough investigation of Lemmens's professional activities in England.

7. Information furnished by Agnes Armstrong.

8. For a more detailed account of Tilborghs's career, see P. Roose, "Jozef Tilborghs," *Orgelkunst* 3/4 (December 1980):3–28.

XVI. Lemmens, a Closer Look

1. Cavaillé-Coll seems to have wanted Lemmens to locate permanently in Paris. From time to time this possibility was mentioned in their correspondence [79, no.60, p.86; 4, p.39].

2. Another edition, with *Nouvelle Edition* printed at the top of the title page, was published by Schott. It is really a reprint of the first edition and appears to have used the same plates. However, the date at the end of the preface is omitted.

3. In 1840 Fétis and Moscheles published *Méthode de méthodes de piano,* an analysis and comparison of selected piano methods. In the "Article" devoted to finger substitution, Fétis observes that this technique is not found in the old works of Marpurg, Türk, or even Dussek. His analysis of the uses of substitution by Kalkbrenner, Adam, and Moscheles shows that he understood the possibilities and limitations of substitution, at least as they were applied to piano playing [118, pp.46–47]. In this context Fétis does not exhibit any special enthusiasm for substitution, and he was obviously aware of its increased use during the earlier decades of the nineteenth century.

4. In regard to articulation and substitution in piano playing, *Méthode de Piano du Conservatoire* by Louis Adam is particularly interesting. Published by the Paris Conservatory in 1804 for use in that institution, it reached many students, including organists who studied piano at the Conservatory. Adam included substitutions on both single and double notes (thirds, sixths, and octaves) [2, pp.43, 45, 51, 53]. He described legato and linked it with vocal legato style. When the choice was left to the performer, he advised the use of legato as the basic touch, reserving staccato for special passages and for contrast [2, p.151]. Adam illustrated three types of articulation: a short staccato, with the notes receiving one-fourth their value; a normal staccato, with the notes receiving one-half value; and a slurred staccato, with the notes receiving three-fourths value [2, pp.154–55]. An 1835 catalogue of the Brussels Conservatory library lists the Adam piano method among its holdings [315].

A late-nineteenth-century view was expressed by another Paris Conservatory piano professor, Antoine-François Marmontel (1816–1898). He attributed the technique of substitution to Bach, stressed the importance of legato style, and maintained that substitution was as indispensable in piano playing as in organ playing [219, pp.24–30].

5. In an open letter of 1859 Fétis contrasted the faith required of the Catholic with the intellectual aspect of Protestantism. He saw "to believe" and "to know" as opposites in this context. The former embraced sentiment and emotion; the latter was calm and cold. In Catholic music it was the heart that spoke, while in Protestant music it was the mind. As grand as the works of Bach and other German composers were, their appeal was still to the intellect rather than the heart. Fétis asserted that in all his travels in north Germany, he had never encountered appreciation for the most beautiful musical works of the Catholic faith, even among the best musicians. "These differences of taste and appreciation have only one single cause: on one side, sentiment and faith; on the other, reason and examination." [Ces différences de goût et d'appréciation n'ont qu'une seule cause: d'un côté, le sentiment et la foi; de l'autre, la raison et l'examen; RGM 26, p.343.]

Lemmens defined the difference between Catholic and Protestant organ music in terms of its emphasis on counterpoint or melody. He, too, acknowledged Bach's genius, but thought his music lacked religious feeling, because of the "coldness" of the Protestant faith.

> One finds there, in the highest degree, the understanding, the intelligence; but from our Catholic point of view, the heart appears to be missing. Harmony and fugue, which are the foundation of his compositions, are not sufficient. Melody ought to play a greater role in Catholic art, because the exterior worship of our religion is intended to respond to all the noble feelings of the soul, from the deepest sorrow to the greatest ecstasy.

> On y trouve, au plus haut degré, l'esprit, l'intelligence; mais, à notre point de vue catholique, le coeur paraît y faire défaut. L'harmonie et la fugue, qui sont la base de ses compositions, ne suffisent pas. La mélodie doit jouer un plus grand rôle dans l'art catholique, par la raison que le culte extérieur de notre religion est destiné à répondre à tous les sentiments nobles de l'âme, depuis la plus profonde douleur jusqu'au plus grand enthousiasme. [Cited in 76, p.xx.]

6. In the Preface to his *Du Chant grégorien: sa mélodie, son rhythme, son harmonisation* (Ghent: C. Annoot-Braeckman, 1886, pp.3–6), Lemmens said he followed Fétis's system of chant accompaniment for three months in the organ class at the Conservatory, by which time he felt it was wrong. He told this to Fétis, who replied: "You are young, my friend; search and you will find a better way." [Vous êtes jeune, mon ami, cherchez et vous trouverez mieux!] Therefore, when the *Ecole* was published ten years later, Lemmens carefully eliminated everything that concerned plainchant accompaniment. Since that time, he said, he had been looking for the true way that Fétis seemed to have promised. *Du Chant grégorien* was the result of his research. It was published posthumously, edited by a former student of Lemmens, Joseph Duclos, who added an essay on Lemmens [76] that is itself a valuable source of information.

7. The position of professor at the Brussels Conservatory was not yet open.

8. For further on the source of Lemmens's style, see [183].

9. In the Preface to his edition of the Lemmens *Ecole,* Widor said he studied with Lemmens "nearly a year" [près d'un an]. According to John Near, Widor had daily lessons with Lemmens and Fétis for about four and a half months and then returned to France [233a, p.44].

10. In 1921 Widor traced the tradition from Bach through Bach's sons to Forkel

(1749–1818), from Forkel to Hesse (1808–63), and from Hesse to Lemmens [331, p.238]. Guilmant, on the other hand, traced the tradition from Bach through his student J. C. Kittel (1732–1809), to Kittel's student J. C. H. Rinck (1770–1846), from Rinck to Hesse and on to Lemmens [145, p.1155].

11. In 1926–28 Jean Huré wrote a scathing denouncement of the Lemmens school. Acknowledging Lemmens's virtuosity, the perfect clarity of his playing, and the great contribution his method made to organ technique in France, Huré described Lemmens as a mediocre musician and a pitiful interpreter. He challenged the notion that there was a connection between the Lemmens method and a Bach tradition, and he blamed Lemmens's disciples for excessive and false claims attributed to their mentor [165]. Although Widor was not named, it is obvious that he was the primary object of Huré's attack. Widor did not hesitate to brand Huré "un âne, doublé d'un fou!" [cited in 4, p.34].

12. Andlauer competed for the post at Notre-Dame-des-Champs early in January and was selected over eight other candidates by a jury that included Gounod, Franck, Widor, Guilmant, Gigout, and several other musicians [ME 43, p.53].

XVII. Widor as Teacher

1. Regarding the enrollment of Vierne and Berger, see Chap. XIV, note 13.

2. Another translation of the same preface is found in [333].

3. One hears the echo of Widor in various statements by Schweitzer, for example: "Bach is played altogether too fast" or "Correct phrasing is to be secured by correct accenting" [292, p.67]. But unlike Widor, Schweitzer was not bound by an allegiance to the Lemmens tradition. While Widor's concept of organ playing remained very much the same throughout his career, Schweitzer's evolved. A striking example is found in his statements about legato. In his 1908 study of Bach, Schweitzer wrote: "Otherwise he [Bach] was distinguished from his contemporaries only by his consistent pursuit of the principle of legato playing" [294, vol.1, p.295].

Several years later, in his introduction to the Widor-Schweitzer edition of Bach's organ works (G. Schirmer, 1912, vol.1, p.vi), he expressed some doubts: "It is generally assumed that the *legato* style of organ-playing was an achievement of Bach and his school. Just how far this assumption is correct historically, remains to be ascertained." By the time his memoirs appeared in 1933 his thinking had turned a corner:

> Whereas down to the middle of the nineteenth century Bach, curiously enough, was generally played staccato, players have since that date gone to the other extreme of rendering him with a monotonous legato. That is how I learned to play him from Widor in 1893. But as time went on, it occurred to me that Bach calls for phrasing which is full of life. He thinks as a violinist. His notes are to be connected with each other and at the same time separated from each other in the way which is natural to the bow of a violin. [292, p.67.]

XVIII. Guilmant as Teacher

1. Vierne said: "From the time that Widor left his class and Guilmant took it over I served as liaison officer between them—that is, I kept my dear *Maître* informed of all that was being done in his former course" [324, vol.30, no.3, p.8].

2. Schmitt and Quef had previously been in Widor's class. Emile Poillot was the prize winner in 1911. Guilmant had actually given up the organ class at the end of January that year, and he died in March.

3. From a list of Guilmant students compiled by Agnes Armstrong.

XIX. The Niedermeyer School

1. This project was at least under consideration. In 1812 the Minister of Churches gave Etienne-Alexandre Choron the task of preparing a plan for the reorganization of *maîtrises* and choirs in cathedrals [114, vol.2, p.289; see also 225, pp.25–26].
2. The organ at the Sorbonne was a new instrument by Louis-Paul Dallery. See also p.25.
3. Actually, Bach fugues were included in Conservatory organ class instruction by 1852. See Chap. XIV, p.149.

XX. Organ Study at the Niedermeyer and Gigout Schools

1. These exercises appeared under the title *Exercise journalier pour le doigter du clavier et des pédales de l'orgue* in *La Maîtrise* 2/5, 6, 7 (August–October 1858).
2. Plainchant was a separate subject at the Niedermeyer School. Thus it was not a part of the organ competition.
3. Information furnished by Agnes Armstrong.
4. Périlhou's birth is given as 1846 in *Larousse de la musique*, ed. Norbert Dufourcq, 1957 (vol.2, p.179), and in *Dictionnaire de la musique*, ed. Marc Honegger, new ed., 1986 (vol.2, p.952). But according to Moulis, Périlhou was born in 1845 [230, p.89].
5. Gigout had already assumed the duties of professor when he received the *Organiste* diploma in 1863 [12, p.19]. He did not teach organ at the Niedermeyer School until after Loret retired in 1900. He then served as organ teacher there until 1905, continuing his own school during the same period [71, p.100].

XXI. The Schola Cantorum

1. Nine according to [46, p.9], ten according to [172, p.3622] and *La Tribune de Saint-Gervais* [TSG 3, no.7, pp.97–101].
2. However, his name does not appear in the lists of students in Widor's organ classes who participated in the examinations [160, pp.59–63]. Decaux may have audited the organ class while he was enrolled in other courses.
3. According to Lejeune-Bonnier, Decaux began teaching at the Schola Cantorum in 1898 [199, p.4]. Records assembled by d'Indy and others indicate that his teaching there began in 1897 [173, p.195; see also TSG, supplement to vol.3, no.10, October 1897].

INDEX

Mutin, Charles, 107, 108. *See also* Cavaillé-Coll-Mutin organs

Nancy Conservatory, 110
Nant, Victor, 94, 117
Near, John R., 260*n*9
Neukomm, Sigismund, 37–38, 252–53*n*1
Ney, Joseph-Napoléon, 205, 219
Niedermeyer, Louis: compositions, 8, 80, 82, 93, 206; and church music style, 126, 136, 205; and plainchant accompaniment, 134–35, 138; and d'Ortigue, 134, 136, 206; career, 205–7; and Gigout, 207, 216; as educator, 208–9, 212; mentioned, 47, 52, 108, 210, 213, 219. *See also* Niedermeyer School
Niedermeyer School: performances and competitions, 8, 97, 99, 208, 211; organ professors, 47, 52, 69, 172, 210; and Saint-Saëns, 55, 73, 212–14; and Gigout, 73, 208, 209, 213, 214, 216–17, 262*n*5; compared with Paris Conservatory, 204, 208, 209, 211; history, administration, curriculum, 205–9, 262*n*2; Loret as organ professor, 210–12; study environment, 214–16; organs, 215, 216; mentioned, 89, 103, 134, 175, 180, 222, 229
Notre-Dame Cathedral, Paris: organists, 13, 15, 29, 45, 105, 106, 116, 125, 148, 251*n*1; services and service music, 15–17, 121–22, 132; organ receptions, inaugurations, recitals, 19, 32–33, 72, 79–82, 84, 108, 229, 233, 252*n*7, 253*n*5; *maîtrise,* 29, 31, 45, 204; mentioned, 26, 78, 113, 131, 193, 212
Notre-Dame-de-Lorette, Paris, 32–33, 35
Notre-Dame-des-Champs, Paris, 70, 117, 172, 180, 261*n*12
Notre-Dame-des-Victoires, Paris, 20
Notre-Dame-du-Mont, Marseille, 34, 254*n*7

Opéra, Paris, 6, 107, 148, 153, 213
Oratoire, Paris, 25
Organ with orchestra, 64–66, 74, 93, 95, 98, 101, 104, 106–112 *passim*, 167–68, 255*n*1
Orgue expressif, 20, 24
d'Ortigue, Joseph, 8, 79, 134, 136, 138, 206, 253*n*1

Palace chapel, Tuileries, Paris, 19, 20, 24, 26, 123, 147, 252*n*1
Palace chapel, Versailles, 123, 230, 233, 256*n*3
Palace of Industry, Amsterdam, 93, 168, 172
Palais Ducal, Brussels, 74, 167, 170
Palais du Trocadéro. *See* Trocadéro
Papot, Marie-Anna, 158, 232
Paris Conservatory: organs, 13, 19, 20, 146–47, 148, 257*n*5; and Séjan, 13, 147–48; and Benoist, 19, 20, 24, 148–55, 225, 257*n*8; admission and enrollment, 26, 145–46, 191, 257*n*3; and Franck, 88, 155–60, 231–32, 258*nn*12,13; and Widor, 105, 183–91,

258*n*13; and Guilmant, 116, 183, 195–99, 221, 261*nn*1,2; history, administration, curriculum, 143–45, 151, 225, 257*nn*2,4,6, 258*nn*10,11; examinations and competitions, 146, 149–58 *passim,* 185, 188–89, 196–97, 199, 257–58*nn*6,7,8,9,12; compared with Niedermeyer School, 204, 208, 209, 211; compared with Schola Cantorum, 221
Parisian rite, 124, 127–31
Pennington, James Alfred, 202
Pentemont, Paris, 41, 43, 48, 253*n*3
Périlhou, Albert-Jacques, 103, 105, 110–11, 213, 214, 262*n*4
Permann (organist in Limoges), 256*n*3
Perne, François-Louis, 144
Peterson, William, 181
Pierné, Henry-Constant-Gabriel, 105, 116, 158, 159–60, 232
Pinel, Stephen, 168
Pirro, André, 186, 221
Plainchant: accompaniment, 123, 125, 131–35, 149, 150, 151, 157, 166, 170, 174, 175, 177–78, 181–82, 185, 196–97, 210, 216, 260*n*6; restoration and reform, 124, 139–40, 181–82, 219, 220; in organ music, 128–30, 131, 138–39; mentioned, 257*n*7, 262*n*2
Poïkilorgue, 28, 92
Poillot, Emile, 198, 261*n*2
Pollet, Joseph, 28, 29
Populus, Nicolas-Adolphe-Alphonse, 106, 117
Pothier, Joseph, 219
Prestat, Marie-Joséphine-Claire, 71, 158, 232
Pugno, Raoul, 117

Quef, Charles, 117, 185, 198, 261*n*2
Querm (organist in Cambrai), 256*n*3

Reicha, Antoine-Joseph, 124, 190
Reichardt, Johann Friedrich, 14
Renaud: Albert, 230; Emile, 230, 233, 256*n*3; Marie-Léonie, 232
Renaud de Vilbac, Alphonse-Zoé-Charles: career, 52, 61–62, 73, 74, 79, 82; mentioned, 75, 89, 103, 152
Riemenschneider, Charles Albert, 192, 202
Rinck, Johann Christian Heinrich, 93, 177, 179, 197, 205, 211, 260–61*n*10
Rogers, James H., 202
Roman rite, 124, 130–31, 134, 138
Romantic period, 27
Ropartz, J.-Guy, 58, 110, 159
Rossini, Gioacchino, 38, 77–78, 79, 84, 205
Rottembourg (Widor student), 185
Roucourt, Jean-Baptiste, 161
Rouen cathedral, 5, 69, 72, 74
Rousseau: Geneviève-Louise, 71, 148; Samuel-Alexandre, 100, 106, 113, 158, 160, 230, 232, 255*n*3
Royal Albert Hall, London, 89, 92, 233

Orpha Ochse, Professor Emerita at Whittier College, is author of *The History of the Organ in the United States.* She is well known as a teacher, church musician, recitalist, and lecturer.